Mastering Windows PowerShell Scripting
Third Edition

Automate and manage your environment using PowerShell Core 6.0

Chris Dent

BIRMINGHAM - MUMBAI

Mastering Windows PowerShell Scripting
Third Edition

Commissioning Editor: Vijin Boricha
Acquisition Editor: Meeta Rajani
Content Development Editor: Nithin George Varghese
Technical Editor: Rutuja Patade
Copy Editor: Safis Editing
Project Coordinator: Drashti Panchal
Proofreader: Safis Editing
Indexer: Pratik Shirodkar
Graphics: Tom Scaria
Production Coordinator: Jisha Chirayil

First published: April 2015
Second edition: October 2017
Third edition: February 2019

Production reference: 1280219

Published by Packt Publishing Ltd.
Livery Place
35 Livery Street
Birmingham
B3 2PB, UK.

ISBN 978-1-78953-666-9

www.packtpub.com

`mapt.io`

Mapt is an online digital library that gives you full access to over 5,000 books and videos, as well as industry leading tools to help you plan your personal development and advance your career. For more information, please visit our website.

Why subscribe?

- Spend less time learning and more time coding with practical eBooks and videos from over 4,000 industry professionals

- Improve your learning with Skill Plans built especially for you

- Get a free eBook or video every month

- Mapt is fully searchable

- Copy and paste, print, and bookmark content

Packt.com

Did you know that Packt offers eBook versions of every book published, with PDF and ePub files available? You can upgrade to the eBook version at `www.packt.com` and as a print book customer, you are entitled to a discount on the eBook copy. Get in touch with us at `customercare@packtpub.com` for more details.

At `www.packt.com`, you can also read a collection of free technical articles, sign up for a range of free newsletters, and receive exclusive discounts and offers on Packt books and eBooks.

Contributors

About the author

Chris Dent is an automation specialist with a deep interest in the PowerShell language. Chris is often found lurking and answering questions about PowerShell in both the UK and virtual PowerShell user groups. Chris has been developing in PowerShell since 2007 and has released several modules over the years.

My thanks, first and foremost, must go to my wife and two children for their forbearance as I have written this book. I want to express my thanks to the technical reviewers, Paul Broadwith and Graham Beer, for their invaluable comments and feedback throughout this journey. Finally, I would like to thank the members of the Virtual PowerShell User Group for putting up with my weekend rambling and musing as I work through each of the chapters.

About the reviewers

Paul Broadwith is a senior technology professional freelancing in Scotland, with over 25 years of experience in diverse sectors, from manufacturing and financial services to the public sector and managed IT services. He has been involved in the open source and PowerShell communities for several years. His love of not doing things twice motivates him to automate as much as possible with PowerShell, and you will find much of it on GitHub. You'll find him working between there and the Chocolatey community, where he works on several open source projects. In what's left of his spare time (which isn't much), you can find him blogging at `pauby.com` and tweeting from `@pauby`.

Graham Beer is an experienced IT professional with excellent PowerShell skills and a flair for automation with Microsoft and AWS products. He is a regular contributor to 4sysops articles and was named in SQLShack's top 50 PowerShell bloggers of 2018. He recently had a chapter published in *The PowerShell Conference Book* about extending type data. He co-founded a PowerShell user group in the South of England, which has been running for over a year.

Packt is searching for authors like you

If you're interested in becoming an author for Packt, please visit `authors.packtpub.com` and apply today. We have worked with thousands of developers and tech professionals, just like you, to help them share their insight with the global tech community. You can make a general application, apply for a specific hot topic that we are recruiting an author for, or submit your own idea.

Table of Contents

Section 3: Automating with PowerShell

Preface

Windows PowerShell is an established language. Over the years, it has become increasingly important to Microsoft Windows-based services, and of course, cloud services such as Azure.

PowerShell Core represents a significant step forward; PowerShell Core expands out to Linux and macOS, opening up more opportunities to use the language.

The move to open source with PowerShell Core has opened the floodgates for new features, tweaks, and fixes. This is clearly where the future of PowerShell lies. Fortunately, the lessons learned using Windows PowerShell are transferable.

PowerShell Core is great but, perhaps, not quite ready to completely replace Windows PowerShell. Module developers need to test, update, and in some cases rewrite modules to make them compatible with PowerShell Core to complete the move. Much of this work must be undertaken by Microsoft themselves. A large number of modules have been written for Windows PowerShell over the years.

This book favors a PowerShell is PowerShell stance. There are differences between Windows PowerShell and PowerShell Core, but these details sit on the edge. Knowing how to use the help system, and how to explore objects, how to use PowerShell to meet an objective, is vital in either case.

Who this book is for

If you are a system administrator who wants to become an expert in controlling and automating your Windows environment, then *Mastering Windows PowerShell Scripting* is for you. It is also ideal for those new to the PowerShell language.

What this book covers

Chapter 1, *Introduction to PowerShell*, offers a brief introduction to some of the most important parts of PowerShell. Including the help subsystem, command naming, providers, and splatting.

Chapter 2, *Modules and Snap-Ins*, explores the use of modules in PowerShell and PowerShell Core, followed by a brief look at snap-ins in Windows PowerShell.

`Chapter 3`, *Working with Objects in PowerShell*, explores the different commands available to interact with objects. These utility commands are used again and again.

`Chapter 4`, *Operators*, takes a look at the different operators available in PowerShell. Operators are a fundamental part of life in PowerShell.

`Chapter 5`, *Variables, Arrays, and Hashtables*, takes a deep dive into the use of variables within PowerShell, including concepts such as variable scope.

`Chapter 6`, *Branching and Looping*, explores different loop operators, such as `foreach`, `for`, `while`, and `do`.

`Chapter 7`, *Working with .NET*, focuses on what .NET means to PowerShell and takes a look at type accelerators and the new `using` keyword.

`Chapter 8`, *Strings, Numbers, and Dates*, explores working with some of the most common datatypes in PowerShell.

`Chapter 9`, *Regular Expressions*, takes a look at the use of regular expressions in PowerShell with a number of detailed examples.

`Chapter 10`, *Files, Folders, and the Registry*, explains that working with the filesystem is an important part of any scripting language. The registry has long been a core part of the Microsoft operating system. This chapter takes a look at the commands used to interact with both the filesystem and the registry.

`Chapter 11`, *Windows Management Instrumentation*, explains that when there are no specific commands, WMI is often the first stop. This chapter explores the commands used to interact with WMI.

`Chapter 12`, *HTML, XML, and JSON*, are common text-based formats that must be either generated or interrogated using PowerShell. This chapter looks at some of the methods available and a number of the common pitfalls.

`Chapter 13`, *Web Requests and Web Services*, explains that the last 5 years has seen the use of web services, particularly REST, soar. This chapter takes a good look at working with REST, using GitHub as a reference site. SOAP is explored in Windows PowerShell using a custom-built site.

`Chapter 14`, *Remoting and Remote Management*, covers PowerShell remoting, which is an import tool stretching PowerShell out from a local machine. The introduction of PowerShell Core adds the ability to use PowerShell remoting to Mac and Linux machines.

`Chapter 15`, *Asynchronous Processing*, starts off with a brief exploration of jobs before taking a look at events and, finally, Runspace Pools.

`Chapter 16`, *Scripts, Functions, and Filters*, covers the building blocks of larger scripts and modules. This chapter explores the structure of scripts and functions and the use of named blocks in relation to the pipeline.

`Chapter 17`, *Parameters, Validation, and Dynamic Parameters*, explores the `param` block in PowerShell. The param block is incredibly versatile, allowing immediately input validation, and offering features such as argument completion.

`Chapter 18`, *Classes and Enumerations*, explores classes in PowerShell and showcases a few possible uses of classes, including parameter validation, argument transformation, and class-based DSC resources.

`Chapter 19`, *Building Modules*, explains that a module draws together groups of functions into a single unit. This chapter also explores differences in structure and requirements between development and runtime.

`Chapter 20`, *Testing*, explores static analysis and unit testing using Pester. Testing requires a great deal of practice but can be used to offer confidence that a script or function behaves they way it was intended to.

`Chapter 21`, *Error Handling*, explores the different types of errors in PowerShell and how they might be handled. This chapter includes the use of `try`, `catch`, `finally`, and `trap`.

To get the most out of this book

Some familiarity with the technologies the scripts interact with is required. A general familiarity with the Windows operating system, the filesystem, web services, and so on is required.

This book is based around PowerShell 5.1, PowerShell Core 6.1, and it includes small references to PowerShell Core 6.2.

The examples are predominantly Windows-based, as it is the most mature.

Download the example code files

You can download the example code files for this book from your account at `www.packt.com`. If you purchased this book elsewhere, you can visit `www.packt.com/support` and register to have the files emailed directly to you.

You can download the code files by following these steps:

1. Log in or register at `www.packt.com`.
2. Select the **SUPPORT** tab.
3. Click on **Code Downloads & Errata**.
4. Enter the name of the book in the **Search** box and follow the onscreen instructions.

Once the file is downloaded, please make sure that you unzip or extract the folder using the latest version of:

- WinRAR/7-Zip for Windows
- Zipeg/iZip/UnRarX for Mac
- 7-Zip/PeaZip for Linux

The code bundle for the book is also hosted on GitHub at `https://github.com/PacktPublishing/Mastering-Windows-PowerShell-Scripting-Third-Edition`. In case there's an update to the code, it will be updated on the existing GitHub repository.

We also have other code bundles from our rich catalog of books and videos available at `https://github.com/PacktPublishing/`. Check them out!

Download the color images

We also provide a PDF file that has color images of the screenshots/diagrams used in this book. You can download it here: `https://www.packtpub.com/sites/default/files/downloads/9781789536669_ColorImages.pdf`.

Conventions used

There are a number of text conventions used throughout this book.

`CodeInText`: Indicates code words in text, database table names, folder names, filenames, file extensions, pathnames, dummy URLs, user input, and Twitter handles. Here is an example: "As seen while looking at syntax in `Get-Help`, commands accept a mixture of parameters."

A block of code is set as follows:

```
Get-Command -CommandType Cmdlet, Function | Where-Object
{
$metadata = New-Object
System.Management.Automation.CommandMetadata($_)
$metadata.ConfirmImpact -eq 'High'
}
```

When we wish to draw your attention to a particular part of a code block, the relevant lines or items are set in bold:

```
Get-Command -CommandType Cmdlet, Function | Where-Object
{
$metadata = New-Object
System.Management.Automation.CommandMetadata($_)
$metadata.ConfirmImpact -eq 'High'
}
```

Any command-line input or output is written as follows:

```
PS> Get-Help Out-Null
```

Bold: Indicates a new term, an important word, or words that you see onscreen. Here is an example: "**Extensible Markup Language (XML)** is a plain text format that's used to store structured data."

Warnings or important notes appear like this.

Tips and tricks appear like this.

Get in touch

Feedback from our readers is always welcome.

General feedback: If you have questions about any aspect of this book, mention the book title in the subject of your message and email us at customercare@packtpub.com.

Errata: Although we have taken every care to ensure the accuracy of our content, mistakes do happen. If you have found a mistake in this book, we would be grateful if you would report this to us. Please visit www.packt.com/submit-errata, selecting your book, clicking on the Errata Submission Form link, and entering the details.

Piracy: If you come across any illegal copies of our works in any form on the Internet, we would be grateful if you would provide us with the location address or website name. Please contact us at copyright@packt.com with a link to the material.

If you are interested in becoming an author: If there is a topic that you have expertise in and you are interested in either writing or contributing to a book, please visit authors.packtpub.com.

Reviews

Please leave a review. Once you have read and used this book, why not leave a review on the site that you purchased it from? Potential readers can then see and use your unbiased opinion to make purchase decisions, we at Packt can understand what you think about our products, and our authors can see your feedback on their book. Thank you!

For more information about Packt, please visit packt.com.

Section 1: Exploring PowerShell Fundamentals

In this section, we will explore the basics of the PowerShell language.

The following chapters are included in this section:

- Chapter 1, *Introduction to PowerShell*
- Chapter 2, *Modules and Snap-ins*
- Chapter 3, *Working with Objects in PowerShell*
- Chapter 4, *Operators*

Introduction to PowerShell

1

PowerShell has reached a point where it has split into Windows PowerShell and PowerShell Core. Windows PowerShell accounts for versions up to, and including, PowerShell 5.1. Windows PowerShell is based on the .NET full framework. PowerShell Core accounts for version 6 and over and is based on the .NET core framework.

The future of PowerShell is in PowerShell Core; it opens up cross-platform scripting with PowerShell, that is, support for Linux and macOS.

As well as the change to .NET, there are an increasing number of differences between Windows PowerShell and PowerShell Core that must be accounted for.

The differences between Windows PowerShell and PowerShell Core will be highlighted throughout this book.

This book is split into a number of sections. Much of this book is intended to act as a reference. We will cover the following topics in this book:

- Exploring PowerShell fundamentals
- Working with data
- Automating with PowerShell
- Extending PowerShell

In the first section of this book, while exploring the PowerShell fundamentals, we will look at the use of language and cover as many building blocks as possible.

In this chapter, we will briefly look at a number of short, diverse topics:

- What is PowerShell?
- PowerShell editors
- Getting help
- Command naming
- Command discovery
- Parameters and parameter sets
- Introduction to providers
- Introduction to splatting

Technical requirements

This chapter makes use of the following on the Windows platform:

- Windows PowerShell 5
- PowerShell Core 6.1

What is PowerShell?

PowerShell is a mixture of a command line, a functional programming language, and an object-oriented programming language. PowerShell is based on Microsoft .NET, which gives it a level of open flexibility that was not available in Microsoft's scripting languages (such as VBScript or batch) before this.

PowerShell is an explorer's scripting language. With built-in help, command discovery, and with access to much of the .NET framework, it is possible to dig down through the layers.

This book is based on PowerShell Core 6.1 with references to PowerShell 5.1; some of the features that are discussed in this book may not be available in the earlier versions of PowerShell.

PowerShell Core may be installed side by side with Windows PowerShell. Preview versions of PowerShell Core can often be installed side by side with full releases of PowerShell Core.

PowerShell editors

While it is possible to write for PowerShell using the notepad application alone, it is rarely desirable. Using an editor that was designed to work with PowerShell can save a lot of time.

Specialized PowerShell editors such as **Visual Studio Code (VS Code)**, PowerShell Studio, and PowerShell ISE offer automatic completion (IntelliSense), which reduces the amount of cross-referencing required while writing code. Finding a comfortable editor early on is a good way to ease into PowerShell; memorizing commands and parameters is not necessary.

PowerShell ISE is not planned to be released to support PowerShell 6 at this time. VS Code is the most commonly recommended editor for PowerShell. VS Code is a free open source editor that was published by Microsoft VS Code and may be downloaded from http://code.visualstudio.com.

The PowerShell extension should be installed, and other extensions may be found on the marketplace: https://marketplace.visualstudio.com/VSCode.

VS Code provides support for PowerShell Core; the following screenshot shows how to change the version of PowerShell that's used when editing a script:

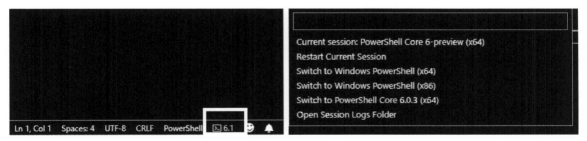

Getting help

Gaining confidence using the built-in help system is an important part of working with PowerShell. In PowerShell, help is extensive; authors can easily write their own help content when working with functions, scripts, and script modules.

A number of commands are available to interact with the help system, as follows:

- `Get-Help`
- `Save-Help`
- `Update-Help`

Before exploring these commands, the concept of *Updatable help* should be discussed, as help may not be present on a system after installation.

Updatable help

Updatable help was introduced with PowerShell 3. It gives authors the option to store the most recent versions of their help documentation outside of PowerShell on web servers.

Which modules support updatable help?

A list of modules that support updatable help may be viewed by running the following command: `Get-Module -ListAvailable | Where-Object HelpInfoURI -like *`.

Help for the core components of PowerShell is no longer a part of the Windows Management Framework package and must be downloaded before it can be viewed. The first time `Get-Help` is run, you will be prompted to update help.

If the previous prompt is accepted, PowerShell will attempt to download content for any module that supports updatable help.

Computers with no internet access or computers behind a restrictive proxy server may not be able to download the help content directly. The `Save-Help` command, which will be discussed later in this section, may be used to work around this problem. If PowerShell is unable to download help, it can only show a small amount of information about a command; for example, without downloading help, the content for the `Out-Null` command is minimal, as shown here:

```
PS> Get-Help Out-Null

NAME
    Out-Null
SYNTAX
    Out-Null [-InputObject <psobject>] [<CommonParameters>]

ALIASES
    None
```

```
REMARKS
    Get-Help cannot find the Help files for this cmdlet on this computer.
    It is displaying only partial help.
        -- To download and install Help files for the module that
           includes this cmdlet, use Update-Help.
        -- To view the Help topic for this cmdlet online, type:
           "Get-Help Out-Null -Online" or go to
           http://go.microsoft.com/fwlink/?LinkID=113366.
```

Updatable help as a `help` file may be viewed using the following command:

Get-Help about_Updatable_Help

The Get-Help command

Without any arguments or parameters, `Get-Help` will show introductory help about the help system. This content is taken from the default `help` file (`Get-Help default`); a snippet of this is as follows:

PS> Get-Help

```
TOPIC
  Windows PowerShell Help System

SHORT DESCRIPTION
  Displays help about Windows PowerShell cmdlets and concepts.

LONG DESCRIPTION
  Windows PowerShell Help describes Windows PowerShell cmdlets,
```

The help content can be long

The help content, in most cases, will not fit on a single screen. The `help` command differs from `Get-Help` in that it pauses (waiting for a key to be pressed) after each page, for example: `help default`.

The previous command is equivalent to running `Get-Help` and piping it into the `more` command:

Get-Help default | more

Alternatively, in Windows PowerShell, but not PowerShell Core, `Get-Help` can be asked to show a window:

```
Get-Help default -ShowWindow
```

The available help content may be listed using either of the following two commands:

```
Get-Help *
Get-Help -Category All
```

Help for a command may be viewed as follows:

```
Get-Help <CommandName>
```

Let's look at an example:

```
Get-Help Get-Variable
```

If a help document includes an online version link, it may be opened in a browser by using this:

```
Get-Help Get-Command -Online
```

The help content is broken down into a number of visible sections: name, synopsis, syntax, description, related links, and remarks. Syntax is covered in the following section in more detail as it is the most complex.

Syntax

The syntax section lists each of the possible combinations of parameters a command will accept; each of these is known as a parameter set.

A command that has more than one parameter set is displayed as follows:

```
SYNTAX
    Get-Process [[-Name] <String[]>] [-ComputerName <String[]>]
    [-FileVersionInfo] [-Module] [<CommonParameters>]

    Get-Process [-ComputerName [<String[]>]] [-FileVersionInfo]
    [-Module] -InputObject <Process[]> [<CommonParameters>]
```

The syntax elements written in square brackets are optional; for example, syntax help for `Get-Process` shows that all of its parameters are optional, as shown in the following code:

```
SYNTAX
    Get-Process [[-Name] <String[]>] [-ComputerName <String[]>] [-
FileVersionInfo] [-Module] [<CommonParameters>]
```

`Get-Process` may be run without any parameters at all, or it may be run with a value only and no parameter name, or it may include the parameter name as well as the value. Each of the following examples is a valid use of `Get-Process`:

```
Get-Process
Get-Process powershell
Get-Process -Name powershell
```

Get-Command can show syntax

`Get-Command` may be used to quickly view the syntax for a command, for example, by running the following code: `Get-Command Get-Variable -Syntax`.

Later in this chapter, we will take a more detailed look at the different parameters and how they might be used.

Examples

The examples section of help is often invaluable. In some cases, a command is sufficiently complex to require a detailed example to accompany parameter descriptions; in others, the command is simple, and a good example may serve in lieu of reading the help documentation.

Examples for a command may be requested using `Get-Help`, as shown in the following example:

```
Get-Help Get-Process -Examples
```

It is common for a command to list several examples of its use, especially if the command has more than one parameter set.

Parameter

Help for specific parameters may be requested as follows:

```
Get-Help Get-Command -Parameter <ParameterName>
```

This option allows for the quick retrieval of specific help for a single parameter; for example, help for the `Path` parameter of the `Import-Csv` command may be quickly viewed:

```
PS> Get-Help Import-Csv -Parameter Path
```

```
-Path [<String[]>]
    Specifies the path to the CSV file to import. You can also pipe
    a path to Import-Csv.
    Required? false
    Position? 1
    Default value None
    Accept pipeline input? true (ByValue)
    Accept wildcard characters? false
```

Detailed and full switches

The `Detailed` switch parameter asks `Get-Help` to return the most help content. This adds information about each parameter and the set of examples to name, synopsis, syntax, and description. Related links are excluded when using this parameter.

The `Detailed` parameter is used as follows:

```
Get-Help Get-Process -Detailed
```

Using a `Full` switch adds more technical details (compared to using the `Detailed` parameter). Inputs, outputs, notes, and related links are added to those that are seen using `Detailed`. For example, the sections detailing input and output types from `Get-Process` may be extracted from the full help document:

```
PS> Get-Help Get-Process -Full
...
INPUTS
    System.Diagnostics.Process
        You can pipe a process object to Get-Process.

OUTPUTS
    System.Diagnostics.Process, System.Diagnotics.FileVersionInfo,
System.Diagnostics.ProcessModule
        By default, Get-Process returns a System.Diagnostics.Process
        object. If you use the FileVersionInfo parameter, it returns a
        System.Diagnostics.FileVersionInfo object. If you use the Module
        parameter (without the FileVersionInfo parameter), it returns a
```

Save-Help

The `Save-Help` command can be used with modules that support updatable help. It saves help content for modules to a folder; for example, the help content for the `DnsClient` module can be saved to `C:\PSHelp` (the directory must already exist):

```
Save-Help -DestinationPath C:\PSHelp -Module DnsClient
```

Alternatively, the help content for all modules may be saved as follows:

```
Save-Help -DestinationPath C:\PSHelp
```

The process creates an XML formatted `HelpInfo` file that holds the source of the help content and a **CAB** (**cabinet**) file that's named after the module and culture.

Opening the `CAB` file shows that it contains a number of XML formatted `help` files, as shown in the following screenshot:

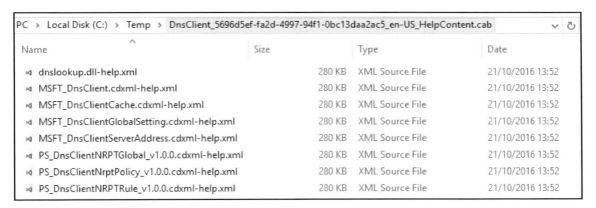

Saved help content can be copied over to another computer and imported using `Update-Help`. This technique is very useful for computers that do not have internet access as it means help content can be made available.

Update-Help

The `Update-Help` command can perform two tasks:

- Update `help` files from the internet
- Import previously saved `help` files

To update help from the internet, Update-Help may be run without any parameters:

Update-Help

Administrator rights are required

 Updating help for some modules will require administrative rights (run as administrator). This applies to modules that are stored in protected areas of the filesystem, such as those in $PSHost (%SystemRoot%\System32\WindowsPowerShell\v1.0) or under program files.

When updating help information from the internet, by default, Update-Help will not download help content more than once every 24 hours. This restriction is documented in the help command and may be seen in action when using the Verbose switch:

```
PS> Update-Help -Module DnsClient -Verbose
VERBOSE: Help was not updated for the module DnsClient, because the Update-
Help command was run on this computer within the last 24 hours.
To update help again, add the Force parameter to your command.
```

As described in the preceding message, using the Force switch parameter will ignore the time restriction. Importing help from a set of saved files uses the SourcePath parameter:

Update-Help -SourcePath C:\temp

The following error message may be generated when attempting to import help from another culture:

```
PS> Update-Help -SourcePath C:\Temp -Module DnsClient
Update-Help : Failed to update Help for the module(s) 'DnsClient' with
UIculture(s) {en-GB} :
Unable to retrieve the HelpInfo XML file for UI culture en-GB. Make sure
the HelpInfoUri property in the module manifest is valid or check your
network connection and then try the command again.
At line:1 char:1
+ Update-Help -SourcePath C:\Temp -Module DnsClient -Verbose -Force
+ ~~~~~~~~~~~~~~~~~~~~~~~~~~~~~~~~~~~~~~~~~~~~~~~~~~~~~~~~~~~~~~~~~~~~
    + CategoryInfo          : ResourceUnavailable: (:) [Update-Help],
Exception
    + FullyQualifiedErrorId :
UnableToRetrieveHelpInfoXml,Microsoft.PowerShell.Commands.UpdateHelpCommand
```

The culture of the computer in question is set to en-GB (Get-UICulture), but the help files are for en-US.

It is possible to work around this problem with the `UICulture` parameter for `Update-Help`, as follows:

```
Update-Help -SourcePath C:\Temp -Module DnsClient -UICulture en-US
```

About help files

`About` documents describe features of a language or concepts that apply to more than one command. These items do not fit into help for individual commands.

PowerShell Core: Where is About?

The PowerShell Core help files are not available as I write this at the time of writing. The examples that are shown here can only be applied to PowerShell 5.1 or lower.

The list of help files may be viewed by running `Get-Help` with the category as `HelpFile`, as demonstrated in the following code:

```
Get-Help -Category HelpFile
```

These files cover a huge variety of topics from aliases, to modules, to WMI:

```
Name                              Category Synopsis
----                              -------- --------
about_Aliases HelpFile            SHORT    DESCRIPTION
about_Arithmetic_Operators HelpFile  SHORT    DESCRIPTION
about_Arrays HelpFile             SHORT    DESCRIPTION
about_Assignment_Operators HelpFile  SHORT    DESCRIPTION
about_Automatic_Variables HelpFile   SHORT    DESCRIPTION
about_Break HelpFile              SHORT    DESCRIPTION
about_Classes HelpFile            SHORT    DESCRIPTION
about_Command_Precedence HelpFile SHORT    DESCRIPTION
about_Command_Syntax HelpFile     SHORT    DESCRIPTION
about_Comment_Based_Help HelpFile SHORT    DESCRIPTION
about_CommonParameters HelpFile   SHORT    DESCRIPTION
about_Comparison_Operators HelpFile  SHORT    DESCRIPTION
about_Continue HelpFile           SHORT    DESCRIPTION
about_Core_Commands HelpFile      SHORT    DESCRIPTION
about_Data_Sections HelpFile      SHORT    DESCRIPTION
...
```

Command naming and discovery

Commands in PowerShell are formed around verb and noun pairs in the form verb-noun.

This feature is useful when finding commands; it allows you to make educated guesses so that there is little need to memorize long lists of commands.

Verbs

The list of verbs is maintained by Microsoft. This formal approach to naming commands greatly assists in discovery.

Verbs are words such as `Add`, `Get`, `Set`, and `New`. In addition to these, we have `ConvertFrom` and `ConvertTo`.

The list of verbs that are available in PowerShell can be accessed as follows:

```
Get-Verb
```

Each verb has a group, such as data, life cycle, or security. Complementary actions such as encryption and decryption tend to use verbs in the same group; for example, the verb `Protect` may be used to encrypt something and the verb `Unprotect` may be used to decrypt something.

Verb descriptions

A detailed list of verbs, along with use cases, is available on MSDN: `https://docs.microsoft.com/en-gb/powershell/developer/cmdlet/approved-verbs-for-windows-powershell-commands`.

It is possible to use verbs other than the approved list. However, if a command using an unapproved verb is part of a module, a warning will be shown every time the module is imported.

Nouns

A noun provides a very short description of the object the command is expecting to act on. The noun part may be a single word, as is the case with `Get-Process`, `New-Item`, or `Get-Help`, or more than one word, as seen with `Get-ChildItem`, `Invoke-WebRequest`, or `Send-MailMessage`.

Finding commands

The verb-noun pairing can make it a lot easier to find commands (without resorting to search engines).

For example, if we want to list firewall rules and we already know of the `NetSecurity` module that's available in Windows PowerShell, we can run the following command, which shows the `Get` commands in that module:

```
PS> Get-Command Get-*Firewall* -Module NetSecurity

CommandType   Name                               Version Source
-----------   ----                               ------- ------
Function      Get-NetFirewallAddressFilter       2.0.0.0 NetSecurity
Function      Get-NetFirewallApplicationFilter   2.0.0.0 NetSecurity
Function      Get-NetFirewallInterfaceFilter     2.0.0.0 NetSecurity
Function      Get-NetFirewallInterfaceTypeFilter 2.0.0.0 NetSecurity
Function      Get-NetFirewallPortFilter          2.0.0.0 NetSecurity
Function      Get-NetFirewallProfile             2.0.0.0 NetSecurity
Function      Get-NetFirewallRule                2.0.0.0 NetSecurity
Function      Get-NetFirewallSecurityFilter      2.0.0.0 NetSecurity
Function      Get-NetFirewallServiceFilter       2.0.0.0 NetSecurity
Function      Get-NetFirewallSetting             2.0.0.0 NetSecurity
```

From the previous list, `Get-NetFirewallRule` closely matches the requirement (to see a list of firewall rules) and should be explored.

Taking a broader approach, if the module was not known, we might still be able to guess by searching for commands containing specific nouns, for example, commands to get existing items that mention a firewall:

```
Get-Command Get-*Firewall*
```

Once a potential command has been found, `Get-Help` can be used to assess whether or not the command is suitable.

NetSecurity and PowerShell Core

The NetSecurity module is not available using PowerShell Core by default. Using modules such as NetSecurity in PowerShell Core is discussed in `Chapter 2`, *Modules and Snap-ins.*

Aliases

An alias in PowerShell is an alternate name for a command. A command may have more than one alias.

The list of aliases may be viewed by using `Get-Alias`, as shown in the following example:

```
PS> Get-Alias

CommandType Name
----------- ----
Alias       % -> ForEach-Object
Alias       ? -> Where-Object
Alias       ac -> Add-Content
Alias       asnp -> Add-PSSnapin
Alias       cat -> Get-Content
Alias       cd -> Set-Location
```

`Get-Alias` may be used to find the command behind an alias:

```
Get-Alias dir
```

It can also be used to find the aliases for a command name:

```
Get-Alias -Definition Get-ChildItem
```

Examples of aliases that are frequently used in examples on the internet include the following:

- `%` for `ForEach-Object`
- `?` for `Where-Object`
- `cd` for `Set-Location`
- `gc` or `cat` for `Get-Content`
- `ls` or `dir` for `Get-ChildItem`
- `man` for `help` (and then `Get-Help`)

An alias does not change how a command is used. There is no practical difference between the following two commands:

```
cd $env:TEMP
Set-Location $env:TEMP
```

New aliases are created with the New-Alias command; for example, we might choose to create an alias named grep for Select-String:

```
New-Alias grep -Value Select-String
```

Each alias exists until the PowerShell session is closed.

 More information is available about aliases in the help file, which may be viewed using the following command: Get-Help about_Aliases.

Parameters and parameter sets

As we saw while looking at syntax in Get-Help, commands accept a mixture of parameters. The following sections show how these parameters are described in help and how to use them.

Parameters

When viewing help for a command, we can see many different approaches to different parameters.

Optional parameters

Optional parameters are surrounded by square brackets. This denotes an optional parameter that requires a value when used:

```
SYNTAX
    Get-Process [-ComputerName <String[]>] ...
```

In this case, if a value for a parameter is to be specified, the name of the parameter must also be specified, as shown in the following example:

```
Get-Process -ComputerName somecomputer
```

Optional positional parameters

It is not uncommon to see an optional positional parameter as the first parameter:

```
SYNTAX
    Get-Process [[-Name] <String[]>] ...
```

In this example, we may use either of the following:

```
Get-Process -Name powershell
Get-Process powershell
```

Mandatory parameters

A mandatory parameter must always be supplied and is written as follows:

```
SYNTAX
    Get-ADUser -Filter <string> ...
```

In this case, the `Filter` parameter name must be written and it must be given a value. For example, to supply a `Filter` for the command, the `Filter` parameter must be explicitly written:

```
Get-ADUser -Filter 'sAMAccountName -eq "SomeName"'
```

Mandatory positional parameters

Parameters that are mandatory and accept values based on position are written as follows:

```
SYNTAX
    Get-ADUser [-Identity] <ADUser> ...
```

In this case, the `Identity` parameter name is optional but the value is not. This command may be used as described by either of the following examples:

```
Get-ADUser -Identity useridentity
Get-ADUser useridentity
```

In both cases, the supplied value fills the `Identity` parameter. A command with more than one mandatory positional parameter may appear as follows:

```
SYNTAX
    Add-Member [-NotePropertyName] <String> [-NotePropertyValue] <Object>
    ...
```

In this case, the command may be called as follows:

```
Add-Member -NotePropertyName Name -NotePropertyValue "value"
Add-Member -NotePropertyValue "value" -NotePropertyName Name
Add-Member Name -NotePropertyValue "value"
Add-Member Name "value"
```

Switch parameters

Switch parameters have no arguments (values); the presence of a switch parameter is sufficient. For example, Recurse is a switch parameter for Get-ChildItem:

```
SYNTAX
    Get-ChildItem ... [-Recurse] ...
```

As with the other types of parameters, optional use is denoted by square brackets. Switch parameters, by default, are false (not set). If a switch parameter is true (set) by default, it is possible to set the value to false using the notation, as shown in the following code:

```
Get-ChildItem -Recurse:$false
```

In the case of Get-ChildItem, this does nothing; this technique is most widely used with the Confirm switch parameter, which we will discuss later in this chapter.

Common parameters

When looking at the syntax, you will see that most commands end with a CommonParameters item:

```
SYNTAX
    Get-Process ... [<CommonParameters>]
```

These common parameters are documented inside PowerShell:

```
Get-Help about_CommonParameters
```

These parameters let you control some of the standardized functionality PowerShell provides, such as verbose output and actions to take when errors occur.

For example, `Stop-Process` does not explicitly state that it has a `Verbose` parameter, but as `Verbose` is a common parameter it may be used. This can be seen if `notepad` is started and immediately stopped:

```
PS> Start-Process notepad -Verbose -PassThru | Stop-Process -Verbose
VERBOSE: Performing the operation "Stop-Process" on target "notepad
(5592)".
```

Not so verbose

Just because a command supports a set of common parameters does not mean it must use them; for example, `Get-Process` supports the `Verbose` parameter, yet it does not write any verbose output.

Parameter values

Value types of arguments (the type of value expected by a parameter) are enclosed in angular brackets, as shown in the following example:

```
<string>
<string[]>
```

If a value is in the `<string>` form, a single value is expected. If the value is in the `<string[]>` form, an array (or list) of values is expected.

For example, `Get-CimInstance` accepts a single value only for the `ClassName` parameter:

```
SYNTAX
    Get-CimInstance [-ClassName] <String> ...
```

The command may be called as follows:

```
Get-CimInstance -ClassName Win32_OperatingSystem
```

In comparison, `Get-Process` accepts multiple values for the `Name` parameter:

```
SYNTAX
    Get-Process [[-Name] <String[]>] ...
```

`Get-Process` may be called as follows:

```
Get-Process -Name powershell, explorer, smss
```

Parameter sets

Many of the commands in PowerShell have more than one parameter set. This was seen while looking at the syntax section of help; for example, Stop-Process has three parameter sets:

```
SYNTAX
    Stop-Process [-Id] <Int32[]> [-Confirm] [-Force] [-PassThru] [-WhatIf]
[<CommonParameters>]
    Stop-Process [-InputObject] <Process[]> [-Confirm] [-Force] [-PassThru]
[-WhatIf] [<CommonParameters>]
    Stop-Process [-Confirm] [-Force] -Name <String[]> [-PassThru] [-WhatIf]
[<CommonParameters>]
```

Each parameter set must have one or more parameters unique to that set. This allows each set to be distinguished from the other. In the previous example, Id, InputObject, and Name are used as differentiators.

The first parameter set expects a process ID, and this ID may be supplied with the parameter name or based on position; for example, both of these commands close the current PowerShell console:

```
Stop-Process -Id $PID
Stop-Process $PID
```

The second parameter set needs a value for InputObject. Again, this may be supplied as a positional parameter. In this case, it will be distinguished based on its type:

```
$process = Start-Process notepad -PassThru
Stop-Process -InputObject $process
Stop-Process $process
$process | Stop-Process
```

Pipeline input

Get-Help should help show which parameters accept pipeline input, and examples are likely to show how.

If Get-Help is incomplete, Get-Command can be used to explore parameters:
```
(Get-Command Stop-
Process).Parameters.InputObject.Attributes.
```

Confirm, WhatIf, and Force

The `Confirm`, `WhatIf`, and `Force` parameters are used with commands that make changes (to files, variables, data, and so on). These parameters are often used with commands that use the verbs `Set` or `Remove`, but the parameters are not limited to specific verbs.

`Confirm` and `WhatIf` have associated preference variables. `Preference` variables have an `about` file, which may be viewed using the following command:

```
Get-Help about_Preference_Variables
```

The `Force` parameter is not one of PowerShell's common parameters, that is, parameters that are automatically added by PowerShell itself.

Force is often seen in commands that might otherwise prompt for confirmation. There is no fixed use of the `Force` parameter. The effect of using `Force` is a choice a command developer must make. The `Help` documentation should state the effect of using `Force`, as is the case with the `Remove-Item` command in the following example:

```
Get-Help Remove-Item -Parameter Force
```

Confirm parameter

The `Confirm` parameter causes a command to prompt before an action is taken; for example, the `Confirm` parameter forces `Remove-Item` to prompt when a file is to be removed:

```
PS> Set-Location $env:TEMP
PS> New-Item IMadeThisUp.txt -Force
PS> Remove-Item .\IMadeThisUp.txt -Confirm
Confirm
Are you sure you want to perform this action?
Performing the operation "Remove File" on target
"C:\Users\whoami\AppData\Local\Temp\IMadeThisUp.txt".
[Y] Yes [A] Yes to All [N] No [L] No to All [S] Suspend [?] Help (default
is "Y"):
```

We have seen that a confirmation prompt may be forcefully requested in the previous example. In a similar manner, confirmation prompts may be suppressed; for example, the value of the `Confirm` parameter may be explicitly set to `false`, as shown in the following code:

```
Remove-Item .\IMadeThisUp.txt -Confirm:$false
```

There is more than one way of prompting

There are two ways of requesting confirmation in PowerShell: Confirm and the associated ConfirmPreference; the variable only acts against one of these.
Using the parameter or changing the variable will not suppress all prompts. For example, Remove-Item will always prompt if you attempt to delete a directory that is not empty without supplying the Recurse parameter.

This technique is useful for commands that prompt by default; for example, Clear-RecycleBin will prompt by default:

```
PS> Clear-RecycleBin
Confirm
Are you sure you want to perform this action?
Performing the operation "Clear-RecycleBin" on target " All of the contents
of the Recycle Bin".
[Y] Yes [A] Yes to All [N] No [L] No to All [S] Suspend [?] Help (default
is "Y"):
```

Setting the Confirm parameter to false for Clear-RecycleBin will bypass the prompt and immediately empty the recycle bin:

```
Clear-RecycleBin -Confirm:$false
```

Finding commands with a specific impact

The following snippet will return a list of all commands that state they have a high impact:

```
Get-Command -CommandType Cmdlet, Function | Where-Object
{
    $metadata = New-Object
System.Management.Automation.CommandMetadata($_)
    $metadata.ConfirmImpact -eq 'High'
}
```

ConfirmPreference

If the Confirm parameter is not set, whether or not a prompt is shown is determined by PowerShell. The value of the ConfirmPreference variable is compared with the stated impact of a command.

By default, the value of `ConfirmPreference` is `High`, as shown in the following code:

```
PS> $ConfirmPreference
High
```

By default, commands have a medium impact.

Finding ConfirmImpact

In scripts and functions, the `ConfirmImpact` setting is part of the `CmdletBinding` attribute: `[CmdletBinding(ConfirmImpact = 'High')]`.
If `CmdletBinding` or `ConfirmImpact` are not present, the impact is medium.

The impact of a function or `cmdlet` may be viewed using the `ConfirmImpact` property of a command's metadata:
`New-Object System.Management.Automation.CommandMetadata(Get-Command Remove-Item)`.

`ConfirmPreference` has four possible values:

- `High`: Prompts when command impact is `High` (default)
- `Medium`: Prompts when command impact is `Medium` or `High`
- `Low`: Prompts when command impact is `Low`, `Medium`, or `High`
- `None`: Never prompts

A new value may be set by assigning it in the console; for example, it can be set to `Low`:

```
$ConfirmPreference = 'Low'
```

ConfirmPreference and the Confirm parameter

While `ConfirmPreference` may be set to `None` to suppress confirmation prompts, confirmation may still be explicitly requested. Let's look at an example:
```
$ConfirmPreference = 'None'
New-Item NewFile.txt -Confirm
```

Since the `Confirm` parameter is supplied, the `ConfirmPreference` value within the scope of the command (`New-Item`) is `Low`, and therefore the prompt displays.

WhatIf parameter

The `WhatIf` parameter replaces the confirmation prompt with a simple statement that should state what would have been done, using `Remove-Item` as an example again:

```
PS> Set-Location $env:TEMP
PS> New-Item IMadeThisUp.txt -Force
PS> Remove-Item .\IMadeThisUp.txt -WhatIf
Confirm
Are you sure you want to perform this action?
What If: Performing the operation "Remove File" on target
"C:\Users\whoami\AppData\Local\Temp\IMadeThisUp.txt".
```

If both `Confirm` and `WhatIf` are used with a command, `WhatIf` takes precedence.

`WhatIf` may be unset on a per-command basis by supplying a value of `false` in the same manner as the `Confirm` parameter. Let's look at the following example:

```
'Some message' | Out-File $env:TEMP\test.txt -WhatIf:$false
```

The previous technique can be useful if a file (such as a log file) should be written to, irrespective of whether `WhatIf` is being used or not.

WhatIfPreference

The `WhatIfPreference` variable holds a Boolean value (`true` or `false`) and has a default value of `false`.

If the preference variable is set to `true`, all commands that support `WhatIf` will act as if the parameter is explicitly set. A new value may be set for the variable, as shown in the following code:

```
$WhatIfPreference = $true
```

The `WhatIf` preference variable takes precedence over the `Confirm` parameter. For example, the `WhatIf` dialog will be shown when running the following `New-Item`, but the `Confirm` prompt will not:

```
$WhatIfPreference = $true
New-Item NewFile.txt -Confirm
```

Force parameter

The Force parameter has a different purpose. With the Force parameter, New-Item will overwrite any existing file with the same path. When used with Remove-Item, the Force parameter allows the removal of files with Hidden or System attributes. The error that's generated when attempting to delete a Hidden file is shown in the following code:

```
PS> Set-Location $env:TEMP
PS> New-Item IMadeThisUp.txt -Force
PS> Set-ItemProperty .\IMadeThisUp.txt -Name Attributes -Value Hidden
PS> Remove-Item IMadeThisUp.txt

Remove-Item : Cannot remove item
C:\Users\whoami\AppData\Local\Temp\IMadeThisUp.txt: You do not have
sufficient access rights to perform this operation.
At line:1 char:1
+ Remove-Item .\IMadeThisUp.txt
+ ~~~~~~~~~~~~~~~~~~~~~~~~~~~~~~
 + CategoryInfo : PermissionDenied:
(C:\Users\uktpcd...IMadeThisUp.txt:FileInfo) [Remove-Item], IOException
 + FullyQualifiedErrorId :
RemoveFileSystemItemUnAuthorizedAccess,Microsoft.PowerShell.Commands.Remove
ItemCommand
```

Adding the Force parameter allows the operation to continue without the error message:

```
Set-Location $env:TEMP
New-Item IMadeThisUp.txt -Force
Set-ItemProperty .\IMadeThisUp.txt -Name Attributes -Value Hidden
Remove-Item IMadeThisUp.txt -Force
```

Introduction to providers

Providers in PowerShell present access to data that is not normally easily accessible. There are providers for the filesystem, registry, certificate store, and so on. Each provider arranges data so that it resembles a filesystem.

 PowerShell Core: What happened to provider help?

PowerShell Core does not include Provider help files. Help may be viewed either online or in Windows PowerShell.

A longer description of Providers may be seen by viewing the about file:

```
Get-Help about_Providers
```

The list of providers available in the current PowerShell session may be viewed by running Get-PSProvider, as shown in the following example:

```
PS> Get-PSProvider
Name             Capabilities                         Drives
----             ------------                         ------
Registry         ShouldProcess, Transactions          {HKLM, HKCU}
Alias            ShouldProcess                        {Alias}
Environment      ShouldProcess                        {Env}
FileSystem       Filter, ShouldProcess, Credentials  {C, D}
Function         ShouldProcess                        {Function}
Variable         ShouldProcess                        {Variable}
Certificate      ShouldProcess                        {Cert}
WSMan            Credentials                          {WSMan}
```

Each of the previous providers has a help file associated with it. These can be accessed using the following code:

```
Get-Help -Name <ProviderName> -Category Provider
```

For example, the help file for the certificate provider may be viewed by running the following code:

```
Get-Help -Name Certificate -Category Provider
```

A list of all help files for providers may be seen by running the following code:

```
Get-Help -Category Provider
```

Drives using providers

The output from Get-PSProvider shows that each provider has one or more drives associated with it.

Alternatively, you can see the list of drives (and the associated provider) using Get-PSDrive, as shown in the following code:

```
PS> Get-PSDrive

Name      Used (GB)  Free (GB)  Provider    Root
----      ---------  ---------  --------    ----
Alias                           Alias
```

```
C 89.13        89.13    111.64 FileSystem   C:\
Cert                           Certificate  \
D               0.45     21.86 FileSystem   D:\
Env                            Environment
Function                       Function
HKCU                           Registry     HKEY_CURRENT_USER
HKLM                           Registry     HKEY_LOCAL_MACHINE
Variable                       Variable
WSMan                          WSMan
```

As providers are presented as a filesystem, accessing a provider is similar to working with a drive. This example shows how Get-ChildItem changes when exploring the Cert drive:

```
PS C:\> Set-Location Cert:\LocalMachine\Root
PS Cert:\LocalMachine\Root> Get-ChildItem

   Directory: Microsoft.PowerShell.Security\Certificate::LocalMachine\Root


Thumbprint                                 Subject
----------                                 -------
CDD4EEAE6000AC7F40C3802C171E30148030C072   CN=Microsoft Root Certif...
BE36A4562FB2EE05DBB3D32323ADF445084ED656   CN=Thawte Timestamping C...
A43489159A520F0D93D032CCAF37E7FE20A8B419   CN=Microsoft Root Author...
```

A similar approach may be taken to access the registry. By default, drives are available for the current user HKCU and local machine HKLM hives. Accessing HKEY_USERS is possible by adding a new drive with the following command:

```
New-PSDrive HKU -PSProvider Registry -Root HKEY_USERS
```

After running the preceding command, a new drive may be used:

```
PS C:\> Get-ChildItem HKU:

    Hive: HKEY_USERS


Name                                 Property
----                                 --------
.DEFAULT
S-1-5-19
S-1-5-20
```

Running HKCU or Cert: does not change the drive

Running `C:` or `D:` in the PowerShell console changes to a new drive letter. This is possible because `C:` is a function that calls `Set-Location: (Get-Command C:).Definition`.

Every letter of the alphabet (A to Z) has a predefined function (`Get-Command *:`) but the other drives (for example, `Cert`, `HKCU`, and so on) do not. `Set-Location` (or its alias `cd`) must be used to switch into these drives.

Using providers

As we saw previously, providers may be accessed in the same way as the filesystem. Commands we might traditionally think of as filesystem commands (such as `Get-ChildItem`, `New` and `Remove-Item`, `Get` and `Set-Acl`, and `Get` and `Set-ItemProperty`) can work with data presented by a provider.

The list of parameters for the filesystem commands changes depending on the provider. The affected parameters are detailed in the help files for individual providers.

If we look at the `FileSystem` provider help file (`Get-Help FileSystem`), we can see that `Get-ChildItem` has a file switch parameter that can be used to filter files only:

```
-File <System.Management.Automation.SwitchParameter>
    Gets files.
    The File parameter was introduced in Windows PowerShell 3.0.
    To get only files, use the File parameter and omit the
    Directory parameter. To exclude files, use the Directory
    parameter and omit the File parameter, or use the
    Attributes parameter.
    Cmdlets Supported: Get-ChildItem
```

Let's look at the following example:

```
Set-Location C:
Get-ChildItem -File
```

Looking at the `Certificate provider` help file (`Get-Help Certificate`), a different set of parameters is available.

PowerShell Core: The certificate provider

The parameters shown next have been removed from PowerShell Core but may return in time. In the meantime, the examples here are valid for Windows PowerShell.

For example, this excerpt shows the `ExpiringInDays` parameter for `Get-ChildItem`:

```
-ExpiringInDays <System.Int32>
    Gets certificates that are expiring in or before
    the specified number of days. Enter an integer. A
    value of 0 (zero) gets certificates that have
    expired.
    This parameter is valid in all subdirectories of
    the Certificate provider, but it is effective only
    on certificates.
    This parameter was introduced in Windows
    PowerShell 3.0.
    Cmdlets Supported: Get-ChildItem
```

The previous parameter may be used to find the `Root` certificates expiring in the next two years, as shown in the following example:

```
Get-ChildItem Cert:\LocalMachine\Root -ExpiringInDays 730
```

Introduction to splatting

Splatting is a technique that was introduced all the way back in PowerShell 2. Splatting is a way of defining the parameters of a command before calling the command. This is an important and often underrated technique.

Individual parameters are written in a hashtable (`@{ }`), and then the `@` symbol is used to tell PowerShell that the content of the hashtable should be read as parameters.

This example supplies the `Name` parameter for the `Get-Process` command, and is normally written as `Get-Process -Name explorer`:

```
$getProcess = @{
    Name = 'explorer'
}
Get-Process @getProcess
```

In this example, `getProcess` is used as the name of the variable for the hashtable. The name is arbitrary; any variable name can be used.

Splatting may be used with cmdlets, functions, and scripts. Splatting may be used when the call operator is present, for example:

```
$getProcess = @{
    Name = 'explorer'
}
& 'Get-Process' @getProcess
```

Splatting to avoid escaped end-of-line

The benefit of splatting is most obvious when working with commands that expect a larger number of parameters.

This first example uses the Windows PowerShell module `ScheduledTasks` to create a fairly basic task that runs once a day at midnight:

```
$taskAction = New-ScheduledTaskAction -Execute pwsh.exe -Argument 'Write-
Host "hello world"'
$taskTrigger = New-ScheduledTaskTrigger -Daily -At '00:00:00'
Register-ScheduledTask -TaskName 'TaskName' -Action $taskAction -Trigger
$taskTrigger -RunLevel 'Limited' -Description 'This line is too long to
read'
```

It is possible to spread the command out, in an attempt to make it easier to read, by escaping the end-of-line character, for example:

```
$taskAction = New-ScheduledTaskAction -Execute pwsh.exe `
                              -Argument 'Write-Host "hello world"'
$taskTrigger = New-ScheduledTaskTrigger -Daily `
                              -At '00:00:00'
Register-ScheduledTask -TaskName 'TaskName' `
                  -Action $taskAction `
                  -Trigger $taskTrigger `
                  -RunLevel 'Limited' `
                  -Description 'This line is too long to read'
```

The approach that's used here is relatively common, but it is fragile. It is easy to miss a tick from the end-of-line, or to accidentally add a space after a tick character. Both will break continuation, and the command will still execute but with an incomplete set of parameters; afterwards, an error may be displayed, or a prompt may be shown, depending on the parameter (or parameters) it missed.

This problem is shown in the following screenshot, where a space character has been accidentally included after the `Daily` switch parameter:

```
PS> $taskTrigger = New-ScheduledTaskTrigger -Daily

cmdlet New-ScheduledTaskTrigger at command pipeline position 1
Supply values for the following parameters:
At:
```

Splatting provides a neater, generally easier to read and more robust alternative. The following example shows one possible way to tackle these commands when using splatting:

```
$newTaskAction = @{
    Execute = 'pwsh.exe'
    Argument = 'Write-Host "hello world"'
}
$newTaskTrigger = @{
    Daily = $true
    At    = '00:00:00'
}
$registerTask = @{
    TaskName    = 'TaskName'
    Action      = New-ScheduledTaskAction @newTaskAction
    Trigger     = New-ScheduledTaskTrigger @newTaskTrigger
    RunLevel    = 'Limited'
    Description = 'Splatting is easy to read'
}
Register-ScheduledTask @registerTask
```

What about switch parameters?

Switch parameters may be treated as if they are Boolean when splatting. The `Daily` parameter that was defined in the previous example is a switch parameter.

The same approach will apply to `Confirm`, `Force`, `WhatIf`, `Verbose`, and so on.

Splatting to avoid repetition

Splatting may be used to avoid repetition when a parameter must be optionally passed on to a number of different commands. It is possible to splat more than one set of parameters.

In this example, the `ComputerName` and `Credential` parameters are used by two different commands:

```
# Parameters used to authenticate remote connections
$remoteParams = @{
    Credential   = Get-Credential
    ComputerName = $env:COMPUTERNAME
}
# Parameters which are specific to Test-WSMan
$testWSMan = @{
    Authentication = 'Default'
    ErrorAction    = 'SilentlyContinue'
}
# By default, do not pass any extra parameters to New-CimSession
$newCimSession = @{}
if (-not (Test-WSMan @testWSMan @remoteParams)) {
    # If WSMan fails, use DCOM (RPC over TCP) to connect
    $newCimSession.Add('SessionOption', (New-CimSessionOption -Protocol
Dcom))
}
# Parameters to pass to Get-CimInstance
$getCimInstance = @{
    ClassName  = 'Win32_Service'
    CimSession = New-CimSession @newCimSession @remoteParams
}
Get-CimInstance @getCimInstance
```

This example takes advantage of a number of features:

- It is possible to splat no parameters using an empty hashtable (`@{}`)
- It is possible to test conditions and dynamically add parameters at run time (if needed)
- It is possible to splat more than one set of parameters into a command

As the preceding example shows, it is possible to dynamically choose the parameters that are passed to a command without having to write the command in full more than once in a script.

Splatting and positional parameters

So far, all of the parameters that have been used were given were names. It is possible, although rare, to splat positional parameters. This will be demonstrated using the `Rename-Item` command, which has two positional parameters: path and new name. It is possible to run `Rename-Item` as follows:

```
Rename-Item oldname.txt newname.txt
```

An array may be used to splat these positional parameters:

```
$renameItem = 'oldname.txt', 'newname.txt'
Rename-Item @renameItem
```

Summary

In this chapter, we explored the help system that's built into PowerShell. We took a brief look at syntax, examples, and parameters. We also looked at how help content may be moved between computers.

Command naming and discovery introduced how we might use the verb-noun pairing to discover commands that can be used. Aliases were introduced briefly.

Parameters and parameter sets were explored, as well as different types of parameters.

We took a basic look at providers and how they are used before taking a look at handling long command lines using splatting.

In `Chapter 2`, *Modules and Snap-ins*, we will explore the commands that are used to find, install, and load modules in PowerShell.

Modules and Snap-ins

2

Modules and snap-ins are packaged collections of commands that may be loaded inside PowerShell. Both modules and snap-ins may be used to extend the set of commands available in PowerShell. Modules are more flexible and are simpler to work with and this will be clear with the several commands that we will be covering in this chapter. We will also look at PowerShell Gallery which is a valuable source of modules published by Microsoft and others. In a nutshell, this chapter will explore the use and discovery of modules within Windows PowerShell and PowerShell Core.

The chapter will cover the following topics:

- Introducing modules
- PowerShell Core and the `WindowsCompatibility` module
- Introducing snap-ins

Introducing modules

Modules were introduced with the release of PowerShell version 2.0. Modules represented a significant step forward over snap-ins. Unlike snap-ins, modules do not have to be formally installed or registered for use with PowerShell.

It is most common to find a module that targets a specific system or focuses on a small set of related operations. For example, the `Microsoft.PowerShell.LocalAccounts` module contains commands for interacting with the local account database (users and groups).

A module may be binary, script, dynamic, or manifest:

- **Binary modules**: These are written in a language such as C# or VB.NET, and then compiled into a **dynamic-link library** (**DLL**).
- **Script modules**: These are a collection of functions written in the PowerShell language. The commands typically reside in a script module file (PSM1).

- **Dynamic modules**: These are created using the `New-Module` command and exists in memory only. The following command creates a very simple dynamic module that adds the `Get-Number` command:

```
New-Module -Name TestModule -ScriptBlock {
    function Get-Number { return 1 }
}
```

- **Manifest modules**: These combines different items to make a single consistent module. For example, a manifest may be used to create a single module out of a DLL containing `cmdlets` and a script containing functions, and `Microsoft.PowerShell.Utility` is a manifest module that combines a binary and script module.

  A manifest module may also be used to build commands based on WMI classes. The `cmdlets-over-objects` feature was added with PowerShell 3, an XML file with a `cdxml` extension (`cmdlet` definition XML). For example, the `Defender` module creates commands based on WMI classes in the `ROOT/Microsoft/Windows/Defender` namespace.

The `cmdlets-over-objects` feature is explored by Richard Siddaway in a series of blog posts on the Scripting Guy site. The first of these is found here: `https://blogs.technet.microsoft.com/heyscriptingguy/2015/02/03/registry-cmdlets-first-steps-with-cdxml/`.

The module manifest file serves a number of purposes, including the following:

- Describing the files that should be loaded (such as a script module file, a binary library, and a `cmdlet` definition XML file)
- Listing any dependencies the module may have (such as other modules, .NET libraries, or other DLL files)
- Listing the commands that should be exported (as in, made available to the end user)
- Recording information about the author or the project

When loading a module with a manifest, PowerShell will try and load any listed dependencies. If a module fails to load because of a dependency, the commands written as part of the module will not be imported.

What is the PowerShell Gallery?

The PowerShell Gallery is a repository and distribution platform for scripts, modules, and **Desired State Configuration (DSC)** resources that have been written by Microsoft or other users of PowerShell.

In February 2016, Microsoft made the PowerShell Gallery public.

The PowerShell Gallery has parallels in other scripting languages, as shown in the following examples:

- Perl has `cpan.org`
- Python has PyPI
- Ruby has RubyGems

Support for the gallery is included by default in PowerShell 5. For PowerShell 3 and 4, PowerShellGet (via the `PackageManagement PowerShell` modules preview package) must be installed: `https://www.microsoft.com/en-us/download/details.aspx?id=51451`.

The PowerShell Gallery may be searched using `https://www.powershellgallery.com` as shown in the following screenshot:

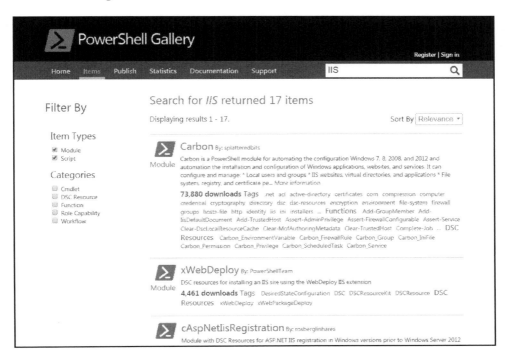

The Get-Module command

The Microsoft Windows operating system, especially the most recent versions, comes with a wide variety of modules installed. These, as well as any other modules that have been installed, can be viewed using the `Get-Module` command.

By default, `Get-Module` shows modules that have been imported (either automatically or using `Import-Module`); for example, if the command is run from PowerShell ISE, it will show that the `ISE` module has been loaded:

```
PS> Get-Module

ModuleType     Version     Name                              ExportedCommands
----------     -------     ----                              ----------------
Script         1.0.0.0     ISE                               {Get-
IseSnippet...}
Manifest       3.1.0.0     Microsoft.PowerShell.Management   {Add-Computer...}
Manifest       3.1.0.0     Microsoft.PowerShell.Utility      {Add-Member...}
```

The `ListAvailable` parameter shows the list of modules that have been loaded, as well as those PowerShell discovers:

```
Get-Module -ListAvailable
```

Modules may exist in more than one location. `Get-Module` and `Import-Module` will consider each path in order. If a matching module is found, the search stops, even if a newer version exists in a different directory.

`Get-Module` can show each instance of a module regardless of the path, using the `All` parameter:

```
Get-Module <ModuleName> -All -ListAvailable
```

`$env:PSMODULEPATH` determines where both Windows PowerShell and PowerShell Core find modules when running `Get-Module` and `Import-Module`. The source of this variable is different for each version, and is explored here.

PSModulePath in Windows PowerShell

Windows PowerShell allows the value of `$env:PSModulePath` to be set using user and machine environment variables. If the environment variables are not set, Windows PowerShell uses the default values shown here:

```
PS> $env:PSModulePath -split ';'
```

```
C:\Users\whoami\Documents\WindowsPowerShell\Modules
C:\Program Files\WindowsPowerShell\Modules
c:\windows\system32\windowspowershell\v1.0\Modules
```

When environment variables are set, the default values are completely replaced, as follows:

- The user path, starting C:\users, is replaced with the content of the user PSModulePath environment variable
- The system path, which starts with C:\windows, is replaced with the machine PSModulePath environment variable

Windows PowerShell merges both instances of the environment variable. C:\Program Files\WindowsPowerShell\Modules is added immediately after the user paths by Windows PowerShell; it will always be present.

The next example sets the user PSModulePath environment variable, adding a new path to the end of the default list. The list is semicolon-delimited. The change will not be visible until Windows PowerShell is restarted:

```
# Get the value of the environment variable
$environmentVariable =
[Environment]::GetEnvironmentVariable('PSMODULEPATH', 'User')
# If it is not set, use the User default path
if (-not $environmentVariable) {
    $environmentVariable = "$home\Documents\WindowsPowerShell\Modules"
}
# Add a new path
$paths = "$environmentVariable;C:\SomeNewModulePath"
# Set the environment variable
[Environment]::SetEnvironmentVariable('PSMODULEPATH', $paths, 'User')
```

PSModulePath in PowerShell Core

In PowerShell Core, PSModulePath is hardcoded and has the following values:

```
PS> $env:PSModulePath -split ';'
C:\Users\whoami\Documents\PowerShell\Modules
C:\Program Files\PowerShell\Modules
c:\program files\powershell\6\Modules
C:\WINDOWS\system32\WindowsPowerShell\v1.0\Modules
```

PowerShell Core disregards the environment variables set for the user or machine. The value may only be overridden by making changes after PowerShell Core has started, for example, by implementing a profile script that explicitly sets a new value for $env:PSModulePath.

The `C:\WINDOWS\system32\WindowsPowerShell\v1.0\Modules` path is included in the list shown in the previous snippet. PowerShell Core performs additional filtering on the content of this directory.

Get-Module, PSCompatibility, and PSEdition

The PSEdition and `PSCompatibleEditions` fields were added to the module manifest (a `.psd1` file that accompanies a module) with PowerShell 5.1. This allows module authors to state whether a module is PowerShell Core (Core), Windows PowerShell (Desk), or both.

By default, PowerShell Core will not find or use modules from `C:\WINDOWS\system32\WindowsPowerShell\v1.0\Modules` when running the `Get-Module -ListAvailable` command or when using `Import-Module`.

Modules in this one location are subject to additional checks as they have not been tested with PowerShell Core and may not load. Modules in this location may be viewed or loaded in the following circumstances:

- The module manifest (`.psd1` file) accompanying the module has PSEdition set to Core
- The module manifest uses the `PSCompatibleEditions` field and includes Core
- The switch parameter `SkipEditionCheck` is used with `Get-Module` or `Import-Module`

For example, the NetSecurity module may be loaded in PowerShell Core directly using this command:

```
Import-Module NetSecurity -SkipEditionCheck
```

Modules loaded from the remaining locations in `$env:PSModulePath` are not filtered.

The Import-Module command

PowerShell 3 and later will attempt to automatically load modules if a command from that module is used and the module is under one of the paths in the `$env:PSModulePath` environment variable. The `Import-Module` command is less important than it was in Windows PowerShell 2.

For example, if PowerShell is started and the PSDesiredStateConfiguration module is not imported, running the Get-DscResource command will cause the module to be imported. This is shown in the following example:

```
PS> Get-Module PSDesiredStateConfiguration
PS> Get-DscResource | Out-Null
PS> Get-Module PSDesiredStateConfiguration

ModuleType    Version    Name                          ExportedCommands
----------    -------    ----                          ----------------
Manifest      1.1        PSDesiredStateConfiguration   ...
```

In the previous example, the first time Get-Module is executed, the PSDesiredStateConfiguration module has not yet been loaded. After running Get-DscResource, a command from the PSDesiredStateConfiguration module, the module is loaded and the command is immediately executed. Once loaded, the module is visible when running Get-Module.

Modules in PowerShell may be explicitly imported using the Import-Module command. Modules may be imported using a name or with a full path, as shown in the following example:

```
Import-Module -Name PSWorkflow
Import-Module -Name
C:\Windows\System32\WindowsPowerShell\v1.0\Modules\PSWorkflow\PSWorkflow.ps
d1
```

Once a module has been imported, the commands within the module may be listed using Get-Command as follows:

```
Get-Command -Module PSWorkflow
```

Modules, Get-Command, and auto-loading

As the commands exported by a module can only be identified by importing the module, the previous command will trigger automatic import.

Modules installed in Windows PowerShell 5 and PowerShell Core are placed in a folder named after the module version. This allows multiple versions of the same module to coexist, as shown in the following example:

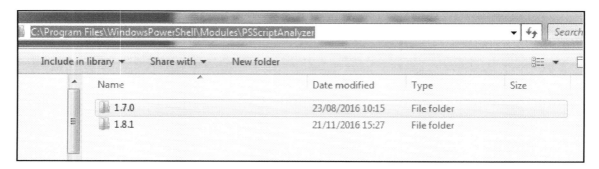

Version 1.8.1 of `PSScriptAnalyzer` will be imported by default, as it is the highest version number. It is possible to import a specific version of a module using the `MinimumVersion` and `MaximumVersion` parameters:

```
Import-Module PSScriptAnalyzer -MaxmimumVersion 1.7.0
```

The Remove-Module command

The `Remove-Module` command attempts to remove a previously imported module from the current session.

For binary modules or manifest modules that incorporate a DLL, commands are removed from PowerShell but DLLs are not unloaded.

`Remove-Module` does not remove or delete the files that make up a module from a computer.

The Find-Module command

The `Find-Module` command allows you to search the PowerShell Gallery or any other registered repository for modules.

Modules can be identified by name, as shown in the following example:

```
Find-Module Carbon
Find-Module -Name Carbon
Find-Module -Name Azure*
```

If the name is not sufficient for the search, the `Filter` parameter may be used. Supplying a value for the `Filter` parameter is equivalent to using the search field in the PowerShell Gallery that expands the search to include tags:

```
Find-Module -Filter IIS
```

The Install-Module command

The `Install-Module` command installs or updates modules from the PowerShell Gallery or any other configured repository. By default, `Install-Module` adds modules to the path for `AllUsers`, at `C:\Program Files\WindowsPowerShell\Modules`.

Access rights

Installing a module under the `AllUsers` scope requires an administrator account.

For example, the `posh-git` module may be installed using either of the following two commands:

```
Find-Module posh-git | Install-Module
Install-Module posh-git
```

Modules may be installed under a user-specific path (`$home\Documents\WindowsPowerShell\Modules`) using the `Scope` parameter:

```
Install-Module carbon -Scope CurrentUser
```

If the most recent version of a module is already installed, the command ends without providing feedback.

In Windows PowerShell, if a newer version is available, it will be automatically installed alongside the original.

In PowerShell Core, a warning is displayed, indicating that the `Force` parameter must be used to install a newer version, such as in the following example:

```
Install-Module carbon -Scope CurrentUser -Force
```

Force may be used to re-install a module in both Windows PowerShell and PowerShell Core:

```
Install-Module posh-git -Force
```

The `Install-Module` command does not provide an option to install modules under the `$PSHOME` (`$env:SYSTEMROOT\System32\WindowsPowerShell\v1.0`) directory. The `$PSHOME` path is reserved for modules created by Microsoft that are deployed with the **Windows Management Framework (WMF)** or the Windows operating system.

The Update-Module command

The `Update-Module` command may only be used after a module has been installed using `Install-Module`. In both Windows PowerShell and PowerShell Core, it will attempt to update the module to the latest, or specified, version.

The Save-Module command

The `Save-Module` command downloads the module from the PowerShell Gallery to a given path without installing it. For example, the following command downloads the `Carbon` module into a `Modules` directory in the root of the `C:` drive:

```
Save-Module -Name Carbon -Path C:\Modules
```

`Save-Module` will do the following:

- Always download the module and overwrite any previously saved version in the specified path.
- Ignore installed or other saved versions.

PowerShell Core and the WindowsCompatibility module

The `WindowsCompatibility` module has been created for PowerShell Core to allow or simplify the use of Windows PowerShell modules and commands in PowerShell Core.

The module may be installed in PowerShell Core by running the command:

```
Install-Module WindowsCompatibility -Scope CurrentUser
```

The module is required for the following sections in which we'll explore its functionality.

The compatibility session

The WindowsCompatibility module uses a technique known as **implicit remoting** to make commands from Windows PowerShell available in PowerShell Core.

A compatibility session is automatically created when any of the commands from the module are run.

By default, the compatibility session is created to use the local computer. To support this, Windows Remoting must be enabled and configured in Windows PowerShell.

Enabling remoting

Remoting is discussed in greater detail in Chapter 14, *Remoting and Remote Management*. Until then, Windows Remoting may be enabled and configured using the wirm command with the quick config argument: winrm qc.

The WindowsCompatibility module can use a session on a remote computer. This may be useful when Windows PowerShell is not available locally, as is the case when running PowerShell Core on Linux or macOS. The Initialize-WinSession command is used to to explicitly create a compatibility session.

Remote commands do not run locally

If a remote computer is used for the compatibility session any imported commands will execute on that remote computer. For example, importing the NetSecurity module and running Get-NetFirewallRule will display the rules on that remote computer.

Each of the remaining commands in the WindowsCompatibility module implements the ComputerName, Credential, and ConfigurationName parameters to support different command sources if necessary.

Add-WindowsPSModulePath

The `Add-WindowsPSModulePath` command adds the default Windows PowerShell module paths and the content of the machine level PSModulePath variable, to the end of the `$env:PSModulePath` variable.

For example, before the command is run, `$env:PSModulePath` may be set to the following:

```
C:\Users\whoami\Documents\PowerShell\Modules
C:\Program Files\PowerShell\Modules
c:\program files\powershell\6-preview\Modules
C:\WINDOWS\system32\WindowsPowerShell\v1.0\Modules
```

After the command has run, `$env:PSModulePath` will have the following added. These values are hardcoded:

```
${env:userprofile}\Documents\WindowsPowerShell\Module
${env:programfiles}\WindowsPowerShell\Modules
```

In addition to these, any paths present in the environment variable are added. This process may result in some duplication. The outcome is shown in this screenshot:

Get-WinModule and Import-WinModule

The `Get-WinModule` command lists the modules available to the compatibility session. This may be considered similar to running `Get-Module -ListAvailable`.

`Import-WinModule` attempts to load the requested module (by name) in the compatibility session. For example, `Import-WinModule Pester` will attempt to load the latest version of the Pester module within the compatibility session.

The version number of the loaded module will display as 1.0 when running `Get-Module` in PowerShell Core this version is not derived from the source module:

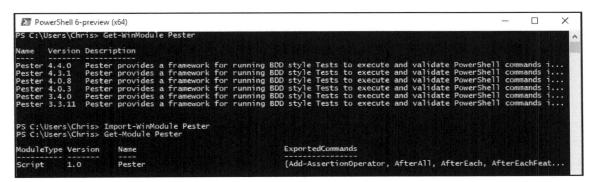

It is not possible at this time to import a specific version of a module in the compatibility session.

Copy-WinModule

The `Copy-WinModule` command copies module content from the current location to either `$pshome\Modules` or a user-specified destination.

`Copy-WinModule` may only be used when the compatibility session is local (the default behavior).

This command is useful where a module has been tested and found working under Core. At this point, it may be desirable to load the module directly rather than through a compatibility session, or from a path that is not listed in PSModulePath.

Invoke-WinCommand

Invoke-WinCommand allows the execution of a script block in the compatibility session. This may be useful when the commands or command output do not work well through Windows Remoting.

Introducing snap-ins

Snap-ins are only available in Windows PowerShell; they are not present in PowerShell Core. A snap-in was the precursor to a module. It was the mechanism available to extend the set of commands in PowerShell 1.0. The `cmdlet` implementation inside a snap-in is similar to a binary module (written in a language such as C#). A snap-in contains a specialized class that holds the fields that were moved into the module manifest with PowerShell 2.0.

Snap-ins must be installed or registered before they can be used. This can be done using `installutil`, which is part of the .NET framework package. Many vendors (including Microsoft) took to releasing **Microsoft Installer (MSI)** packages to simplify the snap-in installation.

Modules have, for the most part, made snap-ins obsolete. Manifest modules, accompanied by a binary module, offer the same performance benefits, without the installation or registration overheads.

The list of snap-ins may be viewed using the following command:

```
Get-PSSnapIn -Registered
```

If the `Registered` parameter is excluded, `Get-PSSnapIn` will show the snap-ins that have been imported into the current PowerShell session.

Windows PowerShell and the Microsoft.PowerShell.Core snap-in

The core commands loaded for Windows PowerShell are a part of the snap-in written into the System.Management.Automation library. This snap-in does not appear in the list of registered snap-ins.

 Registered snap-ins are read from HKLM:\Software\Microsoft\PowerShell\1\PowerShellSnapIns.

If a computer does not have any registered snap-ins, the registry path may not exist. The snap-in list is generated by looping through all commands and reading the PSSnapIn property in a manner similar to the following command: (Get-Command).PSSnapIn.Name | Select-Object – Unique.

Using snap-ins

PowerShell will not automatically load commands from a snap-in. All snap-ins, except Microsoft.PowerShell.Core, must be explicitly imported using the Add-PSSnapIn command:

```
Add-PSSnapIn WDeploySnapin3.0
```

Once a snap-in has been installed (registered) and added, Get-Command may be used to list the commands:

```
Get-Command -Module WDeploySnapin3.0
```

Summary

In this chapter, we primarily looked at modules and snap-ins. We explored that Unlike snap-ins, modules do not have to be formally installed or registered for use with PowerShell. Different commands were covered under the modules section and we saw the various functionalities it handles. In addition to this, PowerShell Core and the WindowsCompatibility module was introduced. Moreover, we saw that Snap-ins are rarely used these days, and support has been removed from PowerShell Core.

With this pre-requisites, we move on to the next challenge, Chapter 3, *Working with Objects in PowerShell*, where we will dive into the commands available to work with objects in PowerShell, including Where-Object, and ForEach-Object.

Working with Objects in PowerShell

3

Everything we do in PowerShell revolves around working with objects. Objects, in PowerShell, may have properties or methods (or both). It is difficult to describe an object without resorting to this; an object is a representation of a thing or item of data. We might use an analogy to attempt to give meaning to the term.

A book is an object and has properties that describe physical characteristics, such as the number of pages, the weight, or size. It has metadata (information about data) properties that describe the author, the publisher, the table of contents, and so on.

The book might also have methods. A method affects the change on the state of an object. For example, there might be methods to open or close the book or methods to jump to different chapters. A method might also convert an object into a different format. For example, there might be a method to copy a page, or even destructive methods such as one to split the book.

PowerShell has a variety of commands that allow us to work with sets (or collections) of objects in a pipeline.

In this chapter, we are going to cover the following topics:

- Pipelines
- Members
- Enumerating and filtering
- Selecting and sorting
- Grouping and measuring
- Comparing
- Importing, exporting, and converting

Pipelines

The pipeline is one of the most prominent features of PowerShell. The pipeline is used to send output from one command (standard out or `Stdout`) into another command (standard in or `Stdin`).

Standard output

The term standard output is used because there are different kinds of output. Each of these different forms of output is referred to as a stream.

When assigning the output of a command to a variable, the values are taken from the standard output (the output stream) of a command. For example, the following command assigns the data from the standard output to a variable:

```
$stdout = Get-CimInstance -ClassName Win32_ComputerSystem
```

Non-standard output

In PowerShell there are other output streams; these include error (`Write-Error`), information (`Write-Information`, introduced in PowerShell 5), warning (`Write-Warning`), and verbose (`Write-Verbose`). Each of these has a stream of its own.

In PowerShell 5 and later, the `Write-Host` command sends output to the information stream.

Prior to PowerShell 5, `Write-Host` did not have a dedicated stream; the output could only be captured via a transcript, that is, using the `Start-Transcript` command to log console output to a file.

For example, if the `Verbose` switch is added to the preceding command, more information is shown. This extra information is not held in the variable, it is sent to a different stream:

```
PS> $stdout = Get-CimInstance Win32_ComputerSystem -Verbose
VERBOSE: Perform operation 'Enumerate CimInstances' with following
parameters, ''namespaceName' = root\cimv2,'className' =
Win32_ComputerSystem'.
VERBOSE: Operation 'Enumerate CimInstances' complete.

PS> $stdout

Name       PrimaryOwnerName      Domain        TotalPhysicalMemory      Model
```

----	----------------	------	--------------------	------
TITAN	**Chris**	**WORKGROUP**	**17076875264**	**All Series**

The object pipeline

Languages such as Batch scripting (on Windows) or Bash scripting (ordinarily on Linux or Unix) use a pipeline to pass text between commands. It is up to the next command to figure out what the text means.

PowerShell, on the other hand, sends objects from one command to another.

The pipe (|) symbol is used to send the standard output between commands.

In the following example, the output of Get-Process is sent to the Where-Object command, which applies a filter. The filter restricts the list of processes to those that are using more than 50MB of memory:

```
Get-Process | Where-Object WorkingSet -gt 50MB
```

Members

At the beginning of this chapter, the idea of properties and methods was introduced. These are part of a set of items collectively known as members. These members are used to interact with an object. A few of the more frequently used members are NoteProperty, ScriptProperty, ScriptMethod, and Event.

What are the member types?

The list of possible member types can be viewed on MSDN, which includes a short description of each member type: https://msdn. microsoft.com/en-us/library/system.management.automation. psmembertypes(v=vs.85).aspx.

This chapter focuses on the different property members: Property, NoteProperty, and ScriptProperty. They are the most relevant to the commands in this chapter.

The Get-Member command

The Get-Member command is used to view the different members of an object. For example, it can be used to list all of the members of a process object (returned by Get-Process):

```
Get-Process -Id $PID | Get-Member
```

Get-Member offers filters using its parameters (MemberType, Static, and View). For example, if we wished to view only the properties of the PowerShell process, we might run the following:

```
Get-Process -Id $PID | Get-Member -MemberType Property
```

The Static parameter will be covered in Chapter 7, *Working with .NET*.

The View parameter is set to all by default. It has three additional values:

- **Base**: It shows properties that are derived from a .NET object
- **Adapted**: It shows members handled by PowerShell's **Adapted Type System (ATS)**
- **Extended**: It shows members added by PowerShell's **Extended Type System (ETS)**

Adapted and Extended Type Systems (ATS and ETS)

ATS and ETS systems make it easy to work with object frameworks other than .NET in PowerShell, for example, objects returned by ADSI, COM, WMI, or XML. Each of these frameworks is discussed later in this book.

Microsoft published an article on ATS and ETS in 2011, which is still relevant today: https://blogs.msdn.microsoft.com/besidethepoint/ 2011/11/22/psobject-and-the-adapted-and-extended-type-systems- ats-and-ets/.

Accessing properties

Properties of an object in PowerShell may be accessed by writing the property name after a period. For example, the Name property of the current PowerShell process may be accessed by using the following code:

```
$process = Get-Process -Id $PID
$process.Name
```

PowerShell also allows us to access these properties by enclosing a command in parentheses:

```
(Get-Process -Id $PID).Name
```

Properties of an object are objects themselves. For example, the StartTime property of a process is a DateTime object. We may access the DayOfWeek property by using the following code:

```
$process = Get-Process -Id $PID
$process.StartTime.DayOfWeek
```

The variable assignment step may be skipped if parentheses are used:

```
(Get-Process -Id $PID).StartTime.DayOfWeek
```

If a property name has a space, it may be accessed using a number of different notation styles. For example, a property named 'Some Name' may be accessed by quoting the name or enclosing the name in curly braces:

```
$object = [PSCustomObject]@{ 'Some Name' = 'Value' }
$object."Some Name"
$object.'Some Name'
$object.{Some Name}
```

A variable may also be used to describe a property name:

```
PS> $object = [PSCustomObject]@{ 'Some Name' = 'Value' }
PS> $propertyName = 'Some Name'
PS> $object.$propertyName
Value
```

Using methods

As we mentioned previously, methods effect a change in state. That may be a change to the object associated with the method, or it may take the object and convert it into something else.

Methods are called using the following notation in PowerShell:

```
<Object>.Method()
```

If a method expects to have arguments (or parameters), the notation becomes the following:

```
<Object>.Method(Argument1, Argument2)
```

When the method is called without parentheses, PowerShell will show the overload definitions. The overload definitions are a list of the different sets of arguments that can be used with a method. For example, the Substring method of System.String has two definitions:

```
PS> 'thisString'.Substring

OverloadDefinitions
-------------------
string Substring(int startIndex)
string Substring(int startIndex, int length)
```

An example of a method that takes an object and converts it into something else is shown here. In this case, a date is converted into a string:

```
PS> $date = Get-Date "01/01/2010"
PS> $date.ToLongDateString()
01 January 2010
```

An example of a method that changes a state might be a TCP socket. TCP connections must be opened before data can be sent over a network:

```
$tcpClient = New-Object System.Net.Sockets.TcpClient
$tcpClient.Connect("127.0.0.1", 135)
```

A TCP client is created, then an attempt is made to connect to the RPC endpoint mapper port (TCP/135) on the localhost.

The `Connect` method does not return anything (although it will throw an error if the connection fails). It affects the state of the object and is reflected by the `Connected` property:

```
PS> $tcpClient.Connected
True
```

The state of the object may be changed again by calling the `Close` method to disconnect:

```
$tcpClient.Close()
```

An example of a method that takes arguments might be the `ToString` method on a `DateTime` object. `Get-Date` can be used to create a `DateTime` object:

```
PS> (Get-Date).ToString('u')
2016-12-08 21:18:49Z
```

In the preceding example, the letter u is one of the standard date and time format strings (`https://msdn.microsoft.com/en-us/library/az4se3k1(v=vs.110).aspx`) and represents a universal sortable date/time pattern. The same result may be achieved by using the `Format` parameter of `Get-Date`:

```
PS> Get-Date -Format u
2016-12-08 21:19:31Z
```

The advantage this method has over the parameter is that the date can be adjusted before conversion by using some of the other properties and methods:

```
(Get-Date).Date.AddDays(-1).ToString('u')
```

The result of this command will be the start of yesterday (midnight, one day before today).

Access modifiers

Depending on the type of object, properties may be read-only or read/write. These may be identified using `Get-Member` and by inspecting the access modifiers.

In the following example, the value in curly braces at the end of each line is the access modifier:

```
PS> $File = New-Item NewFile.txt -Force
PS> $File | Get-Member -MemberType Property

    TypeName: System.IO.FileInfo

Name                MemberType     Definition
----                ----------     ----------
Attributes          Property       System.IO.FileAttributes Attributes
{get;set;}
CreationTime        Property       datetime CreationTime {get;set;}
CreationTimeUtc     Property       datetime CreationTimeUtc {get;set;}
Directory           Property       System.IO.DirectoryInfo Directory {get;}
DirectoryName       Property       string DirectoryName {get;}
Exists              Property       bool Exists {get;}
```

When the modifier is {get;}, the property value is read-only; attempting to change the value will result in an error:

```
PS> $File = New-Item NewFile.txt -Force
PS> $File.Name = 'NewName'
'Name' is a ReadOnly property.
At line:1 char:1
+ $File.Name = 'NewName'
+ ~~~~~~~~~~~~~~~~~~~~~~~
  + CategoryInfo : InvalidOperation: (:) [], RuntimeException
  + FullyQualifiedErrorId : PropertyAssignmentException
```

When the modifier is {get;set;}, the property value may be read and changed. In the preceding example, CreationTime has the set access modifier. The value can be changed; in this case, it may be set to any date after January 1, 1601:

```
$File = New-Item NewFile.txt -Force
$File.CreationTime = Get-Date -Day 1 -Month 2 -Year 1692
```

The result of the preceding command can be seen by reviewing the properties for the file in PowerShell:

```
Get-Item NewFile.txt | Select-Object -ExpandProperty CreationTime
```

Alternatively, you can use explorer, as shown in the following screenshot:

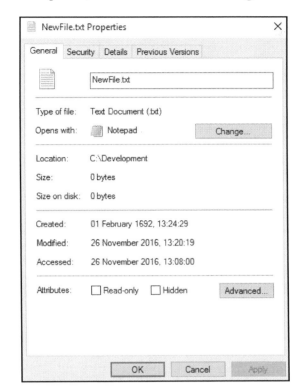

In the preceding example, the change made to `CreationTime` is passed from the object representing the file to the file itself. The object used here, based on the .NET class `System.IO.FileInfo`, is written in such a way that it supports the change. A property may indicate that it can be changed (by supporting the set access modifier in `Get-Member`) and still not pass the change back to whatever the object represents.

The Add-Member command

`Add-Member` allows new members to be added to existing objects.

Starting with an `empty` object, it is possible to add new properties:

```
PS> $empty = New-Object Object
PS> $empty | Add-Member -Name New -Value 'Hello world' -MemberType
NoteProperty
PS> $empty

New
---
Hello world
```

`Add-Member` may also add a `ScriptProperty` or a `ScriptMethod`. When writing script-based properties and methods, the reserved variable `$this` is used to refer to itself.

To add calculated properties, which are evaluated when viewed, use the following code:

```
PS> $empty = New-Object Object
PS> $empty | Add-Member -Name New -Value 'Hello world' -MemberType
NoteProperty
PS> $empty | Add-Member -Name Calculated -Value { $this.New.Length } -
MemberType ScriptProperty
PS> $empty

New            Calculated
---            ----------
Hello world            11
```

Methods may be added as well, for example, a method to replace the word `world` in the new property:

```
PS> $empty = New-Object Object
PS> $empty | Add-Member -Name New -Value 'Hello world' -MemberType
NoteProperty
PS> $params = @{
>>      Name       = 'Replace'
>>      MemberType = 'ScriptMethod'
>>      Value      = { $this.New -replace 'world', 'everyone' }
>> }
PS> $empty | Add-Member @params
PS> $empty.Replace()
Hello everyone
```

Enumerating and filtering

Enumerating, or listing, the objects in a collection in PowerShell does not need a specialized command. For example, if the results of Get-PSDrive were assigned to a variable, enumerating the content of the variable is as simple as writing the variable name and pressing *Enter*:

```
PS> $drives = Get-PSDrive
PS> $drives

Name     Used (GB)    Free (GB)    Provider     Root
----     ---------    ---------    --------     ----
Alias                              Alias
C          319.37       611.60     FileSystem   C:\
Cert                               Certificate  \
Env                                Environment
...
```

ForEach-Object may be used where something complex needs to be done to each object.

Where-Object may be used to filter results.

The ForEach-Object command

ForEach-Object is most often used as a loop (of sorts). For example, the following command works on each of the results from Get-Process in turn:

```
Get-Process | ForEach-Object {
    Write-Host $_.Name -ForegroundColor Green
}
```

In the preceding example, a special variable, $_, is used to access each of the objects from the input pipeline. In the previous example, it is used to access each of the objects returned by the Get-Process command.

ForEach-Object may also be used to get a single property, or execute a single method on each of the objects.

For example, ForEach-Object may be used to return only the Path property when using Get-Process:

```
Get-Process | ForEach-Object Path
```

Or, `ForEach-Object` may be used to run the `ToString` method on a set of dates:

```
PS> (Get-Date '01/01/2019'), (Get-Date '01/01/2020') | ForEach-Object
ToString('yyyyMMdd')
20190101
20200101
```

Where-Object command

Filtering the output from commands may be performed using `Where-Object`. For example, we might filter processes that started after 5 pm today:

```
Get-Process | Where-Object StartTime -gt (Get-Date 17:00:00)
```

The syntax shown in help for `Where-Object` does not quite match the syntax used here. The help text is as follows:

```
Where-Object [-Property] <String> [[-Value] <Object>] -GT ...
```

In the preceding example, we see the following:

- `StartTime` is the argument for the `Property` parameter (first argument by position
- The comparison is greater than, as signified by the `gt` switch parameter
- The date (using the `Get-Date` command) is the argument for the `Value` parameter (second argument by position)

Based on that, the example might be written as follows:

```
Get-Process | Where-Object -Property StartTime -Value (Get-Date 17:00:00) -
gt
```

However, it is far easier to read `StartTime` is greater than `<some date>`, so most examples tend to follow that pattern.

`Where-Object` will also accept filters using the `FilterScript` parameter. `FilterScript` is often used to describe more complex filters, filters where more than one term is used:

```
Get-Service | Where-Object { $_.StartType -eq 'Manual' -and $_.Status -eq
'Running' }
```

When a filter like this is used, the conditions are evaluated in the order they are written. This can be used to avoid conditions that may otherwise cause errors.

In the following example, `Test-Path` is used before `Get-Item`, which is used to test the last time a file was written on a remote computer (via the administrative share):

```
'Computer1', 'Computer2' | Where-Object {
    (Test-Path "\\$_\c$\temp\file.txt") -and
    (Get-Item "\\$_\c$\temp\file.txt").LastWriteTime -lt (Get-
Date).AddDays(-90)
}
```

If `Test-Path` is removed, the snippet will throw an error if either the computer or the file does not exist.

Selecting and sorting

`Select-Object` allows a subset of data to be returned when executing a command. This may be a more restrictive number of elements, or a smaller number of properties.

`Sort-Object` can be used to perform both simple and complex sorting.

The Select-Object command

`Select-Object` is most frequently used to limit the properties returned by a command. The command is extremely versatile as it enables you to do the following:

- Limit the properties returned by a command by name:

```
Get-Process | Select-Object -Property Name, Id
```

- Limit the properties returned from a command using wildcards:

```
Get-Process | Select-Object -Property Name, *Memory
```

- List everything but a few properties:

```
Get-Process | Select-Object -Property * -Exclude *Memory*
```

- Get the first few objects:

```
Get-ChildItem C:\ -Recurse | Select-Object -First 2
```

- Get the last few objects:

```
Get-ChildItem C:\ | Select-Object -Last 3
```

- Skip items at the beginning. In this example, this returns the fifth item:

```
Get-ChildItem C:\ | Select-Object -Skip 4 -First 1
```

- Skip items at the end. This example returns the third from the end:

```
Get-ChildItem C:\ | Select-Object -Skip 2 -Last 1
```

- Expand properties:

```
Get-ChildItem C:\ | Select-Object -ExpandProperty FullName
Get-ChildItem $env:SYSTEMROOT\*.dll | Select-Object Name,
Length -ExpandProperty VersionInfo
```

- Select-Object can return -Unique values from arrays of simple values:

```
1, 1, 1, 3, 5, 2, 2, 4 | Select-Object -Unique
```

About Get-Unique

Get-Unique may also be used to create a list of unique elements. When using Get-Unique, a list must be sorted first, for example: 1, 1, 1, 3, 5, 2, 2, 4 | Sort-Object | Get-Unique.

Select-Object can also return unique values from arrays of objects, but only if a list of properties is specified or a wildcard is used for the list of properties.

In the following example, we create an object with one property called Number. The value for the property is 1, 2, or 3. There are two objects with a value of 1, two with a value of 2, and two with a value of 3:

```
PS> (1..3 + 1..3) | ForEach-Object { [PSCustomObject]@{ Number = $_ } }

Number
------
     1
     2
     3
     1
     2
     3
```

Select-Object can remove the duplicates from the set in this example using the –Unique
parameter if a list of properties (or a wildcard for the properties) is set:

```
PS> (1..3 + 1..3) |
>>    ForEach-Object { [PSCustomObject]@{ Number = $_ } } |
>>    Select-Object -Property * -Unique

Number
------
     1
     2
     3
```

When using Get-Member, you may have noticed the PropertySet member type. Select-
Object can display the properties within the set. In the following example, Get-Member is
used to view property sets, and Select-Object is used to display the first property set
(PSConfiguration):

```
PS> Get-Process -Id $PID | Get-Member -MemberType PropertySet


      TypeName: System.Diagnostics.Process


Name               MemberType      Definition
----               ----------      ----------
PSConfiguration    PropertySet     PSConfiguration {Name, Id, ...
PSResources        PropertySet     PSResources {Name, Id, Hand...

PS> Get-Process -Id $PID | Select-Object PSConfiguration

Name              Id    PriorityClass    FileVersion
----              --    -------------    -----------
powershell_ise    5568           Normal    10.0.14393.103
(rs1_release_inmarket.160819-1924)
```

Select-Object is also able to make new properties. It will build a property if given a
name and a means of calculating it (an expression):

```
Get-Process | Select-Object -Property Name, Id,
    @{Name='FileOwner'; Expression={ (Get-Acl $_.Path).Owner }}
```

In the preceding example, @{} is a hashtable. Hashtables are discussed in Chapter 5,
Variables, Arrays, and Hashtables.

Select-Object can change objects

When `Select-Object` is used with the `Property` parameter, a new object is created (based on the value `Select-Object` is working with). For example, the first process may be selected as shown here. The resulting object type is `Process`: `(Get-Process | Select-Object - First 1).GetType()`.

 If `Select-Object` also requests a list of properties, the object type changes to `PSCustomObject`: `(Get-Process | Select-Object - Property Path, Company -First 1).GetType()`.

This is important if something else is expected to use the process. For example, `Stop-Process` will throw an error because the object being passed is not a process, nor is there sufficient information available to determine which process must stop (either the `Id` or `Name` properties): `Get-Process | Select-Object -Property Path, Company - First 1 | Stop-Process -WhatIf`.

The Sort-Object command

The `Sort-Object` command allows objects to be sorted on one or more properties.

By default, `Sort-Object` will sort numbers in ascending order:

```
PS> 5, 4, 3, 2, 1 | Sort-Object
1
2
3
4
5
```

Strings are sorted in ascending order, irrespective of uppercase or lowercase:

```
PS> 'ccc', 'BBB', 'aaa' | Sort-Object
aaa
BBB
ccc
```

When dealing with complex objects, `Sort-Object` may be used to sort based on a named property. For example, processes may be sorted based on the `Id` property:

```
Get-Process | Sort-Object -Property Id
```

Objects may be sorted on multiple properties; for example, a list of files may be sorted on `LastWriteTime` and then on `Name`:

```
Get-ChildItem C:\Windows\System32 |
    Sort-Object LastWriteTime, Name
```

In the preceding example, items are first sorted on `LastWriteTime`. Items that have the same value for `LastWriteTime` are then sorted based on `Name`.

`Sort-Object` is not limited to sorting on existing properties. A script block (a fragment of script, enclosed in curly braces) can be used to create a calculated value for sorting. For example, it is possible to order items based on a word, as shown in this example:

```
PS> $examResults = @(
>>      [PSCustomObject]@{ Exam = 'Music';   Result = 'N/A';  Mark = 0 }
>>      [PSCustomObject]@{ Exam = 'History'; Result = 'Fail'; Mark = 23 }
>>      [PSCustomObject]@{ Exam = 'Biology'; Result = 'Pass'; Mark = 78 }
>>      [PSCustomObject]@{ Exam = 'Physics'; Result = 'Pass'; Mark = 86 }
>>      [PSCustomObject]@{ Exam = 'Maths';   Result = 'Pass'; Mark = 92 }
>> )
PS> $examResults | Sort-Object {
>>      switch ($_.Result) {
>>          'Pass' { 1 }
>>          'Fail' { 2 }
>>          'N/A'  { 3 }
>>      }
>> }

Exam       Result   Mark
----       ------   ----
Maths      Pass       92
Physics    Pass       86
Biology    Pass       78
History    Fail       23
Music      N/A         0
```

In the preceding example, when `Sort-Object` encounters a pass result, it is given the lowest numeric value (1). As `Sort-Object` defaults to ascending ordering, this means exams with a result of pass appear first in the list. This process is repeated to give a numeric value to each of the other possible results.

Sorting within the set varies depending on the version of PowerShell. Windows PowerShell will change the order of the elements within each set. PowerShell Core on the other hand maintains the original order, listing `Biology`, then `Physics`, then `Maths` within the pass set.

As `Sort-Object` is capable of sorting on more than one property, the preceding example can be taken further to sort on mark next. This makes the output order entirely predictable, regardless of the version of PowerShell:

```
PS> $examResults | Sort-Object {
>>      switch ($_.Result) {
>>          'Pass' { 1 }
>>          'Fail' { 2 }
>>          'N/A'  { 3 }
>>      }
>> }, Mark

Exam        Result    Mark
----        ------    ----
Biology     Pass        78
Physics     Pass        86
Maths       Pass        92
History     Fail        23
Music       N/A          0
```

Adding the `Descending` parameter to `Sort-Object` will reverse the order of both fields:

```
PS> $examResults | Sort-Object {
>>      switch ($_.Result) {
>>          'Pass' { 1 }
>>          'Fail' { 2 }
>>          'N/A'  { 3 }
>>      }
>> }, Mark -Descending

Exam        Result    Mark
----        ------    ----
Music       N/A          0
History     Fail        23
Maths       Pass        92
Physics     Pass        86
Biology     Pass        78
```

The ordering behavior can be made property-specific using the notation that's shown in the following example:

```
PS> $examResults | Sort-Object {
>>      switch ($_.Result) {
>>          'Pass' { 1 }
>>          'Fail' { 2 }
>>          'N/A'  { 3 }
>>      }
>> }, @{ Expression = { $_.Mark }; Descending = $true }
```

Exam	Result	Mark
----	------	----
Maths	Pass	92
Physics	Pass	86
Biology	Pass	78
History	Fail	23
Music	N/A	0

The hashtable, @{}, is used to describe an expression (a calculated property; in this case, the value for mark) and the sorting order, which is either ascending or descending.

In the preceding example, the first sorting property, based on the result property, is sorted in ascending order as this is the default. The second property, mark, is sorted in descending order.

Grouping and measuring

Group-Object is a powerful command that allows you to group objects together based on similar values.

Measure-Object supports a number of simple mathematical operations, such as counting the number of objects, calculating an average, calculating a sum, and so on. It also allows characters, words, or lines to be counted in text fields.

The Group-Object command

The Group-Object command shows a group and count for each occurrence of a value in a collection of objects.

Given the sequence of numbers shown, Group-Object creates a Name that holds the value it is grouping, a Count as the number of occurrences of that value, and a Group as the set of similar values:

```
PS> 6, 7, 7, 8, 8, 8 | Group-Object
```

Count	Name	Group
-----	----	-----
1	6	{6}
2	7	{7, 7}
3	8	{8, 8, 8}

The Group property may be removed using the NoElement parameter, which simplifies the output from the command:

```
PS> 6, 7, 7, 8, 8, 8 | Group-Object -NoElement

Count   Name
-----   ----
    1   6
    2   7
    3   8
```

Group-Object can group based on a specific property. For example, it might be desirable to list the number of occurrences of particular files in an extensive folder structure. In the following example, the C:\Windows\Assembly folder contains different versions of DLLs for different versions of packages, including the .NET Framework:

```
Get-ChildItem C:\Windows\Assembly -Filter *.dll -Recurse |
    Group-Object Name
```

Combining Group-Object with commands such as Where-Object and Sort-Object allows reports about the content of a set of data to be generated extremely quickly, for example, the top five files that appear more than once in a file tree:

```
PS> Get-ChildItem C:\Windows\Assembly -Filter *.dll -Recurse |
>>      Group-Object Name -NoElement |
>>      Where-Object Count -gt 1 |
>>      Sort-Object Count, Name -Descending |
>>      Select-Object Name, Count -First 5

Name                                                    Count
----                                                    -----
Microsoft.Web.Diagnostics.resources.dll                 14
Microsoft.Web.Deployment.resources.dll                  14
Microsoft.Web.Deployment.PowerShell.resources.dll       14
Microsoft.Web.Delegation.resources.dll                  14
Microsoft.Web.PlatformInstaller.resources.dll           13
```

As was seen with Sort-Object, Group-Object can group on more than one property. For example, we might group on both a filename and the size of a file (the Length property of a file):

```
PS> Get-ChildItem C:\Windows\Assembly -Filter *.dll -Recurse |
>>      Group-Object Name, Length -NoElement |
>>      Where-Object Count -gt 1 |
>>      Sort-Object Name -Descending |
>>      Select-Object Name, Count -First 6
```

Name	Count
----	-----
WindowsBase.ni.dll, 4970496	2
System.Xml.ni.dll, 6968320	2
System.Windows.Interactivity.ni.dll, 121856	2
System.Windows.Forms.ni.dll, 17390080	2
System.Web.ni.dll, 16481792	2
System.Web.ni.dll, 13605888	2

In the preceding example, we can see that System.Web.ni.dll appears four times (a count of 2, twice) in the folder structure, and that each pair of files has the same size.

Like Sort-Object, Group-Object is not limited to properties that already exist. It can create calculated properties in much the same way. For example, grouping on an email domain in a list of email addresses might be useful:

```
PS> 'one@one.example', 'two@one.example', 'three@two.example' |
>>     Group-Object { ($_ -split '@')[1] }
```

Count	Name	Group
-----	----	-----
2	one.example	{one@one.example, two@one.example}
1	two.example	{three@two.example}

In this example, the split operator is used to split on the @ character; everything to the left is stored in index 0, while everything to the right is stored in index 1.

By default, Group-Object returns the collection of objects shown in each of the preceding examples. Group-Object is also able to return a hashtable using the AsHashtable parameter.

When using the AsHashTable parameter, the AsString parameter is normally used. The AsString parameter forces the key for each entry in the hashtable to be a string, for example:

```
PS> $hashtable = 'one', 'two', 'two' | Group-Object -AsHashtable -AsString
PS> $hashtable['one']

one
```

By default, `Group-Object` is case insensitive. The strings one, ONE, and One are all considered equal. The `-CaseSensitive` parameter forces `Group-Object` to differentiate between items where cases differ:

```
PS> 'one', 'ONE', 'One' | Group-Object -CaseSensitive

Count Name                     Group
----- ----                     -----
    1 one                      {one}
    1 ONE                      {ONE}
    1 One                      {One}
```

The Measure-Object command

When used without any parameters, `Measure-Object` will return a value for Count, which is the number of items passed in using the pipeline, for example:

```
PS> 1, 5, 9, 79 | Measure-Object

Count    : 4
Average  :
Sum      :
Maximum  :
Minimum  :
Property :
```

Each of the remaining properties is empty, unless requested using their respective parameters. For example, `-Sum` may be requested:

```
PS> 1, 5, 9, 79 | Measure-Object -Sum

Count    : 4
Average  :
Sum      : 94
Maximum  :
Minimum  :
Property :
```

Adding the remaining parameters will fill in the rest of the fields (except `Property`):

```
PS> 1, 5, 9, 79 | Measure-Object -Average -Maximum -Minimum -Sum

Count    : 4
Average  : 23.5
Sum      : 94
Maximum  : 79
```

```
Minimum     : 1
Property    :
```

The value for `Property` is filled in when `Measure-Object` is asked to work against a particular property (instead of a set of numbers), for example:

```
PS> Get-Process | Measure-Object WorkingSet -Average

Count       : 135
Average     : 39449395.2
Sum         :
Maximum     :
Minimum     :
Property    : WorkingSet
```

When working with text, `Measure-Object` can count characters, words, or lines. For example, it can be used to count the number of lines, words, and characters in a text file:

```
PS> Get-Content C:\Windows\WindowsUpdate.log | Measure-Object -Line -Word -Character

Lines      Words     Characters    Property
-----      -----     ----------    --------
    3         32            268
```

Comparing

The `Compare-Object` command allows collections of objects to be compared to one another.

`Compare-Object` must be supplied with a value for the `ReferenceObject` and `DifferenceObject` parameters, which are normally collections or arrays of objects. If both values are equal, `Compare-Object` does not return anything by default. For example, both the `Reference` and `Difference` object in the following example are identical:

```
Compare-Object -ReferenceObject 1, 2 -DifferenceObject 1, 2
```

If there are differences, `Compare-Object` will display the results, as shown here:

```
PS> Compare-Object -ReferenceObject 1, 2, 3, 4 -DifferenceObject 1, 2

InputObject SideIndicator
----------- -------------
          3 <=
          4 <=
```

This shows that the `ReferenceObject` (the collection on the left) has the values, but the `DifferenceObject` (the collection on the right) does not.

`Compare-Object` has a number of other parameters that may be used to change the output. The `IncludeEqual` parameter adds values that are present in both collections to the output:

```
PS> Compare-Object -ReferenceObject 1, 2, 3, 4 -DifferenceObject 1, 2 -
IncludeEqual

InputObject SideIndicator
----------- -------------
          1 ==
          2 ==
          3 <=
          4 <=
```

`ExcludeDifferent` will omit the results that differ. This parameter makes sense if `IncludeEqual` is also set; without this, the command will always return nothing.

The `PassThru` parameter is used to return the original object instead of the representation showing the differences. In the following example, it is used to select values that are common to both the reference and difference objects:

```
PS> Compare-Object -ReferenceObject 1, 2, 3, 4 -DifferenceObject 1, 2 -
ExcludeDifferent -IncludeEqual -PassThru
1
2
```

`Compare-Object` is able to compare based on properties of objects, as well as the simpler values in the preceding examples. This can be a single property, or a list of properties. For example, the following command compares the content of `C:\Windows\System32` with `C:\Windows\SysWOW64`, returning files that have the same name and are the same size in both:

```
$reference = Get-ChildItem C:\Windows\System32 -File
$difference = Get-ChildItem C:\Windows\SysWOW64 -File
Compare-Object $reference $difference -Property Name, Length -IncludeEqual
-ExcludeDifferent
```

By default, `Compare-Object` will write an error if either the reference or difference objects are null. If `Compare-Object` is used when there is a chance of either being empty, the following technique can be used to avoid an error being generated provided neither contains an explicit null value:

```
$reference = Get-ChildItem C:\Windows\System32\tcpmon*.ini
$difference = Get-ChildItem C:\Windows\SysWOW64\tcpmon*.ini
Compare-Object @($reference) @($difference) -Property Name
```

The array, (`@()`), wrapping each parameter value will be discarded by PowerShell. If $difference is empty, it will be treated as an empty array instead of it being a null value.

Importing, exporting, and converting

Getting data in and out of PowerShell is a critical part of using the language. There are a number of commands dedicated to this task by default.

The Export-Csv command

The `Export-Csv` command writes data from objects to a text file, for example:

```
Get-Process | Export-Csv processes.csv
```

By default, `Export-Csv` will write a comma-delimited file using ASCII encoding and will completely overwrite any file using the same name.

`Export-Csv` may be used to add lines to an existing file using the `Append` parameter. When the `Append` parameter is used, the input object must have each of the fields listed in the CSV header or an error will be thrown unless the `Force` parameter is used:

```
PS> Get-Process powershell | Select-Object Name, Id | Export-Csv
.\Processes.csv
PS> Get-Process explorer | Select-Object Name | Export-Csv .\Processes.csv
-Append
Export-Csv : Cannot append CSV content to the following file:
.\Processes.csv.
The appended object does not have a property that corresponds to the
following column: Id. To continue with mismatched properties, add the -
Force parameter, and then retry the command.
At line:2 char:51
      + ... ershell_ise | Select-Object Name | Export-Csv .\Processes.csv -
Append
      + ~~~~~~~~~~~~~~~~~~~~~~~~~~~~~~~~~~
```

```
      + CategoryInfo : InvalidData: (Id:String) [Export-Csv],
InvalidOperationException
      + FullyQualifiedErrorId :
CannotAppendCsvWithMismatchedPropertyNames,Microsoft.PowerShell.Commands.Ex
portCsvCommand
```

If the `Append` parameter is used and the input object has more fields than the CSV, the extra fields will be silently dropped when writing the CSV file. For example, the value held in `Id` will be ignored when writing the results to the existing CSV file:

```
Get-Process powershell | Select-Object Name | Export-Csv .\Processes.csv
Get-Process explorer | Select-Object Name, Id | Export-Csv .\Processes.csv
-Append
```

`Export-Csv` in Windows PowerShell will write a header line to each file, which details the .NET type it has just exported. If the preceding example is used, that will be the following:

```
#TYPE Selected.System.Diagnostics.Process
```

`Export-Csv` can be instructed to exclude this header using the `NoTypeInformation` parameter:

```
Get-Process | Export-Csv processes.csv -NoTypeInformation
```

`ConvertTo-Csv` in Windows PowerShell is similar to `Export-Csv`, except that instead of writing content to a file, content is written as command output:

```
PS> Get-Process powershell | Select-Object Name, Id | ConvertTo-Csv
#TYPE Selected.System.Diagnostics.Process
"Name","Id"
"powershell","404"
```

PowerShell Core: No more type information

In PowerShell Core, this behavior has changed. The `NoTypeInformation` parameter for `Export-Csv` and `ConvertTo-Csv` is present, but it now has a default value of true. The `IncludeTypeInformation` parameter has been added to request this value in the output.

Both `Export-Csv` and `ConvertTo-Csv` are limited in what they can do with arrays of objects. For example, `ConvertTo-Csv` is unable to display the values that are in an array:

```
PS> [PSCustomObject]@{
>>     Name = "Numbers"
>>     Value = 1, 2, 3, 4, 5
```

```
>> } | ConvertTo-Csv -NoTypeInformation
"Name","Value"
"Numbers","System.Object[]"
```

The value it writes is taken from the ToString method, which is called on the property called Value, for example:

```
PS> $object = [PSCustomObject]@{
>>      Name = "Numbers"
>>      Value = 1, 2, 3, 4, 5
>> }
PS> $object.Value.ToString()

System.Object[]
```

If a CSV file is expected to hold the content of an array, code must be written to convert it into a suitable format. For example, the content of the array can be written after converting it in to a string:

```
PS> [PSCustomObject]@{
>>      Name  = "Numbers"
>>      Value = 1, 2, 3, 4, 5
>> } | ForEach-Object {
>>      $_.Value = $_.Value -join ', '
>>      $_
>> } | ConvertTo-Csv -NoTypeInformation

"Name","Value"
"Numbers","1, 2, 3, 4, 5"
```

In the preceding example, the value of the property is joined using a comma followed by a space. The modified object (held in $_) is passed on to the ConvertTo-Csv command.

The Import-Csv command

Comma-Separated Value (CSV) files are plain text. Applications such as Microsoft Excel can work with CSV files without changing the file format, although the advanced features Excel has cannot be saved to a CSV file.

By default, Import-Csv expects input to have a header row, to be comma delimited, and to use ASCII file encoding. If any of these items are different, the command parameters may be used. For example, a tab may be set as the delimiter:

```
Import-Csv TabDelimitedFile.tsv -Delimiter `t
```

A tick followed by t (`t) is used to represent the tab character in PowerShell.

Data that's imported using `Import-Csv` will always be formatted as a string. If `Import-Csv` is used to read a file containing the following text, each of the numbers will be treated as a string:

```
Name,Position
Jim,35
Matt,3
Dave,5
```

Attempting to use `Sort-Object` on the imported CSV file will result in values being sorted as if they were strings, not numbers:

```
PS> Import-Csv .\positions.csv | Sort-Object Position

Name     Position
----     --------
Matt     3
Jim      35
Dave     5
```

`Sort-Object` can be used to consider the value for `Position` as an integer by using a script block expression:

```
PS> Import-Csv .\positions.csv | Sort-Object { [Int]$_.Position }

Name Position
---- --------
Matt 3
Dave 5
Jim  35
```

This conversion problem exists regardless of whether the data in a CSV file is a number, or a date, or any type other than string.

`ConvertFrom-Csv` is similar to `Import-Csv`, except that content is read from PowerShell instead of a file:

```
PS> "powershell,404" | ConvertFrom-Csv -Header Name, Id

Name          Id
----          --
powershell    404
```

Export-Clixml and Import-Clixml

Export-Clixml creates representations of objects in XML files. Export-Clixml is extremely useful where type information about each property must be preserved.

For example, the following object may be exported using Export-Clixml:

```
[PSCustomObject]@{
    Number  = 1
    Decimal = 2.3
    String  = 'Hello world'
} | Export-Clixml .\object.xml
```

The resulting XML file shows the type for each of the properties it has just exported:

```
PS> Get-Content object.xml
<Objs Version="1.1.0.1"
xmlns="http://schemas.microsoft.com/powershell/2004/04">
  <Obj RefId="0">
    <TN RefId="0">
      <T>System.Management.Automation.PSCustomObject</T>
      <T>System.Object</T>
    </TN>
    <MS>
      <I32 N="Number">1</I32>
      <Db N="Decimal">2.3</Db>
      <S N="String">Hello world</S>
    </MS>
  </Obj>
</Objs>
```

I32 is a 32-bit integer (Int32). Db is a double-precision floating-point number (double). S is a string.

With this extra information in the file, PowerShell can rebuild the object, including the different types, using Import-Clixml, as follows:

```
$object = Import-Clixml .\object.xml
```

Once imported, the value types can be inspected using the GetType method:

```
PS> $object.Decimal.GetType()

IsPublic    IsSerial    Name      BaseType
--------    --------    ----      --------
True        True        Double    System.ValueType
```

Summary

In this chapter, we have explored the object pipeline, as well as objects themselves.

Many of the commands for working with objects in a pipeline were introduced. This includes the ability to filter and select from sets of objects to sort, group, and measure.

Finally, we explored exporting, importing, and converting objects. In Chapter 4, *Operators*, we will explore PowerShell's operators.

4
Operators

In programming, an operator is an object that is used to manipulate an item of data. Operators have a wide variety of uses, from comparing two values and replacing values, to allowing command names to be expressed as string. An operator is truly a fundamental part of any programming language and PowerShell is not exception.

PowerShell has a wide variety of operators; most of these will be briefly explored within this chapter.

In this chapter, we are going to cover the following topics:

- Arithmetic operators
- Assignment operators
- Comparison operators
- Regular expression-based operators
- Binary operators
- Logical operators
- Type operators
- Redirection operators
- Other operators

Arithmetic operators

Arithmetic operators are used to perform numeric calculations. The operators that are available are available to us in PowerShell are as follows:

- **Addition**: +
- **Subtraction**: –
- **Multiplication**: *
- **Division**: /
- **Remainder**: %
- **Shift left**: -shl
- **Shift right**: -shr

As well as its use in numeric calculations, the addition operator may also be used with strings, arrays, and hashtables, and the multiplication operator may also be used with strings and arrays.

The sections below explore each of the operators listed above.

Operator precedence

Mathematical operations are executed in a specific order. For example, consider the following two simple calculations:

```
3 + 2 * 2
2 * 2 + 3
```

The result of both of the preceding expressions is 7 (2 multiplied by 2, then add 3).

PowerShell, and most other programming languages, will calculate elements of an expression using multiplication (*), division (/), and remainder (%) first. Addition (+) and subtraction (–) are calculated next.

PowerShell has two additional operators in this category, -shl and -shr. These two have the lowest precedence and are only executed after other operations. For example, the result of the following calculation will be 128:

```
2 * 4 -shl 2 + 2
```

First, 2 * 4 is calculated, followed by 2 + 2, and then -shl is used. The -shl operator is discussed in detail in *Shift left and shift right operators*.

Consider the following example:

```
(3 + 2) * 2
```

Expressions in parentheses are always calculated first to cater for more advanced situations. For example, the result of the above calculation is 10.

Addition and subtraction operators

The addition and subtraction operators, + and -, are most easily recognisable as arithmetic operators. The addition operator also serves as a concatenation operator.

Addition operators

The addition operator may be used to add numeric values. For example, the simple addition operation below will result in the value 5.14159:

```
2.71828 + 3.14159
```

The addition operator may also be used to concatenate strings:

```
'hello' + ' ' + 'world'
```

If an attempt is made to concatenate a string with a number, the number will be converted into a string:

```
'hello number ' + 1
```

This style of operation will fail if the number is used first. PowerShell expects the entire expression to be numeric if that is how it begins:

```
PS> 1 + ' is the number I like to use'
Cannot convert value "is the number I like to use" to type "System.Int32".
Error: "Input string was not in a correct format."
At line:1 char:1
+ 1 + ' is the number I like to use'
+ ~~~~~~~~~~~~~~~~~~~~~~~~~~~~~~~~~~~
    + CategoryInfo : InvalidArgument: (:) [], RuntimeException
    + FullyQualifiedErrorId : InvalidCastFromStringToInteger
```

The addition operator may be used to add single elements to an existing array. As arrays are of fixed size, PowerShell will create a new array containing 1, 2, and 3:

```
@(1, 2) + 3
```

Joining arrays with the addition operator is simple. Each of the following three examples creates an array and each array contains the values 1, 2, 3, and 4:

```
@(1, 2) + @(3, 4)
(1, 2) + (3, 4)
1, 2 + 3, 4
```

Hashtables may be joined in a similar manner:

```
@{key1 = 1} + @{key2 = 2}
```

The addition operation will fail if keys are duplicated as part of the addition operation:

```
PS> @{key1 = 1} + @{key1 = 2}
Item has already been added. Key in dictionary: 'key1' Key being added:
'key1'
At line:1 char:1
+ @{key1 = 1} + @{key1 = 2}
+ ~~~~~~~~~~~~~~~~~~~~~~~~~
    + CategoryInfo : OperationStopped: (:) [], ArgumentException
    + FullyQualifiedErrorId : System.ArgumentException
```

Subtraction operator

The subtraction operator may only be used for numeric expressions. The results of the following expressions are 3 and -18, respectively:

```
5 - 2
2 - 20
```

Subtraction is a simple but important operation. The sections below explore multiplication, division, and remainder.

Multiplication, division, and remainder operators

Like the addition operator, the multiplication operator is capable of acting on strings. The division and remainder operators perform mathematical operations only.

Multiplication operator

The multiplication operator is able to perform simple numeric operations. For example, the result of the following expression is 5:

```
2.5 * 2
```

The multiplication operator may also be used to duplicate strings, resulting in hellohellohello:

```
'hello' * 3
```

As with the addition operator, the multiplication operator will throw an error if a number is on the left of the expression:

```
PS> 3 * 'hello'
Cannot convert value "hello" to type "System.Int32". Error: "Input string
was not in a correct format."
At line:1 char:2
+ 3 * 'hello'
+ ~~~~~~~~~~~
    + CategoryInfo : InvalidArgument: (:) [], RuntimeException
    + FullyQualifiedErrorId : InvalidCastFromStringToInteger
```

The multiplication operator may also be used to duplicate arrays. Each of the following examples creates an array containing one, two, one, and two:

```
@('one', 'two') * 2
('one', 'two') * 2
'one', 'two' * 2
```

Division operator

The division operator performs numeric division:

```
20 / 5
```

An error will be thrown if an attempt to divide by 0 is made:

```
PS> 1 / 0
Attempted to divide by zero.
At line:1 char:1
+ 1 / 0
+ ~~~~~
    + CategoryInfo : NotSpecified: (:) [], RuntimeException
    + FullyQualifiedErrorId : RuntimeException
```

Division using negative numbers is permitted in PowerShell. When a positive number is divided by a negative number, the result will be negative.

Remainder operator

The remainder operator returns the remainder of the whole-number (integer) division. For example, the result of the following operation is 1:

```
3 % 2
```

The remainder operator can also be used for alternation. That is, performing an action on every second, third, fourth, and so on iteration of a loop.

```
1..100 | Where-Object { $_ % 5 -eq 0 } | ForEach-Object {
    Write-Host $_
}
```

The value will show 5, 10, 15, 20, and so on. Each of those values will have a remainder of when divided by 5.

Shift left and shift right operators

The -shl and -shr operators were introduced with PowerShell 3.0. These operators perform bit-shifting.

The possible bit values for a byte can be represented as a table:

Bit position	1	2	3	4	5	6	7	8
Bit value	128	64	32	16	8	4	2	1

For a numeric value of 78, the following bits must be set:

Bit value	128	64	32	16	8	4	2	1
On or off	0	1	0	0	1	1	1	0

When a left shift operation is performed, every bit is moved one to the left. Say we run this expression:

```
78 -shl 1
```

The result is `156`, which is expressed in this bit table:

Bit value	128	64	32	16	8	4	2	1
Before shift	0	1	0	0	1	1	1	0
After shift	1	0	0	1	1	1	0	0

Shifting one bit to the right will reverse the operation:

```
PS> 156 -shr 1
78
```

When converting values using left or right shifting, bits that are set and right-shifted past the rightmost bit (bit value `1`) become `0`, for example:

```
PS> 3 -shr 1
1
```

This is expressed in the following table. Bits that end up in the rightmost column are discarded:

Bit value	128	64	32	16	8	4	2	1	Out of range
Before shift	0	0	0	0	0	0	1	1	
After shift	0	0	0	0	0	0	0	1	1

If the numeric value is of a specific numeric type, the resulting number cannot exceed the maximum value for the type. For example, a `Byte` has a maximum value of `255`; if the value of `255` is shifted one bit to the left, the resulting value will be `254`:

```
PS> ([Byte]255) -shl 1
254
```

Shifting out of range is shown in this table:

Bit value	Out of range	128	64	32	16	8	4	2	1
Before shift		1	1	1	1	1	1	1	1
After shift	1	1	1	1	1	1	1	1	0

If the value were capable of being larger, such as a 16 or 32-bit integer, the value would be allowed to increase as it no longer falls out of range:

```
PS> ([Int16]255) -shl 1
510
```

Bit shifting like this is easiest to demonstrate with unsigned types such as `Byte`, `UInt16`, `UInt32`, and `UInt64`. Unsigned types cannot support values lower than 0 (negative numbers).

Signed types, such as `SByte`, `Int16`, `Int32`, and `Int64`, sacrifice their highest-order bit to indicate whether the value is positive or negative. For example, this table shows the bit positions for a **signed byte (SByte)**:

Bit position	1	2	3	4	5	6	7	8
Bit value	Signing	64	32	16	8	4	2	1

The preceding bit values may be used to express numbers between 127 and −128. The binary forms of 1 and −1 are shown as an example in the following table:

Bit value	Signing	64	32	16	8	4	2	1
1	0	0	0	0	0	0	0	1
-1	1	1	1	1	1	1	1	1

For a signed type, each bit (except for signing) adds to a minimum value:

- When the signing bit is not set, add each value to 0
- When the signing bit is set, add each value to −128

When applying this to left shift, if the value of 64 is shifted one bit to the left, it becomes −128:

```
PS> ([SByte]64) -shl 1
-128
```

The shift into the signing bit is expressed in the following table:

Bit value	Signing	64	32	16	8	4	2	1
Before shift	0	1	0	0	0	0	0	0
After shift	1	0	0	0	0	0	0	0

Shift operations such as these are common in the networking world. For example, the IP address 192.168.4.32 may be represented in a number of different ways:

- **In hexadecimal:** C0A80420
- **As an unsigned 32-bit integer:** 3232236576
- **As a signed 32-bit integer:** −1062730720

The signed and unsigned versions of an IP address are calculated using left shift. For example, the IP address `192.168.4.32` may be written as a signed 32-bit integer (`Int32`):

```
(192 -shl 24) + (168 -shl 16) + (4 -shl 8) + 32
```

Shift operations such as these can be useful but are not common. The next section explores assignment the assignment operator.

Assignment operators

Assignment operators are used to give values to variables. The assignment operators that are available are as follows:

- **Assign**: =
- **Add and assign**: +=
- **Subtract and assign**: −=
- **Multiply and assign**: *=
- **Divide and assign**: /=
- **Modulus and assign**: %=

As with the arithmetic operators, add and assign may be used with strings, arrays, and hashtables. Multiply and assign may be used with strings and arrays.

Assign, add and assign, and subtract and assign

The assignment operator (=) is used to assign values to variables and properties, for example, let's look at assigning a value to a variable:

```
$variable = 'some value'
```

Or, we might change the PowerShell window title by assigning a new value to its property:

```
$host.UI.RawUI.WindowTitle = 'PowerShell window'
```

The add and assign operator (+=) operates in a similar manner to the addition operator. The following example assigns the value 1 to a variable, then += is used to add 20 to that value:

```
$i = 1
$i += 20
```

The preceding example is equivalent to writing the following:

```
$i = 1
$i = $i + 20
```

The += operator may be used to concatenate strings:

```
$string = 'one'
$string += 'one'
```

As we saw with the addition operator, attempting to add a numeric value to an existing string is acceptable. Attempting to add a string to a variable containing a numeric value is not:

```
PS> $variable = 1
PS> $variable += 'one'
Cannot convert value "one" to type "System.Int32". Error: "Input string was
not in a correct format."
At line:2 char:1
+ $variable += 'one'
+ ~~~~~~~~~~~~~~~~~~~
    + CategoryInfo : InvalidArgument: (:) [], RuntimeException
    + FullyQualifiedErrorId : InvalidCastFromStringToInteger
```

It is possible to work around this by assigning a type to the variable:

```
[String]$string = 1
$string += 'one'
```

The += operator may be used to add single elements to an existing array:

```
$array = 1, 2
$array += 3
```

You can also use it to add another array:

```
$array = 1, 2
$array += 3, 4
```

The += operator may be used to join together two hashtables:

```
$hashtable = @{key1 = 1}
$hashtable += @{key2 = 2}
```

As we saw using the addition operator, the operation will fail if one of the keys already exists.

The subtract and assign operator (−=) is intended for numeric operations, as shown in the following examples:

```
$i = 20
$i -= 2
```

After this operation has completed, $i will be assigned a value of 18.

Multiply and assign, divide and assign, and modulus and assign

Numeric assignments using the multiply and assign operator may be performed using *=. The value held by the variable i will be 4:

```
$i = 2 $i *= 2
```

The multiply and assign operator may be used to duplicate a string held in a variable:

```
$string = 'one'
$string *= 2
```

The value on the right-hand side of the *= operator must be numeric or must be able to convert to a number. For example, a string containing the number 2 is acceptable:

```
$string = 'one'
$string *= '2'
```

Using a string that is unable to convert to a number results in an error, as follows:

```
PS> $variable = 'one'
PS> $variable *= 'one'

Cannot convert value "one" to type "System.Int32". Error: "Input string was
not in a correct format."
At line:2 char:1
+ $variable *= 'one'
+ ~~~~~~~~~~~~~~~~~~
    + CategoryInfo : InvalidArgument: (:) [], RuntimeException
    + FullyQualifiedErrorId : InvalidCastFromStringToInteger
```

The multiply and assign operator may be used to duplicate an array held in a variable. In the following example, the variable will hold the values 1, 2 , 1, and 2 after this operation:

```
$variable = 1, 2
$variable *= 2
```

The assign and divide operator is used to perform numeric operations. The variable will hold a value of 1 after the following operation:

```
$variable = 2
$variable /= 2
```

The remainder and assign operator assigns the result of the remainder operation to a variable:

```
$variable = 10
$variable %= 3
```

After the preceding operation, the variable will hold a value of 1, which is the remainder when dividing 10 by 3.

Comparison operators

Comparison operators are used for comparing two mathematical expressions which results in true, false or unknown.

PowerShell has a wide variety of comparison operators which are as follows:

- **Equal to and not equal to**: -eq and -ne
- **Like and not like**: -like and -notlike
- **Greater than and greater than or equal to**: -gt and -ge
- **Less than and less than or equal to**: -lt and -le
- **Contains and not contains**: -contains and -notcontains
- **In and not in**: -in and -notin

Case-sensitivity

None of the comparison operators are case-sensitive by default. Each of the comparison operators has two additional variants, one which explicitly states it is case-sensitive, and another which explicitly states it is case insensitive.

For example, the following statement returns true:

```
'Trees' -eq 'trees'
```

Adding a c modifier in front of the operator name forces PowerShell to make a case-sensitive comparison. The following statement will return `false`:

```
'Trees' -ceq 'trees'
```

In addition to the case-sensitive modifier, PowerShell also has an explicit case insensitive modifier. In the following example, the statement returns `True`:

```
'Trees' -ieq 'trees'
```

However, as case insensitive comparison is the default, it is extremely rare to see examples of the i modifier.

These behaviour modifiers can be applied to all of the comparison operators.

Comparison operators and arrays

When comparison operators are used with scalar values (a single item as opposed to an array), the comparison will result in `true` or `false`.

When used with an array or collection, the result of the comparison is all matching elements, for example:

```
1, $null -ne $null          # Returns 1
1, 2, 3, 4 -ge 3            # Returns 3, 4
'one', 'two', 'three' -like '*e*'   # Returns one and three
```

This behaviour may be problematic if a comparison is used to test whether or not a variable holding an array exists. In the following example, -eq is used to test that a value has been assigned to a variable called `array`:

```
$array = 1, 2
if ($array -eq $null) { Write-Host 'Variable not set' }
```

This test is apparently valid as long as the array does not hold two or more null values. When two or more values are present, the condition unexpectedly returns `true`:

```
PS> $array = 1, 2, $null, $null
PS> if ($array -eq $null) { Write-Host 'No values in array' }

No values in array
```

This happens because the result of the comparison is an array with two `null` values. If it were a single `null` value, PowerShell would flatten the array. With two values, it cannot:

```
[Boolean]@($null)              # Returns false
[Boolean]@($null, $null)       # Returns true
```

To avoid this problem, `null` must be on the left-hand side of the expression. For example, the following `Write-Host` statement will not execute:

```
$array = 1, 2, $null, $null
if ($null -eq $array) { Write-Host 'Variable not set' }
```

In this case, the array is not expanded, null is compared with the entire array. The result will be `false`, the array variable is set.

Equal to and not equal to

The `-eq` (equal to) and `-ne` (not equal to) operators perform exact (and, by default, case insensitive) comparisons. In the example below, the following returns `true`:

```
1 -eq 1
'string' -eq 'string'
[char]'a' -eq 'A'
$true -eq 1
$false -eq 0
```

Similarly, `-ne` (not equal) will return `true` for each of the following:

```
20 -ne 100
'this' -ne 'that'
$false -ne 'false'
```

The last example compares `$false`, the Boolean, with a string containing the word `false`. PowerShell will attempt to convert the word, but as the word is not an empty string, the result will be `true`.

Like and not like

The `-like` and `-notlike` operators support simple wildcards. `*` matches a string of any length (zero or more) and `?` matches a single character. Each of the following examples returns `true`:

```
'The cow jumped over the moon' -like '*moon*'
'Hello world' -like '??llo w*'
'' -like '*'
'' -notlike '?*'
```

Behind the scenes, PowerShell turns expressions used with `-like` and `-notlike` into regular expressions.

Greater than and less than

When comparing numbers, each of the operators `-ge` (greater than or equal to), `-gt` (greater than), `-le` (less than or equal to), and `-lt` (less than) are simple to use:

```
1 -ge 1       # Returns true
2 -gt 1       # Returns true
1.4 -lt 1.9   # Returns true
1.1 -le 1.1   # Returns true
```

String comparison with operators follows the generalised pattern of `0123456789aAbBcCdD...`, rather than basing it on a character table (such as ASCII):

- Cultural variants of characters, for example, the character å, fall between `A` and `b` in the list.
- Other alphabets, for example Cyrillic or Greek, come after the Roman alphabet (after `Z`).

Comparison can be culture sensitive when using commands such as `Sort-Object` with the `culture` parameter, but comparisons are always based on `en-US` when using the operators:

```
'apples' -lt 'pears'    # Returns true
'Apples' -lt 'pears'    # Returns true
'bears' -gt 'Apples'    # Returns true
```

This also occurs when using a case-sensitive comparison:

```
'bears' -gt 'Bears'    # False, they are equal to one another
'bears' -clt 'Bears'   # True, b before B
```

The use of greater than and less than with strings may often be difficult to apply. Careful testing is recommended.

Contains and in

The -contains, -notcontains, -in, and -notin operators are used to test the content of arrays.

When using -contains or -notcontains, the array is expected to be on the left-hand side of the operator:

```
1, 2 -contains 2       # Returns true
1, 2, 3 -contains 4    # Returns false
```

When using -in or -notin, the array is expected to be on the right-hand side of the operator:

```
1 -in 1, 2, 3     # Returns true
4 -in 1, 2, 3     # Returns false
```

Contains or in?

When using comparison operators, I tend to write the subject on the left and the object on the right. Comparisons to null are an exception to this rule. The subject is the variable or property I am testing; the object is the thing I am testing against. For example, I might set the subject to a user in Active Directory:

```
$subject = Get-ADUser -Identity $env:USERNAME -Properties
department, memberOf.
```

I use contains, where the subject is an array, and the object is a single value:

```
$subject.MemberOf -contains
'CN=Group,DC=domain,DC=example'.
```

I use in, where the subject is a single value, and the object is an array:

```
$subject.Department -in 'Department1', 'Department2'.
```

Regular expression-based operators

Regular expressions are an advanced form of pattern matching. In PowerShell, a number of operators have direct support for regular expressions. Regular expressions themselves are covered in greater detail in Chapter 9, *Regular Expressions*.

The following operators use regular expressions:

- **Match**: −match
- **Not match**: −notmatch
- **Replace**: −replace
- **Split**: −split

Match and not match

The −match and −notmatch operators return true or false when testing strings:

```
'The cow jumped over the moon' -match 'cow'   # Returns true
'The        cow' -match 'The +cow'            # Returns true
```

In the preceding example, the + symbol is reserved; it indicates that The is followed by one or more spaces before cow.

Match is a comparison operator

Like the other comparison operators, if match is used against an array, it returns each matching element instead of true or false. The following comparison will return the values one and three:

```
"one", "two", "three" -match 'e'
```

In addition to returning a true or false value about the state of the match, a successful match will add values to a reserved variable, $matches. For example, the following regular expression uses a character class to indicate that it should match any character from 0 to 4, repeated 0 or more times:

```
'1234567689' -match '[0-4]*'
```

Once the match has been executed, the `matches` variable (a hashtable) will be populated with the part of the string that matched the expression:

```
PS> $matches

Name                           Value
----                           -----
0                              1234
```

Regular expressions use parentheses to denote groups. Groups may be used to capture interesting elements of a string:

```
PS> 'Group one, Group two' -match 'Group (.*), Group (.*)'
True

PS> $matches

Name                           Value
----                           -----
2                              two
1                              one
0                              Group one, Group two
```

In the preceding example, the match operator is run first, then the `matches` variable is displayed. The captured value `one` is held in the first group, and is accessible using either of the following statements:

```
$matches[1]
$matches.1
```

Matches is a hashtable, in the example above 1 is being used as a key to access the capture group.

Replace

The `-replace` operator performs replacement based on a regular expression. For example, it can be used to replace several instances of the same thing:

```
PS> 'abababab' -replace 'a', 'c'
cbcbcbcb
```

In the example, `a` is the regular expression that dictates what must be replaced. `'c'` is the value any matching values should be replaced with.

This syntax can be generalised, as follows:

```
<Value> -replace <Match>, <Replace-With>
```

If the `Replace-With` value is omitted, the matches will be replaced with nothing (that is, they are removed):

```
PS> 'abababab' -replace 'a'
bbbb
```

Regular expressions use parentheses to capture groups. The replace operator can use those groups. Each group may be used in the `Replace-With` argument. For example, a set of values can be reversed:

```
'value1,value2,value3' -replace '(.*),(.*),(.*)', '$3,$2,$1'
```

The tokens `$1`, `$2`, and `$3` are references to each of the groups denoted by the parentheses.When performing this operation, the `Replace-With` argument must use single quotes to prevent PowerShell from evaluating the group references as if they were variables. This problem is shown in the following example. The first attempt works as expected; the second shows an expanded PowerShell variable instead:

```
PS> $1 = $2 = $3 = 'Oops'
PS> Write-Host ('value1,value2,value3' -replace '(.*),(.*),(.*)',
'$3,$2,$1') -ForegroundColor Green
PS> Write-Host ('value1,value2,value3' -replace '(.*),(.*),(.*)',
"$3,$2,$1") -ForegroundColor Red

value3,value2,value1
Oops,Oops,Oops
```

The `-replace` operator is a incredibly useful and widely used operator in PowerShell.

Split

The `-split` operator splits a string into an array based on a regular expression.

The following example splits the string into an array containing a, b, c, and d by matching each of the numbers:

```
PS> 'a1b2c3d4' -split '[0-9]'
a
b
c
d
```

The results of as split can be assigned to one or more variables. The split operator also supports a maximum number of split operations, and options for the split operation. Options include `SimpleMatch` which changes `-split` to use a simple wildcard as shown in the example below.

```
'a1b2c3d4' -split 'b2', 0, 'SimpleMatch'
```

The value of 0 in the example above represents an unlimited number of results.

Binary operators

Binary operators are used to perform bitwise operations in PowerShell. That is, operations based around the bits that make up a numeric value. Each operator returns the numeric result of a binary operation.

The available operators are:

- **Binary and**: `-band`
- **Binary or**: `-bor`
- **Binary exclusive or**: `-bxor`
- **Binary not**: `-bnot`

Binary and

The result of `-band` is a number where each of the bits in both the value on the left and the value on the right is set.

In the following example, the result is 2:

```
11 -band 6
```

This operation can be shown in a table:

Bit value		8	4	2	1
Left-hand side	11	1	0	1	1
Right-hand side	6	0	1	1	0
-band	2	0	0	1	0

The result is a number where both the left-hand side and right-hand side include the bit.

Binary or

The result of `-bor` is a number where the bits are set in either the value on the left or right.

In the following example, the result is `15`:

```
11 -bor 12
```

This operation can be shown in a table:

Bit value		8	4	2	1
Left-hand side	11	1	0	1	1
Right-hand side	12	1	1	0	0
-band	15	1	1	1	1

The result is a number made up of the bits from each number where either number has the bit set.

Binary exclusive or

The result of `-bxor` is a number where the bits are set in either the value on the left or the value on the right, but not both.

In the following example, the result is `11`:

```
6 -bxor 13
```

This operation can be shown in a table:

Bit value		8	4	2	1
Left-hand side	6	0	1	1	0
Right-hand side	13	1	1	0	1
-band	11	1	0	1	1

The `-bxor` operator is useful for toggling bit values. For example, `bxor` might be used to toggle the `AccountDisable` bit of `UserAccountControl` in Active Directory:

```
512 -bxor 2 # Result is 514 (Disabled, 2 is set)
514 -bxor 2 # Result is 512 (Enabled, 2 is not set)
```

Binary not

The –bnot operator is applied before a numeric value; it does not use a value on the left-hand side. The result is a value that's composed of all bits that are not set.

The –bnot operator works with signed and unsigned 32-bit and 64-bit integers (Int32, UInt32, Int64, and UInt64). When working with 8-bit or 16-bit integers (SByte, Byte, Int16, and UInt16), the result is always a signed 32-bit integer (Int32).

In the following example, the result is –123:

```
-bnot 122
```

As the preceding result is a 32-bit integer (Int32), it is difficult to show the effect in a small table. If this value were a SByte, the operation could be expressed in a table as follows:

Bit value		Signing	64	32	16	8	4	2	1
Before –bnot	122	0	1	1	1	1	0	1	0
After –bnot	-123	1	0	0	0	0	1	0	1

As shown in the table above, the –bnot operator reverses the value for each bit. The signing bit is not treated any differently.

Logical operators

Logical operators are used to evaluate two or more comparisons or other operations that produce a Boolean (true or false) result.

The following logic operators are available:

- **And**: –and
- **Or**: –or
- **Exclusive or**: –xor
- **Not**: –not and !

And

The –and operator will return true if the values on the left-hand and right-hand side are both true.

For example, each of the following returns `true`:

```
$true -and $true
1 -lt 2 -and "string" -like 's*'
1 -eq 1 -and 2 -eq 2 -and 3 -eq 3
(Test-Path C:\Windows) -and (Test-Path 'C:\Program Files')
```

Or

The `-or` operator will return `true` if either the value on the left, or the value on the right, or both are `true`.

For example, each of the following returns `true`:

```
$true -or $true
2 -gt 1 -or "something" -ne "nothing"
1 -eq 1 -or 2 -eq 1
(Test-Path C:\Windows) -or (Test-Path D:\Windows)
```

Exclusive or

The `-xor` operator will return `true` if either the value on the left is `true`, or the value on the right is `true`, but not both.

For example, each of the following returns `true`:

```
$true -xor $false
1 -le 2 -xor 1 -eq 2
(Test-Path C:\Windows) -xor (Test-Path D:\Windows)
```

The `-xor` operator is perhaps one of the most rarely used in PowerShell.

Not

The `-not` (or `!`) operator may be used to negate the expression that follows it.

For example, each of the following returns `true`:

```
-not $false
-not (Test-Path X:\)
-not ($true -and $false)
!($true -and $false)
```

Double negatives

The `-not` operator has an important place, but it is worth rethinking an expression if it injects a double negative. For example, the following expression will return `true`: `-not (1 -ne 1)`.

The preceding expression is better written using the `-eq` operator: `1 -eq 1`.

Type operators

Type operators are designed to work with .NET types. The following operators are available:

- **As**: `-as`
- **Is**: `-is`
- **Is not**: `-isnot`

These operators may be used to convert an object of one type into another, or to test whether or not an object is of a given type.

As

The `-as` operator is used to convert a value into an object of the specified type. The operator returns `null` (without throwing an error) if the conversion cannot be completed.

For example, the operator may be used to perform the following conversions:

```
"1" -as [Int32]
'String' -as [Type]
```

The `-as` operator can be useful for testing whether or not a value can be cast to a specific type, or whether a specific type exists.

For example, the System.Web assembly is not imported by default and the
System.Web.HttpUtility class does not exist. The -as operator may be used to test for
this condition:

```
PS> if (-not ('System.Web.HttpUtility' -as [Type])) {
>>      Write-Host 'Adding assembly' -ForegroundColor Green
>>      Add-Type -Assembly System.Web
>> }
Adding assembly
```

If the System.Web assembly has not been imported, attempting to turn the string,
System.Web.HttpUtility, into a type will fail. The failure to convert will not generate an
error.

is and isnot

The -is and -isnot operators test whether or not a value is of the specified type.

For example, each of the following returns true:

```
'string' -is [String]
1 -is [Int32]
[String] -is [Type]
123 -isnot [String]
```

The -is and -isnot operators are very useful for testing the exact type of a value without
needing to use more complex methods.

Redirection operators

In Chapter 3, *Working with Objects in PowerShell*, we started exploring the different output
streams PowerShell utilizes.

Information from a command may be redirected using the redirection operator >.
Information may be sent to another stream or a file.

For example, the output from a command can be directed to a file. The file will contain the
output as it would have been displayed in the console:

```
PS> Get-Process -Id $pid > process.txt
PS> Get-Content process.txt

Handles NPM(K)  PM(K)  WS(K) CPU(s)    Id SI  ProcessName
```

```
------- ------  ----- ----- ------    -- --  -----------
    731      57 132264 133156   1.81 11624   1  powershell_ise
```

Each of the streams in PowerShell has a number associated with it. These are shown in the following table:

Stream name	Stream number
Standard out	1
Error	2
Warning	3
Verbose	4
Debug	5
Information	6

Each of the streams above can be redirected. In most cases PowerShell provides parameters for commands which can be used to capture the streams when used. For example, the ErrorVariable and WarningVariable parameters.

About Write-Host

Before PowerShell 5, the output written using the Write-Host command could not be captured, redirected, or assigned to a variable. In PowerShell 5, Write-Host has become a wrapper for Write-Information and is sent to the information stream.

Information written using Write-Host is unaffected by the InformationPreference variable and the InformationAction parameter, except when either is set to Ignore.

When InformationAction for the Write-Host command is set to Ignore, the output will be suppressed. When Ignore is set for the InformationPreference variable, an error is displayed, stating that it is not supported.

Redirection to a file

Output from a specific stream may be directed by placing the stream number on the left of the redirect operator.

For example, the output written by `Write-Warning` can be directed to a file:

```
PS> function Test-Redirect{
>>      'This is standard out'
>>      Write-Warning 'This is a warning'
>> }
PS> $stdOut = Test-Redirect 3> 'warnings.txt'
PS> Get-Content 'warnings.txt'
This is a warning
```

When using the redirect operator, any file of the same name is overwritten. If information must be added to a file, the operator becomes >>:

```
$i = 1
function Test-Redirect{
    Write-Warning "Warning $i"
}
Test-Redirect 3> 'warnings.txt'    # Overwrite
$i++
Test-Redirect 3>> 'warnings.txt'   # Append
```

It is possible to redirect additional streams, for example, warnings and errors, by adding more redirect statements. The following example redirects the error and warning streams to separate files:

```
function Test-Redirect{
    'This is standard out'
    Write-Error 'This is an error'
    Write-Warning 'This is a warning'
}
Test-Redirect 3> 'warnings.txt' 2> 'errors.txt'
```

The wildcard character * may be used to represent all streams if all content was to be sent to a single file:

```
$verbosePreference = 'continue'
function Test-Redirect {
    'This is standard out'

    Write-Information 'This is information'
    Write-Host 'This is information as well'
    Write-Error 'This is an error'
    Write-Verbose 'This is verbose'
    Write-Warning 'This is a warning'
}
Test-Redirect *> 'alloutput.txt'
```

The preceding example starts by setting the `verbosePreference` variable. Without this, or the addition of the `verbose` parameter to the `Write-Verbose` command, the output from `Write-Verbose` will not be shown at all.

Redirecting streams to standard output

Streams can be redirected to standard output in PowerShell. The destination stream is written on the right-hand side of the redirect operator (without a space). Stream numbers on the right-hand side are prefixed with an ampersand (`&`) to distinguish the stream from a filename.

Only Stdout

Each of the following examples shows redirection to `Stdout`. It is not possible to redirect to streams other than standard output.

For example, the `Information` output written by the following command is sent to standard output:

```
PS> function Test-Redirect{
>>      'This is standard out'
>>      Write-Information 'This is information'
>> }
PS> $stdOut = Test-Redirect 6>&1
PS> $stdOut

This is standard out
This is information
```

It is possible to redirect additional streams, for example, warnings and errors, by adding more redirect statements. The following example redirects the error and warning streams to standard output:

```
function Test-Redirect {
    'This is standard out'
    Write-Error 'This is an error'
    Write-Warning 'This is a warning'
}
$stdOut = Test-Redirect 2>&1 3>&1
```

The wildcard character * may be used to represent all streams if all streams were to be sent to another stream:

```
$verbosePreference = 'continue'
function Test-Redirect {
    'This is standard out'
    Write-Information 'This is information'
    Write-Host 'This is information as well'
    Write-Error 'This is an error'
    Write-Verbose 'This is verbose'
    Write-Warning 'This is a warning'
}
$stdOut = Test-Redirect *>&1
```

The preceding example starts by setting the verbose preference variable. Without this, the output from Write-Verbose will not be shown at all.

Redirection to null

Redirecting output to null is a technique that's used to drop unwanted output. The $null variable takes the place of the filename:

```
Get-Process > $null
```

The preceding example redirects standard output (stream 1) to nothing. This is equivalent to using an empty filename:

```
Get-Process > ''
```

The stream number or * may be included to the left of the redirect operator. For example, warnings and errors might be redirected to null:

```
.\somecommand.exe 2> $null 3> $null
.\somecommand.exe *> $null
```

Redirection like this is most commonly used with native executables; redirection is often unnecessary with PowerShell commands.

Other operators

PowerShell has a wide variety of operators, a few of which do not easily fall into a specific category, including the following:

- **Call**: &
- **Comma**: ,
- **Format**: -f
- **Increment and decrement**: ++ and --
- **Join**: -join

Each of these operators is in common use. The call operator can run a command based on a string, to the format operator which can be used to build up complex strings, and so on.

Call

The call operator is used to execute a string or script block. For example, the call operator may be used to execute the ipconfig command using a variable:

```
$command = 'ipconfig'
& $command
```

Or, it may be used to execute a scriptBlock:

```
$scriptBlock = { Write-Host 'Hello world' }
& $scriptBlock
```

The call operator accepts a list of arguments that can be passed to the command. For example, the displaydns parameter can be passed into the ipconfig command:

```
& 'ipconfig' '/displaydns'
```

The call operator is also used when calling a script or a command with a space in the path. The list of arguments can be placed in an array.

Comma

The comma operator may be used to separate elements in an array, for example:

```
$array = 1, 2, 3, 4
```

If the comma operator is used before a single value, it creates an array containing one element:

```
$array = ,1
```

When working with functions, the comma operator can be used to emit an array as an object. PowerShell will expand an array by default. The `Write-Output` command can be used with the `NoEnumerate` parameter to achieve the same thing.

Format

The `-f` operator can be used to create complex formatted strings. The syntax for the format operator is inherited from .NET; MSDN has a number of advanced examples: `https:// msdn.microsoft.com/en-us/library/system.string.format(v=vs.110).aspx#Starting`.

The `-f` operator uses a number in curly braces (`{<number>}`) in a string on the left of the operator to reference a value in an array on the right, for example:

```
'1: {0}, 2: {1}, 3: {2}' -f 1, 2, 3
```

The format operator is one possible way to assemble complex strings in PowerShell. In addition to this, it may be used to simplify some string operations. For example, a decimal may be converted into a percentage:

```
'The pass mark is {0:P}' -f 0.8
```

An integer may be converted into a hexadecimal string:

```
'244 in Hexadecimal is {0:X2}' -f 244
```

A number may be written as a culture-specific currency:

```
'The price is {0:C2}' -f 199
```

Reserved characters

When using the `-f` operator, curly braces are considered reserved characters. If a curly brace is to be included in a string as a literal value, it can be escaped: `'The value in {{0}} is {0}' -f 1.`

Increment and decrement

The ++ and –– operators are used to increment and decrement numeric values. The increment and decrement operators are split into pre-increment and post-increment versions.

The post-increment operators are frequently seen in for loops. The value for $i is used, and then incremented by one after use. In the case of the for loop, this happens after all the statements inside the loop block have executed:

```
for ($i = 0; $i -le 15; $i++) {
    Write-Host $i -ForegroundColor $i
}
```

The post-decrement reduces the value by one after use:

```
for ($i = 15; $i -ge 0; $i--) {
    Write-Host $i -ForegroundColor $i
}
```

Post-increment and post-decrement operators are often seen when iterating through an array:

```
$array = 1..15
$i = 0
while ($i -lt $array.Count) {
    # $i will increment after this statement has completed.
    Write-Host $array[$i++] -ForegroundColor $i
}
```

Pre-increment and pre-decrement are rarely seen. Instead of incrementing or decrementing a value after use, the change happens before the value is used, for example:

```
$array = 1..5
$i = 0
do {
    # $i is incremented before use, 2 will be the first printed.
    Write-Host $array[++$i]
} while ($i -lt $array.Count -1)
```

The post-increment operator, ++, is the most commonly used, typically in looping scenarios like those above.

Join

The -join operator joins arrays using a string. In the following example, the string is split based on a comma, and then joined based on a tab (`t):

```
PS> "a,b,c,d" -split ',' -join "`t"
a       b       c       d
```

The join operator may also be used in front of an array, when there is no need for a separator, for example:

```
PS> -join ('h', 'e', 'l', 'l', 'o', ' ', 'w', 'o', 'r', 'l', 'd')
hello world
```

If the parentheses are excluded from the example, the join operation will be confined to the first element of the array, the first h character.

Summary

In this chapter, we have explored many of the operators PowerShell has to offer, including operators for performing arithmetic, assignment, and comparison. Several specialized operators that use regular expressions were introduced for matching, replacing, and splitting. Binary, logical, and type operators were demonstrated. Finally, a number of other significant operators were introduced, including call, format, increment, and decrement, and the join operator.

In Chapter 5, *Variables, Arrays, and Hashtables,* are explored in detail.

Section 2: Working with Data

In this section, we will work with structured and unstructured data in PowerShell.

The following chapters are included in this section:

5

Variables, Arrays, and Hashtables

This chapter explores variables, along with a detailed look at arrays and hashtables, as these have their own complexities.

A variable in a programming language allows you to assign a label to a piece of information or data. A variable can be used and reused in the console, script, or function or in any other piece of code.

In this chapter, we're going to cover the following topics:

- Naming and creating variables
- Variable commands
- Variable provider
- Variable scope
- Types and type conversion
- Objects assigned to variables
- Arrays
- Hashtables
- Lists, dictionaries, queues, and stacks

A variable may be of any .NET type or object instance. The variable may be a string `Hello World`, an integer `42`, a decimal `3.141`, an array, a hashtable, a ScriptBlock, and so on. Everything a variable might hold is considered to be an object when used in PowerShell.

Naming and creating variables

Variables in PowerShell are preceded by the dollar symbol ($), for example:

```
$MyVariable
```

The name of a variable may contain numbers, letters, and underscores. For example, each of the following is a valid name:

```
$123
$x
$my_variable
$variable
$varIABle
$Path_To_File
```

Variables are frequently written in either camel case or upper-camel case (also known as Pascal case). PowerShell doesn't enforce any naming convention, nor does it exhibit a convention in any of the automatic variables. For example:

- `$myVariable` is camel case
- `$MyVariable` is upper-camel case, or Pascal case

One of the most commonly accepted practices is that variables used as parameters must use Pascal case. Variables used only within a script or a function must use camel case.

I suggest making your variable names meaningful so that when you revisit your script again after a long break, you can identify its purpose. I recommend choosing and maintaining a consistent style in your own code.

It's possible to use more complex variable names using the following notation:

```
${My Variable}
${My-Variable}
```

From time to time, the preceding notation appears in PowerShell, perhaps most often in dynamically generated code. This convention is otherwise rare and harder to read and therefore not desirable.

The bracing style has at least one important use. The following example shows an attempt to embed the var variable in a string:

```
$var = 'var'
"$variable"   # Will not expand correctly
"${var}iable" # Will expand var
```

The braces define a boundary for the variable name. It is otherwise unclear whether PowerShell should attempt to expand the string.

The following notation, where a file path is written as the variable name, allows variables to be stored on the filesystem:

```
${C:\Windows\Temp\variable.txt} = "New value"
```

Inspecting the given file path shows that the variable value has been written there:

```
PS> Get-Content C:\Windows\Temp\variable.txt
New value
```

As with the bracing notation, this is non-standard practice. It may confuse or surprise anyone reading the code.

Variables don't need to be declared prior to use, nor does a variable need to be assigned a specific type, for example:

```
$itemCount = 7
$dateFormat = "ddMMyyyy"
$numbers = @(1, 9, 5, 2)
$psProcess = Get-Process -Name PowerShell
```

It is possible to assign the same value to several variables in one statement. For example, this creates two variables, i and j, both with a value of 0:

```
$i = $j = 0
```

Variable commands

A number of commands are available to interact with the following variables:

- Clear
- Get
- New
- Remove
- Set

When using the * variable commands, the $ preceding the variable name isn't considered part of the name.

Clear

The `Clear` variable removes the value from any existing variable. It does not remove the variable itself. For example, the following example calls `Write-Host` twice: on the first occasion, it writes the variable value; on the second occasion, it does not write anything:

```
PS> $temporaryValue = "Some-Value"
PS> Write-Host $temporaryValue -ForegroundColor Green

Some-Value

PS> Clear-Variable temporaryValue
PS> Write-Host $temporaryValue -ForegroundColor Green
```

Get

The `Get` variable provides access to any variable that has been created in the current session as well as the default (automatic) variables created by PowerShell. For further information on automatic variables, refer to `about_Automatic_Variables` (`Get-Help about_Automatic_Variables`).

Default or automatic variables often have descriptions; these may be seen by using the `Get` variable and selecting the description:

```
Get-Variable | Select-Object Name, Description
```

New

The `New` variable can be used to create a new variable:

```
New-Variable -Name today -Value (Get-Date)
```

This command is the equivalent of using the following:

```
$today = Get-Date
```

The `New` variable gives more control over the created variable. For example, you may wish to create a constant, a variable that can't be changed following its creation:

```
New-Variable -Name startTime -Value (Get-Date) -Option Constant
```

Any attempt to modify the variable after creation results in an error message; this includes changing the variable value or its properties and attempts to remove the variable, as shown here:

```
PS> $startTime = Get-Date
Cannot overwrite variable startTime because it is read-only or constant.
At line:1 char:1
+ $startTime = Get-Date
+ ~~~~~~~~~~~~~~~~~~~~~
    + CategoryInfo : WriteError: (startTime:String) [],
SessionStateUnauthorizedAccessException
    + FullyQualifiedErrorId : VariableNotWritable
```

A variable cannot be changed into a constant after creation.

Remove

As the name suggests, the Remove variable destroys a variable and any data it may hold.

The Remove variable is used as follows:

```
$psProcesses = Get-Process powershell
Remove-Variable psProcesses
```

If more than one variable refers to an object, the object won't be removed. For example, the following command shows the name of the first process running (conhost.exe, in this particular case):

```
PS> $object1 = $object2 = Get-Process | Select-Object -First 1
PS> Remove-Variable object1
PS> Write-Host $object2.Name

conhost
```

Set

The Set variable allows you to change the value and certain aspects of the created variable. For example, the following sets the value of an existing variable:

```
$objectCount = 23
Set-Variable objectCount -Value 42
```

It isn't common to see the `Set` variable being used in this manner; it is simpler to assign the new value directly, as was done when the variable was created. As with the `New` variable, much of the `Set` variable's utility comes from the additional parameters it offers, as shown in the following examples.

Setting a description for a variable is effected as follows:

```
Set-Variable objectCount -Description 'The number of objects in the queue'
```

Rendering a variable private is effected as follows:

```
Set-Variable objectCount -Option Private
```

Private scope

Private scope is accessible using `$private:objectCount`. The `Set` variable may be used but is not required.

Variable provider

PowerShell includes a variable provider that can be queried as a filesystem using `Get-ChildItem`, `Test-Path`, and so on.

`Get-ChildItem` may be used to list all of the variables in the current scope by running the command shown as follows:

```
Get-ChildItem variable:
```

The output will include the default variables, as well as any variables created by modules that might have been imported.

As this behaves much like a filesystem, `Test-Path` may be used to determine whether or not a variable exists:

```
Test-Path variable:\VerbosePreference
```

`Set-Item` may be used to change the value of a variable or create a new variable:

```
Set-Item variable:\new -Value variable
```

`Get-Content` can also be used to retrieve the content of a variable:

```
Get-Content variable:\OutputEncoding
```

The backslash character used in the preceding examples is optional. The output from each command in the following example will be identical:

```
$new = 123
Get-Item variable:\new
Get-Item variable:new
```

Variable scope

Variables may be declared in a number of different scopes. The scopes are as follows:

- Local
- Global
- Private
- Script
- A numeric scope relative to the current scope

More about scopes

The help document, `about_scopes` (`Get-Help about_scopes`), contains further examples and details.

By default, variables are placed in local scope. Access to variables is hierarchical: a child (scopes created beneath a parent) can access variables created by the parent (or ancestors). Variables created in a child scope cannot be accessed from a parent scope.

Local and global scope

When creating a variable in the console (outside of functions or script blocks), the local scope is global. The global scope can be accessed from inside a function (child) because it is a parent scope:

```
Remove-Variable thisValue -ErrorAction SilentlyContinue
$Local:thisValue = "Some value"
"From Local: $local:thisValue"          # Accessible
"From Global: $global:thisValue"        # Accessible

function Test-ThisScope {
    "From Local: $local:thisValue"      # Does not exist
    "From Global: $global:thisValue"    # Accessible
}

Test-ThisScope
```

When scopes are explicitly named as this, the source of a variable value can be reasonably clear. If the scope prefix is removed, PowerShell attempts to resolve the variable by searching the parent scopes, as follows:

```
Remove-Variable thisValue -ErrorAction SilentlyContinue
# This is still "local" scope
$thisValue = "Some value"

function Test-ThisScope {
    "From Local: $local:thisValue"      # Does not exist
    "From Global: $global:thisValue"    # Accessible
    "Without scope: $thisValue"         # Accessible
}

Test-ThisScope
```

The `thisValue` variable was created in the global scope. As the function does not have a similarly named variable in its local scope, it walks up the scope hierarchy and picks out the variable from the parent scope.

Private scope

The private scope may be accessed using the `private` prefix, as follows:

```
$private:thisValue = "Some value"
```

Moving a variable into the private scope will hide the variable from child scopes:

```
Remove-Variable thisValue -ErrorAction SilentlyContinue
# This is still "local" scope
$private:thisValue = "Some value"
"From global: $global:thisValue"           # Accessible

function Test-ThisScope {
    "Without scope: $thisValue"             # Not accessible
    "From private: $private:thisValue"      # Not accessible
    "From global: $global:thisValue"        # Not accessible
}

Test-ThisScope
```

If the stack depth is increased, the variable search can be made to skip a private variable within an intermediate function and reference the variable from an ancestor, as shown here:

```
PS> function bottom {
>>      $thisValue = "Bottom"
>>      Write-Host "Bottom: $thisValue"
>>      middle
>> }
PS> function middle {
>>      # Hide thisValue from children
>>      $private:thisValue = "Middle" # Middle only
>>      Write-Host "Middle: $thisValue"
>>      top
>> }
PS> function top {
>>      Write-Host "Top: $thisValue" # Original value
>> }
PS> bottom

Bottom: Bottom
Middle: Middle
Top: Bottom
```

Script scope

The script scope is shared across all children in a script or script module. The script scope is a useful place to store variables that must be shared without exposing the variable to the global scope (and therefore to anyone with access to the session).

For example, the following short script stores a version number in a script-level variable. The Get-Version and Set-Version functions both interact with the same variable:

```
# Script file: example.ps1
[Version]$Script:Version = "0.1"

function Get-Version {
    Write-Host "Version: $Version"
}

function Set-Version {
    param(
        [Version]$version
    )

    $Script:Version = $version
}

Set-Version 0.2
Write-Host (Get-Version)
```

The Set-Version function implements a local variable in the param block with the same name as the script scope variable. To access the script scope variable version, the name must be prefixed with the scope.

Scope confusion

If variables within a named scope are used, I recommend referencing the scope whenever the variable is used to make it clear where the values originate from.

In the preceding example, that means using $Script:Version in the Get-Version command.

Type and type conversion

Type conversion in PowerShell is used to switch between different types of a value. Types are written between square brackets, in which the type name must be a .NET type, a class, or an enumeration, such as a string, an integer (Int32), and a date (DateTime).

For example, a date may be changed into a string:

```
PS> [String](Get-Date)
10/27/2016 13:14:32
```

Or a string may be changed into a date:

```
PS> [DateTime]"01/01/2016"

01 January 2016 00:00:00
```

In a similar manner, variables may be assigned a fixed type. To assign a type to a variable, the following notation is used:

```
[String]$thisString = "some value"
[Int]$thisNumber = 2
[DateTime]$date = '01/01/2016'
```

This adds an argument-type converter attribute to the variable. The presence of this converter is visible using Get-Variable, although the resultant type is not:

```
PS> [String]$thisString = "some value"
PS> (Get-Variable thisString).Attributes


TransformNullOptionalParameters TypeId
------------------------------- ------
                           True
System.Management.Automation.ArgumentTypeConverterAttribute
```

Subsequent assignments made to the variable will be converted into a string. This remains so for the lifetime of the variable: until the session is closed, the variable falls out of scope, or the variable is removed using Remove-Variable.

Setting the variable value to `$null` does not remove the type conversion attribute. This can be seen here:

```
PS> [String]$thisString = 'A string value'
PS> $thisString = $null
PS> $thisString = Get-Process powershell
PS> $thisString.GetType()


IsPublic IsSerial Name                BaseType
-------- -------- ----                --------
True     True     String              System.Object
```

PowerShell's type conversion is exceptionally powerful. When converting a value, PowerShell uses the following conversions:

- Direct assignment
- Language-based conversion
- Parse conversion
- Static create conversion
- Constructor conversion
- Cast conversion
- IConvertible conversion
- IDictionary conversion
- PSObject property conversion
- TypeConverter conversion

More about type conversion

The conversion process is extensive, but documentation is available. The preceding list can be found on an MSDN blog: `https://blogs.msdn.microsoft.com/powershell/2013/06/11/understanding-powershells-type-conversion-magic/`.

Experimentation with the process is a vital part of learning.

Objects assigned to variables

So far, we've explored one-off assignments of simple value types, and while these values are considered objects, they're still (reasonably) simple objects. Once created, variables holding simple values, such as integers and strings, can diverge without affecting one another.

That is, the numeric value assigned to each variable is independent following creation:

```
$i = $j = 5
```

Each of the following commands increases the value held in the i variable by creating a new integer object (based on the original object):

```
$i = $j = 5
$i++
$i += 1
$i = $i + 1
```

If each statement is executed in turn, the i variable will be 8, and the j will be 5 variable .

When changing the value of a property on a more complex object, the change will be reflected in any variable referencing that object. Consider the following example, where we create a custom object and assign it to two variables, as follows:

```
$object1 = $object2 = [PSCustomObject]@{
    Name = 'First object'
}
```

A change to a property on an object will be reflected in both variables. The action of changing a property value does not create a new copy of the object. The two variables will continue to reference the same object:

```
PS> $object1.Name = 'New name'
PS> Write-Host $object2.Name

New name
```

The same applies when using nested objects; objects that use other objects as properties:

```
PS> $complexObject = [PSCustomObject]@{
>>      OuterNumber = 1
>>      InnerObject = [PSCustomObject]@{
>>          InnerNumber = 2
>>      }
>> }
PS> $innerObject = $complexObject.InnerObject
```

```
PS> $innerObject.InnerNumber = 5
PS> Write-Host $complexObject.InnerObject.InnerNumber
```

5

Arrays

An array contains a set of objects of the same type. Each entry in the array is called an element, and each element has an index (position). Indexing in an array starts from 0.

Arrays are an important part of PowerShell. When the return from a command is assigned to a variable, an array will be the result if the command returns more than one object. For example, the following command will yield an array of objects:

```
$processes = Get-Process
```

Array type

In PowerShell, arrays are, by default, given the System.Object[] type (an array of objects where [] is used to signify that it is an array).

Why System.Object?

All object instances are derived from a .NET type or class, and, in .NET, every object instance is derived from System.Object (including strings and integers). Therefore, a System.Object array in PowerShell can hold just about anything.

Arrays in PowerShell (and .NET) are immutable. The size is declared on creation and cannot be changed. A new array must be created if an element is to be added or removed. The array operations described next are considered less efficient for large arrays because of the recreation overhead involved in changing the array size.

We will explore creating arrays, assigning a type to the array, and selecting elements, as well as adding and removing elements. We will also take a brief look at how arrays may be used to fill multiple variables and conclude with a look at multi-dimensional arrays and jagged arrays.

Creating an array

There are a number of ways to create arrays. An empty array (containing no elements) can
be created as follows:

```
$myArray = @()
```

An empty array of a specific size may be created using the New object. Using [] after the
name of the type denotes that it is an array, and the number following sets the array size:

```
$myArray = New-Object Object[] 10          # 10 objects
$byteArray = New-Object Byte[] 100         # 100 bytes
$ipAddresses = New-Object IPAddress[] 5    # 5 IP addresses
```

An array with a few strings in it can be created as follows:

```
$myGreetings = "Hello world", "Hello sun", "Hello moon"
```

Or it can be created as follows:

```
$myGreetings = @("Hello world", "Hello sun", "Hello moon")
```

An array may be spread over multiple lines in either the console or a script that may make
it easier to read in a script:

```
$myGreetings = "Hello world",
               "Hello sun",
               "Hello moon"
```

You can mix values that are considered to be objects without losing anything:

```
$myThings = "Hello world", 2, 34.23, (Get-Date)
```

Arrays with a type

An array may be given a type in similar manner to a variable holding a single value. The
difference is that the type name is followed by [], as was the case when creating an empty
array of a specific size. For example, each of these is an array type, which may appear
before a variable name:

```
[String[]]    # An array of strings
[UInt64[]]    # An array of unsigned 64-bit integers
[Xml[]]       # An array of XML documents
```

If a type is set for the array, more care must be taken as regards assigning values. If a type is declared, PowerShell will attempt to convert any value assigned to an array element into that type.

In this example, $null will become 0 and 3.45 (a double) will become 3 (normal rounding rules apply when converting integers):

```
[Int32[]]$myNumbers = 1, 2, $null, 3.45
```

The following example shows an error being thrown, as a string cannot be converted into an integer:

```
PS> [Int32[]]$myNumbers = 1, 2, $null, "A string"
Cannot convert value "A string" to type "System.Int32". Error: "Input
string was not in a correct format."
At line:1 char:1
+ [Int32[]]$myNumbers = 1, 2, $null, "A string"
+ ~~~~~~~~~~~~~~~~~~~~~~~~~~~~~~~~~~~~~~~~~~~~~~~
    + CategoryInfo : MetadataError: (:) [],
ArgumentTransformationMetadataException
    + FullyQualifiedErrorId : RuntimeException
```

Adding elements to an array

A single item can be added to the end of an array using the assignment by addition operator:

```
$myArray = @()
$myArray += "New value"
```

The preceding command is equivalent to the following:

```
$myArray = $myArray + "New value"
```

In the background, PowerShell creates a new array with one extra element, copies the existing array in, and then adds the value for the new element before disposing of the original array. The larger the array, the less efficient this operation becomes.

The same technique can be used to join one array to another, demonstrated as follows:

```
$firstArray = 1, 2, 3
$secondArray = 4, 5, 6
$mergedArray = $firstArray + $secondArray
```

Selecting elements from an array

Individual elements from an array may be selected using an index. The index counts from 0 to the end of the array. The first and second elements are available using index, 0 and 1:

```
$myArray = 1, 2, 3, 4, 5, 6, 7, 8, 9, 10
$myArray[0]
$myArray[1]
```

In a similar manner, array elements can be accessed counting backward, from the end. The last element is available using the -1 index, and the penultimate element using the -2 index, for example:

```
$myArray[-1]
$myArray[-2]
```

Ranges of elements may be selected either going forward (starting from 0) or going backward (starting with -1):

```
$myArray[2..4]
$myArray[-1..-5]
```

More than one range can be selected in a single statement:

```
$myArray[0..2 + 6..8 + -1]
```

This requires some care. The first part of the index set must be an array for the addition operation to succeed. The expression in square brackets is evaluated first and converted into a single array (of indexes) before any elements are selected from the array:

```
PS> $myArray[0 + 6..8 + -1]
Method invocation failed because [System.Object[]] does not contain a
method named 'op_Addition'.
At line:1 char:1
+ $myArray[0 + 6..8 + -1]
+ ~~~~~~~~~~~~~~~~~~~~~~~~
    + CategoryInfo : InvalidOperation: (op_Addition:String) [],
RuntimeException
    + FullyQualifiedErrorId : MethodNotFound
```

Exactly the same error would be shown when running the expression within square brackets alone:

```
0..2 + 6..8 + -1
```

The following modified command shows two different ways to achieve the intended result:

```
$myArray[@(0) + 6..8 + -1]
$myArray[0..0 + 6..8 + -1]
```

Changing element values in an array

Elements within an array may be changed by assigning a new value to a specific index, for example:

```
$myArray = 1, 2, 9, 4, 5
$myArray[2] = 3
```

Values in an array may be changed within a loop, as follows:

```
$myArray = 1, 2, 3, 4, 5
for ($i = 0; $i -lt $myArray.Count; $i++) {
    $myArray[$i] = 9
}
```

Removing elements from an array

Removing elements from an array is difficult because arrays are immutable. To remove an element, a new array must be created.

It is possible to appear to remove an element by setting it to null, for example:

```
$myArray = 1, 2, 3, 4, 5
$myArray[1] = $null
$myArray
```

However, observe that the count does not decrease when a value is set to null:

```
PS> $myArray.Count
5
```

Loops (or pipelines) consuming the array will not skip the element with the null value (extra code is needed to guard against the null value):

```
$myArray | ForEach-Object { Write-Host $_ }
```

The Where object may be used to remove the null value, creating a new array:

```
$myArray | Where-Object { $_ } | ForEach-Object { Write-Host $_ }
```

Depending on usage, a number of ways are available to address removal. Removal by index and removal by value are discussed next.

Removing elements by index

Removing elements based on an index requires the creation of a new array and omission of the value in the element in that index. In each of the following cases, an array with 100 elements will be used as an example; the element at index 49 (with the value of 50) will be removed:

```
$oldArray = 1..100
```

This method uses indexes to access and add everything we want to keep:

```
$newArray = $oldArray[0..48] + $oldArray[50..99]
```

Using the .NET `Array.Copy` static method (see `Chapter 7`, *Working with .NET*), we have the following:

```
$newArray = New-Object Object[] ($oldArray.Count - 1)
# Before the index
[Array]::Copy(
    $oldArray,      # Source
    $newArray,      # Destination
    49              # Number of elements to copy
)
# After the index
[Array]::Copy(
    $oldArray,      # Source
    50,             # Copy from index of Source
    $newArray,      # Destination
    49,             # Copy to index of Destination
    50              # Number of elements to copy
)
```

This is the outcome using a `for` loop:

```
$newArray = for ($i = 0; $i -lt $oldArray.Count; $i++) {
    if ($i -ne 49) {
        $oldArray[$i]
    }
}
```

Removing elements by value

Removing an element with a specific value from an array can be achieved in a number of different ways.

Again, we start with an array of 100 elements, as follows:

```
$oldArray = 1..100
```

The Where object may be used to identify and omit the element with the value 50. If 50 were to occur more than once, all instances would be omitted:

```
$newArray = $oldArray | Where-Object { $_ -ne 50 }
```

The index of the element might be identified and removed using the methods explored in removing elements according to the index:

```
$index = $oldArray.IndexOf(50)
```

If the value of the variable index is −1, the value is not present in the array (0 would indicate that it is the first element):

```
$index = $oldArray.IndexOf(50)
if ($index -gt -1) {
    $newArray = $oldArray[0..($index - 1)] +
        $oldArray[($index + 1)..99]
}
```

Unlike the Where object version, which inspects all elements, IndexOf gets the first occurrence of a value only. A complementary method, LastIndexOf, allows the most recent occurrence of a value to be removed.

Clearing an array

Finally, an array may be completely emptied by calling the Clear method:

```
$newArray = 1, 2, 3, 4, 5
$newArray.Clear()
```

Filling variables from arrays

It is possible to fill two (or more) variables from an array:

```
$i, $j = 1, 2
```

This is often encountered when splitting a string:

```
$firstName, $lastName = "First Last" -split " "
$firstName, $lastName = "First Last".Split(" ")
```

If the array is longer than the number of variables, all remaining elements are assigned to the last variable. For example, the k variable will hold 3, 4, and 5, as can be seen as follows:

```
$i, $j, $k = 1, 2, 3, 4, 5
```

If there are too few elements, the remaining variables will not be assigned a value. In this example, k will be null:

```
$i, $j, $k = 1, 2
```

Multi-dimensional and jagged arrays

Given that an array contains objects, an array can therefore also contain other arrays.

For example, an array that contains other arrays (a multi-dimensional array) might be created as follows:

```
$arrayOfArrays = @(
    @(1, 2, 3),
    @(4, 5, 6),
    @(7, 8, 9)
)
```

Be careful to ensure that the comma following each of the inner arrays (except the last) is in place. If that comma is missing, the entire structure will be flattened, merging the three inner arrays.

Elements in the array are accessed by indexing into each array in turn (starting with the outermost). The element with the value 2 is accessible using the following notation:

```
PS> $arrayOfArrays[0][1]
2
```

This states that we wish to retrieve the first element (which is an array) and the second element of that array.

The element with the value 6 is accessible using the following:

```
PS> $arrayOfArrays[1][2]
6
```

Jagged arrays are a specific form of multi-dimensional array. An example of a jagged array is as follows:

```
$arrayOfArrays = @(
    @(1,  2),
    @(4,  5,  6,  7,  8,  9),
    @(10, 11, 12)
)
```

As in the first example, it is an array containing arrays. Instead of containing inner arrays, which all share the same size (dimension), the inner arrays have no consistent size (hence, they are jagged).

In this example, the element with the value 9 is accessed as follows:

```
PS> $arrayOfArrays[1][5]
9
```

Hashtables

A hashtable is an associative array or an indexed array. Individual elements in the array are created with a unique key. Keys cannot be duplicated within the hashtable.

Hashtables are important in PowerShell. They are used to create custom objects, to pass parameters into commands, to create custom properties using the Select object, and as the type for values assigned to parameter values of many different commands, among other things.

For finding commands that use Hashtable as a parameter, we use the following:

```
Get-Command -ParameterType Hashtable
```

This topic explores creating hashtables, selecting elements, enumerating all values in a hashtable, and adding and removing elements.

Creating a hashtable

An empty hashtable is created in the same manner as the following:

```
$hashtable = @{}
```

A hashtable with a few objects appears as follows:

```
$hashtable = @{Key1 = "Value1"; Key2 = "Value2"}
```

Elements in a hashtable may be spread across multiple lines:

```
$hashtable = @{
    Key1 = "Value1"
    Key2 = "Value2"
}
```

Adding and changing elements to a hashtable

Elements may be explicitly added to a hashtable using the Add method:

```
$hashtable = @{}
$hashtable.Add("Key1", "Value1")
```

If the value already exists, using Add will generate an error (as shown here):

```
PS> $hashtable = @{"Existing", "Value0"}
PS> $hashtable.Add("Existing", "Value1")

Exception calling "Add" with "2" argument(s): "Item has already been added.
Key in dictionary: 'Existing' Key being added: 'Existing'"
At line:2 char:1
+ $hashtable.Add("Existing", "Value1")
+ ~~~~~~~~~~~~~~~~~~~~~~~~~~~~~~~~~~~~~
    + CategoryInfo : NotSpecified: (:) [], MethodInvocationException
    + FullyQualifiedErrorId : ArgumentException
```

The Contains method will return true or false, depending on whether or not a key is present in hashtable. This may be used to test for a key before adding:

```
$hashtable = @{}
if (-not $hashtable.Contains("Key1")) {
    $hashtable.Add("Key1", "Value1")
}
```

Alternatively, two different ways of adding or changing elements are available. The first option is as follows:

```
$hashtable = @{ Existing = "Old" }
$hashtable["New"] = "New"              # Add this
$hashtable["Existing"] = "Updated"     # Update this
```

The second option is as follows:

```
$hashtable = @{ Existing = "Old" }
$hashtable.New = "New"                 # Add this
$hashtable.Existing = "Updated"        # Update this
```

If a value only has to be changed if it exists, the Contains method may be used:

```
$hashtable = @{ Existing = "Old" }
 if ($hashtable.Contains("Existing")) {
     $hashtable.Existing = "New"
}
```

This may also be used to ensure a value is only added if it does not exist:

```
$hashtable = @{ Existing = "Old" }
if (-not $hashtable.Contains("New")) {
     $hashtable.New = "New"
}
```

Keys cannot be added nor can values be changed while looping through the keys in a hashtable using the keys property. Doing so changes the underlying structure of the hashtable, invalidating the iterator:

```
PS> $hashtable = @{
    Key1 = 'Value1'
    Key2 = 'Value2'
}
PS> foreach ($key in $hashtable.Keys) {
    $hashtable[$key] = "NewValue"
}

Collection was modified; enumeration operation may not execute.
At line:5 char:10
+ foreach ($key in $hashtable.Keys) {
+ ~~~~
    + CategoryInfo : OperationStopped: (:) [], InvalidOperationException
    + FullyQualifiedErrorId : System.InvalidOperationException
```

It is possible to work around this problem by first creating an array of the keys, as follows:

```
$hashtable = @{
    Key1 = 'Value1'
    Key2 = 'Value2'
}
[Object[]]$keys = $hashtable.Keys
foreach ($key in $keys) {
    $hashtable[$key] = "NewValue"
}
```

Notice that the highlighted keys variable is declared as an array of objects. Earlier in this chapter, we discussed assigning objects to variables, and how an assignment does not always create a new instance of an object. Using the Object[] type conversion forces the creation of a new object (a new array of objects) based on the values held in KeyCollection. Without this step, the preceding error message would repeat.

Another approach uses the ForEach object to create a new array of the keys:

```
$hashtable = @{
    Key1 = 'Value1'
    Key2 = 'Value2'
}
$keys = $hashtable.Keys | ForEach-Object { $_ }
foreach ($key in $keys) {
    $hashtable[$key] = "NewValue"
}
```

Selecting elements from a hashtable

Individual elements may be selected by key. A number of different formats are supported for selecting elements:

```
$hashtable["Key1"]
```

Using dot notation, we have the following:

```
$hashtable.Key1
```

The key is not case sensitive, but it is type sensitive and will not automatically convert. For instance, consider the following hashtable:

```
$hashtable = @{1 = 'one'}
```

The value 1 can be selected if an integer is used as the key, but not if a string is used. In other words, the following works:

```
$hashtable.1
$hashtable[1]
```

The following approach, however, does not:

```
$hashtable."1"
$hashtable["1"]
```

Enumerating a hashtable

A hashtable can return the information it holds in several ways. Start with the hashtable:

```
$hashtable = @{
    Key1 = 'Value1'
    Key2 = 'Value2'
}
```

Keys can be returned using the Keys property of the hashtable, which returns KeyCollection:

```
$hashtable.Keys
```

Values can be returned using the Values property, which returns ValueCollection. The key is discarded when using the Values property:

```
$hashtable.Values
```

A simple loop can be used to retain the association between key and value:

```
foreach ($key in $hashtable.Keys) {
    Write-Host "Key: $key     Value: $($hashtable[$key])"
}
```

Removing elements from a hashtable

Unlike arrays, removing an element from a hashtable is straightforward—an element is removed using the Remove method:

```
$hashtable = @{ Existing = "Existing" }
$hashtable.Remove("Existing")
```

If the requested key does not exist, the command does nothing (and does not throw an error).

The `Remove` method cannot be used to modify the hashtable while looping through the keys in a hashtable using the `Keys` property:

```
PS> $hashtable = @{
    Key1 = 'Value1'
    Key2 = 'Value2'
}
PS> foreach ($key in $hashtable.Keys) {
    $hashtable.Remove($key)
}

Collection was modified; enumeration operation may not execute.
At line:5 char:10
+ foreach ($key in $hashtable.Keys) {
+ ~~~~
    + CategoryInfo : OperationStopped: (:) [], InvalidOperationException
    + FullyQualifiedErrorId : System.InvalidOperationException
```

The same method as discussed in the *Adding and changing elements to a hashtable* section, may be used.

Finally, a hashtable may be emptied completely by calling the `Clear` method:

```
$hashtable = @{one = 1; two = 2; three = 3}
$hashtable.Clear()
```

Lists, dictionaries, queues, and stacks

Arrays and hashtables are integral to PowerShell, and being able to manipulate these is critical. If these simpler structures fail to provide an efficient means of working with a set of data, there are advanced alternatives.

The following .NET collections will be discussed:

- `System.Collections.Generic.List`
- `System.Collections.Generic.Dictionary`
- `System.Collections.Generic.Queue`
- `System.Collections.Generic.Stack`

Each of these collections has detailed documentation (for .NET) available on MSDN: `https://msdn.microsoft.com/en-us/library/system.collections.generic(v=vs.110).aspx`.

Lists

A list is the same as an array, but with a larger set of features, such as the ability to add elements without copying two arrays into a new one. The generic list using the .NET class, `System.Collections.Generic.List`, is shown next.

ArrayList is often used in examples requiring advanced array manipulation in PowerShell. However, ArrayList is older (.NET 2.0) and less efficient (it can use more memory), and cannot be strongly typed, as will be shown when creating a generic list.

Creating a list

A generic list must have a type declared. A generic list, in this case a list of strings, is created as follows:

```
$list = New-Object System.Collections.Generic.List[String]
```

`ArrayList` is created in a similar manner. `ArrayList` cannot have the type declared:

```
$arrayList = New-object System.Collections.ArrayList
```

Once created, `ArrayList` may be used in much the same way as a generic list.

Adding elements to the list

`Add` can be used to add new elements to the end of the list:

```
$list.Add("David")
```

The `Insert` and `InsertRange` methods are available to add items elsewhere in the list. For example, an element may be added at the beginning:

```
$list.Insert(0, "Sarah")
$list.Insert(2, "Jane")
```

Selecting elements from the list

As with the array, elements may be selected by index:

```
$list = New-Object System.Collections.Generic.List[String]
$list.AddRange([String[]]("Tom", "Richard", "Harry"))
$list[1]    # Returns Richard
```

The generic list offers a variety of methods that may be used to find elements when the index is not known, such as the following:

```
$index = $list.FindIndex( { $args[0] -eq 'Richard' } )
```

Predicates

In the preceding example, ScriptBlock is a predicate. Arguments are passed into ScriptBlock and all list items matching the query are returned.

The predicate is similar in syntax to the Where object, except $args[0] is used to refer to the item in the list instead of the pipeline variable, $_.

A param block may be declared for ScriptBlock to assign a more meaningful name to the argument ($args[0]) if desirable.

Alternatively, the IndexOf and LastIndex methods may be used. Both of these methods support additional arguments (as opposed to Array.IndexOf, which only supports a restrictive search for a value) to constrain the search. For example, the search may start at a specific index:

```
$list.IndexOf('Harry', 2)       # Start at index 2
$list.IndexOf('Richard', 1, 2)  # Start at index 1, and 2 elements
```

Finally, a generic list offers a BinarySearch (half-interval) search method. This method may dramatically cut the time to search very large, sorted, datasets when compared to a linear search.

In a binary search, the element in the middle of the list is selected, and compared to the value. If the value is larger, the first half of the list is discarded, and the element in the middle of the new, smaller, set is selected for comparison. This process repeats (always cutting the list in half) until the value is found (or it runs out of elements to test):

```
$list = New-Object System.Collections.Generic.List[Int]
$list.AddRange([Int[]](1..100000000))
# Linear and Binary are roughly comparable
```

```
Measure-Command { $list.IndexOf(24) }              # A linear search
Measure-Command { $list.BinarySearch(24) }         # A binary search
# Binary is more effective
Measure-Command { $list.IndexOf(99767859) }        # A linear search
Measure-Command { $list.BinarySearch(99767859) }   # A binary search
```

The time taken to execute a binary search remains fairly constant, regardless of the element position. The time taken to execute a linear search increases as every element must be read (in sequence).

Removing elements from the list

Elements in a list may be removed based on the index or value:

```
$list = New-Object System.Collections.Generic.List[String]
$list.AddRange([String[]]("Tom", "Richard", "Harry", "David"))
$list.RemoveAt(1)            # By Richard by index
$list.Remove("Richard")      # By Richard by value
```

All instances of a particular value may be removed using the RemoveAll method:

```
$list.RemoveAll( { $args[0] -eq "David" } )
```

Changing element values in a list

Elements within a list may be changed by assigning a new value to a specific index, as in the following example:

```
$list = New-Object System.Collections.Generic.List[Int]
$list.AddRange([Int[]](1, 2, 2, 4))
$list[2] = 3
```

Dictionaries

A dictionary, using the .NET class, System.Collections.Generic.Dictionary, is most similar to a hashtable. Like a hashtable, it is a form of associative array.

Unlike the hashtable, however, a dictionary implements a type for both the key and the value, which may make it easier to use.

Creating a dictionary

A dictionary must declare a type for the key and value when it is created. A dictionary that uses a string for the key and an IP address for the value may be created using either of the following examples:

```
$dictionary = New-Object
System.Collections.Generic.Dictionary"[String,IPAddress]"
$dictionary = New-Object
"System.Collections.Generic.Dictionary[String,IPAddress]"
```

Adding and changing elements in a dictionary

As with the hashtable, the `Add` method may be used to add a new value to a dictionary:

```
$dictionary.Add("Computer1", "192.168.10.222")
```

If the key already exists, using `Add` will generate an error, as was the case with the hashtable.

In a dictionary, the `Contains` method behaves differently from the same method in the hashtable. When checking for the existence of a key, the `ContainsKey` method should be used as follows:

```
if (-not $dictionary.ContainsKey("Computer2")) {
    $dictionary.Add("Computer2", "192.168.10.13")
}
```

The dictionary supports the addition of elements using dot-notation:

```
$dictionary.Computer3 = "192.168.10.134"
```

The dictionary leverages PowerShell's type conversion for both the key and the value. For example, if a numeric key is used, it will be converted into a string. If an IP address is expressed as a string, it will be converted into an `IPAddress` object.

For example, consider the addition of the following element:

```
$dictionary.Add(1, 20)
```

In this case, key `1` is converted into a string, and the value `20` is converted into an IP address. Inspecting the element afterward shows the following:

```
PS> $dictionary."1"

Address              : 20
```

```
AddressFamily        : InterNetwork
ScopeId              :
IsIPv6Multicast      : False
IsIPv6LinkLocal      : False
IsIPv6SiteLocal      : False
IsIPv6Teredo         : False
IsIPv4MappedToIPv6   : False
IPAddressToString    : 20.0.0.0
```

Selecting elements from a dictionary

Individual elements may be selected by a key. As with the hashtable, two different notations are supported:

```
$dictionary["Computer1"]      # Key reference
$dictionary.Computer1         # Dot-notation
```

We've seen that, when adding elements, types are converted. Looking back to selecting elements from a hashtable, we know that the value for the key was sensitive to type. As the dictionary has a type declared for the key, it can leverage PowerShell's type conversion.

Consider a dictionary created using a number as a string for the key:

```
$dictionary = New-Object
System.Collections.Generic.Dictionary"[String,IPAddress]"
$dictionary.Add("1", "192.168.10.222")
$dictionary.Add("2", "192.168.10.13")
```

Each of the following examples works to access the value:

```
$dictionary."1"
$dictionary[1]
$dictionary["1"]
```

Enumerating a dictionary

A dictionary can return the information it holds in several ways. Start with this dictionary:

```
$dictionary = New-Object
System.Collections.Generic.Dictionary"[String,IPAddress]"
$dictionary.Add("Computer1", "192.168.10.222")
$dictionary.Add("Computer2", "192.168.10.13")
```

Keys can be returned using the `Keys` property of the dictionary, which returns `KeyCollection`:

```
$dictionary.Keys
```

Values can be returned using the `Values` property, which returns `ValueCollection`. The key is discarded when using the `Values` property:

```
$dictionary.Values
```

A simple loop can be used to retain the association between `key` and `value`:

```
foreach ($key in $dictionary.Keys) {
    Write-Host "Key: $key     Value: $($dictionary[$key])"
}
```

Removing elements from a dictionary

An element may be removed from a dictionary using the `Remove` method:

```
$dictionary.Remove("Computer1")
```

The `Remove` method cannot be used to modify the dictionary while looping through the keys in a dictionary using the `Keys` property.

Queues

A queue is a first-in, first-out array. Elements are added to the end of the queue and taken from the beginning.

The queue uses the .NET class, `System.Collections.Generic.Queue`, and must have a type set.

Creating a queue

A queue of strings may be created as follows:

```
$queue = New-Object System.Collections.Generic.Queue[String]
```

Enumerating the queue

PowerShell will display the content of a queue in the same way as it would the content of an array. It isn't possible to access elements of the queue by the index. The ToArray method may be used to convert the queue into an array if required:

```
$queue.ToArray()
```

The preceding command returns an array of the same type as the queue. That is, if the queue is configured to hold strings, the array will be an array of strings.

The queue has a Peek method that allows retrieval of the next element in the queue without it being removed:

```
$queue.Peek()
```

The Peek method will throw an error if the queue is empty (refer to the *Removing elements from the queue* section).

Adding elements to the queue

Elements are added to the end of the queue using the Enqueue method:

```
$queue.Enqueue("Tom")
$queue.Enqueue("Richard")
$queue.Enqueue("Harry")
```

Removing elements from the queue

Elements are removed from the end using the Dequeue method:

```
$queue.Dequeue() # This returns Tom.
```

If the queue is empty and the Dequeue method is called, an error will be thrown, as shown here:

```
PS> $queue.Dequeue()
Exception calling "Dequeue" with "0" argument(s): "Queue empty."
At line:1 char:1
+ $queue.Dequeue()
+ ~~~~~~~~~~~~~~~~~
  + CategoryInfo : NotSpecified: (:) [], MethodInvocationException
  + FullyQualifiedErrorId : InvalidOperationException
```

To avoid this, the `Count` property of the queue may be inspected, for example:

```
# Set-up the queue
$queue = New-Object System.Collections.Generic.Queue[String]
"Tom", "Richard", "Harry" | ForEach-Object {
    $queue.Enqueue($_)
}
# Dequeue until the queue is empty
while ($queue.Count -gt 0) {
    Write-Host $queue.Dequeue()
}
```

Stacks

A stack is a collection of objects in which objects are accessed in **Last In First Out (LIFO)**. Elements are added and removed from the top of the stack.

The stack uses the .NET class, `System.Collections.Generic.Stack`, and must have a type set.

Creating a stack

A stack containing strings may be created as follows:

```
$stack = New-Object System.Collections.Generic.Stack[String]
```

Enumerating the stack

PowerShell will display the content of a stack in the same way as it would the content of an array. It isn't possible to index into a stack. The `ToArray()` method may be used to convert the stack into an array if required:

```
$stack.ToArray()
```

The preceding command returns an array of the same type as the stack. That is, if a stack is configured to hold strings, the array will be an array of strings.

The stack has a `Peek` method that allows retrieval of the top element from the stack without it being removed:

```
$stack.Peek()
```

The `Peek` method will throw an error if the stack is empty (refer to the *Removing elements from the stack* section).

Adding elements to the stack

Elements may be added to the stack using the `Push` method:

```
$stack.Push("Up the road")
$stack.Push("Over the gate")
$stack.Push("Under the bridge")
```

Removing elements from the stack

Elements may be removed from the stack using the `Pop` method:

```
$stack.Pop()      # This returns Under the bridge
```

If the stack is empty and the `Pop` method is called, an error will be thrown, as shown here:

```
PS> $stack.Pop()
Exception calling "Pop" with "0" argument(s): "Stack empty."
At line:1 char:1
+ $stack.Pop()
+ ~~~~~~~~~~~~
    + CategoryInfo : NotSpecified: (:) [], MethodInvocationException
    + FullyQualifiedErrorId : InvalidOperationException
```

To avoid this, the `Count` property of the stack may be inspected, for example:

```
# Set-up the stack
$stack = New-Object System.Collections.Generic.Stack[String]
"Up the road", "Over the gate", "Under the bridge" | ForEach-Object {
    $stack.Push($_)
}
# Pop from the stack until the stack is empty
while ($stack.Count -gt 0) {
    Write-Host $stack.Pop()
}
```

Summary

Variables can be created to hold on to information that's to be reused in a function or a script. A variable may be a simple name, or loaded from a file.

The * variable commands are available to interact with variables beyond changing the value, such as setting a description, making a variable in a specific scope, or making a variable private.

A variable scope affects how variables may be accessed. Variables are created in the local scope by default.

Arrays are sets of objects of the same type. Arrays are immutable, and the size of an array cannot change after creation. Adding or removing elements from an array requires the creation of a new array.

Hashtables are associative arrays. An element in a hashtable is accessed using a unique key.

Lists, stacks, queues, and dictionaries are advanced collections that may be used when a particular behavior is required, or if they offer a desirable performance benefit.

In Chapter 6, *Branching and Looping*, we will explore branching and looping in PowerShell.

6
Branching and Looping

A branch in a script or command is created every time an `if`, `switch` statement, or loop is added. The branch represents a different set of instructions. Branches can be conditional, such as one created by an `if` statement, or unconditional, such as a `for` loop.

As a script or command increases in complexity, the branches spread out the same as the limbs of a tree.

In this chapter, we are going to cover the following topics:

- Conditional statements
- Loops
- Branching and assignment

Conditional statements

Statements or lines of code may be executed when certain conditions are met. PowerShell provides `if` and `select` statements for this purpose.

if, else, and elseif

An `if` statement is written as follows; the statements enclosed by the `if` statement will execute if the condition evaluates to `true`:

```
if (<condition>) {
    <statements>
}
```

The `else` statement is optional and will trigger if all previous conditions evaluate to `false`:

```
if (<first-condition>) {
    <first-statements>
} else {
    <second-statements>
}
```

The `elseif` statement allows conditions to be stacked:

```
if (<first-condition>) {
    <first-statements>
} elseif (<second-condition>) {
    <second-statements>
} elseif (<last-condition>) {
    <last-statements>
}
```

The `else` statement may be added after any number of `elseif` statements.

Execution of a block of conditions stops as soon as a single condition evaluates to `true`. For example, both the first and second condition would evaluate to `true`, as shown here, but only the first will execute:

```
$value = 1
if ($value -eq 1) {
    Write-Host 'value is 1'
} elseif ($value -lt 10) {
    Write-Host 'value is less than 10'
}
```

Implicit Boolean

An implicit Boolean is a condition that can evaluate as true (is considered to be something) without using a comparison operator that would explicitly return true or false. For example, the number 1 will evaluate as true:

```
$value = 1
if ($value) {
    Write-Host 'Implicit true'
}
```

In the previous example, the statement executes because casting the value 1 to Boolean results in true. If the variable were set to 0, the condition would evaluate to false.

Each of the following will evaluate to true, as they are considered to be something when used in this manner:

```
[Boolean]1
[Boolean]-1
[Boolean]2016
[Boolean]"Hello world"
```

Each of the following will evaluate to false, as each is considered to be nothing:

```
[Boolean]0
[Boolean]""
[Boolean]$null
```

Assignment within if statements

An if statement can include an assignment step, as follows:

```
if ($i = 1) {
    Write-Host "Implicit true. The variable i is $i"
}
```

This is most commonly used when testing for the existence of a value in a variable, for example:

```
if ($interface = Get-NetAdapter | Where-Object Status -eq 'Up') {
    Write-Host "$($interface.Name) is up"
}
```

In the previous example, the statement to the right of the assignment operator (=) is executed, assigned to the `$interface` variable, and then the value in the variable is treated as an implicit Boolean.

switch

A `switch` statement uses the following generalized notation:

```
switch [-regex|-wildcard] [-casesensitive] (<value>) {
    <condition> { <statements> }
    <condition> { <statements> }
}
```

The `casesensitive` parameter applies when testing conditions against a string value.

The `switch` command can also be used to work on the content of a file using the following notation:

```
switch [-regex|-wildcard] [-casesensitive] -File <Name> {
    <condition> { <statements> }
    <condition> { <statements> }
}
```

The `File` parameter can be used to select from a text file (line by line). The `switch` statement differs from conditions written using `if-elseif` in one important respect. The `switch` statement will not stop testing conditions unless the `break` keyword is used, for example:

```
$value = 1
switch ($value) {
    1 { Write-Host 'value is 1' }
    1 { Write-Host 'value is still 1' }
}
```

Using `break`, as shown here, will exit the `switch` statement after a match:

```
$value = 1
switch ($value) {
    1 { Write-Host 'value is 1'; break }
    1 { Write-Host 'value is still 1' }
}
```

The `default` keyword provides the same functionality as the `else` statement when using `if`, for example:

```
$value = 2
switch ($value) {
    1       { Write-Host 'value is 1' }
    default { Write-Host 'No conditions matched' }
}
```

A switch statement can test more than one value at once; however, `break` applies to the entire statement, not just a single value. For example, without `break`, both of the following `Write-Host` statements execute:

```
switch (1, 2) {
    1 { Write-Host 'Equals 1' }
    2 { Write-Host 'Equals 2' }
}
```

If the `break` keyword is included, as shown here, only the first executes:

```
switch (1, 2) {
    1 { Write-Host 'Equals 1'; break }
    2 { Write-Host 'Equals 2' }
}
```

wildcard and regex

The `wildcard` and `regex` parameters are used when matching strings. The `wildcard` parameter allows for the use of the characters ? (any single character) and * (any character, repeated 0 or more times) in a condition, for example:

```
switch -Wildcard ('cat') {
    'c*'  { Write-Host 'The word begins with c' }
    '???' { Write-Host 'The word is 3 characters long' }
    '*t'  { Write-Host 'The word ends with t' }
}
```

The Regex parameter allows for the use of regular expressions to perform comparisons (Chapter 9, *Regular Expressions*, will explain this syntax in greater detail), for example:

```
switch -Regex ('cat') {
 '^c' { Write-Host 'The word begins with c' } '[a-z]{3}' { Write-Host 'The
word is 3 characters long' } 't$' { Write-Host 'The word ends with t' } }
```

Expressions

Switch allows expressions (a ScriptBlock) to be used in place of a simpler condition. The result of the expression should be an explicit true or false, or an implicit Boolean, for example:

```
switch (Get-Date) {
    { $_ -is [DateTime] } { Write-Host 'This is a DateTime type' }
    { $_.Year -ge 2017 }  { Write-Host 'It is 2017 or later' }
}
```

Loops

Loops may be used to iterate through collections, performing an operation against each element in the collection, or to repeat an operation (or series of operations) until a condition is met.

foreach

The foreach loop executes against each element of a collection using the following notation:

```
foreach (<element> in <collection>) {
    <body-statements>
}
```

For example, the foreach loop may be used to iterate through each of the processes returned by Get-Process:

```
foreach ($process in Get-Process) {
    Write-Host $process.Name
}
```

If the collection is $null or empty, the body of the loop will not execute.

for

The `for` loop is typically used to step through a collection using the following notation:

```
for (<intial>; <exit condition>; <repeat>){
    <body-statements>
}
```

`<initial>` represents the state of a variable before the first iteration of the loop. This is normally used to initialize a counter for the loop.

The exit condition must be `true` as long as the loop is executing.

`<repeat>` is executed after each iteration of the body and is often used to increment a counter.

The `for` loop is most often used to iterate through a collection, for example:

```
$processes = Get-Process
for ($i = 0; $i -lt $processes.Count; $i++) {
    Write-Host $processes[$i].Name
}
```

The `for` loop provides a significant degree of control over the loop and is useful where the step needs to be something other than simple ascending order. For example, `repeat` may be used to execute the body for every third element:

```
for ($i = 0; $i -lt $processes.Count; $i += 3) {
    Write-Host $processes[$i].Name
}
```

The loop parameters may also be used to reverse the direction of the loop, for example:

```
for ($i = $processes.Count - 1; $i -ge 0; $i--) {
    Write-Host $processes[$i].Name
}
```

do until and do while

`do until` and `do while` each execute the body of the loop at least once, as the condition test is at the end of the loop statement. Loops based on `do until` will exit when the condition evaluates to `true`; loops based on `do while` will exit when the condition evaluates to `false`.

do loops are written using the following notation:

```
do {
    <body-statements>
} <until | while> (<condition>)
```

do until is suited to exit conditions that are expected to be positive. For example, a script might wait for a computer to respond to a ping:

```
do {
    Write-Host "Waiting for boot"
    Start-Sleep -Seconds 5
} until (Test-Connection 'SomeComputer' -Quiet -Count 1)
```

The do while loop is more suitable for exit conditions that are negative. For example, a loop might wait for a remote computer to stop responding to a ping:

```
do {
    Write-Host "Waiting for shutdown"
    Start-Sleep -Seconds 5
} while (Test-Connection 'SomeComputer' -Quiet -Count 1)
```

while

As the condition for a while loop comes first, the body of the loop will only execute if the condition evaluates to true:

```
while (<condition>) {
    <body-statements>
}
```

A while loop may be used to wait for something to happen. For example, it might be used to wait for a path to exist:

```
while (-not (Test-Path $env:TEMP\test.txt -PathType Leaf)) {
    Start-Sleep -Seconds 10
}
```

break and continue

break can be used to end a loop early. The loop in the following example would continue to 20; break is used to stop the loop at 10:

```
for ($i = 0; $i -lt 20; $i += 2) {
```

```
        Write-Host $i
        if ($i -eq 10) {
            break     # Stop this loop
        }
    }
```

break acts on the loop it is nested inside. In the following example, the inner loop breaks early when the i variable is less than or equal to 2:

```
PS> $i = 1 # Initial state for i
PS> while ($i -le 3) {
>>      Write-Host "i: $i"
>>      $k = 1 # Reset k
>>      while ($k -lt 5) {
>>          Write-Host " k: $k"
>>          $k++ # Increment k
>>          if ($i -le 2 -and $k -ge 3) {
>>              break
>>          }
>>      }
>>      $i++ # Increment i
>> }

i: 1
k: 1
k: 2
i: 2
k: 1
k: 2
i: 3
k: 1
k: 2
k: 3
k: 4
```

The continue keyword may be used to move on to the next iteration of a loop immediately. For example, the following loop executes a subset of the loop body when the value of the i variable is less than 2:

```
for ($i = 0; $i -le 5; $i++) {
    Write-Host $i
    if ($i -lt 2) {
        continue    # Continue to the next iteration
    }
    Write-Host "Remainder when $i is divided by 2 is $($i % 2)"
}
```

Branching and assignment

PowerShell allows the output from a branching operation (`if`, `switch`, `foreach`, `for`, and so on) to be assigned to a variable.

This example assigns a value based on a switch statement when converting a value. The values of the variables at the top are expected to change:

```
$value = 20
$units = 'TB'
$bytes = switch ($Units) {
    'TB'    { $value * 1TB }
    'GB'    { $value * 1GB }
    'MB'    { $value * 1MB }
    default { $value }
}
```

The same approach may be used when working with a loop, such as `foreach`. The following example shows a commonly used approach to building an array:

```
$serviceProcesses = @()
foreach ($service in Get-CimInstance Win32_Service -Filter
'State="Running"') {
    $serviceProcesses += Get-Process -Id $service.ProcessId
}
```

In this example, a new array must be recreated with one extra element (and the old copied) for every iteration of the loop.

This operation may be simplified by moving the assignment operation in front of `foreach`:

```
$serviceProcesses = foreach ($service in Get-CimInstance Win32_Service -
Filter 'State="Running"') {
    Get-Process -Id $service.ProcessId
}
```

In this case, the assignment occurs once when the loop finishes running. There is no array to continually resize.

Summary

In this chapter, we have explored the `if` and `switch` statements.

Each of the different loops, `foreach`, `for`, `do until`, `do while`, and `while`, have been introduced.

In `Chapter 7`, *Working with .NET*, we will explore working with the .NET Framework.

7
Working with .NET

PowerShell is written in and built on the .NET Framework. Much of the .NET Framework can be used directly, and doing so adds a tremendous amount of flexibility by removing many of the borders the language might otherwise have.

The idea of working with objects was introduced in Chapter 3, *Working with Objects in Powershell*, and this chapter extends on that, moving from objects created by commands to objects created from .NET classes. Many of the chapters that follow this one make extensive use of .NET, simply because it's the foundation of PowerShell.

It's important to understand that the .NET Framework is vast; it isn't possible to cover everything about the .NET Framework in a single chapter. This chapter aims to show how the .NET Framework may be used within PowerShell based on the MSDN reference, which is available at `https://docs.microsoft.com/en-us/dotnet/api/index?view=netframework-4.7.2`.

What can you do with .NET?

I enjoy implementing network protocols in PowerShell. To do this, I use several branches of .NET that specialize in network operations, such as creating sockets, sending and receiving bytes, and reading and converting streams of bytes.

Classes implemented in .NET will come up again and again as different areas of the language are explored. From building strings and working with Active Directory, to writing graphical interfaces and working with web services, everything needs a little .NET.

In this chapter, we're going to cover the following topics:

- Assemblies
- Namespaces
- Types
- Classes
- Constructors
- Properties and methods
- Static properties
- Static methods
- Non-public classes
- Type accelerators
- The `using` keyword

Assemblies

.NET objects are implemented within assemblies. An assembly may be static (based on a file) or dynamic (created in memory).

Many of the most commonly used classes exist in DLL files stored in `%SystemRoot%\Assembly`. The list of currently loaded assemblies in a PowerShell session may be viewed using the following statement:

```
[System.AppDomain]::CurrentDomain.GetAssemblies()
```

Once an assembly, and the types it contains, has been loaded into a session, it can't be unloaded without completely restarting the session.

Much of PowerShell is implemented in the `System.Management.Automation` DLL. Details of this can be shown using the following statement:

```
[System.Management.Automation.PowerShell].Assembly
```

In this statement, the PowerShell type is chosen to get the assembly. Any other type in the same assembly is able to show the same information. The PowerShell type could be replaced with another in the previous command, as follows:

```
[System.Management.Automation.PSCredential].Assembly
[System.Management.Automation.PSObject].Assembly
```

Namespaces

A namespace is used to organize classes into a hierarchy, often to group types with related functionalities.

In PowerShell, the system namespace is implicit. The `System.AppDomain` type was used previously; this command, used when introducing assemblies, can be shortened:

```
[AppDomain]::CurrentDomain.GetAssemblies()
```

The same applies to types with longer names, such as `System.Management.Automation.PowerShell`, which can be shortened as follows:

```
[Management.Automation.PowerShell].Assembly
```

Types

A type is used to represent the generalized functionality of an object. To use this book as an example again, it could have a number of types, including the following:

- `PowerShellBook`
- `TextBook`
- `Book`

Each of these types describes the general functionality of the object. The type doesn't say how this book came to be, nor whether it will do anything (on its own) to help create one.

In PowerShell, types are written between square brackets. The `[System.AppDomain]` and `[System.Management.Automation.PowerShell]` statements, used when discussing previous assemblies, are types.

Type descriptions are objects in PowerShell

`[System.AppDomain]` denotes a type, but the syntax used to denote the type is itself an object. It has properties and methods and a type of its own (`RuntimeType`), which can be seen by running the following command: `[System.AppDomain].GetType()`

To an extent, the terms type and class are synonymous. A class is used to define a type, but it isn't the only way of doing so. Another way is to use what is known as a **structure** (or **struct**), which is used to define value types such as integers (`Int32`, `Int64`, and so on).

A type cannot be used to create an object instance all on its own.

Classes

A class is a set of instructions that dictates how a specific instance of an object is to be created. A class is, in a sense, a recipe.

In the case of this book, a class includes details of authoring, editorial processes, and publication steps. These steps are, hopefully, invisible to anyone reading this book; they're part of the internal implementation of the class. Following these steps will produce an instance of the `PowerShellBook` object.

It's often necessary to look up the instructions for using a class in the .NET class library on MSDN, available at

`https://msdn.microsoft.com/en-us/library/mt472912(v=vs.110).aspx`.

The starting point for creating an instance of an object is often what's known as a constructor.

Constructors

The `System.Text.StringBuilder` class can be used to build complex strings. The `StringBuilder` class has a number of constructors that can be viewed on the MSDN class library, as shown in the following screenshot:

	Name	Description
	StringBuilder()	Initializes a new instance of the StringBuilder class.
	StringBuilder(Int32)	Initializes a new instance of the StringBuilder class using the specified capacity.
	StringBuilder(Int32, Int32)	Initializes a new instance of the StringBuilder class that starts with a specified capacity and can grow to a specified maximum.
	StringBuilder(String)	Initializes a new instance of the StringBuilder class using the specified string.
	StringBuilder(String, Int32)	Initializes a new instance of the StringBuilder class using the specified string and capacity.
	StringBuilder(String, Int32, Int32, Int32)	Initializes a new instance of the StringBuilder class from the specified substring and capacity.

PowerShell is also able to show the list of constructors. However, PowerShell cannot show the descriptive text. Still, this may be useful as a reminder if the general functionality is already known. In PowerShell 5.0, the following syntax may be used to list the constructors:

```
PS> [System.Text.StringBuilder]::new

OverloadDefinitions
-------------------
System.Text.StringBuilder new()
System.Text.StringBuilder new(int capacity)
System.Text.StringBuilder new(string value)
System.Text.StringBuilder new(string value, int capacity)
System.Text.StringBuilder new(string value, int startIndex, int length, int
capacity)
System.Text.StringBuilder new(int capacity, int maxCapacity)
```

For older versions of PowerShell, a longer, less descriptive alternative is available:

```
PS> [System.Text.StringBuilder].GetConstructors() | ForEach-Object ToString
Void .ctor()
Void .ctor(Int32)
Void .ctor(System.String)
Void .ctor(System.String, Int32)
Void .ctor(System.String, Int32, Int32, Int32)
Void .ctor(Int32, Int32)
```

Both MSDN and PowerShell show that there are six possible constructors for `StringBuilder`. Both show that the first of those does not expect any arguments.

Calling constructors

In PowerShell 5.0 and higher, an object instance may be created using the new static method:

```
$stringBuilder = [System.Text.StringBuilder]::new()
```

For earlier versions of PowerShell, the object instance may be created using the following syntax:

```
$stringBuilder = New-Object System.Text.StringBuilder
```

PowerShell has added the static method (discussed later in this chapter); it can be used if required, but it isn't documented on the MSDN page for `StringBuilder`.

Once an instance of `StringBuilder` has been created, it can be viewed:

```
PS> $stringBuilder = New-Object System.Text.StringBuilder
PS> $stringBuilder

Capacity MaxCapacity Length
-------- ----------- ------
      16  2147483647      0
```

The `StringBuilder` object has a number of other constructors. These are used to adjust the initial state of the instance.

Calling constructors with lists of arguments

Arguments may be passed to the class constructor using a number of different approaches.

Using `New-Object` and the `ArgumentList` parameter, passing a single argument will use the second constructor in the list on MSDN (and in PowerShell):

```
PS> New-Object -TypeName System.Text.StringBuilder -ArgumentList 10

Capacity MaxCapacity Length
-------- ----------- ------
      10  2147483647      0
```

Alternatively, the following two approaches may be used:

```
New-Object System.Text.StringBuilder(10)
[System.Text.StringBuilder]::new(10)
```

PowerShell decides which constructor to use based on the numbers and types of the arguments.

In the previous examples, one argument is passed; there are two possible constructors that accept a single argument. One of these expects a value of the `Int32` type, the other a string.

If a string is passed, `StringBuilder` will be created, with an initial value for the string. The following example creates a `StringBuilder` object instance containing the specified (`'Hello world'`) string:

```
PS> $stringBuilder = New-Object System.Text.StringBuilder('Hello world')
PS> $stringBuilder.ToString()

Hello world
```

PowerShell will attempt to find a constructor, even if the value type used does not exactly match one of the definitions. For example, an argument of `$true`, a Boolean, creates a `StringBuilder` object with a capacity set to 1. The value for `$true` is treated as an `Int32` value by PowerShell:

```
PS> New-Object System.Text.StringBuilder($true)

Capacity MaxCapacity Length
-------- ----------- ------
   1 2147483647 0
```

If the value for the argument does not match any of the possible constructors, an error will be thrown:

```
PS> New-Object System.Text.StringBuilder((Get-Date))

New-Object : Cannot convert argument "0", with value: "23/01/2017
15:26:59", for "StringBuilder" to type "System.Int32": "Cannot convert
value "23/01/2017 15:26:59" to type
"System.Int32". Error: "Invalid cast from 'DateTime' to 'Int32'.""
At line:1 char:1
+ New-Object System.Text.StringBuilder((Get-Date))
+ ~~~~~~~~~~~~~~~~~~~~~~~~~~~~~~~~~~~~~~~~~~~~~~~~~~
+ CategoryInfo : InvalidOperation: (:) [New-Object], MethodException
+ FullyQualifiedErrorId :
ConstructorInvokedThrowException,Microsoft.PowerShell.Commands.NewObjectCom
mand
```

Arguments as an array

Arguments for constructors can be passed in as an array. Each of the following may be used to create an instance of a `StringBuilder` object:

```
$params = @{
    TypeName     = 'System.Text.StringBuilder'
    ArgumentList = 'Initial value', 50
}
$stringBuilder = New-Object @params
$stringBuilder = New-Object System.Text.StringBuilder($argumentList)
```

Attempting to pass in a list of arguments using the new method will produce a different result; the initial string will be filled with both values:

```
PS> $argumentList = 'Initial value', 50
PS> $stringBuilder = [System.Text.StringBuilder]::new($argumentList)
PS> Write-Host $stringBuilder.ToString() -ForegroundColor Green
PS> $stringBuilder

Initial value 50
Capacity MaxCapacity Length
-------- ----------- ------
      16  2147483647     16
```

An array can be passed in using new, by adopting a slightly different approach:

```
PS> $stringBuilder = [System.Text.StringBuilder]::new.Invoke($argumentList)
PS> Write-Host $stringBuilder.ToString() -ForegroundColor Green
PS> $stringBuilder

Initial value
Capacity MaxCapacity Length
-------- ----------- ------
      50  2147483647     13
```

The ability to push arguments into an array presents a complication when an argument is an array. For example, the memoryStream (System.IO.MemoryStream) class has a number of constructors; two of these expect an array of bytes, as shown in the following screenshot:

⬀	MemoryStream(Byte[])	Initializes a new non-resizable instance of the MemoryStream class based on the specified byte array.
⬀	MemoryStream(Byte[], Boolean)	Initializes a new non-resizable instance of the MemoryStream class based on the specified byte array with the CanWrite property set as specified.

The first of these only expects an array (of bytes) as input. The following example shows an error generated when attempting to pass in the array:

```
PS> [Byte[]]$bytes = 97, 98, 99
PS> $memoryStream = New-Object System.IO.MemoryStream($bytes)

New-Object : Exception calling ".ctor" with "3" argument(s): "Offset and
length were out of bounds for the array or count is greater than the number
of elements from index to the end of the source collection."
```

```
At line:2 char:17
+ $memoryStream = New-Object System.IO.MemoryStream($bytes)
+                 ~~~~~~~~~~~~~~~~~~~~~~~~~~~~~~~~~~~~~~~~~~~~
+ CategoryInfo : InvalidOperation: (:) [New-Object],
MethodInvocationException
+ FullyQualifiedErrorId :
ConstructorInvokedThrowException,Microsoft.PowerShell.Commands.NewObjectCom
mand
```

PowerShell treats each byte as an individual argument for the constructor, rather than passing all of the values into the intended constructor.

The new static method does not suffer from this problem:

```
[Byte[]]$bytes = 97, 98, 99
$memoryStream = [System.IO.MemoryStream]::new($bytes)
```

To work around the problem in earlier versions of PowerShell, the unary comma operator may be used as follows:

```
$memoryStream = New-Object System.IO.MemoryStream(,$bytes)
```

Using the comma operator prevents PowerShell from expanding the array into a set of arguments. The array, held in bytes, is wrapped in another array that contains a single element. When PowerShell executes this, the wrapper is discarded, and the inner array (bytes) is passed without further expansion.

PowerShell will cast and coerce types

The preceding examples can be significantly shortened, as PowerShell will do a lot to call appropriate constructors when casting. This extended example will do the following:

- Create an array of characters from a string
- Create a byte array from the array of characters
- Create a memory stream from the byte array
- Create a binary reader from the memory stream

```
using namespace System.IO
[BinaryReader][MemoryStream][Byte[]][Char[]]'hello world'
```

Creating objects from hashtables

Many classes (or types) implement a constructor that does not require any arguments, for example, ADSISearcher (the type accelerator for System.DirectoryServices.DirectorySearcher).

An instance of the searcher may be created as follows, using one of the available constructors:

```
$searcher = [ADSISearcher]::new(
    [ADSI]'LDAP://domain.com',
    '(&(objectClass=user)(objectCategory=person))'
)
$searcher.PageSize = 1000
```

Alternatively, it can be created from a hashtable, which can be easier to read, as each of the arguments has a clear name:

```
$searcher = [ADSISearcher]@{
    SearchRoot = [ADSI]'LDAP://domain.com'
    Filter     = '(&(objectClass=user)(objectCategory=person))'
    PageSize   = 1000
}
```

This technique is especially useful for classes that have a large number of properties, for example, those used by the Windows Presentation Framework or Windows Forms.

Properties and methods

In Chapter 3, *Working with Objects in PowerShell*, the idea of using properties and methods was introduced. Get-Member was used to list each of these.

Properties for objects derived from .NET classes, such as those for the
`System.Text.StringBuilder` class, are documented on MSDN:

Properties

	Name	Description
	Capacity	Gets or sets the maximum number of characters that can be contained in the memory allocated by the current instance.
	Chars[Int32]	Gets or sets the character at the specified character position in this instance.
	Length	Gets or sets the length of the current StringBuilder object.
	MaxCapacity	Gets the maximum capacity of this instance.

Similarly, methods are described in detail, often with examples of usage (in C#, VB, F#, and so on):

Methods

	Name	Description
	Append(Boolean)	Appends the string representation of a specified Boolean value to this instance.
	Append(Byte)	Appends the string representation of a specified 8-bit unsigned integer to this instance.
	Append(Char)	Appends the string representation of a specified Char object to this instance.
	Append(Char*, Int32)	Appends an array of Unicode characters starting at a specified address to this instance.

These methods may be used as long as the argument lists can be satisfied. The fourth item on the list is difficult to leverage in PowerShell, as `Char*` represents a pointer to an array of `Unicode` characters. A pointer is a reference to a location in memory, something not often seen in PowerShell and beyond the scope of this chapter.

Static properties

Properties require an instance of a type to be created before they can be accessed. Static properties, on the other hand, don't.

A static property is a piece of data; in some cases, this includes constant values, associated with class definitions, that can be retrieved without creating an object instance.

MSDN shows static properties using an S symbol in the leftmost column. For example, the System.Text.Encoding class has a number of static properties denoting different text encoding types, shown in the following screenshot:

Properties

		Name	Description
	S	ASCII	Gets an encoding for the ASCII (7-bit) character set.
	S	BigEndianUnicode	Gets an encoding for the UTF-16 format that uses the big endian byte order.
		BodyName	When overridden in a derived class, gets a name for the current encoding that can be used with mail agent body tags.
		CodePage	When overridden in a derived class, gets the code page identifier of the current Encoding.
		DecoderFallback	Gets or sets the DecoderFallback object for the current Encoding object.
	S	Default	Gets an encoding for the operating system's current ANSI code page.

PowerShell is also able to list the static properties for a type (or class) using Get-Member with the Static switch:

```
PS> [System.Text.Encoding] | Get-Member -MemberType Property -Static

    TypeName: System.Text.Encoding

Name                   MemberType Definition
----                   ---------- ----------
ASCII                  Property   static System.Text.Encoding ASCII {get;}
BigEndianUnicode       Property   static System.Text.Encoding BigEndianUnicode
{get;}
Default                Property   static System.Text.Encoding Default {get;}
```

```
Unicode           Property   static System.Text.Encoding Unicode {get;}
UTF32             Property   static System.Text.Encoding UTF32 {get;}
UTF7              Property   static System.Text.Encoding UTF7 {get;}
UTF8              Property   static System.Text.Encoding UTF8 {get;}
```

These static properties are accessed using the following generalized notation:

```
[<TypeName>]::<PropertyName>
```

In the case of `System.Text.Encoding`, the `ASCII` property is accessible using the following syntax:

```
[System.Text.Encoding]::ASCII
```

A variable may be used to represent either the type or the property name, as follows:

```
$type = [System.Text.Encoding]
$propertyName = 'ASCII'
$type::$propertyName
```

Fields are often used as part of the internal implementation of a class (or structure). Fields aren't often accessible outside of a class.

The `Int32` structure exposes two static fields, holding the maximum and minimum possible values that the type can hold:

Fields

	Name	Description
⬦ S	MaxValue	Represents the largest possible value of an Int32. This field is constant.
⬦ S	MinValue	Represents the smallest possible value of Int32. This field is constant.

PowerShell does not distinguish between fields and properties. The following statements show the values of each static field in turn:

```
[Int32]::MaxValue
[Int32]::MinValue
```

Static methods

As static properties, static methods do not require that an instance of a class is created.

MSDN shows static methods using an S symbol in the leftmost column. For example, the System.Net.NetworkInformation.NetworkInterface class has a number of static methods. The first of these is shown in the following screenshot:

	Name	Description
♦	Equals(Object)	Determines whether the specified object is equal to the current object.(Inherited from Object.)
♦	Finalize()	Allows an object to try to free resources and perform other cleanup operations before it is reclaimed by garbage collection. (Inherited from Object.)
S	GetAllNetworkInterfaces()	Returns objects that describe the network interfaces on the local computer.
♦	GetHashCode()	Serves as the default hash function. (Inherited from Object.)
♦	GetIPProperties()	Returns an object that describes the configuration of this

Methods

PowerShell is also able to list these methods using Get-Member with the Static switch, as shown here:

```
PS> [System.Net.NetworkInformation.NetworkInterface] | Get-Member -
MemberType Method -Static


   TypeName: System.Net.NetworkInformation.NetworkInterface

Name                       MemberType Definition
----                       ---------- ----------
Equals                     Method     static bool Equals(System.Object objA,
System.Object objB)
GetAllNetworkInterfaces Method        static
System.Net.NetworkInformation.NetworkInterface[] GetAllNetworkInterfaces()
GetIsNetworkAvailable      Method     static bool GetIsNetworkAvailable()
ReferenceEquals            Method     static bool
ReferenceEquals(System.Object objA, System.Object objB)
```

Static methods are accessed using the following generalized notation:

```
[<TypeName>]::<MethodName>(<ArgumentList>)
```

As the `GetAllNetworkInterfaces` method does not require arguments, it may be called as follows:

```
[System.Net.NetworkInformation.NetworkInterface]::GetAllNetworkInterfaces()
```

The parentheses at the end of the statement must be included to tell PowerShell that this is a method.

As was seen with static properties, both `type` and `method` may be assigned to variables:

```
$type = [System.Net.NetworkInformation.NetworkInterface]
$methodName = 'GetAllNetworkInterfaces'
$type::$methodName()
```

The parentheses are not part of the method name.

Static methods often require arguments. The `System.IO.Path` class has many static methods that require arguments, as shown in the following screenshot:

Methods ⚓

	Name	Description
◈S	ChangeExtension(String, String)	Changes the extension of a path string.
◈S	Combine(String, String)	Combines two strings into a path.
◈S	Combine(String, String, String)	Combines three strings into a path.
◈S	Combine(String, String, String, String)	Combines four strings into a path.
◈S	Combine(String[])	Combines an array of strings into a path.
◈S	GetDirectoryName(String)	Returns the directory information for the specified path string.

Arguments are passed in as a comma-separated list. For example, the `ChangeExtension` method may be used, as follows:

```
[System.IO.Path]::ChangeExtension("C:\none.exe", "bak")
```

An array containing a list of arguments cannot be directly supplied. Consider the following example:

```
$argumentList = "C:\none.exe", "bak"
[System.IO.Path]::ChangeExtension($argumentList)
```

If a list of arguments is to be supplied from a variable, the method object must be invoked:

```
$argumentList = "C:\none.exe", "bak"
[System.IO.Path]::ChangeExtension.Invoke($argumentList)
```

The method object (because everything is an object) is accessed by omitting the parentheses that normally follow the name of the method:

```
PS> [System.IO.Path]::ChangeExtension

OverloadDefinitions
-------------------
static string ChangeExtension(string path, string extension)
```

Non-public classes

.NET classes come with a number of access modifiers. Each of these affords a different level of protection and visibility.

Instances of a public class may be created using New-Object (with an appropriate list of arguments) or the new static method via constructors, as shown previously.

Private and internal (non-public) classes are not directly accessible; they are placed out of sight by the developer of the class. They are often part of an implementation of a program or command and are not expected to be directly accessed.

In some cases, the decision to hide something away appears to be counterproductive. One example of this is the TypeAccelerators class.

The type derived from the class may be accessed using the following notation:

```
PS> [System.Management.Automation.PowerShell].Assembly.GetType(
    'System.Management.Automation.TypeAccelerators'
)

IsPublic IsSerial Name                  BaseType
-------- -------- ----                  --------
False    False    TypeAccelerators System.Object
```

Type accelerators

A type accelerator is an alias for a type name. At the beginning of this chapter, the `System.Management.Automation.PowerShell` type was used. This type has an accelerator available. The accelerator allows the following notation to be used:

```
[PowerShell].Assembly
```

Another commonly used example is the `ADSI` accelerator. This represents the `System.DirectoryServices.DirectoryEntry` type. This means that the following two commands are equivalent:

```
[System.DirectoryServices.DirectoryEntry]"WinNT://$env:COMPUTERNAME"
[ADSI]"WinNT://$env:COMPUTERNAME"
```

Getting the list of type accelerators isn't quite as easy as it should be. An instance of the `TypeAccelerators` type is required first. Once that has been retrieved, a static property called `Get` will retrieve the list; the first few results are shown as follows:

```
$type =
[PowerShell].Assembly.GetType('System.Management.Automation.TypeAccelerator
s')
$type::Get
```

New accelerators may be added; for example, an accelerator for the `TypeAccelerators` class would make life easier. To do this, an accelerator with the name `Accelerators` is added, using the `TypeAccelerators` type as the object that it references:

```
$type =
[PowerShell].Assembly.GetType('System.Management.Automation.TypeAccelerator
s')
$type::Add('Accelerators', $type)
```

Once the new accelerator has been added, the previous operations can be simplified. Getting the list of accelerators is now done as follows:

```
[Accelerators]::Get
```

New accelerators may be added using the following syntax:

```
[Accelerators]::Add('<Name>', [<TypeName>])
```

The using keyword

The using keyword was introduced with PowerShell 5.0. The using keyword may be used in a script, a module, or in the console.

The using keyword does a number of different things. It can import and declare the following:

- Assemblies
- Modules
- Namespaces

In the context of working with .NET, assemblies, and namespaces are of particular interest.

Future plans for the using command look to include aliasing, as well as support for type and command objects. For example, we might expect the following to work in the future:

```
using namespace NetInfo = System.Net.NetworkInformation
```

At this time, however, this statement will fail with a not supported error.

Using assemblies

If an assembly is listed in the using statement for a script, it will be loaded. For example, System.Windows.Forms may be loaded in Windows PowerShell; the assembly is not available in PowerShell Core:

```
using assembly System.Windows.Forms
```

Add-Type is able to do much the same thing:

```
Add-Type -AssemblyName System.Windows.Forms
```

Assemblies loaded by name are stored in the **Global Assembly Cache (GAC)**. The GAC is stored in $env:WINDIR\Assembly. gacutil may be used to find assemblies within the cache:

```
gacutil /l System.Windows.Forms
```

The Gac module, on the PowerShell Gallery, provides a more consistent experience:

```
PS> Install-Module Gac -Scope CurrentUser
PS> Get-GacAssembly System.Windows.Forms
```

```
Name Version Culture PublicKeyToken PrArch
---- ------- ------- -------------- ------
System.Windows.Forms 2.0.0.0 b77a5c561934e089 MSIL
System.Windows.Forms 1.0.5000.0 b77a5c561934e089 None
System.Windows.Forms 4.0.0.0 b77a5c561934e089 MSIL
```

As shown in the preceding code block, more than one version of the same assembly can exist on a system. If a specific version is required, the full name of the assembly may be used:

```
using assembly 'System.Windows.Forms, Version=4.0.0.0, Culture=neutral,
PublicKeyToken=b77a5c561934e089'
```

This full name is exposed by both `gacutil` and the `Gac` module, as shown here:

```
PS> Get-GacAssembly System.Windows.Forms | Select-Object FullName

FullName
--------
System.Windows.Forms, Version=2.0.0.0, Culture=neutral,
PublicKeyToken=b77a5c561934e089
System.Windows.Forms, Version=1.0.5000.0, Culture=neutral,
PublicKeyToken=b77a5c561934e089
System.Windows.Forms, Version=4.0.0.0, Culture=neutral,
PublicKeyToken=b77a5c561934e089
```

The `using assembly` statement will load assemblies from a specific path, if one is supplied, as follows:

```
using assembly 'C:\SomeDir\someAssembly.dll'
```

PowerShell allows the `using assembly` statement any number of times in a script, and more than one assembly can be loaded in a single script.

Using namespaces

Many of the examples used in this chapter have involved typing the full namespace path to get to a class name. This requirement can be eased with the `using` keyword.

For example, if a script does a lot of work with the `System.Net.NetworkInformation` class, the requirement to type the namespace every time can be removed. This allows the `System.Net.NetworkInformation.NetworkInterface` class to be used with a much shorter type name:

```
using namespace System.Net.NetworkInformation
```

With this statement in place, classes can be used without the long namespace:

```
[NetworkInterface]::GetAllNetworkInterfaces()
```

If the namespace is present within an assembly that isn't loaded by default, the `using assembly` command should be added first. For example, if a script is to work with `Windows Presentation Framework` in Windows PowerShell, the following might be useful:

```
# Load the Windows Presentation Framework
using assembly PresentationFramework
# Use the System.Windows namespace
using namespace System.Windows

$window = [Window]@{
    Height = 100
    Width = 150
}
# Create a System.Windows.Controls.Button object
$button = [Controls.Button]@{
    Content = 'Close'
}
$button.Add_Click( { $window.Close() } )
$window.Content = $button
$window.ShowDialog()
```

 GUIs and PowerShell Core

Like `System.Windows.Forms`, the Windows Presentation Framework is not available in .NET Core at this time. Both are planned to reappear in .NET Core 3 in 2019 (on Windows systems only).

PowerShell only allows one `using namespace` statement line in the console. If the statements are made on different lines, only the last will be valid. It is possible to *use* more than one namespace in the console by separating the statements with `;`. This is demonstrated in the following code block:

```
PS> using namespace System.IO; using namespace System.Text
PS> [File].FullName
System.IO.File
PS> [StringBuilder].FullName
System.Text.StringBuilder
```

In a script, `using namespace` statements may appear across as many lines as required.

Summary

In this chapter, we've explored assemblies, namespaces, types, and classes, before delving into the creation of objects from a class. Static properties and static methods were introduced, both of which may be used without creating an instance of a class. Non-public classes were introduced, before briefly touching on type accelerators. The `using` keyword was introduced, along with a peek at its possible future direction.

This chapter brings part one of this book to an end. In part two, we'll explore working with data in PowerShell, starting with data parsing and manipulation.

8

Strings, Numbers, and Dates

Access to the .NET framework means that PowerShell comes with a wide variety of ways to work with simple data types, such as strings and numbers.

In this chapter, we're going to cover the following topics:

- Manipulating strings
- Converting strings
- Manipulating numbers
- Converting strings into numeric values
- Manipulating dates and times

Manipulating strings

The .NET `System.String` type offers a wide array of methods for manipulating or inspecting strings. The following methods are case-sensitive, but are, in many cases, faster alternatives to using regular expressions, for situations when the time that it takes for a script to run is important.

Working with data held in strings is an important part of any scripting language.

Indexing into strings

In PowerShell, it's possible to index into a string the same way as we select elements from an array. Consider the following example:

```
$myString = 'abcdefghijklmnopqrstuvwxyz'
$myString[0]      # This is a (the first character in the string)
$myString[-1]     # This is z (the last character in the string)
```

String methods and arrays

In PowerShell, some string methods can be called on an array. The method will be executed against each of the elements in the array. For example, the `Trim` method is used against each of the strings as follows:

```
('azzz', 'bzzz', 'czzz').Trim('z')
```

The `Split` method is also capable of acting against an array:

```
('a,b', 'c,d').Split(',')
```

This remains true as long as the array object doesn't have a conflicting method or property. For example, the `Insert` method can't be used as an array object has a version of its own.

Properties and methods of array elements

The feature demonstrated here has broader scope than methods, and it applies to more than string objects.

In the case of strings, you can view the methods that can be used as follows:
```
$arrayMembers = (Get-Member -InputObject @() -MemberType
Property, Method).Name
'string' | Get-Member -MemberType Property, Method |
Where-Object Name -notin $arrayMembers.
```

Using this feature with `DateTime` objects, the `AddDays` method may be called on each element in an array: `((Get-Date '01/01/2017'), (Get-Date '01/02/2017')).AddDays(5)`.

Likewise, the `DayOfWeek` property may be accessed on each element in the array, as follows: `((Get-Date '01/01/2017'), (Get-Date '01/02/2017')).DayOfWeek`.

A similar `Get-Member` command reveals the list of properties and methods that may be used in this manner: `Get-Date | Get-Member -MemberType Property, Method | Where-Object Name -notin $arrayMembers`.

Substring

The Substring method selects part of a string. Substring can select everything after a specific index:

```
$myString = 'abcdefghijklmnopqrstuvwxyz'
$myString.Substring(20)   # Start at index 20. Returns 'uvwxyz'
```

Substring can also select a specific number of characters from a starting point:

```
$myString = 'abcdefghijklmnopqrstuvwxyz'
$myString.Substring(3, 4) # Start at index 3, get 4 characters.
```

 The index starts at 0, counting from the beginning of the string.

Split

The Split method has a relative in PowerShell: the –split operator. The –split operator expects a regular expression, whereas the split method for a string expects an array of characters by default:

```
$myString = 'Surname,GivenName'
$myString.Split(',')
```

When splitting the following string based on a comma, the resulting array will have three elements. The first element is Surname, the last is GivenName. The second element in the array (index 1) is blank:

```
$string = 'Surname,,GivenName'
$array = $string.Split(',')
$array.Count    # This is 3
$array[1]       # This is empty
```

This blank value may be discarded by setting the StringSplitOptions argument of the Split method:

```
$string = 'Surname,,GivenName'
$array = $string.Split(',', [StringSplitOptions]::RemoveEmptyEntries)
$array.Count    # This is 2
```

When using the `Split` method in this manner, individual variables may be filled from each value as follows:

```
$surname, $givenName = $string.Split(',',
[StringSplitOptions]::RemoveEmptyEntries)
```

The `Split` method is powerful, but care is required when using its different arguments. Each of the different sets of arguments works as follows:

```
PS> 'string'.Split

OverloadDefinitions
-------------------
string[] Split(Params char[] separator)
string[] Split(char[] separator, int count)
string[] Split(char[] separator, System.StringSplitOptions options)
string[] Split(char[] separator, int count, System.StringSplitOptions
options)
string[] Split(string[] separator, System.StringSplitOptions options)
string[] Split(string[] separator, int count, System.StringSplitOptions
options)
```

PowerShell can create a character array from a string, or an array of strings, provided that each string is no more than one character long. Both of the following statements will result in an array of characters (`char[]`):

```
[char[]]$characters = [string[]]('a', 'b', 'c') [char[]]$characters = 'abc'
```

When the `Split` method is used as follows, the separator is any (and all) of the characters in the string. The result of the following expression is an array of five elements (`one`, `<empty>`, `two`, `<empty>`, and `three`):

```
$string = 'one||two||three'
$string.Split('||')
```

To split using a string, instead of an array of characters, PowerShell must be forced to use this overload definition:

```
string[] Split(string[] separator, System.StringSplitOptions options)
```

This can be achieved with the following cumbersome syntax:

```
$string = 'one||two||three'
$string.Split([String[]]'||', [StringSplitOptions]::None)
```

Replace

The `Replace` method will substitute one string value for another:

```
$string = 'This is the first example'
$string.Replace('first', 'second')
```

PowerShell also has a `replace` operator. The `replace` operator uses a regular expression to describe the value that should be replaced.

Regular expressions (discussed in `Chapter 9`, *Regular Expressions*) may be more difficult to work with in some cases, especially when replacing characters that are reserved in regular expressions (such as the period character, `.`):

```
$string = 'Begin the begin.'
$string -replace 'begin.', 'story, please.'
$string.Replace('begin.', 'story, please.')
```

In these cases, the `Replace` method may be easier to work with.

Trim, TrimStart, and TrimEnd

The `Trim` method, by default, removes all white space (spaces, tabs, and line breaks) from the beginning and end of a string. Consider the following example:

```
$string = "
    This string has leading and trailing white space       "
$string.Trim()
```

The `TrimStart` and `TrimEnd` methods limit their operation to either the start or end of the string.

Each of the methods accepts a list of characters to trim. Consider the following example:

```
$string = '*__This string is surrounded by clutter.--#'
$string.Trim('*_-#')
```

The `Trim` method does not remove a string from the end of another. The string supplied in the previous example (`'*_-#'`) is treated as an array. This can be seen in the definition of the method:

```
PS> 'string'.Trim

OverloadDefinitions
-------------------
string Trim(Params char[] trimChars)
string Trim()
```

A failure to appreciate this can lead to unexpected behavior. The domain name in the following example ends with the suffix, `'.uk.net'`. The goal is to trim the suffix from the end of the string. However, the method goes too far here, taking away part of the name:

```
PS> $string = 'magnet.uk.net'
PS> $string.TrimEnd('.uk.net')

mag
```

Insert and remove

The `Insert` method is able to add one string into another. This method expects an index from the beginning of the string, counting from 0, and a string to insert, as follows:

```
$string = 'The letter of the alphabet is a'
$string.Insert(4, 'first ')  # Insert this before "letter", include a
trailing space
```

The `Remove` method removes characters from a string, based on a start position and the length of the string to remove:

```
$string = 'This is is an example'
$string.Remove(4, 3)
```

The previous statement removes the first instance of `is`, including the trailing space.

IndexOf and LastIndexOf

`IndexOf` and `LastIndexOf` may be used to locate a character or string within a string. `IndexOf` finds the first occurrence of a string, and `LastIndexOf` finds the last occurrence of the string. In both cases, the zero-based index of the start of the string is returned. If the character, or string, isn't present, the two methods will return −1:

```
$string = 'abcdefedcba'
$string.IndexOf('b')      # Returns 1
$string.LastIndexOf('b')  # Returns 9
$string.IndexOf('ed')     # Returns 6
```

As −1 is used to indicate that the value is absent, the method is not suitable for statements based on an implicit Boolean. The index 0, a valid position, is considered to be false. The following example correctly handles the return value from `IndexOf` in a conditional statement:

```
$string  = 'abcdef'
if ($string.IndexOf('a') -gt -1) {
    'The string contains an a'
}
```

The scope of the `IndexOf` and `LastIndexOf` methods can be limited using the start index and count arguments.

Methods that are able to locate a position within a string are useful when combined with other string methods, as shown here:

```
PS> $string = 'First,Second,Third'
PS> $string.Substring(
>>     $string.IndexOf(',') + 1, # startIndex (6)
>>     $string.LastIndexOf(',') - $string.IndexOf(',') - 1 # length (6)
>> )

Second
```

PadLeft and PadRight

The `PadLeft` and `PadRight` options endeavor to increase the length of a string up to a given maximum length. Both `PadLeft` and `PadRight` take the same arguments, as follows:

```
PS> ''.PadRight

OverloadDefinitions
-------------------
string PadRight(int totalWidth)
string PadRight(int totalWidth, char paddingChar)

PS> ''.PadLeft

OverloadDefinitions
-------------------
string PadLeft(int totalWidth)
string PadLeft(int totalWidth, char paddingChar)
```

Both methods attempt to make a string up to the total width. If the string is already equal to, or longer than the total width, it won't be changed. Unless another is supplied, the padding character is a space.

The following example pads the right-hand side of strings, using `.` as the padding character argument:

```
PS> ('one', 'two', 'three').PadRight(10, '.')

one.......
two.......
three.....
```

Padding a string on the left, in effect, aligns the string on the right:

```
PS> ('one', 'two', 'three').PadLeft(10, '.')

.......one
.......two
.....three
```

ToUpper, ToLower, and ToTitleCase

ToUpper converts any lowercase characters in a string into uppercase. ToLower converts any uppercase characters in a string into lowercase:

```
'aBc'.ToUpper()      # Returns ABC
'AbC'.ToLower()      # Returns abc
```

Considering that the methods discussed here are case sensitive, converting a string into a known case may be an important first step. Consider the following example:

```
$string = 'AbN'
$string = $string.ToLower()
$string = $string.Replace('n', 'c')
```

The ToTitleCase is not a method of the String object. It is a method of the System.Globalization.TextInfo class. The ToTitleCase method performs limited culture-specific capitalization of words:

```
PS> (Get-Culture).TextInfo.ToTitleCase('some title')
Some Title
```

As this is not a static method, the TextInfo object must be created first. This object cannot be directly created. TextInfo can be obtained via the System.Globalization.CultureInfo object, and this object is returned by the Get-Culture command.

The same TextInfo object may also be accessed using the host automatic variable:

```
$host.CurrentCulture.TextInfo.ToTitleCase('another title')
```

The ToTitleCase method will not convert words that are entirely uppercase as they're considered to be acronyms.

Contains, StartsWith, and EndsWith

The Contains, StartsWith, and EndsWith methods will each return true or false, depending on whether or not the string contains the specified string.

Contains returns true if the value is found within the subject string:

```
$string = 'I am the subject'
$string.Contains('the')     # Returns $true
```

`StartsWith` and `EndsWith` return true if the subject string starts or ends with the specified value:

```
$string = 'abc'
$string.StartsWith('ab')
$string.EndsWith('bc')
```

Chaining methods

As many of the string methods return a string, it is entirely possible to chain methods together. For example, each of the following methods return a string, so another method can be added to the end:

```
' ONe*? '.Trim().TrimEnd('?*').ToLower().Replace('o', 'O')
```

This ability to chain methods is not in any way unique to strings.

Converting strings

PowerShell has a variety of commands that can convert strings. These are explained in the following sections.

Working with Base64

Base64 is a transport encoding that is used to represent binary data, and therefore, any (relatively simple) data type.

Base64 is particularly useful when storing complex strings in files, or in text-based transport protocols, such as SMTP.

The .NET `System.Convert` class contains the following static methods that can be used to work with `Base64`:

- `ToBase64String`
- `FromBase64String`

The `ToBase64String` method takes an array of bytes and converts it into a string. For example, a simple byte array may be converted as follows:

```
PS> [Byte[]]$bytes = 97, 98, 99, 100, 101
PS> [Convert]::ToBase64String($bytes)
YWJjZGU=
```

A more meaningful byte sequence can be made from a few words by getting the byte values for each character:

```
PS> $bytes = [System.Text.Encoding]::ASCII.GetBytes('Hello world')
PS> [Convert]::ToBase64String($bytes)
SGVsbG8gd29ybGQ=
```

If the encoding is ASCII, it is possible in PowerShell to supply the `ToBase64String` method with an array of characters. Consider the following example:

```
PS> [Convert]::ToBase64String('Hello world'.ToCharArray())
SGVsbG8gd29ybGQ=
```

The text encoding type used here is ASCII (1 byte per character); UTF16 text encoding will result in a longer Base64 string, as each character is stored in two bytes:

```
PS> $bytes = [System.Text.Encoding]::Unicode.GetBytes('Hello world')
PS> [Convert]::ToBase64String($bytes)
SABlAGwAbABvACAAdwBvAHIAbABkAA==
```

Unicode encoding is used to create an encoded command

`PowerShell.exe` and `pwsh.exe` both have an `EncodedCommand` parameter. This can be any encoded script. The text must be Unicode-encoded.

Converting from a Base64 string into a sequence of bytes, and then into a string, may be achieved as follows:

```
PS> $base64String = 'YWJjZGU='
PS> $bytes = [Convert]::FromBase64String($base64String)
PS> [System.Text.Encoding]::ASCII.GetString($bytes)
abcde
```

Base64 can be a handy format for storing items such as keys (normally a set of bytes) for use with the `ConvertTo-SecureString` command. Consider the following example:

```
# Create a 16-byte key
[Byte[]]$key = 1..16 | ForEach-Object { Get-Random -Minimum 0 -Maximum 256 }
```

```
# Convert the key to a string and save it in a file
[Convert]::ToBase64String($key) | Out-File 'KeepThisSafe.txt'

# Create a secure string (from plain text) to encrypt
$secure = ConvertTo-SecureString -String 'Secure text' -AsPlainText -Force
# Encrypt the password using the key (from the file)
$convertFromSecureString = @{
    SecureString = $secure
    Key          = [Convert]::FromBase64String((Get-Content
.\KeepThisSafe.txt))
}
$encrypted = ConvertFrom-SecureString @convertFromSecureString

# Decrypt the password using the same key
$convertToSecureString = @{
    String = $encrypted
    Key    = [Convert]::FromBase64String((Get-Content .\KeepThisSafe.txt))
}
$secure = ConvertTo-SecureString @convertToSecureString

# Show the original password
[PSCredential]::new('.', $secure).GetNetworkCredential().Password
```

Working with comma-separated value strings

ConvertTo-Csv turns objects in PowerShell into **comma-separated value (CSV)** strings:

```
PS> Get-Process -Id $pid | Select-Object Name, Id, Path | ConvertTo-Csv
"Name","Id","Path"
"powershell_ise","9956","C:\WINDOWS\System32\WindowsPowerShell\v1.0\powersh
ell_ise.exe"
```

In the preceding example, Windows PowerShell will also include type data by default.

ConvertFrom-Csv turns CSV-formatted strings into objects:

```
"David,0123456789,28" | ConvertFrom-Csv -Header Name, Phone, Age
```

As ConvertFrom-Csv is specifically written to read CSV-formatted data, it will discard quotes surrounding strings but will allow fields to spread across lines and so on. Consider the following example:

```
'David,0123456789,28,"1 Some street, A Lane"' | ConvertFrom-Csv -Header
Name, Phone, Age, Address | Format-Table -Wrap
```

If the `Header` parameter is not defined, the first line read by `ConvertFrom-Csv` is expected to be a header. If there's only one line of data, nothing will be returned:

```
'Name,Age', 'David,28' | ConvertFrom-Csv
```

`Export-Csv` and `Import-Csv` complement these two commands by writing and reading information to a file instead:

```
Get-Process -Id $pid | Select-Object Name, Id, Path | Export-Csv
'somefile.csv'
Import-Csv somefile.csv
```

Convert-String

 `Convert-String` and PowerShell Core: Convert-String is not available in PowerShell Core 6.1. It may reappear in a later version, or may be moved to a separate module.

The `Convert-String` command may be used to simplify some string conversion operations. The conversion is performed based on an example that must be supplied. For example, `Convert-String` can generate account names from a list of users:

```
'Michael Caine', 'Benny Hill', 'Raf Vallone' | Convert-String -Example
'Michael Caine=MCaine'
```

The `Example` parameter uses the generalized syntax as follows:

```
<Before>=<After>
```

This example text does not have to be one of the set being converted. For example, the following will work:

```
'Michael Caine', 'Benny Hill', 'Raf Vallone' | Convert-String -Example
'First Second=FSecond'
```

The following alternate syntax is also supported:

```
'Michael Caine', 'Benny Hill', 'Raf Vallone' | Convert-String -Example @{
    Before = 'First Second'
    After = 'FSecond'
}
```

The `Convert-String` command is not without its limitations. `After` may only include strings, or partial strings, from `Before`, along with a subset of punctuation characters. Characters that aren't permitted in `After` include @, $, ~, `, and !. Because of these limitations, `Convert-String` cannot, for example, build an email address for each user in the list in a single step.

ConvertFrom-String

Convert-FromString and PowerShell Core

`ConvertFrom-String` is not available in PowerShell Core 6.1. It may reappear in a later version, or may be moved to a separate module.

`ConvertFrom-String` has two different styles of operation. The first behaves much as `ConvertFrom-Csv` does, except that it doesn't discard characters that make up the CSV format. In the following example, the quotation marks surrounding the first name are preserved:

```
PS> '"bob",tim,geoff' | ConvertFrom-String -Delimiter ',' -PropertyNames
name1, name2, name3


name1 name2 name3
----- ----- -----
"bob" tim   geoff
```

The default delimiter (if the parameter is not supplied) is a space. The second operating mode of `ConvertFrom-String` is far more complex. A template must be defined for each element of data that's to be pushed into a property.

The following example uses `ConvertFrom-String` to convert the output from the `tasklist` command into an object:

```
$template = '{Task*:{ImageName:System Idle Process} {[Int]PID:0}
{SessionName:Services} {Session:0} {Memory:24 K}}'

tasklist |
    Select-Object -Skip 3 |
    ConvertFrom-String -TemplateContent $template |
    Select-Object -ExpandProperty Task
```

The `Task*` element denotes the start of a data record. It allows each of the remaining fields to be grouped together under a single object.

The `ConvertFrom-String` command is good at dealing with well formatted data that's already divided correctly. In the case of the `tasklist` command, the end of a single task (or data record) is denoted by a line break.

Manipulating numbers

Basic mathematical operations in PowerShell make use of the operators discussed in `Chapter 4`, *Operators*.

Formatting numbers using the format operators are introduced, along with a number of features, as follows:

```
'{0:x}' -f 24244     # Lower-case hexadecimal. Returns 5eb4
'{0:X}' -f 24244     # Upper-case hexadecimal. Returns 5EB4
'{0:P}' -f 0.28232   # Percentage. Returns 28.23%
'{0:N2}' -f 32583.122 # Culture specific number format.
                     # 2 decimal places.
                     # Returns 32,583.12 (for en-GB)
```

The format operator is powerful, but it has one major shortcoming: it returns a string. It is great for when you want to display a number to a user, but will prevent sorting or work with the numeric form.

Large byte values

PowerShell provides operators for working with bytes. These operators are as follows:

- **nKB**: Kilobytes (n * 1024^1)
- **nMB**: Megabytes (n * 1024^2)
- **nGB**: Gigabytes (n * 1024^3)
- **nTB**: Terabytes (n * 1024^4)
- **nPB**: Petabytes (n * 1024^5)

These operators can be used to represent large values:

```
PS> 22.5GB
24159191040
```

The operators may also be used to convert large byte values into shorter values. For example, a shorter value might be added to a message using the format operator, as shown here:

```
PS> '{0:F} TB available' -f (123156235234522 / 1TB)
112.01 TB available
```

Power of 10

PowerShell uses the e operator to represent a scientific notation (power-of-10, "* 10^n") that can be used to represent very large numbers. The exponent can be either positive or negative:

```
2e2     # Returns 200 (2 * 102)
2e-1    # Returns 0.2 (2 * 10-1)
```

Hexadecimal

Hexadecimal formats are accessible in PowerShell without any significant work. PowerShell will return the decimal form of any given hexadecimal number. The hexadecimal number should be prefixed with 0x:

```
PS> 0x5eb4

24244
```

Using System.Math

While PowerShell itself comes with reasonably basic mathematical operators, the .NET System.Math class has a far wider variety.

The Round static method can be used to round up to a fixed number of decimal places. In the following example, the value is rounded to two decimal places:

```
[Math]::Round(2.123456789, 2)
```

By default, the Round method in .NET performs what's known as bankers rounding. It will always prefer to round to an even number. For example, 1.5 will round to 2, and 2.5 will round to 2.

This behavior can be changed using the `MidpointRounding` enumeration, as shown here:

```
[Math]::Round(2.225, 2)                                    # Results in
2.22
[Math]::Round(2.225, 2, [MidpointRounding]::AwayFromZero)  # Results in
2.23
```

The `Ceiling` and `Floor` methods are used when performing whole-number rounding:

```
[Math]::Ceiling(2.1234)     # Returns 3
[Math]::Floor(2.9876)       # Returns 2
```

The `Abs` converts a positive or negative integer into a positive integer (and multiplies by -1 if the value is negative):

```
[Math]::Abs(-45748)
```

Numbers may be raised to a power using the following syntax:

```
[Math]::Pow(2, 8) # Returns 256 (28)
```

A square root can be calculated as follows:

```
[Math]::Sqrt(9)       # Returns 3
```

The `System.Math` class also contains static properties for mathematical constants:

```
[Math]::pi     # π, 3.14159265358979
[Math]::e      # e, 2.71828182845905
```

Methods are also available to work with log, tan, sin, cos, and so on.

 For a deeper dive into math in PowerShell, Tim Curwick's blog uncovers more detail. The article is available at `https://www.madwithpowershell.com/2013/10/math-in-powershell.html`.

Converting strings into numeric values

In most cases, strings may be cast back to numeric values. Consider the following example:

```
[Int]"2"            # String to Int32
[Decimal]"3.141"    # String to Decimal
[UInt32]10          # Int32 to UInt32
[SByte]-5           # Int32 to SByte
```

For advanced conversions, the `System.Convert` class may be used. The `Convert` class includes static methods that can take a string and convert it into a number using a specified base.

A binary (base 2) value is converted as follows:

```
[Convert]::ToInt32('01000111110101', 2)   # Returns 4597
```

A hexadecimal (base 16) value can be converted like so:

```
[Convert]::ToInt32('FF9241', 16)   # Returns 16749121
```

The bases that `Convert` supports are 2 (binary), 8 (octal), 10 (denary), and 16 (hexadecimal).

Manipulating dates and times

`DateTime` objects may be created in a number of ways. The `Get-Date` command is one of these. The methods on the `DateTime` type has a number of static methods that might be used, and an instance of `DateTime` has methods that might be used.

DateTime parameters

While most commands deal with dates in a culture-specific format, care must be taken when passing dates as strings to parameters that cast to `DateTime`.

Casting to `DateTime` does not account for a cultural bias. For example, in the UK, the format `dd/MM/yyyy` is often used. Casting this format to `DateTime` will switch the format to `MM/dd/yyyy` (as used in the US):

```
$string = "11/10/2000"    # 11th October 2000
[DateTime]$string         # 10th November 2000
```

If a function is created that accepts `DateTime` as a parameter, the result may not be as expected, depending on the local culture:

```
function Test-DateTime {
    param(
        [DateTime]$Date
    )
    $Date
}
Test-DateTime -Date "11/10/2000"
```

It is possible to work around this problem using the `Get-Date` command, to ensure the culture specific conversion is more appropriately handled:

```
Test-DateTime -Date (Get-Date "11/10/2000")
```

Parsing dates

The `Get-Date` command is the best first stop for converting strings into dates. `Get-Date` deals with a reasonable number of formats.

If, however, `Get-Date` is unable to help, the `DateTime` class has two static methods that may be used:

- `ParseExact`
- `TryParseExact`

The format strings used by these methods are documented on MSDN, available at `https://msdn.microsoft.com/en-us/library/8kb3ddd4(v=vs.110).aspx`.

The `ParseExact` method accepts one or more format strings, and returns a `DateTime` object:

```
$string = '20170102-2030'  # Represents 1st February 2017, 20:30
[DateTime]::ParseExact($string, 'yyyyddMM-HHmm', (Get-Culture))
```

The culture, returned from `Get-Culture`, used previously, fills in the format provider argument.

The format string uses the following syntax:

- yyyy to represent a four-digit year
- dd for a two-digit day
- MM for a two-digit month
- HH for the hours in the day (this is for 24 hour format; hh is used for 12 hour format)

This can be extended to account for more than one date format. In this case, two variations of the format are accepted, the second of which expects seconds (ss):

```
$strings = '20170102-2030', '20170103-0931.24'
[String[]]$formats = 'yyyyddMM-HHmm', 'yyyyddMM-HHmm.ss'
foreach ($string in $strings) {
    [DateTime]::ParseExact(
```

```
        $string,
        $formats,
        (Get-Culture),
        'None'
    )
}
```

The final argument, None, grants greater control over the parsing process. The other possible values and the effects are documented on MSDN, available at https://msdn. microsoft.com/en-us/library/91hfhz89(v=vs.110).aspx.

The TryParseExact method has a safer failure control than ParseExact, which will throw an exception if it fails. The TryParseExact method itself returns true or false, depending on whether or not it was able to parse the string.

The parsed date can be extracted using a reference to an existing date. This is an existing variable that holds DateTime. The method updates the value held in the variable, if parsing is successful, as follows:

```
$date = Get-Date 01/01/1601    # A valid DateTime object with an obvious
date
$string = '20170102-2030'
if ([DateTime]::TryParseExact($string, 'yyyyddMM-HHmm', $null, 'None',
[Ref]$date)) {
    $date
}
```

The updated value of the $date variable is shown when the TryParseExact method returns true, and the body of the if statement executes.

Changing dates

A date object can be changed in a number of ways.

A Timespan object can be added to or subtracted from a date:

```
(Get-Date) + (New-Timespan -Hours 6)
```

The Date property can be used, representing the start of the day:

```
(Get-Date).Date
```

The Add<Interval> methods can be used to add and subtract time, as follows:

```
(Get-Date).AddDays(1)   # One day from now
(Get-Date).AddDays(-1)  # One day before now
```

In addition to AddDays, the DateTime object makes the following available:

```
(Get-Date).AddTicks(1)
(Get-Date).AddMilliseconds(1)
(Get-Date).AddSeconds(1)
(Get-Date).AddMinutes(1)
(Get-Date).AddHours(1)
(Get-Date).AddMonths(1)
(Get-Date).AddYears(1)
```

By default, dates returned by Get-Date are local (that is, within the context of the current timezone). A date may be converted into UTC as follows:

```
(Get-Date).ToUniversalTime()
```

The ToUniversalTime method only changes the date if the Kind property of the date is set to Local or Unspecified. This is shown in the following snippet:

```
PS> Get-Date | Select-Object DateTime, Kind

DateTime                    Kind
--------                    ----
30 October 2018 18:38:41    Local
```

The ToLocalTime method adjusts the date in accordance with the system's current timezone. This operation may be performed if Kind is Utc or unspecified.

A date of a specific Kind may be created as follows, enabling appropriate use of ToLocalTime or ToUniversalTime:

```
$UtcDate = [DateTime]::new((Get-Date).Ticks, 'Utc')
```

Dates may be converted into a string, either immediately using Get-Date with the Format parameter or using the ToString method. The Format parameter and ToString method accept the same arguments.

The date strings created by the following statements are equal:

```
Get-Date -Format 'dd/MM/yyyy HH:mm'
(Get-Date).ToString('dd/MM/yyyy HH:mm')
```

The ToString method is useful, as it means a date can be adjusted by chaining properties and methods before conversion into a string:

```
(Get-Date).ToUniversalTime().Date.AddDays(-7).ToString('dd/MM/yyyy HH:mm')
```

When storing dates, it might be good practice to store them in an unambiguous format, such as a universal date-time string. Consider the following:

```
(Get-Date).ToUniversalTime().ToString('u')
```

Comparing dates

DateTime objects may be compared using PowerShell's comparison operators:

```
$date1 = (Get-Date).AddDays(-20)
$date2 = (Get-Date).AddDays(1)
$date2 -gt $date1
```

Dates can be compared to a string; the value on the right-hand side will be converted into DateTime. As with casting with parameters, a great deal of care is required for date formats other than those used in the US.

For example, in the UK, I might write the following code, yet the conversion will fail. The value on the left will convert into 13th January, 2017, but the value on the right will convert into 1st December, 2017:

```
(Get-Date "13/01/2017") -gt "12/01/2017"
```

The corrected conversion is as follows:

```
(Get-Date "13/01/2017") -gt "01/12/2017"
```

Summary

In this chapter, some of the methods used to work with strings were introduced. Alternate formats, such as Base64, were explored, along with the PowerShell commands for working with CSV formats.

Two new commands from PowerShell 5 were introduced: `Convert-String` and `ConvertFrom-String`.

Working with byte values in PowerShell was explored, as well as the `power-of-10` operator.

The `System.Math` class adds a great deal of functionality, which was briefly demonstrated. Finally, we took a brief look at working with `DateTime` objects.

In `Chapter 9`, *Regular Expressions*, we'll look at regular expressions.

Regular Expressions

9

Regular expressions (regex) are used to perform advanced searches against a text. For the uninitiated, anything but a trivial regular expression can be a confusing mess. To make the topic more difficult, regular expressions differ slightly across different programming languages, platforms, and tools. Given that PowerShell is built on .NET, PowerShell uses .NET style regular expressions. There are often several different ways to achieve a goal when using regular expressions.

In this chapter, we'll cover the following topics:

- Regex basics
- Anchors
- Repetition
- Character classes
- Alternation
- Grouping
- Examples

Regex basics

A few basic characters can go a long way. A number of the most widely used characters and operators introduced in this section are summarized in the following table:

Description	Character	Example
Literal character	Any, except: `[\^$.|?*+()`	`'a' -match 'a'`
Any single character (except carriage return, line feed, \r, and \n)	`.`	`'a' -match '.'`
The preceding character repeated zero or more times	`*`	`'abc' -match 'a*'` `'abc' -match '.*'`
The preceding character repeated one or more times	`+`	`'abc' -match 'a+'` `'abc' -match '.+'`
Escape a character's special meaning	`\`	`'*' -match '\*'` `'\' -match '\\'`
Optional character	`?`	`'abc' -match 'ab?c'` `'ac' -match 'ab?c'`

Debugging regular expressions

Regular expressions can quickly become complicated and difficult to understand. Modifying a complex regular expression isn't a particularly simple undertaking.

While PowerShell indicates whether there's a syntax error in a regular expression, it can't do more than that. For example, in the following expression, PowerShell announces that there is a syntax error:

```
PS> 'abc' -match '*'
parsing "*" - Quantifier {x,y} following nothing.
At line:1 char:1
+ 'abc' -match '*'
+ ~~~~~~~~~~~~~~~~
    + CategoryInfo : OperationStopped: (:) [], ArgumentException
    + FullyQualifiedErrorId : System.ArgumentException
```

Fortunately, there are a number of websites that can visualize a regular expression and lend an understanding of how it works against a string.

Debuggex is one such site. This service can pick apart regular expressions, showing how each element applies to an example. Debuggex can be found at `https://www.debuggex.com/`.

Debuggex uses Java regular expressions, so some of the examples used in this chapter may not be compatible.

Online engines that are .NET-specific, but don't include visualization, are as follows:

- `https://regextester.github.io/`
- `http://www.regexplanet.com/advanced/dotnet/index.html`

Finally, the website (`http://www.regular-expressions.info`) is an important learning resource that provides detailed descriptions, examples, and references.

Literal characters

The best place to begin is with the simplest of expressions, that is, expressions that contain no special characters. These expressions contain what are known as literal characters. A literal character can be anything except `[\^$.|?*+()`. Special characters must be escaped using `\` to avoid errors. See the following example:

```
'9*8'-match '\*'    # * is reserved
'1+5' -match '\+'   # + is reserved
```

Curly braces (`{}`) are considered literal in many contexts.

Curly braces become reserved characters if they enclose either a number, two numbers separated by a comma, or one number followed by a comma.

In the following two examples, `{` and `}` are literal characters:
```
'{string}' -match '{'
'{string}' -match '{string}'
```

In the preceding example, the curly braces take on a special meaning. To match, the string would have to be `string` followed by `123` of the character, "g". We'll explore `'string{123}' -match 'string{123}'` `{}` in detail when discussing repetition.

The following statement returns True and fills the matches automatic variable with what matched. The matches variable is a hash table; it's only updated when something successfully matches when using the -match operator:

```
PS> 'The first rule of regex club' -match 'regex'

True

PS> $matches

Name                            Value
----                            -----
0                               regex
```

If a -match fails, the matches variable will continue to hold the last matching value:

```
PS> 'This match will fail' -match 'regex'

False

PS> $matches

Name                                            Value
----                                            -----
0                                               regex
```

Any character (.)

The next step is to introduce the period, or dot (.). The dot matches any single character, except the end-of-line characters. The following statement will return True:

```
'abcdef' -match '......'
```

As the previous expression matches any six characters anywhere in a string, it will also return True when a longer string is provided. There are no implied boundaries on the length of a string, only on the number of characters matched:

```
'abcdefghijkl' -match '......'
```

Repetition with * and +

+ and * are two of a set of characters known as quantifiers. Quantifiers are discussed in great detail later in this chapter.

The * character can be used to repeat the preceding character zero or more times. Consider the following example:

```
'aaabc' -match 'a*'# Returns true, matches 'aaa'
```

However, zero or more means the character in question doesn't have to be present at all:

```
'bcd' -match 'a*'   # Returns true, matches nothing
```

If a character must be present in a string, the + quantifier is more appropriate:

```
'aaabc' -match 'a+'# Returns true, matches 'aaa'
'bcd' -match 'a+'    # Returns false
```

Combining * or + with . produces two very simple expressions: .* and .+. These expressions may be used as follows:

```
'Anything' -match '.*'    # 0 or more. Returns true
'' -match '.*'            # 0 or more. Returns true
'Anything' -match '.+'    # 1 or more. Returns true
```

Attempting to use either * or + as a match, without a preceding character, will result in an error:

```
PS> '*' -match '*'
parsing "*" - Quantifier {x,y} following nothing.
At line:1 char:1
+ '*' -match '*'
+ ~~~~~~~~~~~~~~
    + CategoryInfo : OperationStopped: (:) [], ArgumentException
    + FullyQualifiedErrorId : System.ArgumentException
```

The escape character (\)

In this context, \ is an escape character, but it is perhaps more accurate to say that \ changes the behavior of the character that follows. For example, finding a string that contains the normally reserved character, *, may be accomplished using \, as follows:

```
'1 * 3' -match '\*'
```

In the following example, \ is used to escape the special meaning of \, making it a literal character:

```
'domain\user' -match 'domain\\user'
'domain\user' -match '.*\\.*'
```

This technique may be used with `-replace` to change the domain prefix:

```
'domain\user' -replace 'domain\\', 'newdomain\'
```

Using \ alone will result in either an invalid expression or an unwanted expression. For example, the following expression is valid, but it doesn't act as you might expect. The . character is treated as a literal value because it is escaped. The following `-match` will return `false`:

```
'domain\user' -match 'domain\.+'
```

The following string will be matched by the previous expression, as the string contains a literal .:

```
'domain.user' -match 'domain\.+'
```

The `-replace` operator will allow access to parts of these strings as follows:

```
'Domain\User' -replace '.+\\'  # Everything up to and including \
```

Alternatively, it can `-replace` everything after a character:

```
'Domain\User' -replace '\\.+' # Everything including and after \
```

Optional characters

The question mark character (?) can be used to make the preceding character optional. For example, there might be a need to look for either the singular or plural form of a certain word:

```
'There are 23 sites in the domain' -match 'sites?'
```

The regular expression will match the optional s if it can; the ? character is greedy. A greedy expression will match as many characters as it possibly can..

Non-printable characters

Regular expressions support searches for non-printable characters. The most common of these are shown in the following table:

Description	Character
Tab	\t
Line feed	\n
Carriage return	\r

Anchors

An anchor does not match a character; instead, it matches what comes before (or after) a character:

Description	Character	Example
Beginning of a string	^	'aba' -match '^a'
End of a string	$	'cbc' -match 'c$'
Word boundary	\b	'Band and Land' -match '\band\b'

Anchors are useful where a character, string, or word may appear elsewhere in a string and the position is critical.

For example, there might be a need to get values from the PATH environment variable that starts with a specific drive letter. One approach to this problem is to use the start of a string anchor; in this case, retrieving everything that starts with the C drive:

```
$env:PATH -split ';' | Where-Object { $_ -match '^C' }
```

Alternatively, there may be a need to get every path that is three or more directories deep from a given set:

```
$env:PATH -split ';' | Where-Object { $_ -match '\\.+\\.+\\.+$' }
```

The word boundary anchor matches both before and after a word. It allows a pattern to look for a specific word, rather than a string of characters that may be a word or a part of a word.

For example, if the intent is to `-replace` the word day in the following string, then attempting this without the word boundary replaces too much:

```
'The first day is Monday' -replace 'day', 'night'
'Monday is the first day' -replace 'day', 'night'
```

Adding the word boundary avoids the problem without significantly increasing the complexity:

```
'The first day is Monday' -replace '\bday\b', 'night'
'Monday is the first day' -replace '\bday\b', 'night'
```

Repetition

A quantifier is used to repeat an element. Three examples of quantifiers have already been introduced: *, +, and ?. The quantifiers are as follows:

Description	Character	Example
The preceding character repeated zero or more times	*	`'abc'-match 'a*'` `'abc'-match '.*'`
The preceding character repeated one or more times	+	`'abc'-match 'a+'` `'abc'-match '.+'`
Optional character	?	`'abc' -match 'ab?c'` `'ac' -match 'ab?c'`
A fixed number of characters	{exactly}	`'abbbc' -match 'ab{3}c'`

A number of characters within a range	{min,max}	`'abc' -match 'ab{1,3}c'`
		`'abbc' -match 'ab{1,3}c'`
		`'abbbc' -match 'ab{1,3}c'`

Specifies a minimum number of characters	{min, }	`'abbc' -match 'ab{2,}c'` `'abbbbbc' -match 'ab{2,}c'`

Each *, +, and ? can be described using a curly brace notation:

- * is the same as {0, }
- + is the same as {1, }
- ? is the same as {0,1}

It's extremely uncommon to find examples where the functionality of special characters is replaced with curly braces. It is equally uncommon to find examples where the quantifier {1} is used, as it adds unnecessary complexity to an expression.

Exploring the quantifiers

Each of these different quantifiers is greedy. A greedy quantifier will grab as much as it possibly can before allowing the regex engine to move on to the next character in the expression.

In the following example, the expression has been instructed to match everything it can, ending with a \ character. As a result, it takes everything up to the last \, because the expression is greedy:

```
PS> 'C:\long\path\to\some\files' -match '.*\\'; $matches[0]
True
C:\long\path\to\some\
```

The repetition operators can be made lazy by adding the ? character. A lazy expression, by contrast, will get as little as it can before it ends:

```
PS> 'C:\long\path\to\some\files' -match '.*?\\'; $matches[0]
True
C:\
```

A possible use of a lazy quantifier is parsing HTML. The following line describes a very simple HTML table. The goal is to get the first table's data (td) element:

```
<table><tr><td>Value1</td><td>Value2</td></tr></table>
```

Using a greedy quantifier will potentially take too much:

```
PS> $html = '<table><tr><td>Value1</td><td>Value2</td></tr></table>'
$html -match '<td>.+</td>'; $matches[0]
True
<td>Value1</td><td>Value2</td>
```

Using a character class is one possible way to solve this problem. The character class is used to take all characters except >, which denotes the end of the next </td> tag:

```
PS> $html = '<table><tr><td>Value1</td><td>Value2</td></tr></table>'
PS> $html -match '<td>[^>]+</td>'
True
PS> $matches[0]
<td>Value1</td>
```

Another way to solve a problem is to use a lazy quantifier:

```
PS> $html = '<table><tr><td>Value1</td><td>Value2</td></tr></table>'
PS> $html -match '<td>.+?</td>'
True
PS> $matches[0]
<td>Value1</td>
```

Character classes

A character class is used to match a single character to a set of possible characters. A character class is denoted using square brackets ([ ]).

For example, a character class may contain each of the vowels:

```
'get' -match 'g[aeiou]t'
'got' -match 'g[aeiou]'
```

Within a character class, the special or reserved characters are as follows:

- −: Used to define a range
- \: Escape character
- ^: Negates the character class

Ranges

The hyphen is used to define a range of characters. For example, we might want to match any number that's repeated one or more times in a set (using +):

```
'1st place' -match '[0-9]+'    # $matches[0] is "1"
'23rd place' -match '[0-9]+'   # $matches[0] is "23"
```

A range in a character class can be any range of ASCII characters, such as the following examples:

- a-z
- A-K
- 0-9
- 1-5
- !-9 (0-9 and the ASCII characters 33 to 47)

The following code returns `true`, as " is ASCII character 34, and # is ASCII character 35; that is, they're within the specified `!-9` range:

```
PS> '"#' -match '[!-9]+'; $matches[0]
True
"#
```

The range notation allows hexadecimal numbers within strings to be identified. A hexadecimal character can be identified by a character class containing `0-9` and `a-f`:

```
PS> 'The registry value is 0xAF9B7' -match '0x[0-9a-f]+'; $matches[0]
True
0xAF9B7
```

If the comparison operator were case-sensitive, the character class may also define `A-F`:

```
'The registry value is 0xAF9B7' -cmatch '0x[0-9a-fA-F]+'
```

Alternatively, a range might be used to tentatively find an IP address in a string, as follows:

```
PS> (ipconfig) -match 'IPv4 Address.+: *[0-9]+\.[0-9]+\.[0-9]+\.[0-9]+'
   IPv4 Address. . . . . . . . . . : 172.16.255.30
```

The range used to find the IP address here is very simple. It matches any string containing four numbers separated by a period. For example, the following version number matches this range:

```
'version 0.1.2.3234' -match '[0-9]+\.[0-9]+\.[0-9]+\.[0-9]+'
```

This IP address-matching regular expression will be improved as the chapter progresses.

The hyphen is not a reserved character when it is put in a position where it does not describe a range. If it is the first character (with no start to the range), it will be treated as a literal. The following split operation demonstrates this:

```
PS> 'one-two_three,four' -split '[-_,]'
one
two
three
four
```

The same output is seen when – is placed at the end (that is, when there is no end to the range):

```
'one-two_three,four' -split '[_,-]'
```

Elsewhere in the class, the escape character may be used to remove the special meaning from the hyphen:

```
'one-two_three,four' -split '[_\-,]'
```

Negated character class

Within a character class, the caret (^) is used to negate the class. The character class, [aeiou], matches vowels, negating it with the caret, [^aeiou], which matches any character except a vowel (including spaces, punctuation, tabs, and everything else).

As with the hyphen, the caret is only effective if it is in the right position. In this case, it only negates the class if it is the first character. Elsewhere in the class, it is a literal character.

A negated character class is sometimes the fastest way to tackle a problem. If the list of expected characters is small, negating that list is a quick way to perform a match.

In the following example, the negated character class is used with the -replace operator to fix a problem:

```
'Ba%by8 a12315tthe1231 k#.,154eyboard' -replace '[^a-z ]'
```

Character class subtraction

Character class subtraction is supported by .NET (and hence PowerShell). Character class subtraction is not commonly used at all.

Inside a character class, one character class may be subtracted from another, reducing the size of the overall set. One of the best examples of this extends to the character class containing vowels. The following matches the first vowel in a string:

```
'The lazy cat sat on the mat' -match '[aeiou]'
```

To match the first consonant, one approach can be to list all of the consonants:

```
'The lazy cat sat on the mat' -match '[b-df-hj-np-tv-z]'
```

Another approach to the problem is to take a larger character class, then subtract the vowels:

```
'The lazy cat sat on the mat' -match '[a-z-[aeiou]]'
```

Shorthand character classes

A number of shorthand character classes are available. The following table shows each of these:

Shorthand	Description	Character class
\d	Digit character	[0-9]
\s	White space (space, tab, carriage return, new line, and form feed)	[\t\r\n\f]
\w	Word character	[A-Za-z0-9_]

Each of these shorthand classes can be negated by capitalizing the letter. [^0-9] may be represented using \D and \S is for any character except white space, and \W for any character except a word character.

Alternation

The alternation (or) character in a regular expression is a pipe (|). This is used to combine several possible regular expressions. A simple example is to match a list of words:

```
'one', 'two', 'three' | Where-Object { $_ -match 'one|three' }
```

The alternation character has the lowest precedence; in the previous expression, every value is first tested against the expression to the left of the pipe and then against the expression to the right of the pipe.

The goal of the following expression is to extract strings that only contain the words one or three. Adding the start and the end of string anchors ensures that there is a boundary. However, because the left and right are treated as separate expressions, the result might not be as expected when using the following expression:

```
PS> 'one', 'one hundred', 'three', 'eighty three' | Where-Object { $_ -
match '^one|three$' }
one
one hundred
three
eighty three
```

The two expressions are evaluated as follows:

- Look for all strings that start with one
- Look for all strings that end with three

There are at least two possible solutions to this problem. The first is to add the start and end of string characters to both expressions:

```
'one', 'one hundred', 'three', 'eighty three' |
Where-Object { $_ -match '^one$|^three$' }
```

Another possible solution is to use a group:

```
'one', 'one hundred', 'three', 'eighty three' | Where-Object { $_ -match
'^(one|three)$' }
```

Grouping is discussed in detail in the following section.

Grouping

A group in a regular expression serves a number of different possible purposes:

- To denote repetition (of more than a single character)
- To restrict alternation to a part of the regular expression
- To capture a value

Repeating groups

Groups may be repeated using any of the quantifiers. The regular expression that tentatively identifies an IP address can be improved using a repeated group. The starting point for this expression is as follows:

```
[0-9]+\.[0-9]+\.[0-9]+\.[0-9]+
```

In this expression, the `[0-9]+` term followed by a literal `.` character is repeated three times. Therefore, the expression can become as follows:

```
([0-9]+\.){3}[0-9]+
```

The expression itself is not very specific—it will match much more than an IP address, but is also now more concise. This example will be taken further later in this chapter.

If `*` is used as the quantifier for the group, it becomes optional. If faced with a set of version numbers ranging in formats from `1` to `1.2.3.4`, a similar regular expression might be used:

```
[0-9]+(\.[0-9]+)*
```

The result of applying this to a number of different version strings is shown in the following code:

```
PS> 'v1', 'Ver 1.000.232.14', 'Version: 0.92', 'Version-7.92.1-alpha' |
    Where-Object { $_ -match '[0-9]+(\.[0-9]+)*' } |
    ForEach-Object { $matches[0] }
1
1.000.232.14
0.92
7.92.1
```

In the case of the last example, −alpha is ignored; if that were an interesting part of the version number, the expression would need to be modified to account for that.

Restricting alternation

Alternation is the lowest precedence operator. In a sense, it might be wise to consider it as describing an ordered list of regular expressions to test.

Placing an alternation statement in parentheses reduces the scope of the expression.

For example, it is possible to match a multi-line string using alternation as follows:

```
PS> $string = @'
First line
second line
third line
'@

PS> if ($string -match 'First(.|\r?\n)*line') { $matches[0] }
First line
second line
third line
```

In this example, as . does not match the end of line character, using alternation allows each character to be tested against a broader set. In this case, each character is tested to see whether it is any character, \r\n or \n.

A regular expression might be created to look for files with specific words, or parts of words, in the name:

```
Get-ChildItem -Recurse -File |
    Where-Object { $_.Name -match '(pwd|pass(word|wd)?).*\.(txt|doc)$' }
```

The expression that compares filenames looks for strings that contain `pwd`, `pass`, `password`, or `passwd`, followed by anything with the `.txt` or `.doc` extensions.

This expression will match any of the following (and more):

```
pwd.txt
server passwords.doc
passwd.txt
my pass.doc
private password list.txt
```

Capturing values

The ability to capture values from a string is an incredibly useful feature of regular expressions.

When using the `-match` operator, groups that have been captured are loaded into the `matches` variable (hash table) in the order that they appear in the expression. Consider the following example:

```
PS> 'first second third' -match '(first) (second) (third)'
True

PS> $matches

Name Value
---- -----
3    third
2    second
1    first
0    first second third
```

The first key, `0`, is always the string that matched the entire expression. Numbered keys are added to the hash table for each of the groups in the order that they appear. This applies to nested groups as well, counting from the leftmost `(`:

```
PS> 'first second third' -match '(first) ((second) (third))'
True

PS> $matches

Name Value
---- -----
4    third
3    second
```

```
2      second third
1      first
0      first second third
```

When using the `-replace` operator, the `matches` variable is not filled, but the contents of individual groups are available as tokens for use in `Replace-With`:

```
PS>'first second third' -replace '(first) ((second) (third))', '$1, $4, $2'
first, third, second third
```

 Use single quotes when tokens are included: As was mentioned in `Chapter 4`, *Operators*, single quotes should be used when using capture groups in `Replace-With`. Tokens in double quotes will expand as if they were PowerShell variables.

Named capture groups

Capture groups can be given names. The name must be unique within the regular expression.

The following syntax is used to name a group:

```
(?<GroupName>Expression)
```

This may be applied to the previous simple example as follows:

```
PS> 'first second third' -match '(?<One>first) (?<Two>second)
(?<Three>third)'
True

PS> $matches

Name        Value
----        -----
One         first
Three       third
Two         second
0           first second third
```

In PowerShell, this adds a pleasant additional capability. If the goal is to tear apart text and turn it into an object, one approach is as follows:

```
if ('first second third' -match '(first) (second) (third)') {
    [PSCustomObject]@{
        One   = $matches[1]
        Two   = $matches[2]
        Three = $matches[3]
    }
}
```

This produces an object that contains the result of each (unnamed) -match group in a named property.

An alternative is to use named matches and create an object from the matches hash table. When using this approach, $matches[0] should be removed:

```
PS> if ('first second third' -match '(?<One>first) (?<Two>second)
(?<Three>third)') {
    $matches.Remove(0)
    [PSCustomObject]$matches
}

One    Three Two
---    ----- ---
first  third second
```

A possible disadvantage of this approach is that the output is not ordered, as it has been created from a hash table.

Non-capturing groups

By default, every group is a capture group. A group can be marked as non-capturing by using ?: before the expression. In the following example, the third group has been marked as a non-capturing group:

```
PS> 'first second third' -match '(?<One>first) (?<Two>second) (?:third)'
True

PS> $matches

Name Value
---- -----
Two  second
One  first
```

```
0 first second third
```

The outer group, which previously added `second third` to the `matches` list, is now excluded from the results:

```
PS> 'first second third' -match '(first) (?:(second) (third))'; $matches
True

PS> $matches
```

Name	Value
3	third
2	second
1	first
0	first second third

This technique may be useful when using `-replace`—it simplifies the list of tokens available, even if an expression grows in complexity:

```
PS> 'first second third' -replace '(first) (?:(second) (third))', '$1, $2,
$3'
first, second, third
```

Examples of regular expressions

The following examples walk you through creating regular expressions for a number of different formats.

MAC addresses

Media Access Control (MAC) is a unique identifier for network interface addresses with 6-byte fields normally written in hexadecimal.

Tools such as `ipconfig` show the value of a MAC address with each hexadecimal byte separated by a hyphen, for example, `1a-2b-3c-4d-5f-6d`.

Linux or Unix-based systems tend to separate each hexadecimal byte with `:`, such as `1a:2b:3c:4d:5f:6d`. This includes Linux and Unix variants, VMWare, JunOS (the Juniper network device operating system, based on FreeBSD), and so on.

Cisco IOS shows a MAC address as three two-byte pairs, separated by a period (`.`).

A regular expression can be created to simultaneously match all of these formats.

To match a single hexadecimal character, the following character class may be used:

```
[0-9a-f]
```

To account for the first two formats, a pair of hexadecimal characters is followed by a hyphen or a colon:

```
[0-9a-f]{2}[-:]
```

This pattern is repeated 5 times, followed by one last pair:

```
([0-9a-f]{2}[-:]){5}[0-9a-f]{2}
```

Adding the Cisco format into the mix will make the expression a little longer:

```
(([0-9a-f]{2}[-:]?){2}[-:.]){2}([0-9a-f]{2}[-:]?){2}
```

Another approach is to keep the formats separate and use the alternation operator to divide the two possibilities:

```
([0-9a-f]{2}[-:]){5}[0-9a-f]{2}|([0-9a-f]{4}\.){2}[0-9a-f]{4}
```

A small script can be written to test the regular expressions against some strings. In the following tests, the first pattern is expected to fail when testing against the Cisco IOS format:

```
$patterns = '^([0-9a-f]{2}[-:]){5}[0-9a-f]{2}$',
            '^(([0-9a-f]{2}[-:]?){2}[-:.]){2}([0-9a-f]{2}[-:]?){2}$',
            '^([0-9a-f]{2}[-:]){5}[0-9a-f]{2}|([0-9a-f]{4}\.){2}[0-9a-
f]{4}$'
$strings = '1a-2b-3c-4d-5f-6d',
           '1a:2b:3c:4d:5f:6d',
           '1c2b.3c4d.5f6d'
foreach ($pattern in $patterns) {
    Write-Host "Testing pattern: $pattern" -ForegroundColor Cyan
    foreach ($string in $strings) {
        if ($string -match $pattern) {
            Write-Host "${string}: Matches" -ForegroundColor Green
        } else {
            Write-Host "${string}: Failed" -ForegroundColor Red
        }
    }
}
```

IP addresses

Validating an IPv4 address using a regular expression is not necessarily a trivial task.

The IP address consists of four octets; each octet can be a value between 0 and 255. When using a regular expression, the values are considered strings, therefore, the following strings must be considered:

- `[0-9]`: 0 to 9
- `[1-9][0-9]`: 1 to 9, then 0 to 9 (10 to 99)
- `1[0-9]{2}`: 1, then 0 to 9, then 0 to 9 (100 to 199)
- `2[0-4][0-9]`: 2, then 0 to 4, then 0 to 9 (200 to 249)
- `25[0-5]`: 2, then 5, then 0 to 5 (250 to 255)

Each of these is an exclusive set, so alternation is used to merge all of the previous small expressions into a single expression. This generates the following group, that matches a single octet (0 to 255):

```
([0-9]|[1-9][0-9]|1[0-9]{2}|2[0-4][0-9]|25[0-5])
```

The IP address validation expression contains repetition now, it contains four octets with a period between each of them:

```
(([0-9]|[1-9][0-9]|1[0-9]{2}|2[0-4][0-9]|25[0-5])\.){3}([0-9]|[1-9][0-9]|1[
0-9]{2}|2[0-4][0-9]|25[0-5])
```

There are other, perhaps better, ways to do this than using such a long regex. If a string is a strong candidate for being an IP address, consider using the `TryParse` static method on the `IPAddress` type. It will handle both v4 and v6 addressing, as follows:

```
$ipAddress = [IPAddress]0 # Used as a placeholder
if ([IPAddress]::TryParse("::1", [ref]$ipAddress)) {
$ipAddress
}
```

The netstat command

The `netstat` command produces tab-delimited, fixed-width tables. The following example converts the active connections that list active TCP connections, as well as listening TCP and UDP ports, into an object.

A snippet of the output that the example is intended to parse is shown in the following code:

```
PS> netstat -ano

Active Connections

    Proto  Local Address    Foreign Address    State        PID
    TCP    0.0.0.0:135      0.0.0.0:0          LISTENING    124
    TCP    0.0.0.0:445      0.0.0.0:0          LISTENING    4
    TCP    0.0.0.0:5357     0.0.0.0:0          LISTENING    4
```

When handling text such as this, a pattern based on white space (or not white space) can be used:

```
^\s*\S+\s+\S+
```

For each column, the following expression with a named group is created:

```
(?<ColumnName>\S+)\s+
```

The trailing `\s+` is omitted for the last column (`PID`):

```
^\s*(?<Protocol>\S+)\s+(?<LocalAddress>\S+)\s+(?<ForeignAddress>\S+)\s+(?<State>\S+)\s+(?<PID>\d+)$
```

The expression is long, but incredibly repetitive. The repetition is desirable in this case, where each column value is pushed into a differently named group.

The expression can be applied using `Where-Object`:

```
$regex =
'^\s*(?<Protocol>\S+)\s+(?<LocalAddress>\S+)\s+(?<ForeignAddress>\S+)\s+(?<State>\S+)\s+(?<PID>\d+)$'
netstat -ano | Where-Object { $_ -match $regex } | ForEach-Object {
    $matches.Remove(0)
    [PSCustomObject]$matches
}
```

Unfortunately, the output from this command will be missing information about UDP ports. The regular expression makes having a value in the state column mandatory. Marking this group as optional will add UDP connection information to the output:

```
(State>\S+)?
```

Inserting it back into the regular expression is achieved as follows:

```
$regex =
'^\s*(?<Protocol>\S+)\s+(?<LocalAddress>\S+)\s+(?<ForeignAddress>\S+)\s+(?<
State>\S+)?\s+(?<PID>\d+)$'
netstat -ano | Where-Object { $_ -match $regex } | ForEach-Object {
    $matches.Remove(0)
    [PSCustomObject]$matches
}
```

Finally, if it is desirable to return the fields in the same order as `netstat` does, `Select-Object` may be used:

```
PS>$regex =
'^\s*(?<Protocol>\S+)\s+(?<LocalAddress>\S+)\s+(?<ForeignAddress>\S+)\s+(?<
State>\S+)\s+(?<PID>\d+)$'
PS> netstat -ano | Where-Object { $_ -match $regex } | ForEach-Object {
    $matches.Remove(0)
    [PSCustomObject]$matches
} | Select-Object Protocol, LocalAddress, ForeignAddress, State, PID |
    Format-Table


Protocol LocalAddress ForeignAddress State     PID
-------- ------------ -------------- -----     ---
TCP      0.0.0.0:135  0.0.0.0:0      LISTENING 124
TCP      0.0.0.0:445  0.0.0.0:0      LISTENING 4
TCP      0.0.0.0:5357 0.0.0.0:0      LISTENING 4
```

Formatting certificates

It is occasionally necessary to create certificates in very specific formats to appease other systems requiring such a certificate.

A certificate may be exported as a Base64 string as follows. The `InsertLineBreaks` option splits the string every 76 characters:

```
$certificate = Get-ChildItem Cert:\LocalMachine\Root | Select-Object -First
1
[Convert]::ToBase64String(
    $certificate.Export('Cert'),
    [System.Base64FormattingOptions]::InsertLineBreaks
)
```

If a different width is required, a regular expression may be used to tweak the format of the certificate—in this case, we split the lines every 64 characters:

```
$certificate = Get-ChildItem Cert:\LocalMachine\Root | Select-Object -First
1
@(
    '-----BEGIN CERTIFICATE-----'
    [Convert]::ToBase64String(
        $certificate.Export('Cert')
    ) -split '(?<=\G.{64})'
    '-----END CERTIFICATE-----'
) -join "`n"
```

This makes use of the \G anchor that continues from the end of the previous match. This anchor is difficult to demonstrate, but is very useful in situations such as this. The anchor is placed inside a positive look-behind assertion. The length of the string is important, but the content shouldn't be removed by -split.

Summary

In this chapter, we took a look at regular expressions and their use in PowerShell.

The *Regex basics* section introduced a number of heavily used characters. Anchors showing how the start and end of a string or word boundary may be used to restrict the scope of an expression.

Character classes were introduced as a powerful form of alternation, providing a range of options for matching a single character. Alternation was demonstrated using different sets of expressions to be evaluated.

We looked at repetition using "*", +, ?, and curly braces, and discussed the notion of greedy and lazy expressions.

Grouping was introduced as a means of limiting the scope of alternation in order to repeat larger expressions or to capture strings.

Finally, a number of examples were included, bringing together the areas covered in this chapter to solve specific problems.

In Chapter 10, *Files, Folders, and the Registry*, we will discuss working with files, folders, and the registry.

Files, Folders, and the Registry
10

The filesystem and the registry are two from among a number of providers available in PowerShell. A provider represents a data store as a filesystem.

The commands used to work with data within a particular provider, such as filesystems, are common to all providers.

In this chapter, we will cover the following topics:

- Working with providers
- Items
- Item properties
- Item attributes
- Windows permissions
- Transactions
- File catalogs

Working with providers

Each provider shares a common set of commands, such as `Set-Location`, `Get-Item`, and `New-Item`.

Navigating

Set-Location, which has the alias cd, is used to navigate around a provider's hierarchy, for example:

```
Set-Location \            # The root of the current drive
Set-Location Windows      # A child container named Windows
Set-Location ..           # Navigate up one level
Set-Location ..\..        # Navigate up two levels
Set-Location Cert:        # Change to a different drive
Set-Location HKLM:\Software # Change to a specific child container under
a drive
```

Set-Location may only be used to switch to a container object.

The print working directory pwd variable shows the current location across all providers:

PS> $pwd

Path

HKLM:\Software\Microsoft\Windows\CurrentVersion

pwd and .NET

.NET classes and methods are oblivious to PowerShell's current directory. When the following command is executed, the file will be created in the Start in path (if a shortcut started PowerShell: [System.IO.File]::WriteAllLines('file.txt', 'Some content').

.NET constructors and methods are an ideal place to use the pwd variable:[System.IO.File]::WriteAllLines("$pwd\file.txt", 'Some content').

Getting items

The Get-Item command is used to get an object represented by a path:

```
Get-Item \ # The root container
Get-Item .  # The current container
Get-Item .. # The parent container
Get-Item C:\Windows\System32\cmd.exe  # A leaf item
Get-Item Cert:\LocalMachine\Root      #A container item
```

The `Get-ChildItem` command, which has `dir` and `ls` aliases, is used to list the children of the current item.

Neither `Get-ChildItem` nor `Get-Item` will show hidden files and folders by default. The following error will be returned for a hidden item:

```
PS> Get-Item $env:USERPROFILE\AppData
Get-Item : Could not find item C:\Users\Someone\AppData.
At line:1 char:1
+ Get-Item $env:USERPROFILE\AppData
+ ~~~~~~~~~~~~~~~~~~~~~~~~~~~~~~~~~~
 + CategoryInfo : ObjectNotFound: (C:\Users\Someone \AppData:String) [Get-
Item], IOException
 + FullyQualifiedErrorId :
ItemNotFound,Microsoft.PowerShell.Commands.GetItemCommand
```

The `Force` parameter may be added to access hidden items:

```
PS> Get-Item $env:USERPROFILE\AppData -Force


    Directory: C:\Users\Someone


Mode                LastWriteTime         Length Name
----                -------------          ------ ----
d--h--        23/09/2016     18:22                AppData
```

Drives

PowerShell will automatically create a drive for any disk with a drive letter, any existing shared drive, the `HKEY_LOCAL_MACHINE` and `HKEY_CURRENT_USER` registry hives, the certificate store, and so on.

Additional drives may be added using `New-PSDrive`; for example, a network drive can be created:

```
New-PSDrive X -PSProvider FileSystem -Root \\Server\Share
New-PSDrive HKCR -PSProvider Registry -Root HKEY_CLASSES_ROOT
```

Existing drives may be removed using `Remove-PSDrive`. PowerShell allows filesystem drives to be removed; however, this is not a destructive operation, and it only removes the reference to the drive from PowerShell.

The filesystem provider supports the use of credentials when creating a drive, allowing network shares to be mapped using specific credentials.

Items

Support for each of the `*-Item` commands varies from one provider to another. The filesystem provider supports all of the commands, while the `Registry` provider supports a smaller number.

Testing for existing items

The `Test-Path` command may be used to test for the existence of a specific item under a drive:

```
Test-Path HKLM:\Software\Publisher
```

`Test-path` distinguishes between item types with the `PathType` parameter. The container and leaf terms are used across providers to broadly classify items.

When working with the filesystem, a container is a directory (or folder) and a leaf is a file. In the registry, a key is a container and there are no leaves. In a certificate provider, a store or store location is a container and a certificate is a leaf.

The following commands test for items of differing types:

```
Test-Path C:\Windows -PathType Container
Test-Path C:\Windows\System32\cmd.exe -PathType Leaf
```

The `Test-Path` command is often used in an `if` statement prior to creating a file or directory:

```
if (-not (Test-Path C:\Temp\NewDirectory -PathType Container)) {
    New-Item C:\Temp\NewDirectory -ItemType Directory
}
```

Get-Item, Test-Path, and pagefile.sys

Some files in Windows are locked, with the result that `Get-Item` and `Test-Path` are unable to correctly return results. The `pagefile.sys` file is one of these.

 `Get-Item` returns an error, indicating that the file does not exist, even when the `Force` parameter is used. `Test-Path` always returns `false`.

This may be considered to be a bug. To work around the problem, `Get-ChildItem` is able to get the file: `Get-ChildItem C:\ -Filter pagefile.sys -Force`.

To replace the functionality of `Test-Path`, the static method `Exists` may be used: `[System.IO.File]::Exists('c:\pagefile.sys')`.

Creating and deleting items

The `New-Item` command is able to create files, directories, keys, and so on depending on the provider:

```
New-Item $env:Temp\newfile.txt -ItemType File
New-Item $env:Temp\newdirectory -ItemType Directory
New-Item HKLM:\Software\NewKey -ItemType Key
```

When creating a file using `New-Item` in PowerShell, the file is empty (0 bytes).

In PowerShell 5, `New-Item` gained the ability to create symbolic links, junctions, and hard links:

- A symbolic link is a link to another file or directory. Creating a symbolic link requires administrator privileges (run as administrator).
- A hard link is a link to another file on the same drive.
- A junction is a link to another directory on any local drive. Creating a junction does not require administrative privileges.

Links may be created as follows:

```
New-Item LinkName -ItemType SymbolicLink -Value \\Server\Share New-Item
LinkName.txt -ItemType HardLink -Value OriginalName.txt New-Item LinkName -
ItemType Junction -Value C:\Temp
```

Temporary files

If a script needs a file to temporarily store data, the `New-TemporaryFile` command may be used.

This command was introduced with PowerShell 5. Earlier versions of PowerShell may use the `Path.GetTempFileName` static method: `[System.IO.Path]::GetTempFileName()`.

Both commands create an empty file. The resulting file may be used with `Set-Content`, `Out-File`, or any commands that write data to a file.

The `Remove-Item` command may be used to remove an existing item under a provider, for example:

```
$file = New-TemporaryFile
Set-Content -Path $file -Value 'Temporary: 10'
Remove-Item $file
```

Providers such as filesystem and registry are reasonably flexible about removing items. When removing a directory or key with children, the `recurse` parameter should be used.

The `certificate` provider restricts the use of `Remove-Item` to certificates; certificate stores cannot be removed.

Invoking items

`Invoke-Item` (which has an alias, ii) has a number of different uses. `Invoke-Item` will open or execute an object using the default settings for that file:

```
Invoke-Item .                           # Open the current directory in
explorer
Invoke-Item test.ps1                    # Open test.ps1 in the default
editor
Invoke-Item $env:windir\system32\cmd.exe  # Open cmd
Invoke-Item Cert:                       # Open the certificate store
MMC for the current user
```

The registry provider does not support `Invoke-Item`.

Item properties

The `Get-ItemProperty` and `Set-ItemProperty` commands allow individual properties to be modified.

Filesystem properties

When working with the filesystem provider, `Get-ItemProperty` and `Set-ItemProperty` are rarely needed. For example, `Set-ItemProperty` might be used to make a file read-only. The following example assumes that the `somefile.txt` file already exists:

```
Set-ItemProperty .\somefile.txt -Name IsReadOnly -Value $true
```

The same property may be directly set from a file object retrieved using `Get-Item` (or `Get-ChildItem`):

```
(Get-Item 'somefile.txt').IsReadOnly = $true
```

The `IsReadOnly` flag affects the attributes of the file object, adding the `ReadOnly` flag.

Adding and removing file attributes

The attributes property of a file object is a bit field presented as a number and given an easily understandable value by the `System.IO.FileAttributes` enumeration.

Bit fields

A bit field is a means of exposing multiple settings that have two states (on or off binary states) using a single number.

A byte, an 8-bit value, can therefore hold eight possible settings. A 32-bit integer, 4-bytes long, can hold 32 different settings.

The following table, whose state is described by 4 bits, has four settings:
Name: Setting4 Setting3 Setting2 Setting1
State: On Off On Off
Binary: 1 0 1 0
Decimal: 8 4 2 1

When settings 2 and 4 are toggled on, the value of the field is the conversion of 1010 to decimal. This value is the result of 8 -bor 2, that is, 10.

A number of the possible attributes are shown in the following table:

Name	Compressed	Archive	System	Hidden	Read-only
Bit value	2048	32	4	2	1

When a file is hidden and read-only, the value of the attributes property is 3 (2 + 1). The value 3 can be cast to the FileAttributes type, which shows the names of the individual flags:

```
PS> [System.IO.FileAttributes]3
ReadOnly, Hidden
```

While the value is numeric, the use of the enumeration means words can be used to describe each property:

```
PS> [System.IO.FileAttributes]'ReadOnly, Hidden' -eq 3
True
```

This opens up a number of possible ways to set attributes on a file.

Attributes may be replaced entirely:

```
(Get-Item 'somefile.txt').Attributes = 'ReadOnly, Hidden'
```

Attributes may be toggled:

```
$file = Get-Item 'somefile.txt'
$file.Attributes = $file.Attributes -bxor 'ReadOnly'
```

Attributes may be added:

```
$file = Get-Item 'somefile.txt'
$file.Attributes = $file.Attributes -bor 'ReadOnly'
```

The +, −, +=, and −= operators may be used, as this is a numeric operation. Addition or subtraction operations are not safe, as they do not account for existing flags. For example, if a file was already read-only and += was used to attempt to make the file read-only, the result would be a hidden file:

```
PS> $file = Get-Item 'somefile.txt'
PS> $file.Attributes = 'ReadOnly'
PS> $file.Attributes += 'ReadOnly'
PS> $file.Attributes

Hidden
```

Finally, regardless of whether or not a flag is present, attributes may be written as a string:

```
$file = Get-Item 'somefile.txt'
$file.Attributes = "$($file.Attributes), ReadOnly"
```

This is a feasible approach because casting to the enumeration type will ignore any duplication:

```
PS> [System.IO.FileAttributes]'ReadOnly, Hidden, ReadOnly'
ReadOnly, Hidden
```

Registry values

`Get-ItemProperty` and `Set-ItemProperty` are most useful when manipulating registry values.

The following method may be used to get values from the registry:

```
Get-ItemProperty -Path HKCU:\Environment
Get-ItemProperty -Path HKCU:\Environment -Name Path
Get-ItemProperty -Path HKCU:\Environment -Name Path, Temp
```

Individual values may be written back to the registry under an existing key:

```
Set-ItemProperty -Path HKCU:\Environment -Name NewValue -Value 'New'
```

A value may be subsequently removed:

```
Remove-ItemProperty -Path HKCU:\Environment -Name NewValue
```

The `Set-ItemProperty` command does not directly allow the value type to be influenced. The command will do as much as it can to fit the value into the existing type. For a property with type `REG_SZ`, numbers will be converted to strings.

If a value does not already exist, a registry type will be created according to the value type:

- `Int32`: `REG_DWORD`
- `Int64`: `REG_QWORD`
- `String`: `REG_SZ`
- `String[]`: `REG_MULTI_SZ` (must use `"[String[]]@('value', 'value')"`)
- `Byte[]`: `REG_BINARY`
- **Any other type**: `REG_SZ`

If a value of a specific type is required, the `New-ItemProperty` command should be used instead, for instance, if an expanding string must be created:

```
New-ItemProperty HKCU:\Environment -Name Expand -Value 'User: %USERNAME%' -PropertyType ExpandString
```

`New-ItemProperty` will throw an error if a property already exists. The `Force` parameter may be used to overwrite an existing value with the same name.

Windows permissions

The filesystem and registry providers both support `Get-Acl` and `Set-Acl`, which allow the different access control lists to be modified.

Working with permissions in PowerShell involves a mixture of PowerShell commands and .NET objects and methods.

While some values and classes differ between the different providers, many of the same concepts apply.

The following snippet creates a set of files and folders in `C:\Temp`. These files and folders are used in the examples that follow:

```
New-Item C:\Temp\ACL -ItemType Directory -Force
1..5 | ForEach-Object {
    New-Item C:\Temp\ACL\$_ -ItemType Directory -Force
    'content' | Out-File "C:\Temp\ACL\$_\$_.txt"

    New-Item C:\Temp\ACL\$_\$_ -ItemType Directory -Force
    'content' | Out-File "C:\Temp\ACL\$_\$_\$_.txt"
}
```

The `Get-Acl` command is used to retrieve an existing **Access Control List (ACL)** for an object. `Set-Acl` is used to apply an updated `ACL` to an object.

If `Get-Acl` is used against a directory, the `ACL` type is `DirectorySecurity`; for a file, the `ACL` type is `FileSecurity` and, for a registry key, the `ACL` type is `RegistrySecurity`.

Alternatives to .NET classes

The NtfsSecurity module found in the PowerShell Gallery may be an easier alternative to the native methods discussed in this section.

Ownership

Ownership of a file or directory may be changed using the `SetOwner` method of the `ACL` object. Changing the ownership of a file requires administrative privileges.

The owner of the `C:\Temp\ACL\1` file is the current user:

```
PS> Get-Acl C:\Temp\ACL\1 | Select-Object Owner

Owner
-----
COMPUTER\Chris
```

The owner may be changed (in this case, to the `Administrator` account) using the `SetOwner` method:

```
$acl = Get-Acl C:\Temp\ACL\1
$acl.SetOwner([System.Security.Principal.NTAccount]'Administrator')
Set-Acl C:\Temp\ACL\1 -AclObject $acl
```

This is not taking ownership

Setting ownership when the current user already has full control is one thing. Very specific privileges are required to take ownership without existing permissions: `SeRestorePrivilege`, `SeBackupPrivilege`, and `SeTakeOwnershipPrivilege`.

Access and audit

Access lists come with two different types of access controls.

The **discretionary access control list (DACL)** is used to grant (or deny) access to a resource. The DACL is referred to as access in PowerShell.

The **system access control list (SACL)** is used to define which activities should be audited. The SACL is referred to as audit in PowerShell.

Reading and setting the audit `ACL` requires administrator privileges (run as administrator). `Get-Acl` will only attempt to read the audit `ACL` if it is explicitly requested. The `-Audit` switch parameter is used to request the list:

```
Get-Acl C:\Temp\ACL\1 -Audit | Format-List
```

As none of the folders created have audit ACLs at this time, the `-Audit` property will be blank.

Rule protection

Access control lists, by default, inherit rules from parent container objects. Access rule protection blocks the propagation of rules from a parent object.

Rule protection can be enabled for the access ACL using the `SetAccessRuleProtection` method or for the audit ACL using the `SetAuditRuleProtection` method.

Setting rule protection has the same effect as disabling inheritance in the GUI.

Each of the methods expects two arguments. The first argument, `isProtected`, dictates whether or not the list should be protected. The second argument, `preserveInheritance`, dictates what should be done with existing inherited entries. Inherited entries can either be copied or discarded.

In the following example, access rule protection is enabled (inheritance is disabled) and the previously inherited rules are copied into the ACL:

```
$acl = Get-Acl C:\Temp\ACL\2
$acl.SetAccessRuleProtection($true, $true)
Set-Acl C:\Temp\ACL\2 -AclObject $acl
```

Copied rules will only appear on the ACL (as explicit rules) after `Set-Acl` has been run.

If access rule protection is subsequently re-enabled, copied rules are not removed. The resulting ACL will contain both inherited and explicit versions of each of the rules. Inheritance can be re-enabled as follows:

```
$acl = Get-Acl C:\Temp\ACL\2
$acl.SetAccessRuleProtection($false, $false)
Set-Acl C:\Temp\ACL\2 -AclObject $acl
```

The access control list will have doubled in length:

```
PS> Get-Acl 2 |
>>      Select-Object -ExpandProperty Access |
>>      Select-Object FileSystemRights, IdentityReference, IsInherited


FileSystemRights              IdentityReference
IsInherited
----------------              -----------------
---
-536805376                    NT AUTHORITY\Authenticated Users    False
Modify, Synchronize           NT AUTHORITY\Authenticated Users    False
FullControl                   NT AUTHORITY\SYSTEM                  False
268435456                     NT AUTHORITY\SYSTEM                  False
```

268435456	BUILTIN\Administrators	False
FullControl	BUILTIN\Administrators	False
ReadAndExecute, Synchronize	BUILTIN\Users	False
FullControl	BUILTIN\Administrators	True
268435456	BUILTIN\Administrators	True
FullControl	NT AUTHORITY\SYSTEM	True
268435456	NT AUTHORITY\SYSTEM	True
ReadAndExecute, Synchronize	BUILTIN\Users	True
Modify, Synchronize	NT AUTHORITY\Authenticated Users	True
−536805376	NT AUTHORITY\Authenticated Users	True

Discarding access rules will result in an empty ACL:

```
$acl = Get-Acl C:\Temp\ACL\3
$acl.SetAccessRuleProtection($true, $false)
Set-Acl C:\Temp\ACL\3 -AclObject $acl
```

Once this operation completes, any attempt to access the directory will result in access being denied:

```
PS> Get-ChildItem C:\Temp\ACL\3
Get-ChildItem : Access to the path 'C:\Temp\ACL\3' is denied.
At line:1 char:1
+ Get-ChildItem C:\Temp\ACL\3
+ ~~~~~~~~~~~~~~~~~~~~~~~~~~~
    + CategoryInfo : PermissionDenied: (C:\Temp\ACL\3:String) [Get-
ChildItem], UnauthorizedAccessException
    + FullyQualifiedErrorId :
DirUnauthorizedAccessError,Microsoft.PowerShell.Commands.GetChildItemComman
d
```

Access to the folder can be restored provided the current user has the SeSecurityPrivilege privilege, granted to users with administrative privileges (run as administrator). Re-enabling inheritance is the simplest way to do this, although we might have taken the opportunity to add rules:

```
$acl = Get-Acl C:\Temp\ACL\3
$acl.SetAccessRuleProtection($false, $false)
Set-Acl C:\Temp\ACL\3 -AclObject $acl
```

In the previous example, the second argument for SetAccessRuleProtection, preserveInheritance, is set to false. This value has no impact; it only dictates behavior when access rule protection is enabled.

This loss of access does not apply when using the SetAuditRuleProtection method, as it does not describe who or what can access an object.

Inheritance and propagation flags

Inheritance and propagation flags dictate how individual access control entries are pushed down to child objects.

Inheritance flags are described by the `System.Security.AccessControl.InheritanceFlags` **enumeration. The possible** values are as follows:

- `None`: Objects will not inherit this access control entry
- `ContainerInherit`: Only container objects (such as directories) will inherit this entry
- `ObjectInherit`: Only leaf objects (such as files) will inherit this entry

Propagation flags are described by the `System.Security.AccessControl.PropagationFlags` **enumeration. The possible** values are as follows:

- `None`: Propagation of inheritance is not changed
- `NoPropagateInherit`: Do not propagate inheritance flags
- `InheritOnly`: This entry does not apply to this object, only children

These two flag fields are used to build the `Applies to` option shown in the graphical user interface when setting security on a folder. The following table shows how each option is created:

Option	Flags
This folder only	• Inheritance: `None` • Propagation: `None`
This folder, subfolders, and files	• Inheritance: `ContainerInherit, ObjectInherit` • Propagation: `None`
This folder and subfolders	• Inheritance: `ContainerInherit` • Propagation: `None`
This folder and files	• Inheritance: `ObjectInherit` • Propagation: `None`
Subfolders only	• Inheritance: `ContainerInherit` • Propagation: `InheritOnly`
Files only	• Inheritance: `ObjectInherit` • Propagation: `InheritOnly`

The `NoPropagateInherit` propagation flag comes into play when the tick box only applies these permissions to objects and/or containers ticked within this container. This may be used with all but in this folder, only right (where it has no effect).

Removing access control entries

Individual rules may be removed from an access control list using a number of different methods:

- `RemoveAccessRule`: Matches `IdentityReference` and `AccessMask`
- `RemoveAccessRuleAll`: Matches `IdentityReference`
- `RemoveAccessRuleSpecific`: Exact match

Access mask is a generic term used to refer to specific rights granted (filesystem rights for a file or directory and registry rights for a registry key).

To demonstrate rule removal, explicit entries might be added to ACL. Enabling then disabling access rule protection will add new rules: the original inherited set and an explicitly set copy of the same rules.

To enable access rule protection and copy inherited rules, do the following:

```
$acl = Get-Acl C:\Temp\ACL\3
$acl.SetAccessRuleProtection($true, $true)
Set-Acl C:\Temp\ACL\3 -AclObject $acl
```

In disable protection, once committed, the inherited rules will appear alongside the copied rules:

```
$acl = Get-Acl C:\Temp\ACL\3
$acl.SetAccessRuleProtection($false, $true)
Set-Acl C:\Temp\ACL\3 -AclObject $acl
```

Rules may be viewed in ACL:

```
PS> $acl = Get-Acl C:\Temp\ACL\3
PS> $acl.Access | Select-Object IdentityReference, FileSystemRights,
IsInherited

IdentityReference                       FileSystemRights IsInherited
-----------------                       ---------------- -----------
NT AUTHORITY\Authenticated Users              -536805376       False
NT AUTHORITY\Authenticated Users     Modify, Synchronize       False
NT AUTHORITY\SYSTEM                          FullControl       False
```

```
NT AUTHORITY\SYSTEM                              268435456         False
BUILTIN\Administrators                           268435456         False
BUILTIN\Administrators                           FullControl       False
BUILTIN\Users                 ReadAndExecute, Synchronize          False
BUILTIN\Administrators                           FullControl       True
BUILTIN\Administrators                           268435456         True
NT AUTHORITY\SYSTEM                              FullControl       True
NT AUTHORITY\SYSTEM                              268435456         True
BUILTIN\Users                 ReadAndExecute, Synchronize          True
NT AUTHORITY\Authenticated Users     Modify, Synchronize           True
NT AUTHORITY\Authenticated Users          -536805376              True
```

The following example finds each explicit rule and removes it from ACL:

```
$acl = Get-Acl C:\Temp\ACL\3
$acl.Access | Where-Object IsInherited -eq $false | ForEach-Object {
    $acl.RemoveAccessRuleSpecific($_)
}
Set-Acl C:\Temp\ACL\3 -AclObject $acl
```

Copying lists and entries

Access lists can be copied from one object to another; for example, a template ACL might have been prepared:

```
$acl = Get-Acl C:\Temp\ACL\4
$acl.SetAccessRuleProtection($true, $true)
$acl.Access |
    Where-Object IdentityReference -like '*\Authenticated Users' |
    ForEach-Object { $acl.RemoveAccessRule($_) }
Set-Acl C:\Temp\ACL\4 -AclObject $acl
```

This ACL can be applied to another object:

```
$acl = Get-Acl C:\Temp\ACL\4
Set-Acl C:\Temp\ACL\5 -AclObject $acl
```

If ACL contains a mixture of inherited and explicit entries, the inherited entries will be discarded.

Access control rules may be copied in a similar manner:

```
# Get the ACE to copy
$ace = (Get-Acl C:\Temp\ACL\3).Access | Where-Object {
    $_.IdentityReference -like '*\Authenticated Users' -and
    $_.FileSystemRights -eq 'Modify, Synchronize' -and
```

```
        -not $_.IsInherited
}

# Get the target ACL
$acl = Get-Acl C:\Temp\ACL\5

# Add the entry
$acl.AddAccessRule($ace)

# Apply the change
Set-Acl C:\Temp\ACL\5 -AclObject $acl
```

Adding access control entries

Access control entries must be created before they can be added to an access control list.

Creating an **access control entry (ACE)** for the filesystem or the registry, and for access or audit purposes, uses a set of .NET classes:

- System.Security.AccessControl.FileSystemAccessRule
- System.Security.AccessControl.FileSystemAuditRule
- System.Security.AccessControl.RegistryAccessRule
- System.Security.AccessControl.RegistryAuditRule

There are a number of different ways to use these classes; this section focuses on the most common.

Filesystem rights

The filesystem access control entry uses the System.Security.AccessControl.FileSystemRights enumeration to describe the different rights that might be granted.

PowerShell is able to list each name using the GetNames (or GetValues) static methods of the Enum type:

```
[System.Security.AccessControl.FileSystemRights].GetEnumNames()
```

PowerShell might be used to show the names, numeric values, and even the binary values associated with each. Several of these rights are composites, such as write, which summarizes `CreateFiles`, `AppendData`, `WriteExtendedAttributes`, and `WriteAttributes`:

```
[System.Security.AccessControl.FileSystemRights].GetEnumValues() | ForEach-
Object {
    [PSCustomObject]@{
        Name    = $_
        Value   = [Int]$_
        Binary  = [Convert]::ToString([Int32]$_, 2).PadLeft(32, '0')
    }
}
```

Microsoft Docs is a better place to find a descriptive meaning of each of the different flags: `https://docs.microsoft.com/en-us/dotnet/api/system.security.accesscontrol.filesystemrights?view=netframework-4.7.2`. This is a bit field, and can therefore be treated in the same way as `FileAttributes` earlier in this chapter. The simplest way to present rights is in a comma-separated list. There is a large number of possible combinations; the graphical user interface shows a small number of these before heading into advanced. These options are shown in the following table:

GUI option	Filesystem rights
Full control	`FullControl`
Modify	`Modify, Synchronize`
Read and execute	`ReadAndExecute, Synchronize`
List folder contents	`ReadAndExecute, Synchronize`
Read	`Read, Synchronize`
Write	`Write, Synchronize`

The previous table shows that both read and execute and list folder contents have the same value. This is, in essence, because the access mask is the same. The difference is in the inheritance flags:

GUI option	Inheritance flags
Read and execute	`ContainerInherit, ObjectInherit`
List folder contents	`ContainerInherit`

In all other cases, the inheritance flags are set to `ContainerInherit, ObjectInherit`. Propagation flags are set to `None` for all examples.

Using these, a full control ACE can be created using one of the constructors for `FileSystemAccessRule`:

```
$ace = [System.Security.AccessControl.FileSystemAccessRule]::new(
    'DOMAIN\User',                        # Identity reference
    'FullControl',                        # FileSystemRights
    'ContainerInherit, ObjectInherit',    # InheritanceFlags
    'None',                               # PropagationFlags
    'Allow'                               # ACE type (allow or deny)
)
```

This ACE can be applied to ACL:

```
$acl = Get-Acl C:\Temp\ACL\5
$acl.AddAccessRule($ace)
Set-Acl C:\Temp\ACL\5 -AclObject $acl
```

Registry rights

Creating access control entries for registry keys follows exactly the same pattern as for filesystem rights. The rights are defined in the `System.Security.AccessControl.RegistryRights` enumeration.

PowerShell is able to list these rights, but the descriptions on MSDN are more useful: https://msdn.microsoft.com/en-us/library/system.security.accesscontrol.registryrights(v=vs.110).aspx.

A rule is created in the same way as a filesystem rule:

```
$ace = [System.Security.AccessControl.RegistryAccessRule]::new(
    'DOMAIN\User',                        # Identity reference
    'FullControl',                        # RegistryRights
    'ContainerInherit, ObjectInherit',    # InheritanceFlags
    'None',                               # PropagationFlags
    'Allow'                               # ACE type (allow or deny)
)
```

The rule can be applied to a key (in this case, a newly created key):

```
$key = New-Item HKCU:\TestKey -ItemType Key -Force
$acl = Get-Acl $key.PSPath
$acl.AddAccessRule($ace)
Set-Acl $key.PSPath -AclObject $acl
```

Numeric values in the access control list

The `FileSystemRights` enumeration used in the previous examples does not quite cover all of the possible values one might see when inspecting an ACL. In some cases, the rights will be shown as numeric values rather than names.

The `-536805376` and `268435456` values were both included in some earlier examples. The missing values are part of the generic portion of the access control entry in Microsoft docs: https://docs.microsoft.com/en-us/windows/desktop/SecAuthZ/access-mask-format.

This generic portion is not accounted for by the `FileSystemRights` enumeration. These generic values, in turn, represent summarized rights, as shown on this page: https://docs.microsoft.com/en-us/windows/desktop/FileIO/file-security-and-access-rights.

Converting each of the values to binary goes a long way to showing their composition:

```
PS> foreach ($value in -536805376, 268435456) {
>>    '{0,-10}: {1}' -f $value, [Convert]::ToString($value, 2).PadLeft(32,
'0')
>> }

-536805376: 11100000000000010000000000000000
268435456 : 00010000000000000000000000000000
```

This script uses a `GenericAccessRights` enumeration toward show how these values may be deconstructed:

```
using namespace System.Security.AccessControl

# Define an enumeration which describes the generic access mask (only)
[Flags()]
enum GenericAccessRights {
    GenericRead    = 0x80000000
    GenericWrite   = 0x40000000
    GenericExecute = 0x20000000
    GenericAll     = 0x10000000
}

# For each value to convert
foreach ($value in -536805376, 268435456) {
    # For each enum that describes the values
    $accessRights = foreach ($enum in [GenericAccessRights],
[FileSystemRights]) {
        # Find values from the enum where the value in question has that
```

```
exact bit set.
        [Enum]::GetValues($enum) | Where-Object { ($value -band $_) -eq $_
}
    }
    # Output the original value and the values from the enum (as a string)
    '{0} : {1}' -f $value, ($accessRights -join ', ')
}
```

The two values discussed are therefore the following:

- −536805376: `GenericExecute`, `GenericWrite`, `GenericRead`, **and** `Delete`
- 268435456: `GenericAll`

Transactions

A transaction allows a set of changes to be grouped together and committed at the same time. Transactions are only supported under Windows PowerShell.

The registry provider supports transactions, as shown in the following code:

```
PS> Get-PSProvider
```

Name	Capabilities	Drives
Registry	ShouldProcess, Transactions	{HKLM, HKCU}
Alias	ShouldProcess	{Alias}
Environment	ShouldProcess	{Env}
FileSystem	Filter, ShouldProcess, Credentials	{B, C, D}
Function	ShouldProcess	{Function}
Variable	ShouldProcess	{Variable}

A transaction may be created as follows:

```
Start-Transaction
$path = 'HKCU:\TestTransaction'
New-Item $path -ItemType Key -UseTransaction
Set-ItemProperty $path -Name 'Name' -Value 'Transaction' -UseTransaction
Set-ItemProperty $path -Name 'Length' -Value 20 -UseTransaction
```

At this point, the transaction may be undone:

```
Undo-Transaction
```

Alternatively, the transaction may be committed:

```
Complete-Transaction
```

A list of the commands that support transactions may be viewed, although not all of these may be used with the registry provider:

```
Get-Command -ParameterName UseTransaction
```

File catalogs

A file catalog is a new feature with Windows PowerShell 5.1. A file catalog is a reasonably lightweight form of **File Integrity Monitoring (FIM)**. The file catalog generates and stores SHA1 hashes for each file within a folder structure and writes the result to a catalog file.

About hashing

Hashing is a one-way process; a hash is not an encryption or encoding. A hash algorithm converts data of any length to a fixed-length value. The length of the value depends on the hashing algorithm used.

MD5 hashing is one of the more common algorithms; it produces a 128-bit hash that can be represented by a 32-character string.

SHA1 is rapidly becoming the default; it produces a 160-bit hash that can be represented by a 40-character string.

PowerShell has a `Get-FileHash` command that can be used to calculate the hash for a file.

As the catalog is the basis for determining integrity, it should be maintained in a secure location, away from the set of files being analyzed.

New-FileCatalog

The `New-FileCatalog` command is used to generate (or update) a catalog:

```
New-FileCatalog -Path <ToWatch> -CatalogFilePath <StateFile>
```

A hash can only be generated for files that are larger than 0 bytes. However, filenames are recorded irrespective of the size.

The following command creates a file catalog from the files and folders created when exploring permissions:

```
New-FileCatalog -Path C:\Temp\ACL -CatalogFilePath
C:\Temp\Security\example.cat
```

If the `CatalogFilePath` had been a directory instead of a file, `New-FileCatalog` would have automatically created a file named `catalog.cat`.

Test-FileCatalog

The `Test-FileCatalog` command compares the content of the catalog file to the filesystem. Hashes are recalculated for each file.

If none of the content has changed, `Test-FileCatalog` will return `Valid`:

```
PS> Test-FileCatalog -Path C:\Temp\ACL -CatalogFilePath
C:\Temp\Security\example.cat
Valid
```

If a file has been added, removed, or changed, the `Test-FileCatalog` command will return `ValidationFailed`.

At this point, the `Detailed` parameter can be used to see which file changed.

Is it faster without Detailed?

 The `Detailed` parameter does not change the amount of work `Test-FileCatalog` must do. If the result is to be used, it might be better to use the `Detailed` parameter right away. This saves the CPU cycles and I/O operations required to list the content of a directory and generate the hashes a second time.

The command does not provide a summary of changes; instead, it returns all files and hashes from the catalog and all files and hashes from the path being tested:

```
PS> Set-Content C:\Temp\ACL\3\3.txt -Value 'New content'
PS> $params = @{
>>      Path = 'C:\Temp\ACL'
>>      CatalogFilePath = 'C:\Temp\Security\example.cat'
>>      Detailed        = $true
>> }
PS> Test-FileCatalog @params
```

```
Status       : ValidationFailed
HashAlgorithm : SHA1
CatalogItems : {[1\1.txt, 3B88969F774811E6A5D634832BE099EDA42B5E72], ...}
PathItems    : {[1\1.txt, 3B88969F774811E6A5D634832BE099EDA42B5E72], ...}
Signature    : System.Management.Automation.Signature
```

These values can be used to find changes. First, assign the result of the command to a variable:

```
$params = @{
    Path            = 'C:\Temp\ACL'
    CatalogFilePath = 'C:\Temp\Security\example.cat'
    Detailed        = $true
}
$result = Test-FileCatalog @params
```

Once done, files that have been added can be listed with the following code:

```
$result.PathItems.Keys | Where-Object { -not
$result.CatalogItems.ContainsKey($_) }
```

Files that have been removed are listed with the following code:

```
$result.CatalogItems.Keys | Where-Object { -not
$result.PathItems.ContainsKey($_) }
```

Files that have been modified are listed with the following code:

```
$result.PathItems.Keys | Where-Object { $result.CatalogItems[$_] -ne
$result.PathItems[$_]}
```

As the file catalog only stores hashes, the command is unable to describe exactly what has changed about a file, only that something has.

Summary

This chapter took a look at working with providers, focusing on filesystem and registry providers. How PowerShell works with items and item properties was demonstrated. Working with permissions in PowerShell for both filesystem and registry providers was also demonstrated. Using transactions with supported providers was demonstrated using the registry provider. Finally, file catalogs were introduced.

Chapter 11, *Windows Management Instrumentation*, will explore how to work with WMI using the CIM commands built into Windows PowerShell and PowerShell Core.

11
Windows Management Instrumentation

Windows Management Instrumentation (WMI) was introduced as a downloadable component with Windows 95 and NT. Windows 2000 had WMI pre-installed, and it has since become a core part of the operating system.

WMI can be used to access a huge amount of information about the computer system. This includes printers, device drivers, user accounts, ODBC, and so on; there are hundreds of classes to explore.

In this chapter, we will be covering the following topics:

- Working with WMI
- CIM cmdlets
- WMI cmdlets
- Permissions

Working with WMI

The scope of WMI is vast, which makes it a fantastic resource for automating processes. WMI classes are not limited to the core operating system; it is not uncommon to find classes created after software or device drivers have been installed.

Given the scope of WMI, finding an appropriate class can be difficult. PowerShell itself is well equipped to explore the available classes.

WMI classes

PowerShell, as a shell for working with objects, presents WMI classes in a very similar manner to .NET classes or any other object. There are a number of parallels between WMI classes and .NET classes.

A WMI class is used as the recipe to create an instance of a WMI object. The WMI class defines properties and methods. The WMI class `Win32_Process` is used to gather information about running processes in a similar manner to the `Get-Process` command.

The `Win32_Process` class has properties such as `ProcessId`, `Name`, and `CommandLine`. It has a terminate method that can be used to kill a process, as well as a create static method that can be used to spawn a new process.

WMI classes reside within a WMI namespace. The default namespace is `root\cimv2`; classes such as `Win32_OperatingSystem` and `Win32_LogicalDisk` reside in this namespace.

WMI commands

PowerShell has two different sets of commands dedicated to working with WMI.

The CIM cmdlets were introduced with PowerShell 3.0. They are compatible with the **Distributed Management Task Force (DMTF)** standard DSP0004. A move towards compliance with open standards is critical as the Microsoft world becomes more diverse.

WMI itself is a proprietary implementation of the CIM server, using the **Distributed Component Object Model (DCOM)** API to communicate between the client and server.

Standards compliance and differences in approach aside, there are solid, practical reasons to consider when choosing which one to use.

Some properties of CIM cmdlets are as follows:

- They are available in both Windows PowerShell and PowerShell Core.
- They handle date conversion natively.
- They have a flexible approach to networking. They use `WSMAN` for remote connections by default, but can be configured to use DCOM over RPC.

Some properties of WMI cmdlets are as follows:

- They are only available in Windows PowerShell, not in PowerShell Core
- They do not automatically convert dates
- They use DCOM over RPC exclusively
- They can be used for all WMI operations
- They have been superseded by the CIM cmdlets

The WMI Query Language

Before diving into the individual commands, it will help to have a grasp of the query language used for **WMI** queries. The query language is useful when querying classes that return multiple values.

The **WMI Query Language** (**WQL**) is used to build queries in WMI for both the CIM and WMI commands.

WQL implements a subset of **Structured Query Language** (**SQL**). The keywords that we will look at are traditionally written in uppercase; however, WMI queries are not case-sensitive.

Both the CIM and WMI cmdlets support `Filter` and `Query` parameters, which accept WQL queries.

Understanding SELECT, WHERE, and FROM

The SELECT, WHERE, and FROM keywords are used with the `Query` parameter.

The generalized syntax for the `Query` parameter is as follows:

```
SELECT <Properties> FROM <WMI Class>
SELECT <Properties> FROM <WMI Class> WHERE <Condition>
```

The wildcard, `*`, may be used to request all available properties or a list of known properties may be requested:

```
Get-CimInstance -Query "SELECT * FROM Win32_Process"
Get-CimInstance -Query "SELECT ProcessID, CommandLine FROM Win32_Process"
```

The WHERE keyword is used to filter results returned by SELECT; for example, see the following:

```
Get-CimInstance -Query "SELECT * FROM Win32_Process WHERE ProcessID=$PID"
```

WQL and arrays
WQL cannot filter array-based properties (for example, the capabilities property of Win32_DiskDrive).

Escape sequences and wildcard characters

The backslash character, \, is used to escape the meaning of characters in a WMI query. This might be used to escape a wildcard character, quotes, or itself. For example, the following WMI query uses a path; each instance of \ in the path must be escaped:

```
Get-CimInstance Win32_Process -Filter
"ExecutablePath='C:\\Windows\\Explorer.exe'"
```

About Win32_Process and the Path property

The Path property is added to the output from the Win32_Process class by PowerShell. While it appears in the output, the property cannot be used to define a filter, nor can Path be selected using the Property parameter of either Get-CimInstance or Get-WmiObject.

Get-Member shows that it is a ScriptProperty as follows:
```
Get-CimInstance Win32_Process -Filter "ProcessId=$pid" |
Get-Member -Name Path
Get-WmiObject Win32_Process -Filter "ProcessId=$pid" |
Get-Member -Name Path
```

WQL defines two wildcard characters that can be used with string queries:

- The % (percentage) character matches any number of characters and is equivalent to using * in a filesystem path or with the -like operator
- The _ (underscore) character matches a single character and is equivalent to using ? in a filesystem path or with the -like operator

The following query filters the results of Win32_Service, including services with paths starting with a single drive letter and ending with .exe:

```
Get-CimInstance Win32_Service -Filter 'PathName LIKE "_:\\%.exe"'
```

Logic operators

Logic operators may be used with the `Filter` and `Query` parameters.

The examples in the following table are based on the following command:

```
Get-CimInstance Win32_Process -Filter "<Filter>"
```

Description	Operator	Syntax	Example
Logical and	AND	`<Condition1> AND` `<Condition2>`	`ProcessID=$pid AND` `Name='powershell.exe'`
Logical or	OR	`<Condition1> OR` `<Condition2>`	`ProcessID=$pid OR ProcessID=0`
Logical not	NOT	`NOT <Condition>`	`NOT ProcessID=$pid`

Comparison operators

Comparison operators may be used with the `Filter` and `Query` parameters.

The examples in the following table are based on the following command:

```
Get-CimInstance Win32_Process -Filter "<Filter>"
```

Description	Operator	Example
Equal to	=	`Name='powershell.exe' AND ProcessId=0`
Not equal to	<>	`Name<>'powershell.exe'`
Greater than	>	`WorkingSetSize>$(100MB)`
Greater than or equal to	>=	`WorkingSetSize>=$(100MB)`
Less than	<	`WorkingSetSize<$(100MB)`
Less than or equal to	<=	`WorkingSetSize<=$(100MB)`
Is	IS	`CommandLine IS NULL` `CommandLine IS NOT NULL`
Like	LIKE	`CommandLine LIKE '%.exe'`

Quoting values

When building a WQL query, string values must be quoted; numeric and Boolean values do not need quotes.

As the filter is also a string, this often means nesting quotes within one another. The following techniques may be used to avoid needing to use PowerShell's escape character.

For filters or queries containing fixed string values, use either of the following styles. Use single quotes outside and double quotes inside:

```
Get-CimInstance Win32_Process -Filter 'Name="powershell.exe"'
```

Alternatively, use double quotes outside and single quotes inside:

```
Get-CimInstance Win32_Process -Filter "Name='powershell.exe'"
```

For filters or queries containing PowerShell variables or sub-expressions, use double quotes outside, as variables within a single-quoted string that will not expand:

```
Get-CimInstance Win32_Process -Filter "ProcessId=$PID"
Get-CimInstance Win32_Process -Filter "ExecutablePath LIKE '$($pshome -
replace '\\', '\\')%'"
```

Regex recap

The regular expression ' \ \ ' represents a single literal ' \ ', as the backslash is normally the escape character. Each ' \ ' in the `pshome` path is replaced with ' \ \ ' to account for WQL using ' \ ' as an escape character as well.

Finally, if a filter contains several conditions, consider using the format operator, as shown in this splatting block:

```
$params = @{
    ClassName = 'Win32_Process'
    Filter    = 'ExecutablePath LIKE "{0}%" AND WorkingSetSize<{1}' -f
        ($env:WINDIR -replace '\\', '\\'),
        100MB
}
Get-CimInstance @params
```

Associated classes

WMI classes often have several different associated or related classes; for example, each instance of Win32_Process has an associated class, CIM_DataFile.

Associations between two classes are expressed by a third class. In the case of Win32_Process and CIM_DataFile, the relationship is expressed by the CIM_ProcessExecutable class.

The relationship is defined by using the antecedent and dependent properties, as shown in the following example:

```
PS> Get-CimInstance CIM_ProcessExecutable |
>>      Where-Object Dependent -match $PID |
>>      Select-Object -First 1


Antecedent              : CIM_DataFile (Name =
"C:\WINDOWS\System32\WindowsPowerShell\v...)
Dependent               : Win32_Process (Handle = "11672")
BaseAddress             : 2340462460928
GlobalProcessCount      :
ModuleInstance          : 4000251904
ProcessCount            : 0
PSComputerName          :
```

This CIM_ProcessExecutable class does not need to be used directly.

WMI object paths

A WMI path is required to find classes associated with an instance. The WMI object path uniquely identifies a specific instance of a WMI class.

The object path is made up of a number of components:

```
<Namespace>:<ClassName>.<KeyName>=<Value>
```

The namespace can be omitted if the class is under the default namespace, root\cimv2.

The KeyName for a given WMI class can be discovered in a number of ways. In the case of Win32_Process, the key name might be discovered by using any of the following methods.

It can be discovered by using the CIM cmdlets:

```
(Get-CimClass Win32_Process).CimClassProperties |
    Where-Object { $_.Flags -band 'Key' }
```

It can be discovered by using the MSDN website, which provides the descriptions of each property (and method) exposed by the class: https://msdn.microsoft.com/en-us/library/aa394372(v=vs.85).aspx.

Having identified a key, only the value remains to be found. In the case of `Win32_Process`, the `key` (handle) has the same value as the process ID. The object path for the `Win32_Process` instance associated with a running PowerShell console is, therefore, the following:

```
root\cimv2:Win32_Process.Handle=$PID
```

The namespace does not need to be included if it uses the default, `root\cimv2`; the object path can be shortened to the following:

```
Win32_Process.Handle=$PID
```

`Get-CimInstance` and `Get-WmiObject` will not retrieve an instance from an object path, but the `Wmi` type accelerator can:

```
PS> [Wmi]"Win32_Process.Handle=$PID" | Select-Object Name, Handle

Name                  Handle
----                  ------
powershell_ise.exe    13020
```

Using ASSOCIATORS OF

The `ASSOCIATORS OF` query may be used for any given object path; for example, using the preceding object path results in the following command:

```
Get-CimInstance -Query "ASSOCIATORS OF {Win32_Process.Handle=$PID}"
```

This query will return objects from three different classes: `Win32_LogonSession`, `Win32_ComputerSystem`, and `CIM_DataFile`. The classes returned are shown in the following example:

```
PS> Get-CimInstance -Query "ASSOCIATORS OF {Win32_Process.Handle=$PID}" |
>>      Select-Object CimClass -Unique

CimClass
--------
root/cimv2:Win32_ComputerSystem
root/cimv2:Win32_LogonSession
root/cimv2:CIM_DataFile
```

The query can be refined to filter a specific resulting class; an example is as follows:

```
Get-CimInstance -Query "ASSOCIATORS OF {Win32_Process.Handle=$PID} WHERE
ResultClass = CIM_DATAFILE"
```

The value in the `ResultClass` condition is deliberately not quoted.

The result of this operation is a long list of files that are used by the PowerShell process. A snippet of this is shown as follows:

```
PS> Get-CimInstance -Query "ASSOCIATORS OF {Win32_Process.Handle=$PID}
WHERE ResultClass = CIM_DATAFILE" |
>>      Select-Object Name

Name
----
c:\windows\system32\windowspowershell\v1.0\powershell_ise.exe
c:\windows\system32\ntdll.dll
c:\windows\system32\mscoree.dll
c:\windows\system32\sysfer.dll
c:\windows\system32\kernel32.dll
```

CIM cmdlets

The **Common Information Model (CIM)** commands are as follows:

- Get-CimAssociatedInstance
- Get-CimClass
- Get-CimInstance
- Get-CimSession
- Invoke-CimMethod
- New-CimInstance
- New-CimSession
- New-CimSessionOption
- Register-CimIndicationEvent
- Remove-CimInstance
- Remove-CimSession
- Set-CimInstance

Each of the CIM cmdlets uses either the `ComputerName` or `CimSession` parameter to target the operation at another computer.

Getting instances

The `Get-CimInstance` command is used to execute queries for instances of WMI objects, an example is as follows:

```
Get-CimInstance -ClassName Win32_OperatingSystem
Get-CimInstance -ClassName Win32_Service
Get-CimInstance -ClassName Win32_Share
```

A number of different parameters are available when using `Get-CimInstance`. The command can be used with a filter, as follows:

```
Get-CimInstance Win32_Directory -Filter "Name='C:\\Windows'"
Get-CimInstance CIM_DataFile -Filter
"Name='C:\\Windows\\System32\\cmd.exe'"
Get-CimInstance Win32_Service -Filter "State='Running'"
```

When returning large amounts of information, the `Property` parameter can be used to reduce the number of fields returned by a query:

```
Get-CimInstance Win32_UserAccount -Property Name, SID
```

The `Query` parameter can also be used, although it is rare to find a use for this that cannot be served by the individual parameters:

```
Get-CimInstance -Query "SELECT * FROM Win32_Process"
Get-CimInstance -Query "SELECT Name, SID FROM Win32_UserAccount"
```

Getting classes

The `Get-CimClass` command is used to return an instance of a WMI class:

```
PS> Get-CimClass Win32_Process

NameSpace: ROOT/cimv2

CimClassName        CimClassMethods            CimClassProperties
-----------         ---------------            ------------------
Win32_Process       {Create, Terminate, Get...}  {Caption, Description,
InstallDate, Name...}
```

The `Class` object describes the capabilities of that class. By default, `Get-CimClass` lists classes from the `root\cimv2` namespace.

The `Namespace` parameter will fill using tab completion; that is, if the following partial command is entered, pressing *Tab* repeatedly will cycle through the possible root namespaces:

```
Get-CimClass -Namespace <tab, tab, tab>
```

The child namespaces of a given namespace are listed in a __Namespace class instance. For example, the following command returns the namespaces under `root`:

```
Get-CimInstance __Namespace -Namespace root
```

Extending this technique, it is possible to recursively query __Namespace to find all of the possible namespace values. Certain WMI namespaces are only available to administrative users (run as administrator); the following function may display errors for some namespaces:

```
function Get-CimNamespace {
    param (
        $Namespace = 'root'
    )
    Get-CimInstance __Namespace -Namespace $Namespace | ForEach-Object {
        $childNamespace = Join-Path $Namespace $_.Name
        $childNamespace

        Get-CimNamespace -Namespace $childNamespace
    }
}
Get-CimNamespace
```

Calling methods

The `Invoke-CimMethod` command may be used to call a method. The CIM class can be used to find details of the methods that a class supports:

```
PS> (Get-CimClass Win32_Process).CimClassMethods

Name ReturnType Parameters Qualifiers
---- ---------- ---------- ----------
Create UInt32 {CommandLine...} {Constructor...}
Terminate UInt32 {Reason} {Destructor...}
GetOwner UInt32 {Domain...} {Implemented...}
GetOwnerSid UInt32 {Sid} {Implemented...}
```

The method with the `Constructor` qualifier can be used to create a new instance of `Win32_Process`.

The `Parameters` property of a specific method can be explored to find out how to use a method:

```
PS> (Get-CimClass Win32_Process).CimClassMethods['Create'].Parameters

Name                           CimType    Qualifiers
----                           -------    ----------
CommandLine                    String     {ID, In, MappingStrings}
CurrentDirectory               String     {ID, In, MappingStrings}
ProcessStartupInformation      Instance   {EmbeddedInstance, ID, In,
MappingStrings}
ProcessId                      UInt32     {ID, MappingStrings, Out}
```

If an argument has the `In` qualifier, it can be passed in when creating an object. If an argument has the `Out` qualifier, it will be returned after the instance has been created. Arguments are passed in using a hashtable.

When creating a process, the `CommandLine` argument is required; the rest can be ignored until later:

```
$params = @{
    ClassName  = 'Win32_Process'
    MethodName = 'Create'
    Arguments  = @{
        CommandLine = 'notepad.exe'
    }
}
$return = Invoke-CimMethod @params
```

The `return` object holds three properties in the case of `Win32_Process`, as follows:

```
PS> $return

ProcessId    ReturnValue    PSComputerName
---------    -----------    --------------
    15172              0
```

`PSComputerName` is blank when the request is local. The `ProcessId` is the `Out` property listed under the method parameters. `ReturnValue` indicates whether or not the operation succeeded, and 0 indicates that it was successful.

A nonzero value indicates that something went wrong, but the values are not translated in PowerShell. The return values are documented on MSDN at https://msdn.microsoft.com/en-us/library/aa389388(v=vs.85).aspx.

The `Create` method used here creates a new instance. The other methods for `Win32_Process` act against an existing instance (an existing process).

Extending the preceding example, a process can be created and then terminated:

```
$params = @{
    ClassName  = 'Win32_Process'
    MethodName = 'Create'
    Arguments  = @{
        CommandLine = 'notepad.exe'
    }
}
$return = Invoke-CimMethod @params

pause

Get-CimInstance Win32_Process -Filter "ProcessID=$($return.ProcessId)" |
    Invoke-CimMethod -MethodName Terminate
```

The pause command will wait for `return` to be pressed before continuing; this gives us the opportunity to show that Notepad was opened before it is terminated.

The `Terminate` method has an optional argument that is used as the exit code for the terminate process. This argument may be added using hashtable; in this case, a (made up) value of 5 is set as the exit code:

```
$invokeParams = @{
    ClassName  = 'Win32_Process'
    MethodName = 'Create'
    Arguments  = @{
        CommandLine = 'notepad.exe'
    }
}
$return = Invoke-CimMethod @invokeParams

$getParams = @{
    ClassName = 'Win32_Process'
    Filter    = 'ProcessId={0}' -f $return.ProcessId
}
Get-CimInstance @getParams |
    Invoke-CimMethod -MethodName Terminate -Arguments @{Reason = 5}
```

`Invoke-CimMethod` returns an object with a `ReturnValue`. A return value of 0 indicates that the command succeeded. A nonzero value indicates an error condition. The meaning of the value will depend on the WMI class.

The return values associated with the `Terminate` method of `Win32_Process` are documented on MSDN at `https://msdn.microsoft.com/en-us/library/aa393907(v=vs.85).aspx`.

Creating instances

The arguments for `Win32_Process`, create include a `ProcessStartupInformation` parameter. `ProcessStartupInformation` is described by a WMI class, `Win32_ProcessStartup`.

There are no existing instances of `Win32_ProcessStartup` (`Get-CimInstance`), and the class does not have a `Create` method (or any other constructor).

`New-CimInstance` can be used to create a class:

```
$class = Get-CimClass Win32_ProcessStartup
$startupInfo = New-CimInstance –CimClass $class –ClientOnly
```

`New-Object` can also be used:

```
$class = Get-CimClass Win32_ProcessStartup
$startupInfo = New-Object CimInstance $class
```

Finally, the `new` method may be used:

```
$class = Get-CimClass Win32_ProcessStartup
$startupInfo = [CimInstance]::new($class)
```

Properties may be set on the created instance; the effect of each property is documented on MSDN at `https://msdn.microsoft.com/en-us/library/aa394375(v=vs.85).aspx`.

In the following example, properties are set to dictate the position and title of a `cmd.exe` window:

```
$class = Get-CimClass Win32_ProcessStartup
$startupInfo = New-CimInstance –CimClass $class –ClientOnly
$startupInfo.X = 50
$startupInfo.Y = 50
$startupInfo.Title = 'This is the window title'

$params = @{
    ClassName   = 'Win32_Process'
    MethodName  = 'Create'
    Arguments   = @{
        CommandLine             = 'cmd.exe'
```

```
            ProcessStartupInformation = $startupInfo
    }
}
$returnObject = Invoke-CimMethod @params
```

Working with CIM sessions

As mentioned earlier in this chapter, a key feature of the CIM cmdlets is their ability to change how connections are formed and used.

The Get-CimInstance command has a ComputerName parameter, and when this is used, the command automatically creates a session to a remote system using WSMAN. The connection is destroyed as soon as the command completes.

While Get-CimInstance supports basic remote connections, it does not provide a means of authenticating a connection, nor can the protocol be changed.

The Get-CimSession, New-CimSession, New-CimSessionOption, and Remove-CimSession commands are optional commands that can be used to define the behavior of remote connections.

The New-CimSession command creates a connection to a remote server an example is as follows:

```
PS> $cimSession = New-CimSession -ComputerName Remote1
PS> $cimSession

Id          : 1
Name        : CimSession1
InstanceId  : 1cc2a889-b649-418c-94a2-f24e033883b4
ComputerName : Remote1
Protocol    : WSMAN
```

Alongside the other parameters, New-CimSession has a Credential parameter that can be used in conjunction with Get-Credential to authenticate a connection.

If the remote system does not, for any reason, present access to WSMAN, it is possible to switch the protocol down to DCOM by using the New-CimSessionOption command:

```
PS> $option = New-CimSessionOption -Protocol DCOM
PS> $cimSession = New-CimSession -ComputerName Remote1 -SessionOption $option
PS> $cimSession

Id          : 2
```

```
Name        : CimSession2
InstanceId  : 62b2cb56-ec84-472c-a992-4bee59ee0618
ComputerName : Remote1
Protocol    : DCOM
```

The New-CimSessionOption command is not limited to protocol switching; it can affect many of the other properties of the connection, as shown in the help and the examples for the command.

Once a session has been created, it exists in the memory until it is removed. The Get-CimSession command shows a list of connections that have been formed, and the Remove-CimSession command permanently removes connections.

Associated classes

The Get-CimAssociatedClass command replaces the use of the ASSOCIATORS OF query type when using the CIM cmdlets.

The following command gets the class instances associated with Win32_NetworkAdapterConfiguration. As the arguments for the Get-CimInstance command are long strings, splatting is used to pass the parameters into the command:

```
$params = @{
    ClassName = 'Win32_NetworkAdapterConfiguration'
    Filter    = 'IPEnabled=TRUE AND DHCPEnabled=TRUE'
}
Get-CimInstance @params | Get-CimAssociatedInstance
```

The following example uses Get-CimAssociatedClass to get the physical interface associated with the IP configuration:

```
$params = @{
    ClassName = 'Win32_NetworkAdapterConfiguration'
    Filter    = 'IPEnabled=TRUE AND DHCPEnabled=TRUE'
}
Get-CimInstance @params | ForEach-Object {
    $adapter = $_ | Get-CimAssociatedInstance -ResultClassName
Win32_NetworkAdapter

    [PSCustomObject]@{
        NetConnectionID = $adapter.NetConnectionID
        Speed           = [Math]::Round($adapter.Speed / 1MB, 2)
        IPAddress       = $_.IPAddress
        IPSubnet        = $_.IPSubnet
        Index           = $_.Index
```

```
    Gateway              = $_.DefaultIPGateway
  }
}
```

The WMI cmdlets

The WMI cmdlets have been superseded by the CIM cmdlets. The WMI cmdlets are not available in PowerShell Core, but the type accelerators are.

The WMI commands are as follows:

- Get-WmiObject
- Invoke-WmiMethod
- Register-WmiEvent
- Remove-WmiObject
- Set-WmiInstance

In addition to the commands, three type accelerators are available:

- [Wmi]: System.Management.ManagementObject
- [WmiClass]: System.Management.ManagementClass
- [WmiSearcher]: System.Management.ManagementObjectSearcher

Each of the WMI cmdlets uses the ComputerName parameter to aim the operation at another computer. The WMI cmdlets also support a credential parameter and other authentication options affecting the authentication method.

Both the Wmi and WmiClass type accelerators can be written to use a remote computer by including the computer name an example is as follows:

```
[Wmi]"\\RemoteComputer\root\cimv2:Win32_Process.Handle=$PID"
[WmiClass]"\\RemoteComputer\root\cimv2:Win32_Process"
```

Getting instances

The `Get-WmiObject` command is used to execute queries for instances of WMI objects an example is as follows:

```
Get-WmiObject -Class Win32_ComputerSystem
```

The type accelerator, `WmiSearcher`, may also be used to execute queries:

```
([WmiSearcher]"SELECT * FROM Win32_Process").Get()
```

Working with dates

The WMI cmdlets do not convert date-time properties found in WMI. Querying the `Win32_Process` class for the creation date of a process returns the date-time property as a long string:

```
PS> Get-WmiObject Win32_Process -Filter "ProcessId=$PID" | Select-Object
Name, CreationDate

Name              CreationDate
----              ------------
powershell_ise.exe 20170209120229.941677+000
```

The .NET namespace used by the WMI cmdlet, `System.Management`, includes a class called `ManagementDateTimeConverter`, dedicated to converting date and time formats found in WMI.

The string in the preceding example may be converted, as follows:

```
Get-WmiObject Win32_Process -Filter "ProcessId=$PID" |
    Select-Object Name, @{Name='CreationDate'; Expression={
[System.Management.ManagementDateTimeConverter]::ToDateTime($_.CreationDate
)
    }}
```

Getting classes

The `Get-WmiObject` command is used to get classes:

```
Get-WmiObject Win32_Process -List
```

The WMI cmdlets are able to recursively list classes in namespaces. The following command lists the classes in root\cimv2 and any child namespaces:

```
Get-WmiObject -List -Recurse
```

In addition to the list parameter, the WmiClass type accelerator can be used:

```
[WmiClass]"Win32_Process"
```

Calling methods

Calling a method on an existing instance of an object found using Get-WmiObject is similar to any .NET method call.

The following example gets and restarts the DNS Client service. The following operation requires administrative access:

```
$service = Get-WmiObject Win32_Service -Filter "DisplayName='DNS Client'"
$service.StopService()     # Call the StopService method
$service.StartService()    # Call the StartService method
```

The WMI class can be used to find the details of a method; for example, the Create method of Win32_Share, as follows:

```
PS> (Get-WmiObject Win32_Share -List).Methods['Create']

Name          : Create
InParameters  : System.Management.ManagementBaseObject
OutParameters : System.Management.ManagementBaseObject
Origin        : Win32_Share
Qualifiers    : {Constructor, Implemented, MappingStrings, Static}
```

Where the Invoke-CimMethod command accepts a hashtable, the Invoke-WmiMethod command expects arguments to be passed as an array, in a specific order. The order can be retrieved by using the GetMethodParameters method of the WMI class:

```
PS> (Get-WmiObject Win32_Share -List).GetMethodParameters('Create')


__GENUS          : 2
__CLASS          : __PARAMETERS
__SUPERCLASS     :
__DYNASTY        : __PARAMETERS
__RELPATH        :
__PROPERTY_COUNT : 7
```

```
__DERIVATION    : {}
__SERVER        :
__NAMESPACE     :
__PATH          :
Access          :
Description     :
MaximumAllowed  :
Name            :
Password        :
Path            :
Type            :
PSComputerName  :
```

To create a share, the argument list must therefore contain an argument for Access, then Description, then MaximumAllowed, and so on. If the argument is optional, it can be set to null; however, PowerShell is unable to say which are mandatory, so a trip to MSDN is required: https://msdn.microsoft.com/en-us/library/aa389393(v=vs.85).aspx.

Having established that Path, Name, and Type are mandatory; an array of arguments can be created in the order described by GetMethodParameters:

```
$argumentList = $null,            # Access
                $null,            # Description
                $null,            # MaximumAllowed
                'Share1',         # Name
                $null,            # Password
                'C:\Temp\Share1', # Path
                0                 # Type (Disk Drive)
Invoke-WmiMethod Win32_Share -Name Create -ArgumentList $argumentList
```

The return value describes the result of the operation; a ReturnValue of 0 indicates success. As this operation requires administrator privileges (run as administrator), a return value of 2 is used to indicate that it was run without sufficient rights.

If the folder used in the previous example does not exist, the ReturnValue will be set to 24.

Adding the ComputerName parameter to Invoke-WmiMethod will create a share on a remote machine.

Arrays of null values are messy

This method of supplying arguments to execute a method is difficult to work with for all but the simplest of methods. An alternative is to use the .NET method InvokeMethod on the class object:

```
$class = Get-WmiObject Win32_Share -List
$inParams = $class.GetMethodParameters('Create')
$inParams.Name = 'Share1'
$inParams.Path = 'C:\Temp\Share1'
$inParams.Type = 0
$return = $class.InvokeMethod('Create', $inParams, $null)
```

The last argument, set to null here, is InvokeMethodOptions, which is most often used to define a timeout for the operation. Doing so is beyond the scope of this chapter.

To create a share on a remote computer, use the ComputerName parameter with Get-WmiObject.

Creating instances

An instance of a WMI class can be created using the CreateInstance method of the class. The following example creates an instance of Win32_Trustee:

```
(Get-WmiObject Win32_Trustee -List).CreateInstance()
```

Associated classes

Objects returned by Get-WmiObject have a GetRelated method that can be used to find associated instances.

The GetRelated method accepts arguments that can be used to filter the results. The first argument, relatedClass, is used to limit the instances returned to specific classes, as shown here:

```
Get-WmiObject Win32_LogonSession | ForEach-Object {
    [PSCustomObject]@{
        LogonName      = $_.GetRelated('Win32_Account').Caption
        SessionStarted =
[System.Management.ManagementDateTimeConverter]::ToDateTime($_.StartTime)
```

```
      }
   }
```

Permissions

Working with permissions in WMI is more difficult than in .NET as the values in use are not given friendly names. However, the .NET classes can still be used, even if not quite as intended.

The following working examples demonstrate configuring the permissions.

Sharing permissions

Get-Acl and Set-Acl are fantastic tools for working with filesystem permissions, or permissions under other providers. However, these commands cannot be used to affect sharing permissions.

The SmbShare **module**

The SmbShare module has commands that affect share permissions. This example uses the older WMI classes to modify permissions. It might be used if the SmbShare module cannot be.

The Get-SmbShareAccess command might be used to verify the outcome of this example.

The following operations require administrative privileges; run ISE or PowerShell as an administrator if attempting to use the examples.

Creating a shared directory

The following snippet creates a directory and shares that directory:

```
$path = 'C:\Temp\WmiPermissions'
New-Item $path -ItemType Directory

$params = @{
    ClassName = 'Win32_Share'
    MethodName = 'Create'
    Arguments = @{
        Name = 'WmiPerms'
```

```
        Path = $path
        Type = [UInt32]0
    }
}
Invoke-CimMethod @params
```

The `Create` method used here will fail if the argument for `Type` is not correctly defined as a `UInt32` value. PowerShell will otherwise use `Int32` for a value of `0`.

The requirement for `UInt32`, in this case, may be viewed by exploring the parameters required for the method:

```
PS> (Get-CimClass Win32_Share).CimClassMethods['Create'].Parameters |
Where-Object Name -eq Type

Name CimType Qualifiers ReferenceClassName
---- ------- ---------- ------------------
Type UInt32 {ID, In, MappingStrings}
```

Getting a security descriptor

When `Get-Acl` is used, the object that it gets is a security descriptor. The security descriptor includes a set of control information (ownership, and so on), along with the discretionary and system access control lists.

The WMI class `Win32_LogicalShareSecuritySetting` is used to represent the security for each of the shares on a computer:

```
$security = Get-CimInstance Win32_LogicalShareSecuritySetting -Filter
"Name='WmiPerms'"
```

The security settings object can be used to retrieve a security descriptor by calling the `GetSecurityDescriptor` method:

```
$return = $security | Invoke-CimMethod -MethodName GetSecurityDescriptor
$aclObject = $return.Descriptor
```

The security descriptor held in the `aclObject` variable is very different from the result returned by `Get-Acl`:

```
PS> $aclObject

ControlFlags   : 32772
DACL           : {Win32_ACE}
Group          :
Owner          :
```

```
SACL          :
TIME_CREATED  :
PSComputerName :
```

The DACL, or discretionary access control list, is used to describe the permission levels for each security principal (a user, group, or computer account). Each entry in this list is an instance of Win32_ACE:

```
PS> $aclObject.DACL

AccessMask                : 1179817
AceFlags                  : 0
AceType                   : 0
GuidInheritedObjectType   :
GuidObjectType            :
TIME_CREATED              :
Trustee                   : Win32_Trustee
PSComputerName            :
```

The Win32_ACE object has a Trustee property that holds the Name, Domain, and SID of the security principal (in this case, the Everyone principal):

```
PS> $aclObject.DACL.Trustee

Domain :
Name : Everyone
SID : {1, 1, 0, 0...}
SidLength : 12
SIDString : S-1-1-0
TIME_CREATED :
PSComputerName :
```

AceFlags describes how an ACE is to be inherited. As this is a share, the AceFlags property will always be 0. Nothing can, or will, inherit this entry; .NET can be used to confirm this:

```
PS> [System.Security.AccessControl.AceFlags]0
None
```

The AceType is either AccessAllowed (0) or AccessDenied (1). Again, .NET can be used to confirm this:

```
PS> [System.Security.AccessControl.AceType]0
AccessAllowed
```

Finally, the `AccessMask` property can be converted into a meaningful value with .NET, as well. The access rights that can be granted on a share are a subset of those that might be assigned to a file or directory:

```
PS> [System.Security.AccessControl.FileSystemRights]1179817
ReadAndExecute, Synchronize
```

Putting this together, the entries in a shared `DACL` can be made much easier to understand:

```
using namespace System.Security.AccessControl

$aclObject.DACL | ForEach-Object {
    [PSCustomObject]@{
        Rights   = [FileSystemRights]$_.AccessMask
        Type     = [AceType]$_.AceType
        Flags    = [AceFlags]$_.AceFlags
        Identity = $_.Trustee.Name
    }
}
```

In the preceding example, the domain of the trustee is ignored. If this is something other than `Everyone`, it should be included.

Adding an access control entry

To add an **access control entry (ACE)** to this existing list, an entry must be created. Creating an ACE requires a `Win32_Trustee`. The following `trustee` is created from the current user:

```
$trustee = New-CimInstance (Get-CimClass Win32_Trustee) -ClientOnly
$trustee.Domain = $env:USERDOMAIN
$trustee.Name = $env:USERNAME
```

The `SID` does not need to be set on the `trustee` object, but if the security principal is invalid, the attempt to apply the change to security will fail.

Then, the `Win32_ACE` can be created. The following ACE grants full control of the share to the `trustee`:

```
$ace = New-CimInstance (Get-CimClass Win32_ACE) -ClientOnly
$ace.AccessMask = [UInt32][FileSystemRights]'FullControl'
$ace.AceType = [UInt32][AceType]'AccessAllowed'
$ace.AceFlags = [UInt32]0
$ace.Trustee = $trustee
```

The ACE is added to the DACL by using the += operator:

```
$aclObject.DACL += $ace
```

Setting the security descriptor

Once the ACL has been changed, the modified security descriptor must be set. The instance returned by Win32_LogicalShareSecuritySetting contains a SetSecurityDescriptor method:

```
$security | Invoke-CimMethod -MethodName SetSecurityDescriptor -Arguments
@{
    Descriptor = $aclObject
}
```

WMI permissions

Getting and setting WMI security in PowerShell uses the same approach as share security. WMI permissions might be set using wmimgmt.msc if the GUI is used. The content of the DACL differs slightly.

The __SystemSecurity class is used to access the security descriptor. Each WMI namespace has its own instance of the __SystemSecurity class; an example is as follows:

```
Get-CimClass __SystemSecurity -Namespace root
Get-CimClass __SystemSecurity -Namespace root\cimv2
```

Getting a security descriptor

The security descriptor for a given namespace can be retrieved from the __SystemSecurity class. By default, administrator privileges are required to get the security descriptor:

```
$security = Get-CimInstance __SystemSecurity -Namespace root\cimv2
$return = $security | Invoke-CimMethod -MethodName GetSecurityDescriptor
$aclObject = $return.Descriptor
```

The access mask

The values of the access mask in the DACL are documented on MSDN: https://msdn.microsoft.com/en-us/library/aa392710(v=vs.85).aspx.

The standard access rights `ReadSecurity` and `WriteSecurity` are also relevant. The access mask is a composite of the values listed here:

- `EnableAccount`: 1
- `ExecuteMethods`: 2
- `FullWrite`: 4
- `PartialWrite`: 8
- `WriteProvider`: 16
- `RemoteEnable`: 32
- `ReadSecurity`: 131072
- `WriteSecurity`: 262144

WMI and SDDL

Security descriptor definition language (SDDL) is used to describe the content of a security descriptor as a string.

A security descriptor returned by `Get-Acl` has a method that can convert the entire security descriptor to a string, as follows:

```
PS> (Get-Acl C:\).GetSecurityDescriptorSddlForm('All')
O:S-1-5-80-956008885-3418522649-1831038044-1853292631-2271478464G:S-1-5-80-
956008885-3418522649-1831038044-1853292631-2271478464D:PAI(A;;LC;;;AU)(A;OI
CIIO;SDGXGWGR;;;AU)(A;;FA;
;;SY)(A;OICIIO;GA;;;SY)(A;OICIIO;GA;;;BA)(A;;FA;;;BA)(A;OICI;0x1200a9;;;BU)
```

A security descriptor defined using `SDDL` can also be imported. If the `sddlString` variable is assumed to hold a valid security descriptor, the following command might be used:

```
$acl = Get-Acl C:\
$acl.SetSecurityDescriptorSddlForm($sddlString)
```

The imported security descriptor will not apply to the directory until `Set-Acl` is used.

WMI security descriptors can be converted to and from different formats, including `SDDL`. WMI has a specialized class for this: `Win32_SecurityDescriptorHelper`. The methods for the class are shown here:

```
PS> (Get-CimClass Win32_SecurityDescriptorHelper).CimClassMethods
```

Name	ReturnType	Parameters	Qualifiers

Win32SDToSDDL static}	UInt32	{Descriptor, SDDL}	{implemented,
Win32SDToBinarySD static}	UInt32	{Descriptor, BinarySD}	{implemented,
SDDLToWin32SD static}	UInt32	{SDDL, Descriptor}	{implemented,
SDDLToBinarySD static}	UInt32	{SDDL, BinarySD}	{implemented,
BinarySDToWin32SD static}	UInt32	{BinarySD, Descriptor}	{implemented,
BinarySDToSDDL static}	UInt32	{BinarySD, SDDL}	{implemented,

A WMI security descriptor might be converted to SDDL to create a backup before making a change, as follows:

```
$security = Get-CimInstance __SystemSecurity -Namespace root\cimv2
$return = $security | Invoke-CimMethod -MethodName GetSecurityDescriptor
$aclObject = $return.Descriptor

$params = @{
    ClassName = 'Win32_SecurityDescriptorHelper'
    MethodName = 'Win32SDToSDDL'
    Arguments  = @{
        Descriptor = $aclObject
    }
}
$return = Invoke-CimMethod @params
```

If the operation succeeds (that is, if the ReturnValue is 0), the security descriptor in the SDDL form will be available:

```
PS> $return.SDDL
O:BAG:BAD:AR(A;CI;CCDCWP;;;S-1-5-21-2114566378-1333126016-908539190-1001)(A
;CI;CCDCLCSWRPWPRCWD;;;BA)(A;CI;CCDCRP;;;NS)(A;CI;CCDCRP;;;LS)(A;CI;CCDCRP;
;;AU)
```

A security descriptor expressed as an SDDL string can be imported:

```
$params = @{
    ClassName = 'Win32_SecurityDescriptorHelper'
    MethodName = 'SDDLToWin32SD'
    Arguments  = @{
        SDDL =
'O:BAG:BAD:AR(A;CI;CCDCWP;;;S-1-5-21-2114566378-1333126016-908539190-1001)(
A;CI;CCDCLCSWRPWPRCWD;;;BA)(A;CI;CCDCRP;;;NS)(A;CI;CCDCRP;;;LS)(A;CI;CCDCRP
;;;AU)'
    }
```

```
}
$return = Invoke-CimMethod @params
$aclObject = $return.Descriptor
```

If the `ReturnValue` is 0, the `aclObject` variable will contain the imported security descriptor:

```
PS> $aclObject

ControlFlags    : 33028
DACL            : {Win32_ACE, Win32_ACE, Win32_ACE, Win32_ACE...}
Group           : Win32_Trustee
Owner           : Win32_Trustee
SACL            :
TIME_CREATED    :
PSComputerName  :
```

Summary

In this chapter, we explored working with WMI classes, the different commands that are available, and the WMI query language. Both the CIM and WMI cmdlets were explored as a means of working with WMI. We explored getting and setting permissions with WMI, using shared security and WMI security as examples.

Chapter 12, *HTML, XML, and JSON*, will explore working with generating and consuming data from a variety of different text-based formats.

HTML, XML, and JSON 12

PowerShell has a number of commands for working with HTML, XML, and **JavaScript Object Notation (JSON)**. These commands, combined with some of the available .NET classes, provide a rich set of tools for creating or modifying these formats.

In this chapter, the following topics will be covered:

- HTML
- XML
- System.Xml
- System.Xml.Linq
- JSON

HTML

HTML is frequently used in PowerShell as a means of generating reports by email. PowerShell includes ConvertTo-Html, which may be used to generate HTML content.

ConvertTo-Html

ConvertTo-Html generates an HTML document with a table based on an input object. The following example generates a table based on the output from Get-Process:

```
Get-Process | ConvertTo-Html -Property Name, Id, WorkingSet
```

Multiple tables

`ConvertTo-Html` may be used to build more complex documents by using the `Fragment` parameter. The `Fragment` parameter generates an HTML table only (instead of a full document). Tables may be combined to create a larger document:

```
# Create the body
$body = '<h1>Services</h1>'
$body += Get-Service |
    Where-Object Status -eq 'Running' |
    ConvertTo-Html -Property Name, DisplayName -Fragment
$body += '<h1>Processes</h1>'
$body += Get-Process |
    Where-Object WorkingSet -gt 50MB |
    ConvertTo-Html -Property Name, Id, WorkingSet-Fragment
# Create a document with the merged body
ConvertTo-Html -Body $body -Title Report | Set-Content report.html
```

Adding style

HTML content can be enhanced by adding a **Cascading Style Sheet** (CSS) fragment. When CSS is embedded in an HTML document, it is added between style tags in the head element.

The following style uses CSS to change the font, color the table headers, define the table borders, and justify the table content:

```
$css = @'
<style>
    body { font-family: Arial; }
    table {
        width: 100%;
        border-collapse: collapse;
    }
    table, th, td {
        border: 1px solid Black;
        padding: 5px;
    }
    th {
        text-align: left;
        background-color: LightBlue;
    }
    tr:nth-child(even) {
        background-color: GainsBoro;
    }
```

```
    </style>
    '@
```

The Head parameter of ConvertTo-Html is used to add the element to the document:

```
Get-Process |
    ConvertTo-Html -Property Name, Id, WorkingSet -Head $css |
    Set-Content report.html
```

The CSS language is complex and very capable. The elements that are used in the preceding code, and many more, are documented with examples on the W3schools website: https://www.w3schools.com/css/.

Different browsers support different parts of the CSS language, and email clients tend to support a smaller set still. Testing in the expected client is an important part of developing content.

ConvertTo-Html and Send-MailMessage

ConvertTo-Html outputs an array of strings, while Send-MailMessage will only accept a body as a string. Attempting to use the output from ConvertTo-Html with Send-MailMessage directly will raise an error.

The Out-String command may be added to ensure the output from ConvertTo-Html is a string:

```
$messageBody = Get-Process |
    ConvertTo-Html Name, Id, WorkingSet -Head $css |
    Out-String
```

HTML and special characters

HTML defines a number of special characters; for example, a literal ampersand (&) in HTML must be written as &.

ConvertTo-Html will handle the conversion of special characters in input objects, but it will not work with special characters in raw HTML that are added using the Body, Head, PreContent, or PostContent parameters.

The Sytem.Web.HttpUtility class includes methods that are able to convert strings containing such characters.

Before `System.Web.HttpUtility` can be used, the assembly must be added:

```
Add-Type -AssemblyName System.Web
```

The `HtmlEncode` static method will take a string and replace any reserved characters with HTML code. For example, the following snippet will replace > with `&gt;`:

```
PS>'<h1>{0}</h1>' -f [System.Web.HttpUtility]::HtmlEncode('Files > 100MB')
<h1>Files &gt; 100MB</h1>
```

The `HtmlDecode` static method can be used to reverse the process:

```
PS> [System.Web.HttpUtility]::HtmlDecode("<h1>Files &gt; 100MB</h1>")
<h1>Files > 100MB</h1>
```

XML

Extensible Markup Language (XML) is a plain text format that's used to store structured data. XML is written to be both human and machine readable.

XML documents often begin with a declaration, as shown here:

```
<?xml version="1.0"?>
```

This declaration has three possible attributes. The version attribute is mandatory when a declaration is included:

- `version`: The XML version, 1.0 or 1.1
- `encoding`: The file encoding, most frequently `utf-8` or `utf-16`
- `standalone`: Whether or not the XML file uses an internal or external **Document Type Definition (DTD)**; permissible values are yes or no

Elements and attributes

XML is similar in appearance to HTML. Elements begin and end with a tag name. The tag name describes the name of an element, for example:

```
<?xml version="1.0"?>
<rootElement>value</rootElement>
```

An XML document can only have one root element, but an element may have many descendants:

```
<?xml version="1.0"?>
<rootElement>
    <firstChild>1</firstChild>
    <secondChild>2</secondChild>
</rootElement>
```

An element may also have attributes. The rootElement element in the following example has an attribute named `attr`:

```
<?xml version="1.0"?>
<rootElement attr="value">
    <child>1</child>
</rootElement>
```

Namespaces

XML documents can use one or more namespaces, which can be used to provide uniquely named elements within a document.

XML namespaces are declared in an attribute with a name prefixed by `xmlns:`, for example:

```
<?xml version="1.0"?>
<rootElement xmlns:item="http://namespaces/item">
    <item:child>1</item:child>
</rootElement>
```

The XML namespace uses a URL as a unique identifier. The identifier is often used to describe an element as belonging to a schema.

Schemas

An XML schema can be used to describe and constrain the elements, attributes, and values within an XML document.

About DTD

A document type definition, or DTD, may be used to constrain the content of an XML file. As a DTD has little bearing on the use of XML in PowerShell, it is considered beyond the scope of this book.

XML schema definitions are saved with an XSD extension. Schema files can be used to validate the content of an XML file.

The following is a simple schema that validates the item namespace:

```
<?xml version="1.0"?>
<xs:schema xmlns:xs="http://www.w3.org/2001/XMLSchema"
        targetNamespace="http://namespaces/item"
        xmlns="https://www.w3schools.com"
        elementFormDefault="qualified">
   <xs:element name="rootElement">
      <xs:element name="child" type="xs:string" />
   </xs:element>
</xs:schema>
```

System.Xml

PowerShell primarily uses the `System.Xml.XmlDocument` type to work with XML content. A number of commands are available to work with XML documents based on this type.

ConvertTo-Xml

The `ConvertTo-XML` command creates an XML representation of an object as an `XmlDocument`. For example, the current PowerShell process object might be converted into XML:

```
Get-Process -Id $pid | ConvertTo-Xml
```

XML is text

The command that we used in the previous code creates an XML representation of the object. All numeric values are stored as strings. The following example shows that the `WorkingSet` property, normally an integer, is held as a string:

```
$xml = Get-Process -Id $pid | ConvertTo-Xml
$property = $xml.Objects.Object.Property | Where-Object
Name -eq WorkingSet
$property.'#text'.GetType()
```

XML type accelerator

The XML type accelerator (`[Xml]`) can be used to create instances of `XmlDocument`, as shown in the following code:

```
[Xml]$xml = @"
<?xml version="1.0"?>
<cars>
    <car type="Saloon">
        <colour>Green</colour>
        <doors>4</doors>
        <transmission>Automatic</transmission>
        <engine>
            <size>2.0</size>
            <cylinders>4</cylinders>
        </engine>
    </car>
</cars>
"@
```

Elements and attributes of an `XmlDocument` object may be accessed as if they were properties. This is a feature of the PowerShell language rather than the .NET object:

```
PS> $xml.cars.car

type         : Saloon
colour       : Green
doors        : 4
transmission : Automatic
engine       : engine
```

If the document contains more than one car element, each of the instances will be returned.

XPath and Select-Xml

`XPath` can be used to navigate or search an XML document. PowerShell (and .NET) uses `XPath 1.0`.

 The structure and format of `XPath` queries are beyond the scope of this chapter. However, a number of web resources are available, including `https://msdn.microsoft.com/en-us/library/ms256115(v=vs.110).aspx`.

Terms and values used in XPath queries, and XML in general, are case-sensitive.

Given the following XML snippet, Select-Xml might use an XPath expression to select the engines of green cars:

```
$string = @"
<?xml version="1.0"?>
<cars>
    <car type="Saloon">
        <colour>Green</colour>
        <doors>4</doors>
        <transmission>Automatic</transmission>
        <engine>
            <size>2.0</size>
            <cylinders>4</cylinders>
        </engine>
    </car>
</cars>
"@
```

The -XPath expression and the result are shown here:

```
PS> Select-Xml -XPath '//car[colour="Green"]/engine' -Content $string |
    Select-Object -ExpandProperty Node

size    cylinders
----    ---------
2.0     4
```

A similar result can be achieved using the SelectNodes method of an XML document:

```
([Xml]$string).SelectNodes('//car[colour="Green"]/engine')
```

Select-Xml has an advantage, in that it can be used to work against files directly using the Path parameter:

SelectNodes **and** XPathNodeList

If the SelectNodes method is called, and there are no results, an empty XPathNodeList object is returned. The following condition is flawed:

```
$nodes = $xml.SelectNodes('//car[colour="Blue"]')
if ($nodes) {
    Write-Host "A blue car record exists"
}
```

In this case, using the Count property is a better approach:

```
if ($nodes.Count -gt 1) {
    Write-Host "A blue car record exists"
}
```

If the search is only concerned with the first matching entry, or the search always returns a unique result, the SelectSingleNode method can be used instead.

Working with namespaces

If an XML document includes a namespace, then queries for elements within the document are more difficult. Not only must the namespace tag be included, but XmlNamespaceManager **must be defined.**

`Select-Xml` builds a namespace manager based on the content of a hashtable when the `Namespace` parameter is used:

```
[Xml]$xml = @"
<?xml version="1.0"?>
<cars xmlns:c="http://example/cars">
    <car type="Saloon">
        <c:colour>Green</c:colour>
        <c:doors>4</c:doors>
        <c:transmission>Automatic</c:transmission>
        <c:engine>
            <size>2.0</size>
            <cylinders>4</cylinders>
        </c:engine>
    </car>
</cars>
"@
Select-Xml '//car/c:engine' -Namespace @{c='http://example/cars'} -Xml $xml
```

If the `SelectNodes` method is being used, `XmlNamespaceManager` must be built first and passed as an argument:

```
$namespaceManager = New-Object
System.Xml.XmlNamespaceManager($xml.NameTable)
$namespaceManager.AddNamespace('c', 'http://example/cars')
$xml.SelectNodes(
    '//car[c:colour="Green"]/c:engine',
    $namespaceManager
)
```

XML documents, such as group policy reports, are difficult to work with as they often contain many different namespaces. Each of the possible namespaces must be added to a namespace manager.

Creating documents

PowerShell can be used to create XML documents from scratch. One possible way to do this is by using the `XmlWriter` class:

```
$writer = [System.Xml.XmlWriter]::Create("$pwd\newfile.xml")
$writer.WriteStartDocument()
$writer.WriteStartElement('cars')
$writer.WriteStartElement('car')
$writer.WriteAttributeString('type', 'Saloon')
$writer.WriteElementString('colour', 'Green')
$writer.WriteEndElement()
$writer.WriteEndElement()
$writer.Flush()
$writer.Close()
```

Elements opened by `WriteStartElement` must be closed to maintain a consistent document.

The `XmlWriter` class is a buffered writer. The `Flush` method is called at the end to push the content of the buffer back to the file.

The format of generated XML can be changed by supplying an `XmlWriterSettings` object when calling the `Create` method. For example, it might be desirable to write line breaks and indent elements, as shown in the following example:

```
$writerSettings = New-Object System.Xml.XmlWriterSettings
$writerSettings.Indent = $true
$writer = [System.Xml.XmlWriter]::Create(
    "$pwd\newfile.xml",
    $writerSettings
)
$writer.WriteStartDocument()
$writer.WriteStartElement('cars')
$writer.WriteStartElement('car')
$writer.WriteAttributeString('type', 'Saloon')
$writer.WriteElementString('colour', 'Green')
$writer.WriteEndElement()
$writer.WriteEndElement()
$writer.Flush()
$writer.Close()
```

Modifying element and attribute values

Existing elements in an XML document can be modified by assigning a new value. For example, the misspelling of `Appliances` could be corrected:

```
[Xml]$xml = @"
<?xml version="1.0"?>
<items>
    <item name='Fridge'>
        <category>Appliancse</category>
    </item>
    <item name='Cooker'>
        <category>Appliances</category>
    </item>
</items>
"@
($xml.items.item | Where-Object name -eq 'Fridge').category = 'Appliances'
```

Attributes may be changed in the same way; the interface does not distinguish between the two value types.

A direct assignment of a new value cannot be used if the XML document contains more than one element or attribute with the same name (at the same level). For example, the following XML snippet has two values with the same name:

```
[Xml]$xml = @"
<?xml version="1.0"?>
<list>
    <name>one</name>
    <name>two</name>
</list>
"@
```

The first value may be changed if it is uniquely identified and selected:

```
$xml.list.SelectSingleNode('./name[.="one"]').'#text' = 'three'
```

The following example shows a similar change being made to the value of an attribute:

```
[Xml]$xml = @"
<?xml version="1.0"?>
<list name='letters'>
<name>1</name>
</list>
"@
$xml.SelectSingleNode('/list[@name="letters"]').SetAttribute('name',
'numbers')
```

The @ symbol preceding `name` in the `XPath` expression denotes that the value type is an attribute. If the attribute referred to by the `SetAttribute` method does not exist, it will be created.

Adding elements

Elements must be created before they can be added to an existing document. Elements are created in the context of a document:

```
[Xml]$xml = @"
<?xml version="1.0"?>
<list type='numbers'>
    <name>1</name>
</list>
"@
$newElement = $xml.CreateElement('name')
$newElement.InnerText = 2
$xml.list.AppendChild($newElement)
```

Complex elements may be built up by repeatedly using the `Create` method of the `XmlDocument` (held in the `$xml` variable).

If the new node is substantial, it may be easier to treat the new node set as a separate document and merge one into the other.

Copying nodes between documents

Nodes (elements, attributes, and so on) may be copied and moved between different XML documents. To bring a node from an external document into another, it must first be imported.

The following example creates two simple XML documents. The first (the `xml` variable) is the intended destination. The `newNodes` variable contains a set of elements that should be copied:

```
[Xml]$xml = @"
<?xml version="1.0"?>
<list type='numbers'>
    <name>1</name>
</list>
"@
[Xml]$newNodes = @"
<root>
```

```
        <name>2</name>
        <name>3</name>
        <name>4</name>
</root>
"@
```

Copying the name nodes requires each node to be selected in turn, imported into the original document, and added to the desired node:

```
foreach ($node in $newNodes.SelectNodes('/root/name')) {
    $newNode = $xml.ImportNode($node, $true)
    $null = $xml.list.AppendChild($newNode)
}
```

The ImportNode method requires two parameters: the node from the foreign document (newNodes) and whether or not the import is deep (one level or fully recursive).

The resulting XML can be viewed by inspecting the OuterXml property of the xml variable:

```
PS> $xml.OuterXml
<?xml version="1.0"?><list
type="numbers"><name>1</name><name>2</name><name>3</name><name>4</name></li
st>
```

Removing elements and attributes

Elements may be removed from a document by selecting the node, then calling the RemoveChild method on the parent:

```
[Xml]$xml = @"
<?xml version="1.0"?>
<list type='numbers'>
    <name>1</name>
    <name>2</name>
    <name>3</name>
</list>
"@
$node = $xml.SelectSingleNode('/list/*[.="3"]')
$null = $node.ParentNode.RemoveChild($node)
```

The RemoveAll method is also available; however, this removes all children (and attributes) of the selected node.

Attributes are also easy to remove from a document:

```
$xml.list.RemoveAttribute('type')
```

Schema validation

XML documents that reference a schema can be validated.

.NET Core and schema validation

.NET Core appears to be unwilling to expand include references in an XML schema. This apparent bug is exhibited in PowerShell Core. Windows PowerShell will produce schema validation errors; PowerShell Core will not at this time.

Windows PowerShell comes with a number of XML files with associated schema in the help files. For example, the help file for ISE is available:

```
PS> Get-Item C:\Windows\System32\WindowsPowerShell\v1.0\modules\ISE\en-US\ISE-help.xml


    Directory: C:\Windows\System32\WindowsPowerShell\v1.0\modules\ISE\en-US


Mode                LastWriteTime         Length Name
----                -------------         ------ ----
-a----        29/11/16     07:57          33969 ISE-help.xml
```

The schema documents used by the help content are saved in C:\Windows\System32\WindowsPowerShell\v1.0\Schemas\PSMaml.

The following snippet may be used to load the schema files and then test the content of the document:

```
$path = 'C:\Windows\System32\WindowsPowerShell\v1.0\modules\ISE\en-US\ISE-help.xml'

$document = [Xml]::new()
$document.Load($path)

# Add the schema to the XmlDocument
$document.Schemas.Add(
    'http://schemas.microsoft.com/maml/2004/10',
    'C:\Windows\System32\WindowsPowerShell\v1.0\Schemas\PSMaml\maml.xsd'
)

# Validate the document
$ErrorsAndWarnings = [System.Collections.Generic.List[String]]::new()
$document.Validate({
    param ($sender, $eventArgs)
```

```
    if ($eventArgs.Severity -in 'Error', 'Warning') {
        $Global:ErrorsAndWarnings.Add($eventArgs.Message)
    }
})
```

The argument for `Validate` is a script block that is executed each time an error is encountered. `Write-Host` is used to print a message to the console. A value cannot be directly returned as the script block is executed in the background.

Line number and line position information is not available using this technique for a number of reasons. The `XmlDocument` object is built from a string (returned by `Get-Content`) and not attached to the file.

System.Xml.Linq

The `System.Xml.Linq` namespace was added with .NET 3.5. This is known as LINQ to XML. **Language Integrated Query** (**LINQ**) is used to describe a query in the same language as the rest of a program. Therefore, interacting with a complex XML document does not require the use of `XPath` queries.

`System.Xml.Linq` is loaded by default in PowerShell Core. Windows PowerShell can make use of `System.Xml.Linq` once the required assembly has been added:

```
Add-Type -AssemblyName System.Xml.Linq
```

This can also be phrased as follows:

```
using assembly System.Xml.Linq
```

As a newer interface, `System.Xml.Linq` tends to be more consistent. The same syntax is used to create a document from scratch that is used to add elements and so on.

Opening documents

The `XDocument` class is used to load or parse a document. XML content may be cast to an `XDocument` in the same way that content is cast using the `[Xml]` type accelerator:

```
[System.Xml.Linq.XDocument]$xDocument = @"
<?xml version="1.0"?>
<cars>
    <car type="Saloon">
        <colour>Green</colour>
```

```
            <doors>4</doors>
            <transmission>Automatic</transmission>
            <engine>
                <size>2.0</size>
                <cylinders>4</cylinders>
            </engine>
        </car>
    </cars>
"@
$xDocument.Save("$pwd\cars.xml")
```

If the content has been saved to a file, the Load method may be used with a filename:

```
$xDocument = [System.Xml.Linq.XDocument]::Load("$pwd\cars.xml")
```

Selecting nodes

LINQ to XML uses PowerShell to query the content of XML files. This is achieved by combining the methods that are made available through an XDocument (or XContainer or XElement). Methods are available to find attributes and elements, either as immediate children or deeper within a document:

```
$xDocument = [System.Xml.Linq.XDocument]::Load("$pwd\cars.xml")
$xDocument.Descendants('car').
    Where( { $_.Element('colour').Value -eq 'Green' } ).
    Element('engine')
```

The XML-specific methods are supplemented by .Linq extension methods, such as the Where method, to filter content.

As the query a script block encapsulated by the Where method—is native PowerShell, the comparison operation (-eq) is case insensitive. The selection of the element by name is case-sensitive.

Although it is not the preferred approach, XPath can still be used by calling the XPathSelectElements static method, as shown here:

```
[System.Xml.XPath.Extensions]::XPathSelectElements(
    $xDocument,
    '//car[colour="Green"]/engine'
)
```

Creating documents

`System.Xml.Linq` can be used to create a document from scratch, for example:

```
using namespace System.Xml.Linq

$xDocument = [XDocument]::new(
    [XDeclaration]::new('1.0', 'utf-8', 'yes'),
    [XElement]::new('list', @(
        [XAttribute]::new('type', 'numbers'),
        [XElement]::new('name', 1),
        [XElement]::new('name', 2),
        [XElement]::new('name', 3)
    ))
)
```

Converting the xDocument object into a string shows the document without the declaration:

```
PS> $xDocument.ToString()

<list type="numbers">
    <name>1</name>
    <name>2</name>
    <name>3</name>
</list>
```

The Save method may be used to write the document to a file:

```
$xDocument.Save("$pwd\test.xml")
```

Reviewing the document shows the declaration:

```
PS> Get-Content test.xml
<?xml version="1.0" encoding="utf-8" standalone="yes"?>
<list type="numbers">
    <name>1</name>
    <name>2</name>
    <name>3</name>
</list>
```

Working with namespaces

LINQ to XML handles the specification of namespaces by adding an XNamespace object to an XName object, for example:

```
PS> [XNameSpace]'http://example/cars' + [XName]'engine'
```

LocalName	Namespace	NamespaceName
engine	http://example/cars	http://example/cars

As XNamespace expects to have an XName added to it, casting to that type can be skipped, simplifying the expression:

```
[XNamespace]'http://example/cars' + 'engine'
```

A query for an element in a specific namespace will use the following format:

```
using namespace System.Xml.Linq

[XDocument]$xDocument = @"
<?xml version="1.0"?>
<cars xmlns:c="http://example/cars">
    <car type="Saloon">
        <c:colour>Green</c:colour>
        <c:doors>4</c:doors>
        <c:transmission>Automatic</c:transmission>
        <c:engine>
            <size>2.0</size>
            <cylinders>4</cylinders>
        </c:engine>
    </car>
</cars>
"@

$xNScars = [XNameSpace]'http://example/cars'
$xDocument.Descendants('car').ForEach( {
    $_.Element($xNScars + 'engine')
} )
```

Modifying element and attribute values

Modifying an existing node, whether it is an attribute or an element value, can be done by assigning a new value:

```
[XDocument]$xDocument = @"
<?xml version="1.0"?>
<items>
    <item name='Fridge'>
        <category>Appliancse</category>
    </item>
    <item name='Cooker'>
        <category>Appliances</category>
    </item>
</items>
"@

$xDocument.Element('items').
    Elements('item').
    Where( { $_.Attribute('name').Value -eq 'Fridge' } ).
    ForEach( { $_.Element('category').Value = 'Appliances' } )
```

Modifying the value of an attribute uses the same syntax:

```
[XDocument]$xDocument = @"
<?xml version="1.0"?>
<list name='letters'>
    <name>1</name>
</list>
"@
$xDocument.Element('list').Attribute('name').Value = 'numbers'
```

If the attribute does not exist, an error will be thrown:

```
PS> $xDocument.Element('list').Attribute('other').Value = 'numbers'

The property 'Value' cannot be found on this object. Verify that the
property exists and can be set.
At line:1 char:1
+ $xDocument.Element('list').Attribute('other').Value = 'numbers'
+ ~~~~~~~~~~~~~~~~~~~~~~~~~~~~~~~~~~~~~~~~~~~~~~~~~~~~~~~~~~~~~~~~~~
    + CategoryInfo          : InvalidOperation: (:) [], RuntimeException
    + FullyQualifiedErrorId :PropertyNotFound
```

Adding nodes

Nodes can be added by using the Add methods, which include Add, AddAfterSelf, AddBeforeSelf, and AddFirst, for example:

```
[XDocument]$xDocument = @"
<?xml version="1.0"?>
<list type='numbers'>
    <name>1</name>
</list>
"@
$xDocument.Element('list').
    Element('name').
    AddAfterSelf(@(
        [XElement]::new('name', 2),
        [XElement]::new('name', 3),
        [XElement]::new('name', 4)
    ))
```

The different Add methods afford a great deal of flexibility over the content of a document; in this case, the new elements appear after the <name>1</name> element.

Removing nodes

The Remove method of XElement or XAttribute is used to remove the current node.

In the following example, the first name element is removed from the document:

```
[XDocument]$xDocument = @"
<?xml version="1.0"?>
<list type='numbers'>
    <name>1</name>
    <name>2</name>
    <name>3</name>
</list>
"@
$xDocument.Element('list').FirstNode.Remove()
```

Schema validation

LINQ to XML can be used to validate an XML document against a schema file.

.NET Core and schema validation

.NET Core appears to be unwilling to expand include references in an XML schema. This apparent bug is exhibited in PowerShell Core. Windows PowerShell will produce schema validation errors; PowerShell Core will not at this time.

The ISE-help.xml XML document is validated against its schema in the following example:

```
using namespace System.Xml.Linq

$path = 'C:\Windows\System32\WindowsPowerShell\v1.0\modules\ISE\en-
US\PSISE-help.xml'
$xDocument = [XDocument]::Load(
    $path,
    [LoadOptions]::SetLineInfo
)

$xmlSchemaSet = [System.Xml.Schema.XmlSchemaSet]::new()
$null = $xmlSchemaSet.Add(
    'http://schemas.microsoft.com/maml/2004/10',
    'C:\Windows\System32\WindowsPowerShell\v1.0\Schemas\PSMaml\maml.xsd'
)
[System.Xml.Schema.Extensions]::Validate(
    $xDocument,
    $xmlSchemaSet,
    {
        param($sender, $eventArgs)

        if ($eventArgs.Severity -in 'Error', 'Warning') {
            Write-Host $eventArgs.Message
            Write-Host ('  At {0} column {1}' -f
                $sender.LineNumber,
                $sender.LinePosition
            )
        }
    }
)
```

Positional information is made available by loading XDocument with the SetLineInfo option.

JSON

JSON is similar to XML in some respects. It is intended to be both human and machine readable, and is written in plain text.

Very similar to a hashtable, JSON-formatted objects are made up of key and value pairs, for example:

```
{
    "key1":  "value1",
    "key2":  "value2"
}
```

ConvertTo-Json

The `ConvertTo-Json` command can be used to convert a PowerShell object (or hashtable) into JSON:

```
PS> Get-Process -Id $PID |
    Select-Object Name, Id, Path |
    ConvertTo-Json

{
    "Name":  "powershell_ise",
    "Id":  3944,
    "Path":
"C:\\Windows\\System32\\WindowsPowerShell\\v1.0\\powershell_ise.exe"
}
```

By default, `ConvertTo-Json` will convert objects into a depth of two. Running the following code will show how the value for three is simplified as a string:

```
@{
    one = @{    # 1st iteration
        two = @{    # 2nd iteration
            three = @{
                four = 'value'
            }
        }
    }
} | ConvertTo-Json
```

The three property is present, but the value is listed as `System.Collections.Hashtable`, as acquiring the value would need a third iteration. Setting the value of the `Depth` parameter to `three` allows `ConvertTo-Json` to fully inspect the properties of three.

Going too deep

JSON serialization is a recursive operation. The depth may be increased, which is useful when converting a complex object.
Some value types may cause `ConvertTo-Json` to apparently hang. This is caused by the complexity of those value types. Such value types may include circular references.

A `ScriptBlock` object, for example, cannot be effectively serialized as JSON. The following command takes over 15 seconds to complete and results in a string that's over 50 million characters long:

```
Measure-Command { { 'ScriptBlock' } | ConvertTo-Json -
Depth 6 -Compress }
```

Increasing the recursion depth to 7 results in an error as keys (property names) begin to duplicate.

ConvertFrom-Json

The `ConvertFrom-Json` command is used to turn a JSON document into an object, for example:

```
'{ "Property": "Value" }' | ConvertFrom-Json
```

`ConvertFrom-Json` creates a `PSCustomObject`.

JSON understands a number of different data types, and each of these types is converted into an equivalent .NET type. The following example shows how each different type might be represented:

```
$object = @"
{
    "Decimal": 1.23,
    "String": "string",
    "Int32": 1,
    "Int64": 2147483648,
    "Boolean": true
}
"@ | ConvertFrom-Json
```

Inspecting individual elements after conversion reflects the type, as demonstrated in the following example:

```
PS> $object.Int64.GetType()
PS> $object.Boolean.GetType()

IsPublic IsSerial Name                                    BaseType
-------- -------- ----                                    --------
True     True     Int64                                   System.ValueType
True     True     Boolean                                 System.ValueType
```

JSON serialization within PowerShell is useful, but it is not perfect. For example, consider the result of converting `Get-Date`:

```
PS> Get-Date | ConvertTo-Json
{
    "value":  "\/Date(1489321529249)\/",
    "DisplayHint":  2,
    "DateTime":  "12 March 2017 12:25:29"
}
```

The value includes a `DisplayHintNoteProperty` and a `DateTimeScriptProperty`, added to the `DateTime` object. These add an extra layer of properties when converting back from JSON:

```
PS> Get-Date | ConvertTo-Json | ConvertFrom-Json

value DisplayHint DateTime ----- ----------- -------- 12/03/2017 12:27:25 2
12 March 2017 12:27:25
```

The `DateTime` property can be removed using the following code:

```
Get-TypeData System.DateTime | Remove-TypeData
```

Dates without type data

 `Get-Date` will appear to return nothing after running the previous command. The date is still present; this is an aesthetic problem only. Without the type data, PowerShell does not know how to display the date, which is ordinarily composed as follows:

```
$date = Get-Date
'{0} {1}' -f $date.ToLongDateString(),
$date.ToLongTimeString()
```

`DisplayHint` is added by `Get-Date`, and therefore the command cannot be used in this context.

Any extraneous members such as this would have to be tested for invalid members prior to conversion, which makes the solution more of a problem:

```
PS> Get-TypeData System.DateTime | Remove-TypeData
PS> [DateTime]::Now | ConvertTo-Json | ConvertFrom-Json | Select-Object *

Date        : 12/03/2017 00:00:00
Day         : 12
DayOfWeek   : Sunday
DayOfYear   : 71
Hour        : 12
Kind        : Utc
Millisecond : 58
Minute      : 32
Month       : 3
Second      : 41
Ticks       : 636249187610580000
TimeOfDay   : 12:32:41.0580000
Year        : 2017
```

Summary

This chapter took a brief look at working with HTML content, and how HTML content is formatted.

Working with XML content is a common requirement. This chapter introduced the structure of XML, along with two different approaches to working with XML.

Finally, JSON serialization was introduced, along with the `ConvertTo-Json` and `ConvertFrom-Json` commands.

Chapter 13, *Web Requests and Web Services*, explores working with **Representational State Transfer (REST)** and **Simple Object Access Protocol (SOAP)**-based web services in PowerShell.

13
Web Requests and Web Services

Representational State Transfer (REST) and **Simple Object Access Protocol (SOAP)** are often used as labels to refer two different approaches to implementing a web-based **Application Programming Interface (API)**.

The growth of cloud-based services in recent years has pushed the chances of working with such interfaces from rare to almost certain.

In this chapter, we are going to cover the following topics:

- Web requests
- Working with REST
- Working with SOAP

SOAP interfaces typically use the `New-WebServiceProxy` command in Windows PowerShell. This command is not available in PowerShell Core as the assembly it depends on is not available. The command is unlikely to be available in PowerShell Core unless it is rewritten.

Technical requirements

In addition to PowerShell and PowerShell Core, Visual Studio 2015 or 2017 Community Edition or better is required to use the SOAP service example.

Web requests

A background in web requests is valuable before delving into interfaces that run over the top of **Hyper-Text Transfer Protocol (HTTP)**.

PowerShell can use `Invoke-WebRequest` to send HTTP requests. For example, the following command will return the response to a GET request for the *Hey, Scripting Guy* blog:

```
Invoke-WebRequest https://blogs.technet.microsoft.com/heyscriptingguy/ -
UseBasicParsing
```

Parsing requires Internet Explorer

In Windows PowerShell, `UseBasicParsing` was an important parameter. Use was mandatory when working on Core installations of Windows server as Internet Explorer is not installed. It was also often used to improve the performance of the command where parsing was not actually required.

In PowerShell Core, all requests use basic parsing. The parameter is deprecated and present to support backward compatibility only. The parameter does not affect the output of the command.

HTTP methods

HTTP supports a number of different methods, including the following:

- GET
- HEAD
- POST
- PUT
- DELETE
- CONNECT
- OPTIONS
- TRACE
- PATCH

These methods are defined in the HTTP 1.1 specification: `https://www.w3.org/Protocols/rfc2616/rfc2616-sec9.html`.

It is common to find that a web server only supports a subset of these. In many cases, supporting too many methods is deemed to be a security risk. The `Invoke-WebRequest` command can be used to verify the list of HTTP methods supported by a site, for example:

```
PS> Invoke-WebRequest www.indented.co.uk -Method OPTIONS |
>>     Select-Object -ExpandProperty Headers

Key            Value
---            -----
Allow          GET, HEAD
```

HTTPS

If a connection to a web service uses HTTPS (HTTP over **Secure Sockets Layer (SSL)**), the certificate must be validated before a connection can complete and a request can be completed. If a web service has an invalid certificate, an error will be returned.

How PowerShell reacts to different scenarios can be tested. The badssl site can be used to test how PowerShell might react to different SSL scenarios: https://badssl.com/.

For example, when attempting to connect to a site with an expired certificate (using `Invoke-WebRequest`), the following message will be displayed in Windows PowerShell:

```
PS> Invoke-WebRequest https://expired.badssl.com/

Invoke-WebRequest : The underlying connection was closed: Could not
establish trust relationship for the SSL/TLS secure channel.
At line:1 char:1
+ Invoke-WebRequest https://expired.badssl.com/
+ ~~~~~~~~~~~~~~~~~~~~~~~~~~~~~~~~~~~~~~~~~~~~~~~
    + CategoryInfo          : InvalidOperation:
(System.Net.HttpWebRequest:HttpWebRequest) [Invoke-WebRequest],
WebException
    + FullyQualifiedErrorId :
WebCmdletWebResponseException,Microsoft.PowerShell.Commands.InvokeWebReques
tCommand
```

In PowerShell Core, this message changes to `The remote certificate is invalid according to the validation procedure`.

In Windows PowerShell, `Invoke-WebRequest` cannot bypass or ignore an invalid certificate on its own (using a parameter). Certificate validation behavior may be changed by adjusting the `CertificatePolicy` on the `ServicePointManager`: https://msdn.microsoft.com/en-us/library/system.net.servicepointmanager(v=vs.110).aspx.

In PowerShell Core, `Invoke-WebRequest` has a new parameter allowing certificate errors to be ignored, as shown here:

```
Invoke-WebRequest https://expired.badssl.com/ -SkipCertificateCheck
```

Chain of trust

Certificates are based on a chain of trust. Authorities are trusted to carry out sufficient checks to prove the identity of the certificate holder. Skipping certificate validation is insecure and should only be used against known hosts which can be trusted.

Bypassing SSL errors in Windows PowerShell

If a service has an invalid certificate, the best response is to fix the problem. When it is not possible or practical to address the real problem, a workaround can be created.

The approach described here applies to Windows PowerShell only. PowerShell Core does not include the `ICertificatePolicy` type.

This modification applies to the current PowerShell session and will reset to default behavior every time a new PowerShell session is opened.

The certificate policy used by the `ServicePointManager` may be replaced with a customized handler by writing a class (PowerShell, version 5) that replaces the `CheckValidationResult` method:

```
Class AcceptAllPolicy: System.Net.ICertificatePolicy {
    [Boolean] CheckValidationResult(
        [System.Net.ServicePoint] $servicePoint,
        [System.Security.Cryptography.X509Certificates.X509Certificate]
$certificate,
        [System.Net.WebRequest] $webRequest,
        [Int32] $problem
    ) {
        return $true
    }
}
[System.Net.ServicePointManager]::CertificatePolicy =
[AcceptAllPolicy]::new()
```

Once the policy is in place, certificate errors will be ignored as the previous method returns true no matter its state:

```
PS> Invoke-WebRequest "https://expired.badssl.com/"

StatusCode      : 200
StatusDescription : OK
...
```

CertificatePolicy is obsolete

The `CertificatePolicy` property is marked as obsolete in the documentation on MSDN.

Until recently, adjusting `ServerCertificateValidationCallback` was sufficient. However, with PowerShell 5 this appears to only fix part of the problem for `Invoke-WebRequest`.

Requests made by `System.Net.WebClient` in Windows PowerShell are satisfied by this simpler approach, which trusts all certificates:

```
[System.Net.ServicePointManager]::ServerCertificateValida
tionCallback = { $true }
```

This approach is not feasible with PowerShell Core. Requests made using `WebClient` may either by replaced by `Invoke-WebRequest` or the `HttpClient`.

Capturing SSL errors

The `ServerCertificateValidationCallback` property of `ServicePointManager` does not work as expected in PowerShell Core. Attempts to assign and use a script block may result in an error being displayed, as shown here, when making a web request:

```
PS> [System.Net.ServicePointManager]::ServerCertificateValidationCallback =
{ $true }
PS>
[System.Net.WebClient]::new().DownloadString('https://expired.badssl.com/')
Exception calling "DownloadString" with "1" argument(s): "The SSL
connection could not be established, see inner exception. There is no
Runspace available to run scripts in this thread. You can provide one in
the DefaultRunspace property of the
System.Management.Automation.Runspaces.Runspace type. The script block you
```

```
attempted to invoke was: $true "
At line:1 char:1
+ [System.Net.WebClient]::new().DownloadString('https://expired.badssl. ...
+ ~~~~~~~~~~~~~~~~~~~~~~~~~~~~~~~~~~~~~~~~~~~~~~~~~~~~~~~~~~~~~~~~~~~~~~~
+ CategoryInfo : NotSpecified: (:) [], MethodInvocationException
+ FullyQualifiedErrorId : WebException
```

The `SslStream` type (`System.Net.Security.SslStream`) offers a potential alternative for capturing detailed certificate validation information. The method used in the following example works in both Windows PowerShell and PowerShell Core.

This example converts certificate validation information using `Export-CliXml`. Assigning the parameters to a global variable is possible, but certain information is discarded when the callback ends, including the elements of the certificate chain:

```powershell
$remoteCertificateValidationCallback = {
    param (
        [Object]$sender,
[System.Security.Cryptography.X509Certificates.X509Certificate2]$certificat
e,
        [System.Security.Cryptography.X509Certificates.X509Chain]$chain,
        [System.Net.Security.SslPolicyErrors]$sslPolicyErrors
    )

    $psboundparameters | Export-CliXml C:\temp\CertValidation.xml
    # Always indicate SSL negotiation was successful
    $true
}

try {
    [Uri]$uri = 'https://expired.badssl.com/'

    $tcpClient = [System.Net.Sockets.TcpClient]::new()
    $tcpClient.Connect($Uri.Host, $Uri.Port)
    $sslStream = [System.Net.Security.SslStream]::new(
        $tcpClient.GetStream(),
        $false,     # leaveInnerStreamOpen: Close the inner stream when
complete
        $remoteCertificateValidationCallback
    )
    $sslStream.AuthenticateAsClient($Uri.Host)
} catch {
    throw
} finally {
    if ($tcpClient.Connected) {
        $tcpClient.Close()
    }
```

```
}
```

```
$certValidation = Import-CliXml C:\temp\CertValidation.xml
```

Once the content of the XML file has been loaded, the content may be investigated. For example, the certificate that was exchanged can be viewed:

```
$certValidation.Certificate
```

Or, the response can be used to inspect all of the certificates in the key chain:

```
$certValidation.Chain.ChainElements | Select-Object -ExpandProperty
Certificate
```

The ChainStatus property exposes details of any errors during chain validation:

```
$certValidation.Chain.ChainStatus
```

ChainStatus is summarized by the SslPolicyErrors property.

Removing the policy

PowerShell should be restarted to reset the certificate policies to system defaults.

Working with REST

REST is a compliant web service that allows a client to interact with the service using a set of predefined stateless operations. REST is not a protocol, it is an architectural style.

Whether or not an interface is truly REST compliant is not particularly relevant when the goal is to use one in PowerShell. Interfaces must be used according to any documentation that has been published.

Invoke-RestMethod

The Invoke-RestMethod command is able to execute methods exposed by web services. The name of a method is part of the **Uniform Resource Identifier (URI)**; it is important not to confuse this with the Method parameter. The Method parameter is used to describe the HTTP method. By default, Invoke-RestMethod uses HTTP GET.

Simple requests

The REST API provided by GitHub may be used to list repositories made available by the PowerShell team.

The API entry point is `https://api.github.com` as documented in this reference: `https://developer.github.com/v3/`.

When working with REST, documentation is very important. The manner in which an interface is used is common, but the manner is which it may respond is not (as this is an architectural style, not a strict protocol).

The specific method being called is documented on a different page of the following reference: `https://developer.github.com/v3/repos/#list-user-repositories`.

The name of the user forms part of the URI; there are no arguments for this method. Therefore, the following command will execute the method and return detailed information about the repositories owned by the PowerShell user (or organization):

```
Invoke-RestMethod -Uri https://api.github.com/users/powershell/repos
```

Windows PowerShell is likely to throw an error relating to SSL/TLS when running this command. This is because the site uses TLS 1.2 whereas, by default, `Invoke-RestMethod` reaches as far as TLS 1.0. PowerShell Core users should not experience this problem.

This Windows PowerShell problem can be fixed by tweaking the `SecurityProtocol` property of `ServicePointManager` as follows:

```
using namespace System.Net
[ServicePointManager]::SecurityProtocol =
[ServicePointManager]::SecurityProtocol -bor 'Tls12'
```

The bitwise `-bor` operator is used to add TLS 1.2 to the default list, which includes `Ssl3` and `Tls`. TLS 1.1 (`Tls11`) may be added in a similar manner if required.

All examples use TLS 1.2

This setting is required for the examples that follow when running Windows PowerShell.

Older versions of Windows may require a patch from Windows Update to gain support for TLS 1.2.

Requests with arguments

The search code method of the GitHub REST API is used to demonstrate how arguments can be passed to a REST method.

The documentation for the method is found in the following API reference: `https://developer.github.com/v3/search/#search-code`.

The following example uses the search code method by building a query string and appending that to the end of the URL. The search looks for occurrences of the `Get-Content` term in PowerShell language files in the PowerShell repository. The search term is therefore the following:

```
Get-Content language:powershell repo:powershell/powershell
```

This `Get-Content` is not PowerShell's `Get-Content`.

PowerShell has a `Get-Content` command. The `Get-Content` term used in the previous string should not be confused with the PowerShell command.

Converting the example from the documentation, the URL required is as follows. Spaces may be replaced by + when encoding the URL:

```
https://api.github.com/search/code?q=Get-Content+language:powershell+repo:p
owershell/powershell
```

In Windows PowerShell, which can use the `HttpUtility` type within the `System.Web` assembly, the task of encoding the URL can be simplified:

```
using assembly System.Web

$queryString = [System.Web.HttpUtility]::ParseQueryString('')
$queryString.Add('q', 'Get-Content language:powershell
repo:powershell/powershell')
Invoke-RestMethod ('https://api.github.com/search/code?{0}' -f
$queryString)
```

Running `$queryString.ToString()` will show that the colon character has been replaced by %3, and the forward slash in the repository name by %2.

PowerShell Core cannot use the `HttpUtility` type, which would leave an author trying to find a means of properly encoding the URL. However, the arguments for the search do not necessarily have to be passed as a query string. Instead, a body for the request may be set, as shown here:

```
Invoke-RestMethod -Uri https://api.github.com/search/code -Body @{
    q = 'Get-Content language:powershell repo:powershell/powershell'
}
```

`Invoke-RestMethod` converts the body (a hashtable) to JSON and handles any encoding required. The result of the search is the same whether the body is set or a query string is used.

In both cases, details of issues are held within the items property of the response:

```
Invoke-RestMethod -Uri https://api.github.com/search/code -Body @{
    q = 'Get-Content language:powershell repo:powershell/powershell'
} | Select-Object -ExpandProperty items | Select-Object number, title
```

This pattern, where the actual results are nested under a property in the response, is frequently seen with REST interfaces. Exploration is often required.

It is critical to note that REST interfaces are case-sensitive; using a parameter named `Q` would result in an error message, as shown here:

```
PS> Invoke-RestMethod -Uri https://api.github.com/search/code -Body @{
>>      Q = 'Get-Content language:powershell repo:powershell/powershell'
>> }
Invoke-RestMethod : {"message":"Validation
Failed","errors":[{"resource":"Search","field":"q","code":"missing"}],"docu
mentation_url":"https://developer.github.com/v3/search"}
At line:1 char:1
+ Invoke-RestMethod -Uri https://api.github.com/search/code -Body @{
+ ~~~~~~~~~~~~~~~~~~~~~~~~~~~~~~~~~~~~~~~~~~~~~~~~~~~~~~~~~~~~~~~~~~~~~
+ CategoryInfo : InvalidOperation: (Method: GET, Re...rShell/6.1.0
}:HttpRequestMessage) [Invoke-RestMethod], HttpResponseException
+ FullyQualifiedErrorId :
WebCmdletWebResponseException,Microsoft.PowerShell.Commands.InvokeRestMetho
dCommand
```

The GitHub API returns an easily understood error message in this case. This will not be true of all REST APIs; it is not uncommon to see a generic error returned by an API. An API may return a simple HTTP 400 error and leave it to the user or developer to figure out what went wrong.

Working with paging

Many REST interfaces will return large result sets from searches in pages, a sub-set of the results. The techniques used to retrieve each subsequent page can vary from one API to another.

The GitHub API exposes the link to the next page in the HTTP header. This is consistent with RFC 5988 (`https://tools.ietf.org/html/rfc5988#page-6`).

In PowerShell Core, it is easy to retrieve and view the header when using `Invoke-RestMethod`:

```
$params = @{
    Uri                   = 'https://api.github.com/search/issues'
    Body                  = @{
        q = 'documentation state:closed repo:powershell/powershell'
    }
    ResponseHeadersVariable = 'httpHeader'
}
Invoke-RestMethod @params | Select-Object -ExpandProperty items
```

Once run, the link field of the header may be inspected via the `httpHeader` variable:

```
PS> $httpHeader['link']
<https://api.github.com/search/issues?q=documentation+state%3Aclosed+repo%3
Apowershell%2Fpowershell&page=2>; rel="next",
<https://api.github.com/search/issues?q=documentation+state%3Aclosed+repo%3
Apowershell%2Fpowershell&page=34>; rel="last"
```

PowerShell Core can also automatically follow this link by using the `FollowRelLink` parameter. This might be used in conjunction with the `MaximumFollowRelLink` parameter to ensure a request stays within any rate limiting imposed by the web service. See `https://developer.github.com/v3/#rate-limiting` for the GitHub API, for example:

```
$params = @{
    Uri                  = 'https://api.github.com/search/issues'
    Body                 = @{
        q = 'documentation state:closed repo:powershell/powershell'
    }
    FollowRelLink        = $true
    MaximumFollowRelLink = 2
}
Invoke-RestMethod @params | Select-Object -ExpandProperty items
```

Windows PowerShell, unfortunately, cannot automatically follow this link. Nor does the `Invoke-RestMethod` command expose the header from the response. When working with complex REST interfaces in Windows PowerShell, it is often necessary to fall back to `Invoke-WebRequest` or even `HttpWebRequest` classes.

The example that follows uses `Invoke-WebRequest` in Windows PowerShell to follow the next link in a similar manner to `Invoke-RestMethod` in PowerShell Core:

```
# Used to limit the number of times "next" is followed
$followLimit = 2
# The initial set of parameters, describes the search
$params = @{
    Uri = 'https://api.github.com/search/issues'
    # PowerShell will convert this to JSON
    Body = @{
        q = 'documentation state:closed repo:powershell/powershell'
    }
    ContentType = 'application/json'
}
# Just a counter, works in conjunction with followLimit.
$followed = 0

do {
    # Get the next response
    $response = Invoke-WebRequest @params
    # Convert and leave the results as output
    $response.Content | ConvertFrom-Json | Select-Object -ExpandProperty
items

    # Retrieve the links from the header and find the next URL
    if ($response.Headers['link'] -match '<([^>]+?)>;\s*rel="next"') {
        $next = $matches[1]
    } else {
        $next = $null
    }

    # Parameters which will be used to get the next page (next loop
iteration)
    $params = @{
        Uri = $next
    }

    # Increment the followed counter
    $followed++
} until (-not $next -or $followed -ge $followLimit)
```

Because of the flexible nature of REST, implementations of page linking may vary. For example, links may appear in the body of a response instead of the header. Exploration is a requirement when working around a web API.

Working with authentication

There are a large number of authentication systems that might be used when working with web services.

For services that expect to use the current user account to authenticate, the UseDefaultCredential parameter may be used to pass authentication tokens without explicitly passing a username and password. A service that is integrated into an Active Directory domain, expecting to use Kerberos authentication, might be an example of such a service.

REST interfaces written to provide automation access tend to offer reasonably simple approaches to automation, often including basic authentication.

GitHub offers a number of different authentication methods, including basic and OAuth. These are shown here when attempting to request the email addresses for a user, which requires authentication.

Using basic authentication

Basic authentication with a username and password is the simplest method available:

```
$params = @{
    Uri        = 'https://api.github.com/user/emails'
    Credential = Get-Credential
}
Invoke-RestMethod @params
```

In PowerShell Core, the Authentication parameter should be added:

```
$params = @{
    Uri            = 'https://api.github.com/user/emails'
    Credential     = Get-Credential
    Authentication = 'Basic'
}
Invoke-RestMethod @params
```

If the account is configured to use two-factor authentication, this request may fail with the following error message:

```
PS> Invoke-RestMethod @params
Invoke-RestMethod : {"message":"Must specify two-factor authentication OTP
code.","documentation_url":"https://developer.github.com/v3/auth#working-wi
th-two-factor-authentication"}
At line:1 char:1
+ Invoke-RestMethod https://api.github.com/user/emails -Credential $cre ...
+ ~~~~~~~~~~~~~~~~~~~~~~~~~~~~~~~~~~~~~~~~~~~~~~~~~~~~~~~~~~~~~~~~~~~~~~~
+ CategoryInfo : InvalidOperation: (Method: GET, Re...rShell/6.1.0
}:HttpRequestMessage) [Invoke-RestMethod], HttpResponseException
+ FullyQualifiedErrorId :
WebCmdletWebResponseException,Microsoft.PowerShell.Commands.InvokeRestMetho
dCommand
```

GitHub provides documentation showing how to add the second authentication factor, although it is not clear how SMS tokens can be requested: `https://developer.github.com/v3/auth/`.

In this case, it may be more appropriate to use a personal access token. Personal access tokens can be generated by visiting account settings, then developer settings. Once generated, the personal access token cannot be viewed. The personal access token is used in place of a password.

OAuth

OAuth is offered by a wide variety of web services. The details of this process will vary slightly between different APIs. The GitHub documentation describes the process that must be followed: `https://developer.github.com/v3/oauth/#web-application-flow`.

OAuth needs a web browser

It is difficult to avoid the need for a web browser willing to execute JavaScript code when working with OAuth.
The example that follows can only be used with Windows PowerShell (not PowerShell Core) as it requires a **Windows Presentation Framework (WPF)**-based browser to extract a code from query string in a redirected web request.

Creating an application

Before starting with code, an application has to be registered with GitHub. This is done by visiting account settings, and then developer settings.

An application must be created to acquire a `clientid` and `clientsecret`. Creation of the application requires a homepage URL and an authorization callback URL. Both should be set to `http://localhost`. This does not have to be a valid web service for the purposes of this example; it is used to acquire the authorization code in a web browser.

The values from the web page will fill the following variables:

```
$clientId = 'FromGitHub'
$clientSecret = 'FromGitHub'
```

Getting an authorization code

Once an application is registered, an authorization code is required. Obtaining the authorization code gives the end user the opportunity to grant the application access to a GitHub account. If the user is not currently logged in to GitHub, it will also prompt him/her to log on.

A URL must be created that will prompt for authorization:

```
$authorize =
'https://github.com/login/oauth/authorize?client_id={0}&scope={1}' -f
    $clientId,
    'user:email'
```

The `'user:email'` scope describes the rights the application would like to have. The web API guide contains a list of possible scopes: `https://developer.github.com/apps/building-oauth-apps/understanding-scopes-for-oauth-apps/`.

GitHub does not support Internet Explorer

WPF and Windows Forms both include browser controls that can be used. However, both are based on Internet Explorer, which is not supported by GitHub. An alternative is required.

Before creating the web request, an appropriate browser control must be found. The WebView control uses the Microsoft Edge browser and is available from `https://www.nuget.org/`: `https://www.nuget.org/packages/Microsoft.Toolkit.Win32.UI.Controls/`.

The following script will download and extract the package to the current directory:

```
$params = @{
    Uri =
'https://www.nuget.org/api/v2/package/Microsoft.Toolkit.Win32.UI.Controls/4
.0.2'
    OutFile = 'Microsoft.Toolkit.Win32.UI.Controls.zip'
}
Invoke-WebRequest @params
Expand-Archive Microsoft.Toolkit.Win32.UI.Controls.zip
```

The downloaded assembly may be used to implement a small browser to handle the OAuth callback process:

```
using assembly PresentationFramework
using assembly
.\Microsoft.Toolkit.Win32.UI.Controls\lib\net462\Microsoft.Toolkit.Win32.UI
.Controls.dll

$window = [System.Windows.Window]@{
    Height = 650
    Width = 450
}
$browser = [Microsoft.Toolkit.Win32.UI.Controls.WPF.WebView]@{
    Height = 650
    Width = 450
}
# Add an event handler to close the window when
# interaction with GitHub is complete.
$browser.add_NavigationCompleted( {
    param ( $sender, $eventargs )

    if ($eventArgs.Uri -notmatch 'GitHub') {
        $Global:authorizationCode = $eventArgs.Uri -replace '^.+code='

        $sender.Parent.Close()
    } else {
        $Global:authorizationCode = $null
    }
} )
$browser.Navigate($authorize)
$window.Content = $browser
$null = $window.ShowDialog()
```

The window will close as soon as it leaves the GitHub pages, when the request is redirected to the callback URL for the application.

If the application has already been authorized and the user is logged in, the window will close without prompting for user interaction.

The `authroizationCode` global variable should contain code that can be used to request an access token.

Requesting an access token

The next step is to create an access token. The access token is valid for a limited time.

The `clientSecret` is sent with this request; if this were an application that was given to others, keeping the secret would be a challenge to overcome:

```
$params = @{
    Uri = 'https://github.com/login/oauth/access_token'
    Method = 'POST'
    Body = @{
        client_id = $clientId
        client_secret = $clientSecret
        code = $authorizationCode
    }
}
$response = Invoke-RestMethod @params
$token =
[System.Web.HttpUtility]::ParseQueryString($response)['access_token']
```

The previous request used the HTTP method POST. The HTTP method, which should be used with a REST method, is documented for an interface in the Developer Guides.

Each of the requests that follow will use the access token from the previous request. The access token is placed in a HTTP header field named Authorization.

Using a token

We can call methods that require authentication by adding a token to the HTTP header.

The format of the authorization header field is shown here:

```
Authorization: token OAUTH-TOKEN
```

OAUTH-TOKEN is replaced and the authorization head is constructed as shown here:

```
$headers = @{
    Authorization = 'token {0}' -f $token
}
```

The token can be used in subsequent requests for the extent of its lifetime:

```
$headers = @{
    Authorization = 'token {0}' -f $token
}
Invoke-RestMethod 'https://api.github.com/user/emails' -Headers $headers
```

Working with SOAP

Unlike REST, which is an architectural style, SOAP is a protocol. It is perhaps reasonable to compare working with SOAP to importing a .NET assembly (DLL) to work with the types inside. As a result, a SOAP client is much more strongly tied to a server than is the case with a REST interface.

SOAP uses XML to exchange information between the client and server.

Finding a SOAP service

SOAP-based web APIs are quite rare, less popular by far than REST. The examples in this section are based on a simple SOAP service I wrote for this book.

The service is available on GitHub as a Visual Studio solution: `https://github.com/indented-automation/SimpleSOAP`.

The solution should be downloaded, opened in Visual Studio (2015 or 2017, Community Edition or better), and debugging should be started by pressing *F5*. A browser page will be opened, which will show the port number the service is operating on. A 403 error may be displayed; this can be ignored.

This service is not a well designed service; it has been contrived to expose similar patterns in its method calls to those seen in real SOAP services.

A `ReadMe` file accompanies the project. Common problems running the project will be noted there.

> **Alternatives?**
>
>
>
> Alternative services include older versions of SQL Server Reporting Services, which are extensively documented: `https://docs.microsoft.com/en-us/dotnet/api/reportservice2010?view=sqlserver-2016`. SQL Server Reporting Services 2017 and newer use a REST API.

The discovery based approaches explored in this section should be applicable to any SOAP based service.

New-WebServiceProxy

The `New-WebServiceProxy` command is used to connect to a SOAP web service. This can be a service endpoint, such as a .NET `service.asmx` URL, or a WSDL document.

New-WebServiceProxy and PowerShell Core

The New-WebServiceProxy command has not been implemented in PowerShell Core. The examples in this section only apply when using Windows PowerShell.

The web service will include methods, and may also include other object types and enumerations.

The command accesses a service anonymously by default. If the current user should be passed on, the `UseDefaultCredential` parameter should be used. If explicit credentials are required, the `Credential` parameter can be used.

Localhost and a port

Throughout this section, localhost and a port are used to connect to the web service. The port is set by Visual Studio when debugging the simple SOAP web service and must be updated to use these examples.

By default, `New-WebServiceProxy` creates as dynamic namespace. This is as follows:

```
PS> $params = @{
>>      Uri = 'http://localhost:62369/Service.asmx'
>> }
>> $service = New-WebServiceProxy @params
>> $service.GetType().Namespace
Microsoft.PowerShell.Commands.NewWebserviceProxy.AutogeneratedTypes.WebServ
iceProxy4__localhost_62369_Service_asmx
```

The dynamic namespace is useful as it avoids problems when multiple connections are made to the same service in the same session.

To simplify exploring the web service in, a fixed namespace might be defined:

```
$params = @{
    Uri = 'http://localhost:62369/Service.asmx'
    Namespace = 'SOAP'
}
$service = New-WebServiceProxy @params
```

The $ service object returned by `New-WebServiceProxy` describes the URL used to connect, the timeout, the HTTP user agent, and so on. The object is also the starting point for exploring the interface; it is used to expose web services methods.

Methods

The methods available may be viewed in a number of ways. The URL used can be visited in a browser, or `Get-Member` may be used. A subset of the output from `Get-Member` follows:

```
PS> $service | Get-Member

Name                  MemberType   Definition
----                  ----------   ----------
GetElement            Method       SOAP.Element GetElement(string Name)
GetAtomicMass         Method       string GetAtomicMass(string Name)
GetAtomicNumber       Method       int GetAtomicNumber(string Name)
GetElements           Method       SOAP.Element[] GetElements()
GetElementsByGroup    Method       SOAP.Element[]
GetElementsByGroup(SOAP.Group group)
GetElementSymbol      Method       string GetElementSymbol(string Name)
SearchElements        Method       SOAP.Element[]
SearchElements(SOAP.SearchCondition[] searchConditions)
```

The preceding `GetElements` method requires no arguments and may be called immediately, as shown here:

```
PS> $service.GetElements() | Select-Object -First 5 | Format-Table
```

AtomicNumber	Symbol	Name	AtomicMass	Group
1	H	Hydrogen	1.00794(4)	Nonmetal
2	He	Helium	4.002602(2)	NobleGas
3	Li	Lithium	6.941(2)	AlkaliMetal
4	Be	Beryllium	9.012182(3)	AlkalineEarthMetal
5	B	Boron	10.811(7)	Metalloid

Methods requiring string or numeric arguments may be similarly easy to call, although the value the method requires is often open to interpretation. In this case, the name argument may be either an element name or an element symbol. Documentation is difficult to replace when working with web services:

```
PS> $service.GetAtomicNumber('oxygen')
8

PS> $service.GetAtomicMass('H')
1.00794(4)
```

Methods and enumerations

The `GetElementsByGroup` method shown by Get-Member requires an argument of type `SOAP.Group`. This is an enumeration, as indicated by the `BaseType` shown here:

```
PS> [SOAP.Group]
```

IsPublic	IsSerial	Name	BaseType
True	True	Group	System.Enum

The values of the enumeration may be shown by running the `GetEnumValues` method as shown here:

```
PS> [SOAP.Group].GetEnumValues()

Actinoid
AlkaliMetal
AlkalineEarthMetal
Halogen
Lanthanoid
Metal
Metalloid
NobleGas
Nonmetal
PostTransitionMetal
TransitionMetal
```

PowerShell will help cast to enumeration values; a string value is sufficient to satisfy the method:

```
PS> $service.GetElementsByGroup('Nonmetal') | Format-Table
```

AtomicNumber	Symbol	Name	AtomicMass	Group
1	H	Hydrogen	1.00794(4)	Nonmetal
6	C	Carbon	12.0107(8)	Nonmetal
7	N	Nitrogen	14.0067(2)	Nonmetal
8	O	Oxygen	15.9994(3)	Nonmetal
15	P	Phosphorus	30.973762(2)	Nonmetal
16	S	Sulfur	32.065(5)	Nonmetal
34	Se	Selenium	78.96(3)	Nonmetal

If the real value of the enumeration must be used, it may be referenced as a static property of the enumeration:

```
$service.GetElementsByGroup([SOAP.Group]::Nonmetal)
```

Methods and SOAP objects

When working with SOAP interfaces, it is common to encounter methods that need instances of objects presented by the SOAP service. The SearchElements method is an example of this type.

The SearchElements method requires an array of SOAP.SearchCondition as an argument. This is shown in the following by accessing the definition of the method:

```
PS> $service.SearchElements

OverloadDefinitions
-------------------
SOAP.Element[] SearchElements(SOAP.SearchCondition[] searchConditions)
```

An instance of `SearchCondition` may be created as follows:

```
$searchCondition = [SOAP.SearchCondition]::new()
```

Exploring the object with `Get-Member` shows that the operator property is another type from the SOAP service. This is an enumeration, as shown here:

```
PS> [SOAP.ComparisonOperator]
```

IsPublic	IsSerial	Name	BaseType
True	True	ComparisonOperator	System.Enum

A set of search conditions may be constructed and passed to the method:

```
$searchConditions = @(
    [SOAP.SearchCondition]@{
        PropertyName = 'AtomicNumber'
        Operator     = 'ge'
        Value        = 1
    }
    [SOAP.SearchCondition]@{
        PropertyName = 'AtomicNumber'
        Operator     = 'lt'
        Value        = 6
    }
)
$service.SearchElements($searchConditions)
```

Overlapping services

When testing a SOAP interface, it is easy to get into a situation where `New-WebServiceProxy` has been called several times against the same web service. This can be problematic if using the `Namespace` parameter.

Consider the following example, which uses two instances of the web service:

```
$params = @{
    Uri = 'http://localhost:62369/Service.asmx'
    Namespace = 'SOAP'
}
# Original version
$service = New-WebServiceProxy @params
# New version
$service = New-WebServiceProxy @params

$searchConditions = @(
    [SOAP.SearchCondition]@{
        PropertyName = 'Symbol'
        Operator     = 'eq'
        Value        = 'H'
    }
)
```

In theory, there is nothing wrong with this example. In practice, the
SOAP.SearchCondition object is created based on the original version of the service
created using New-WebServiceProxy. The method is, on the other hand, executing against
the newer version.

As the method being called and the type being used are in different assemblies, an error is
shown; this is repeated in the following:

```
PS> $service.SearchElements($searchConditions)
Cannot convert argument "searchConditions", with value: "System.Object[]",
for "SearchElements" to type
"SOAP.SearchCondition[]": "Cannot convert the "SOAP.SearchCondition" value
of type "SOAP.SearchCondition" to type
"SOAP.SearchCondition"."
At line:1 char:1
+ $service.SearchElements($searchConditions)
+ ~~~~~~~~~~~~~~~~~~~~~~~~~~~~~~~~~~~~~~~~~~~~
  + CategoryInfo : NotSpecified: (:) [], MethodException
  + FullyQualifiedErrorId : MethodArgumentConversionInvalidCastArgument
```

It is still possible to access the second version of SearchCondition by searching for the type, then creating an instance of that:

```
$searchCondition = ($service.GetType().Module.GetTypes() |
    Where-Object Name -eq 'SearchCondition')::new()

$searchCondition.PropertyName = 'Symbol'
$searchCondition.Operator = 'eq'
$searchCondition.Value = 'H'

$searchConditions = @($searchCondition)

$service.SearchElements($searchConditions)
```

However, it is generally better to avoid the problem by allowing New-WebServiceProxy to use a dynamic namespace. At which point, an instance of the SearchCondition may be created, as shown here:

```
('{0}.SearchCondition' -f $service.GetType().Namespace -as [Type])::new()
```

Summary

This chapter explored the use of Invoke-WebRequest and how to work with and debug SSL negotiation problems.

Working with REST explored simple method calls, authentication, and OAuth negotiation, before exploring REST methods that require authenticated sessions.

SOAP is hard to find these days; a sample project was used to show how the capabilities of a SOAP service might be discovered and used.

Chapter 14, *Remoting and Remote Management*, explores remoting and remote management.

Section 3: Automating with PowerShell

3

In this section, we will look at using PowerShell to administer and automate.

The following chapters are included in this section:

14
Remoting and Remote Management

Windows remoting came to PowerShell with the release of version 2.0. Windows remoting is a powerful feature that allows administrators to move away from RPC-based remote access.

In this chapter, we will cover the following topics:

- WS-Management
- PSSessions
- Remoting on Linux
- Remoting over SSH
- The double-hop problem
- CIM sessions

Technical requirements

This chapter makes use of a remote Windows system named PSTest, which runs Windows 10, Windows PowerShell 5.1, and PowerShell Core 6.1.

Remoting between Windows and Linux is demonstrated using a system that runs CentOS 7, PowerShell 6.1, and the PSRP package.

WS-Management

Windows remoting uses WS-Management as its communication protocol. Support for WS-Management and remoting were introduced with PowerShell 2.0. WS-Management uses the **Simple Object Access Protocol (SOAP)** to pass information between the client and the server.

Enabling remoting

Before remoting can be used, it must be enabled. In a domain environment, remoting can be enabled using a group policy:

- **Policy name**: Allow remote server management through WinRM
- **Path**: `Computer configuration\Administrative Templates\Windows Components\Windows Remote Management (WinRM)\WinRM Service`

If remoting is enabled using a group policy, a firewall rule should be created to allow access to the service:

- **Policy name**: Define inbound port exceptions
- **Path**: `Computer Configuration\Administrative Templates\Network\ Network Connections\Windows Firewall\Domain Profile`
- **Port exception example**: `5985:TCP:*:enabled:WSMan`

Windows remoting can be enabled on a per-machine basis using the `Enable-PSRemoting` command.

Remoting may be disabled in PowerShell using `Disable-PSRemoting`. Disabling remoting will show the following warning:

```
PS> Disable-PSRemoting

WARNING: Disabling the session configurations does not undo all the changes
made by the Enable-PSRemoting or Enable-PSSessionConfiguration cmdlet. You
might have to manually undo the changes by following these steps:
1. Stop and disable the WinRM service.
2. Delete the listener that accepts requests on any IP address.
3. Disable the firewall exceptions for WS-Management communications.
4.Restore the value of the LocalAccountTokenFilterPolicy to 0, which
restricts remote access to members of the Administrators group on the
computer.
```

If `Enable-PSRemoting` is run in the PowerShell 6 console, additional session configurations will be created that allow a choice of either Windows PowerShell (the default) or PowerShell Core when creating a remote session. Accessing PowerShell Core sessions is explored later in this chapter.

Get-WSManInstance

`Get-WSManInstance` provides access to instances of resources at a lower level than commands such as `Get-CimInstance`.

For example, `Get-WSManInstance` can be used to get the `Win32_OperatingSystem` WMI class:

```
Get-WSManInstance -ResourceUri wmicimv2/win32_operatingsystem
```

The response is an `XmlElement` that PowerShell presents as an object with properties for each child element.

`Get-WSManInstance` has been superseded by `Get-CimInstance`, which was introduced in PowerShell 3.0.

The WSMan drive

The `WSMan` drive is accessible when PowerShell is running as the administrator. The drive can be used to view and change the configuration of remoting.

For example, the provider can be used to update settings, such as `MaxEnvelopeSize`, which affects the maximum permissible size of SOAP messages sent and received by `WSMan`:

```
Set-Item WSMan:\localhost\MaxEnvelopeSizekb 1024
```

The WinRM service may need to be restarted after values are changed:

```
Restart-Service winrm
```

Remoting and SSL

By default, Windows remoting requests are unencrypted. An HTTPS listener can be created to support encryption. Before attempting to create an HTTPS listener, a certificate is required.

Using a self-signed certificate is often the first step when configuring SSL. Windows 10 comes with a PKI module that can be used to create a certificate. The PKI module is only available in Windows PowerShell. In the following example, a self-signed certificate is created in the computer's personal store:

```
PS> New-SelfSignedCertificate -DnsName $env:COMPUTERNAME

PSParentPath: Microsoft.PowerShell.Security\Certificate::LocalMachine\MY

Thumbprint                                Subject
----------                                -------
D8D2F174EE1C37F7C2021C9B7EB6FEE3CB1B9A41  CN=SSLTEST
```

Once the certificate has been created, an HTTPS listener may be created using the WSMan drive:

```
$params = @{
    Path                 = 'WSMan:\localhost\Listener'
    Address              = '*'
    Transport            = 'HTTPS'
    CertificateThumbprint = 'D8D2F174EE1C37F7C2021C9B7EB6FEE3CB1B9A41'
    Force                = $true
}
New-Item @params
```

The Force parameter is used to suppress a confirmation prompt.

If Windows Firewall is running, a new rule must also be created to allow the connection:

```
$params = @{
    DisplayName = $name = 'Windows Remote Management (HTTPS-In)'
    Name        = $name
    Profile     = 'Any'
    LocalPort   = 5986
    Protocol    = 'TCP'
}
New-NetFirewallRule @params
```

Set-WSManQuickConfig

Certificates used by remoting have the following requirements:

- The subject must contain the computer name (without a domain).
- The certificate must support the server authentication enhanced key usage.
- The certificate must not be expired, revoked, or self-signed.

If a certificate that meets these requirements is present, the Set-WSManQuickConfig command may be used:

```
Set-WSManQuickConfig -UseSSL
```

HTTPS listeners may be viewed as follows:

```
PS> Get-ChildItem WSMan:\localhost\Listener\* |
>>     Where-Object { (Get-Item "$($_.PSPath)\Transport").Value -eq 'HTTPS'
}


WSManConfig: Microsoft.WSMan.Management\WSMan::localhost\Listener

Type       Keys                             Name
----       ----                             ----
Container  {Transport=HTTPS, Address=*}     Listener_1305953032
```

The preceding example may be extended by exploring the properties for the listener:

```
Get-ChildItem WSMan:\localhost\Listener | ForEach-Object {
    $listener = $_ | Select-Object Name
    Get-ChildItem $_.PSPath | ForEach-Object {
        $listener | Add-Member $_.Name $_.Value
    }
    $listener
} | Where-Object Transport -eq 'HTTPS'
```

The self-signed certificate can be assigned in this manner, but, for an SSL connection to succeed, the client must trust the certificate. Without trust, the following error is shown:

```
PS> Invoke-Command -ScriptBlock { Get-Process } -ComputerName
$env:COMPUTERNAME -UseSSL


[SSLTEST] Connecting to remote server SSLTEST failed with the following
error message : The server certificate on the destination computer
(SSLTEST:5986) has the following errors:
The SSL certificate is signed by an unknown certificate authority. For more
information, see the about_Remote_Troubleshooting Help topic.
+ CategoryInfo : OpenError: (SSLTEST:String) [],
PSRemotingTransportException
+ FullyQualifiedErrorId : 12175,PSSessionStateBroken
```

A number of options are available to bypass this option:

- Disable certificate verification.
- Add the certificate from the remote server to the local root certificate store.

Disabling certificate verification can be achieved by configuring the options of a PSSession:

```
$options = New-PSSessionOption -SkipCACheck
$session = New-PSSession computerName -SessionOption $options
```

Either of the preceding options will allow the connection to complete. This can be verified using Test-WSMan:

```
Test-WSMan -UseSSL
```

If a new certificate is obtained, the certificate for the listener may be replaced by using Set-Item:

```
$params = @{
    Path  =
'WSMan:\localhost\Listener\Listener_1305953032\CertificateThumbprint'
    Value = 'D8D2F174EE1C37F7C2021C9B7EB6FEE3CB1B9A41'
}
Set-Item @params
```

Remoting and permissions

By default, Windows remoting requires administrative access. A summary of granted permissions may be viewed using Get-PSSessionConfiguration. The summary does not include the permission level:

```
Get-PSSessionConfiguration Microsoft.PowerShell
```

Remoting permissions GUI

Permissions can be changed using the graphical interface. The interface will be displayed when the following command is run:

```
Set-PSSessionConfiguration Microsoft.PowerShell -ShowSecurityDescriptorUI
```

The following screenshot displays a standard GUI for assigning permissions:

The session configuration defines four different permission levels:

- Full
- Read
- Write
- Execute

Remoting permissions by script

Permissions may also be changed using a script. The following commands retrieve the current security descriptor:

```
using namespace System.Security.AccessControl

$sddl = Get-PSSessionConfiguration microsoft.powerShell |
    Select-Object -ExpandProperty SecurityDescriptorSddl
```

```
$acl = [CommonSecurityDescriptor]::new(
    $false,
    $false,
    $sddl
)
$acl.DiscretionaryAcl
```

The object created here does not translate access masks into meaningful names. There are a small number of possible values for the access mask (shown here as 32-bit integers):

- Full (All operations): 268435456
- Read (Get, Enumerate, Subscribe): −2147483648
- Write (Put, Delete, Create): 1073741824
- Execute (Invoke): 536870912

Permissions may be combined by using the −bor operator. For example, read and write may be defined using the following:

```
$readAndWrite = -2147483648 -bor 1073741824
```

Granting Read, Write, and Execute individually should be equivalent to Full Control. However, the result of binary (or the composite of all values) is −536870912, not the expected value for Full.

Understanding these values allows the current settings to be displayed in more detail than Get-PSSessionConfiguration displays. The function adds two script properties to each of the access control entries in the discretionary ACL. The first translates the SID into an account name; the second translates the access mask into a name (or set of names).

The example uses an enumeration (enum) to describe the possible access rights:

```
using namespace System.Security.AccessControl; using namespace
System.Security.Principal
[Flags()]
enum SessionAccessRight {
    All     = -536870912
    Full    = 268435456
    Read    = -2147483648
    Write   = 1073741824
    Execute = 536870912
}

function Get-PSSessionAcl {
    [CmdletBinding()]
    param (
```

```
        [Parameter(Mandatory)]
        [String[]]$Name
    )
    Get-PSSessionConfiguration -Name $Name | ForEach-Object {
        [CommonSecurityDescriptor]::new(
            $false,
            $false,
            $_.SecurityDescriptorSddl
        )
    }
}

function Get-PSSessionAccess {
    [CmdletBinding()]
    param (
        [Parameter(Mandatory)]
        [String[]]$Name
    )

    (Get-PSSessionAcl -Name $Name).DiscretionaryAcl |
        Add-Member Identity -MemberType ScriptProperty -Value {
            $this.SecurityIdentifier.Translate([NTAccount])
        } -PassThru |
        Add-Member AccessRight -MemberType ScriptProperty -Value {
            [SessionAccessRight]$this.AccessMask
        } -PassThru
}
```

Additional access may be granted by using the AddAccess method on DiscretionaryAcl. Granting access requires the SID of an account. The SID can be retrieved using the same Translate method that was used to get an account name from an SID. For example, the security identifier of the local administrator account may be retrieved as follows:

```
using namespace System.Security.Principal

([NTAccount]"Administrator").Translate([SecurityIdentifier])
```

Adding to the discretionary ACL may be achieved as shown in the following snippet. The example makes use of the Get-PSSessionAcl function and the SessionAccessRight enumeration created previously to grant access to the current user. The current user is identified using environment variables:

```
using namespace System.Security.AccessControl; using namespace
System.Security.Principal

$identity = "$env:USERDOMAIN\$env:USERNAME"
```

```
$acl = Get-PSSessionAcl -Name "Microsoft.PowerShell"
$acl.DiscretionaryAcl.AddAccess(
    'Allow',
    ([NTAccount]$identity).Translate([SecurityIdentifier]),
    [Int][SessionAccessRight]'Full',
    'None',    # Inheritance flags
    'None'     # Propagation flags
)
```

The updated ACL must be converted back to an SDDL string to apply the change:

```
$sddl = $acl.GetSddlForm('All')
Set-PSSessionConfiguration Microsoft.PowerShell -SecurityDescriptorSddl
$sddl
```

User Account Control

User Account Control (UAC) restricts local (not domain) user accounts that log on using a remote connection. By default, the remote connection will be made as a standard user account, that is, a user without administrative privileges.

The `Enable-PSRemoting` command disables UAC remote restrictions. If another method has been used to enable remoting, and a local account is being used to connect, it is possible that remote restrictions are still in place.

The current value can be viewed using the following:

```
$params = @{
    Path =
'HKLM:\SOFTWARE\Microsoft\Windows\CurrentVersion\Policies\System'
    Name = 'LocalAccountTokenFilterPolicy'
}
Get-ItemPropertyValue @params
```

If the key or value is missing, an error will be thrown. UAC remote restrictions can be disabled as follows. Using the `Force` parameter will allow the creation of both the key and the value:

```
$params = @{
    Path  =
'HKLM:\SOFTWARE\Microsoft\Windows\CurrentVersion\Policies\System'
    Name  = 'LocalAccountTokenFilterPolicy'
    Value = 1
    Force = $true
}
Set-ItemProperty @params
```

The change used previously, and UAC remote restrictions, are described in the following Microsoft's Knowledge Base article 951016: `https://support.microsoft.com/en-us/help/951016/description-of-user-account-control-and-remote-restrictions-in-windows-vista`.

Trusted hosts

If a remote system is not part of a domain, or is part of an untrusted domain, an attempt to connect using remoting may fail. The remote system must either be listed in trusted hosts or use SSL.

Use of trusted hosts also applies when connecting from a computer on a domain to another computer that is using a local user account.

Trusted hosts are set on the client, that is, the system making the connection. The following command gets the current value:

```
Get-Item WSMan:\localhost\Client\TrustedHosts
```

The value is a comma-delimited list. Wildcards are supported in the list. The following function may be used to add a value to the list:

```
function Add-TrustedHost {
    param (
        [String]$Hostname
    )

    $item = Get-Item WSMan:\localhost\Client\TrustedHosts
    $trustedHosts = @($item.Value -split ',')
    $trustedHosts = $trustedHosts + $Hostname |
        Where-Object { $_ } |
        Select-Object -Unique

    $item | Set-Item -Value ($trustedHosts -join ',')
}
```

PSSessions

PSSessions use Windows remoting to communicate between servers. PSSessions can be used for anything from remote commands and script execution to providing a remote shell.

By default, PSSessions use the `Microsoft.PowerShell` configuration, described by the built-in `$PSSessionConfigurationName` variable. Administrative rights are required to view and change session-configuration information.

If you are creating a session to the local system, the `-EnableNetworkAccess` parameter should be added to the following commands. This parameter is only applicable to sessions that are created from and connect to the same system.

New-PSSession

Sessions are created using the `New-PSSession` command. In the following example, a session is created on a computer named `PSTEST`:

```
PS> New-PSSession -ComputerName PSTEST

Id    Name      ComputerName    State    ConfigurationName      Availability
--    ----      ------------    -----    -----------------      ------------
1     Session1  PSTEST          Opened   Microsoft.PowerShell   Available
```

Get-PSSession

Sessions created using `New-PSSession` persist until the PSSession is removed (by `Remove-PSSession`) or the PowerShell session ends. The following example returns sessions created in the current PowerShell session:

```
PS> Get-PSSession | Select-Object Id, ComputerName, State

Id ComputerName State
-- ------------ -----
 1 PSTEST       Opened
```

If the `ComputerName` parameter is supplied, `Get-PSSession` will show sessions created on that computer. For example, imagine a session is created in one PowerShell console:

```
$session = New-PSSession -ComputerName PSTest -Name Example
```

A second administrator console session will be able to view details of that session:

```
PS> Get-PSSession -ComputerName PSTest | Select-Object Name, ComputerName,
State

Name       ComputerName  State
----       ------------  -----
Example    PSTest        Disconnected
```

Invoke-Command

Invoke-Command may be used with a PSSession to execute a command or script on a remote system:

```
$session = New-PSSession -ComputerName $env:COMPUTERNAME
Invoke-Command { Get-Process -Id $PID } -Session $session
```

> $env:COMPUTERNAME is localhost

Connecting to a session requires administrative access by default. The preceding command will fail if PowerShell is not running with an administrative token (run as administrator).

A PowerShell session with the administrator token can be started using the Start-Process powershell -Verb RunAs command.

Invoke-Command has a wide variety of different uses, as shown in the command help. For example, a single command can be executed against a list of computers:

```
Invoke-Command { Get-Process -Id $PID } -ComputerName 'first', 'second',
'third'
```

This technique can be useful when combined with AsJob. Pushing the requests into the background allows each server to get on with its work, pushing it back when the work is complete.

Once the job created by the previous command has completed, any data may be retrieved using the Receive-Job command.

A number of advanced techniques may be used with Invoke-Command.

Local functions and remote sessions

The following example executes a function created on the local machine in a remote system using positional arguments:

```
function Get-FreeSpace {
    param (
        [Parameter(Mandatory = $true)]
        [String]$Name
    )

    [Math]::Round((Get-PSDrive $Name).Free / 1GB, 2)
}
Invoke-Command ${function:Get-FreeSpace} -Session $session -ArgumentList C
```

This technique succeeds because the body of the function is declared as a script block. ArgumentList is used to pass a positional argument into the DriveLetter parameter.

If the function depends on other locally-defined functions, the attempt will fail.

Using splatting with ArgumentList

The ArgumentList parameter of Invoke-Command does not offer a means of passing named arguments to a command.

The following example uses splatting to pass parameters. The function is defined on the local system, and the definition of the function is passed to the remote system:

```
# A function which exists on the current system
function Get-FreeSpace {
    param (
        [Parameter(Mandatory = $true)]
        [String]$Name
    )

    [Math]::Round((Get-PSDrive $Name).Free / 1GB, 2)
}

# Define parameters to pass to the function
$params = @{
    Name = 'c'
}

# Execute the function with a named set of parameters
Invoke-Command -ScriptBlock {
```

```
    param ( $definition, $params )

    & ([ScriptBlock]::Create($definition)) @params
} -ArgumentList ${function:Get-FreeSpace}, $params -ComputerName
$computerName
```

In the preceding example, the definition of the Get-FreeSpace function is passed as an argument along with the requested parameters. The script block used with Invoke-Command converts the definition into a ScriptBlock and executes it.

The AsJob parameter

The AsJob parameter can be used with Invoke-Command, for example:

```
$session = New-PSSession PSTest
Invoke-Command -Session $session -AsJob -ScriptBlock { Start-Sleep -Seconds
120 'Done sleeping' }
```

The command finishes immediately, and returns the job that has been created.

While the job is running, the session availability is set to Busy:

```
PS> $session | Select-Object Name, ComputerName, Availability

Name      ComputerName Availability
----      ------------ ------------
Session1  PSTest       Busy
```

Attempts to run another command against the same session will result in an error message.

Once the job has completed, the Receive-Job command may be used.

Disconnected sessions

The InDisconnectedSession of Invoke-Command starts the requested script and immediately disconnects the session. This allows a script to be started and collected from a different console session or a different computer.

The session parameter cannot be used with InDisconnectedSession; Invoke-Command creates a new session for a specified computer name. The session is returned by the following command:

```
Invoke-Command { Start-Sleep -Seconds 120; 'Done' } -ComputerName PSTest -
InDisconnectedSession
```

A second PowerShell session or computer is able to connect to the disconnected session to retrieve the results. The following command assumes that only one session exists with the PSTest computer:

```
Get-PSSession -ComputerName PSTest |
    Connect-PSSession |
    Receive-PSSession
```

Tasks started with AsJob will also continue to run if a session is disconnected. The following example creates a session, starts a long-running process, and disconnects the session:

```
$session = New-PSSession PSTest -Name 'Example'
Invoke-Command { Start-Sleep -Seconds (60 * 60) } -Session $session -AsJob
Disconnect-PSSession $session
```

Once the session has been created and disconnected, the PowerShell console can be closed. A second PowerShell console can find and connect to the existing session:

```
$session = Get-PSSession -ComputerName PSTest -Name 'Example'
Connect-PSSession $session
```

Reviewing the details of the session will show that it is busy running Start-Sleep:

```
PS> Get-PSSession | Select-Object Name, ComputerName, State, Availability

Name     ComputerName State  Availability
----     ------------ -----  ------------
Example  PSTest       Opened Busy
```

The using variable scope

When working with Invoke-Command, PowerShell makes the using variable scope available.

The using variable scope allows access to variables created on a local machine within a script block used with Invoke-Command.

The following example shows the use of a variable that contains parameters for Get-Process. The local variable may contain any reasonable value:

```
$params = @{
    Name            = 'powershell'
    IncludeUserName = $true
}
Invoke-Command -ComputerName PSTest -ScriptBlock {
```

```
    $params = $using:params
    Get-Process @params
}
```

The using scope is a handy alternative to the ArgumentList parameter.

The Enter-PSSession command

Enter-PSSession may be employed to use a session as a remote console. By default, Enter-PSSession accepts a computer name as the first argument:

```
Enter-PSSession PSTest
```

In a similar way, an existing session might be used:

```
$session = New-PSSession -ComputerName PSTest
Enter-PSSession -Session $session
```

Enter-PSSession uses WS-Management as a means of exchanging information between the client and the server. Once a command is typed and the return key is pressed, the entire command is sent to the remote host. The result of the command is sent back using the same mechanism. This exchange can inject a small amount of latency into the shell.

Import-PSSession

Import-PSSession brings commands from a remote computer into the current session. Microsoft Exchange uses this technique to provide remote access to the Exchange Management Shell.

The following example imports the NetAdapter module from a remote server into the current session:

```
$computerName = 'PSTest'
$session = New-PSSession -ComputerName $computerName
Import-PSSession -Session $session -Module NetAdapter
```

Any commands used within this module are executed against the session target, not against the local computer.

If the session is removed, the imported module and its commands will be removed from the local session.

Export-PSSession

In the preceding example, `Import-PSSession` is used to immediately import commands from a remote system into a local session. `Export-PSSession` writes a persistent module that can be used to achieve the same goal.

The following example creates a module in the current user's module path:

```
$computerName = 'PSTest'
$session = New-PSSession -ComputerName $computerName
Export-PSSession -Session $session -Module NetAdapter -OutputModule
"NetAdapter-$computerName"
```

Once the module has been created, it can be imported by name:

```
Import-Module "NetAdapter-$computerName"
```

This process replaces the need to define and import a session, and is useful for remote commands that are used on a regular basis.

Copying items between sessions

PowerShell 5 introduced the ability to copy between sessions using the `Copy-Item` command.

The `FromSession` parameter is used to copy a file to the local system:

```
$session1 = New-PSSession PSTest1
Copy-Item -Path C:\temp\doc.txt -Destination C:\Temp -FromSession $session1
```

In the preceding example, `Path` is on `PSTest1`.

The `ToSession` parameter is used to copy a file to a remote system:

```
$session2 = New-PSSession PSTest2
Copy-Item -Path C:\temp\doc.txt -Destination C:\Temp -ToSession $session2
```

In the previous example, the path used for the destination parameter is on `PSTest2`.

The `FromSession` and `ToSession` parameters cannot be specified together; two separate commands are required to copy a file between two remote sessions.

Remoting on Linux

Microsoft provides instructions for installing PowerShell on Linux; these should be followed before attempting to configure remoting: https://docs.microsoft.com/en-us/powershell/scripting/install/installing-powershell-core-on-linux?view=powershell-6.

Once installed, it is possible to make PowerShell the default shell. This is optional and does not affect remoting. First, check that PowerShell is listed in the shells file:

```
Get-Content /etc/shells    # Use cat or less in Bash
```

The native chsh (change shell) command can be used to change the default shell for the current user, as shown in the following example:

```
chsh -s /usr/bin/pwsh
```

To configure remoting using WSMan, the OMI and PSRP packages must be installed. The following example uses yum since the operating system in use is CentOS 7:

```
yum install omi.x86_64 omi-psrp-server.x86_64
```

By default, CentOS has a firewall configured. The network interface in use, in this case eth0, must be added to an appropriate zone, and WinRM must be allowed:

```
firewall-cmd --zone=home --change-interface=eth0
firewall-cmd --zone=home --add-port=5986/tcp
```

Once configured, it should be possible to connect to the remote host. SSL is required to form the connection. The certificate is self-signed so certificate validity tests must be skipped at this stage:

```
$params = @{
    ComputerName    = 'LinuxSystemNameOrIPAddress'
    Credential      = Get-Credential
    Authentication  = 'Basic'
    UseSsl          = $true
    SessionOption   = New-PSSessionOption -SkipCACheck -SkipCNCheck
}
Enter-PSSession @params
```

The state of the certificate leaves the identity of the host in question, but it does ensure that traffic is encrypted. If SSL is to be used beyond testing, a valid certificate chain should be established.

At this point, the remote computer should be accessible using both Windows PowerShell and PowerShell Core.

Remoting over SSH

PowerShell Core introduces the concept of remoting over SSH. This provides a useful alternative to remoting over HTTPS, which avoids the burden of managing certificates: `https://github.com/PowerShell/PowerShell/blob/866b558771a20cca3daa47f300e830b31a24ee95/docs/new-features/remoting-over-ssh/README.md`.

The SSH transport for remoting cannot be used from Windows PowerShell, only PowerShell Core.

Connecting from Windows to Linux

If connecting from Windows, an SSH client must be installed. The following command uses the Chocolatey package manager (`http://chocolatey.org`) to install OpenSSH for Windows:

```
choco install openssh
```

Depending on the desired configuration, public key authentication may be enabled in the SSH daemon configuration file. A subsystem must be added to the file.

To enable public key authentication, set `PubkeyAuthentication`:

```
PubkeyAuthentication yes
```

An existing subsystem entry will likely exist toward the end of the file; this new entry can be added beneath the existing entry:

```
Subsystem        powershell      /opt/microsoft/powershell/6/pwsh -sshs -
NoLogo -NoProfile
```

The `sshd` service should be restarted after changing the configuration file:

```
service sshd restart
```

The connection in this example uses SSH-key authentication. This requires an SSH key on Windows. If an existing key is not available, the `ssh-keygen` command can be used to create a new key pair. The command will prompt for any information it requires.

The private key created by this command will be used when connecting to a remote host. The public key is used to authorize a user and will be placed on the Linux system.

The public key can be obtained by running the following command on the system on which it was generated. This command assumes default filenames were used when generating the key:

```
Get-Content ~\.ssh\id_rsa.pub | Set-Clipboard
```

~ is home

The tilde character may be used as shorthand for the path to the home directory. On Linux it is typically /home/<username>, and on Windows it is typically similar to C:\users\<username>.

~ may be replaced with the $home variable, or the $env:USERPROFILE environment variable on Windows, if desired.

The public key should be added to the authorized_keys files on Linux:

```
$publicKey = 'ssh-rsa AAAABG...'
New-Item ~/.ssh -ItemType Directory
Set-Content -Path ~/.ssh/authorized_keys -Value $publicKey
```

Once complete, a session can be created and used to interact with the Linux system:

```
$params = @{
    HostName     = 'LinuxSystemNameOrIPAddress'
    UserName     = $env:USERNAME
    SSHTransport = $true
    KeyFilePath  = '~\.ssh\id_rsa'
}
Enter-PSSession @params
```

Connecting from Linux to Windows

Connecting from Linux to Windows is a harder path; it is clearly undergoing rapid change and is much less mature than connections in the other direction.

Before moving on to configuring SSH, verify that WSMan functions. An HTTPS listener must be set up; HTTP connections are prohibited by newer versions of the PSRP package. If HTTPS is not already available, a self-signed certificate may be created and used as shown in the *Remoting and SSL* section.

If remoting is not yet configured for PowerShell Core, run the `Enable-PSRemoting` command in the Core console (as an administrator). Once enabled, find the name of the configuration entry using the `Get-PSSessionConfiguration` command.

The configuration name may be used to create a session to PowerShell Core that runs on the Windows system:

```
$params = @{
    HostName          = 'WindowsSystemNameOrIPAddress'
    Credential        = (Get-Credential)
    Authentication    = 'Basic'
    UseSSL            = $true
    ConfigurationName = 'PowerShell.6.1.1'
}
Enter-PSSession @params
```

At the time of writing, attempting to connect from Linux to a PowerShell 5.1 session results in an "access denied" error message.

The OpenSSH package must be installed on Windows to continue, as described when configuring the connection from Windows to Linux.

The SSHD service must be installed to allow incoming connections using SSH. A service installation script is included with the OpenSSH package:

```
& "C:\Program Files\OpenSSH-Win64\install-sshd.ps1"
Start-Service sshd
```

If used, Windows Firewall must also be opened:

```
$params = @{
    DisplayName = $name = 'SSH Daemon (SSH-In)'
    Name        = $name
    Profile     = 'Any'
    LocalPort   = 22
    Protocol    = 'TCP'
}
New-NetFirewallRule @params
```

Once this step is complete, it should be possible to create an SSH connection from Linux to Windows:

```
ssh user@WindowsSystemNameOrIPAddress
```

As with configuring Linux, public key authentication may be allowed, and a subsystem must be configured, this time on the Windows system. The `C:\ProgramData\ssh\sshd_config` file must be edited.

To enable public key authentication, set `PubkeyAuthentication`:

```
PubkeyAuthentication yes
```

Add a subsystem to the file. This may be specified in addition to any existing subsystem:

```
Subsystem       powershell     C:/progra~1/PowerShell/6/pwsh.exe -sshs -NoLogo
-NoProfile
```

The `sshd` service should be restarted after changing the configuration file:

```
Restart-Service sshd
```

At this point, it will be possible to create a remoting session using SSH, by entering a password when prompted:

```
$params = @{
    HostName     = 'WindowsSystemNameOrIPAddress'
    UserName     = $env:USERNAME
    SSHTransport = $true
}
Enter-PSSession @params
```

Public key authentication may be configured in the same way as was done for Linux. A key can be generated on Linux using the `ssh-keygen` command.

The public key, by default `~/.ssh/id_rsa.pub`, may be added to an `authorized_keys` file on Windows. The following command, when run on Linux, displays the public key:

```
Get-Content ~/.ssh/id_rsa.pub
```

This public key may be added to an `authorized_keys` file for a user on the Windows system:

```
$publicKey = 'ssh-rsa AAAABG...'
Set-Content -Path ~/.ssh/authorized_keys -Value $publicKey
```

At this point, the Linux system will be able to use public key authentication to access the Windows system:

```
$params = @{
    HostName     = 'WindowsSystemNameOrIPAddress'
    UserName     = $env:USERNAME
    SSHTransport = $true
    KeyFilePath  = '~\.ssh\id_rsa'
}
Enter-PSSession @params
```

Extending this further, Windows systems running PowerShell Core and the SSH daemon may use SSH as a remoting transport to access other Windows systems.

The double-hop problem

The double-hop problem describes a scenario in PowerShell where remoting is used to connect to a host and the remote host tries to connect to another resource. In this scenario, the second connection, the second hop, fails because authentication cannot be implicitly passed.

Over the years, there have been numerous articles that discuss this problem. Ashley McGlone published a blog post in 2016 that describes the problem and the possible solutions: https://blogs.technet.microsoft.com/ashleymcglone/2016/08/30/powershell-remoting-kerberos-double-hop-solved-securely/.

This section briefly explores using CredSSP, as well as how to pass explicit credentials to a remote system. Neither of these options is considered secure, but they require the least amount of work to implement.

These two options are useful in the following situations:

- The remote endpoint is trusted and has not been compromised.
- Critical authentication tokens can be extracted by any administrator on the remote system.
- They are not used for wide-scale regular or scheduled automation, as the methods significantly increase exposure.

CredSSP

A session can be created using CredSSP as the authentication provider:

```
New-PSSession -ComputerName PSTest -Credential (Get-Credential) -
Authentication CredSSP
```

CredSSP must be enabled on the client to support passing credentials to a remote system. The DelegateComputer parameter can be used with either a specific name or a wildcard (*):

```
Enable-WSManCredSSP -Role Client -DelegateComputer PSTest
```

`CredSSP` must also be enabled on the server to receive credentials:

```
Enable-WSManCredSSP -Role Server
```

If this approach is used as a temporary measure, the `CredSSP` roles might be removed afterward.

On the server making the connection, the `Client` role can be disabled:

```
Disable-WSManCredSSP -Role Client
```

On the remote system, the `Server` role can be disabled:

```
Disable-WSManCredSSP -Role Server
```

Passing credentials

Passing credentials into a remote session means the second hop can authenticate without being dependent on authentication tokens from the original system.

In this example, the `using` variable scope is used to access a credential variable. The credential is used to run a query against Active Directory from a remote system:

```
$Credential = Get-Credential
Invoke-Command -ComputerName PSTest -ScriptBlock {
    Get-ADUser -Filter * -Credential $using:Credential
}
```

CIM sessions

CIM sessions are used to work with CIM services, predominantly WMI or commands that base their functionality on WMI. Such commands include those in the `NetAdapter` and `Storage` modules available on Windows 2012 and Windows 8. A list of commands that support CIM sessions may be viewed by entering the following:

```
Get-Command -ParameterName CimSession
```

The list will only include commands from modules that have been imported.

New-CimSession

CIM sessions are created using the New-CimSession command. The following example creates a CIM session using the current system as the computer name using WSMan as the protocol:

```
PS> New-CimSession -ComputerName $env:COMPUTERNAME

Id          : 1
Name        : CimSession1
InstanceId  : bc03b547-1051-4af1-a41d-4d16b0ec0402
ComputerName : PSTEST
Protocol    : WSMAN
```

If the computer name parameter is omitted, the protocol will be set to DCOM:

```
PS> New-CimSession

Id          : 2
Name        : CimSession2
InstanceId  : 804595f4-0144-4590-990a-92b2f22f894f
ComputerName : localhost
Protocol    : DCOM
```

New-CimSession can be used to configure operation timeout settings and whether or not an initial network test should be performed.

The protocol used by New-CimSession can be changed using New-CimSessionOption. Changing the protocol can be useful if there is a need to interact with systems where WinRM is not running or configured:

```
PS> New-CimSession -ComputerName $env:COMPUTERNAME -SessionOption (New-CimSessionOption -Protocol Dcom)

Id          : 3
Name        : CimSession3
InstanceId  : 29bba117-c899-4389-b874-5afe43962a1e
ComputerName : PSTEST
Protocol    : DCOM
```

Get-CimSession

Sessions created using `New-CimSession` persist until the CIM session is removed (by `Remove-CimSession`) or the PowerShell session ends:

```
PS> Get-CimSession | Select-Object Id, ComputerName, Protocol

Id   ComputerName Protocol
--   ------------ --------
 1   PSTEST       WSMAN
 2   localhost    DCOM
 3   PSTEST       DCOM
```

Using CIM sessions

Once a CIM session has been created, it can be used for one or more requests. In the following example, a CIM session is created and then used to gather disk and partition information:

```
$ErrorActionPreference = 'Stop'
try {
    $session = New-CimSession -ComputerName $env:COMPUTERNAME
    Get-Disk -CimSession $session
    Get-Partition -CimSession $session
} catch {
    throw
}
```

In the preceding script, if the attempt to create the session succeeds, the session will be used to get disk and partition information.

Error handling with `try` and `catch` is discussed in Chapter 21, *Error Handling*. The block is treated as a transaction; if a single command fails, the block will stop running. If the attempt to create a new session fails, `Get-Disk` and `Get-Partition` will not run.

Summary

In this chapter, we explored remoting in PowerShell, starting with WS-Management, and took a look at the new SSH-transport features introduced with PowerShell Core. We discussed the double-hop problem, along with a number of possible ways to work around the issue. Finally, we covered CIM sessions briefly.

In the next chapter, we'll explore systems management using a number of the more common Microsoft systems.

15 Asynchronous Processing

PowerShell prefers to run things synchronously, that is, sequentially, or one after another. However, it is frequently necessary to run many things simultaneously, without waiting for another command to complete. This is known as an asynchronous operation.

Operations of this nature may be local to the current machine, or might be used to run queries or code against remote systems.

PowerShell includes a number of different commands and classes that can be used to do more than one thing at a time. The most obvious of these are the job commands.

In addition to the job commands, PowerShell can react to .NET events, and can use Runspaces and Runspace pools.

This chapter explores the following topics:

- Working with jobs
- Reacting to events
- Using Runspaces and Runspace pools

Working with jobs

The job commands in PowerShell provide a means of executing code asynchronously by creating a new PowerShell process for each job.

As each job executes within a new process, data cannot be shared between jobs. Any required modules, functions, or variables all need to be imported into each job.

In addition, jobs might be considered resource heavy as each job must start both a PowerShell process and a console window's host process.

PowerShell provides a number of commands to create and interact with jobs. In addition to the following commands, `Invoke-Command` with the `AsJob` parameter might be used when acting against remote systems.

The Start-Job, Get-Job, and Remove-Job commands

The `Start-Job` command is most commonly used to execute a script block in a very similar manner to `Invoke-Command`. `Start-Job` may also be used to execute a script using the `FilePath` parameter.

When `Start-Job` is executed, a job object, `System.Management.Automation.PSRemotingJob` is created. The job object continues to be available using the `Get-Job` command regardless of whether the output from `Start-Job` is assigned. This is shown as follows:

```
PS> Start-Job -ScriptBlock { Start-Sleep -Seconds 10 }

Id    Name    PSJobTypeName    State    HasMoreData    Location
Command
--    ----    -------------    -----    -----------    --------    -----
--
1     Job1    BackgroundJob    Running         True    localhost
Start-Sleep -Seconds 10

PS> Get-Job

Id    Name    PSJobTypeName    State    HasMoreData    Location
Command
--    ----    -------------    -----    -----------    --------    -----
--
1     Job1    BackgroundJob    Running         True    localhost
Start-Sleep -Seconds 10
```

When a script is using jobs, the common practice is to capture the jobs created instead of relying entirely on `Get-Job`. This avoids problems if module used in a script also creates jobs. The state of the job is reflected on the job object; `Get-Job` is not required to update the status.

Job objects and any data the job has returned remain available until they are removed using the `Remove-Job` command.

`Start-Job` includes a `RunAs32` parameter to run code under the 32-bit version of PowerShell if required.

The `InitializationScript` parameter of `Start-Job` may be used to isolate setup steps, such as importing modules, creating functions, and setting up variables. Each job executes in a separate thread, which means that values cannot be automatically shared.

`Start-Job` does not offer a throttling capability. PowerShell will simultaneously execute every job. Each job will compete for system resources. A `while` or `do` loop may be implemented to maintain a pool of running jobs:

```
$listOfJobs = 1..50
foreach ($job in $listOfJobs) {
 while (@(Get-Job -State Running).Count -gt 10) {
 Start-Sleep -Seconds 10
 }
 Start-Job { Start-Sleep -Seconds (Get-Random -Minimum 10 -Maximum 121) }
}
```

The jobs created here do not return any data and can therefore be removed as soon as they have completed. Data must be retrieved from a job before is it removed.

The Receive-Job command

`Receive-Job` is used to retrieve data from a job. `Receive-Job` may be both as a script runs and when the script is finished. If `Receive-Job` is run before a job is finished, any existing values will be returned. Running `Receive-Job` again will get any new values that have been added, not previously filesystem, which retrieved values. This is shown in the following example:

```
PS> $job = Start-Job { 1..10 | ForEach-Object { $_; Start-Sleep -Seconds 2
} }
>> Write-Host 'Sleeping 2'
>> Start-Sleep -Seconds 2
>> $job | Receive-Job
>> Write-Host 'Sleeping 5'
>> Start-Sleep -Seconds 5
>> $job | Receive-Job

Sleeping 2
1
Sleeping 5
2
3
```

4

The remaining results will be available to Receive-Job as they are returned, or when the job has completed.

The Wait parameter of Receive-Job will receive data from the job as it becomes available and send it to the output pipeline. Receive-Job, along with the Wait parameter, may be useful when Start-Job is running a 32-bit process.

The Wait-Job command

The Wait-Job command waits for all of the jobs in the input pipeline to complete. Wait-Job supports a degree of filtering and offers a timeout to define jobs to wait for.

In some cases, it is desirable to pull off output from jobs as they complete. This can be solved by creating a while or do loop in PowerShell, reacting to jobs as the state changes:

```
while (Get-Job -State Running) {
    $jobs = Get-Job -State Completed
    $jobs | Receive-Job
    $jobs | Remove-Job
    Start-Sleep -Seconds 1
}
```

A while loop does not have an output pipeline, if output is to be piped to another command it would need to be piped within the loop. For example, if the job output were filling a CSV file, Export-Csv would be added inside the loop and the Append parameter would be used:

```
while (Get-Job -State Running) {
    $jobs = Get-Job -State Completed
    $jobs | Receive-Job | Export-Csv output.csv -Append
    $jobs | Remove-Job
    Start-Sleep -Seconds 1
}
```

This technique is useful if the job is returning a large amount of data. Streaming output to a file as jobs complete will potentially help manage memory usage across a larger number of jobs.

This approach can be combined with the snippet, which limits the number of concurrent jobs. The tweak is shown as follows:

```
$listOfJobs = 1..50
```

```
$jobs = foreach ($job in $listOfJobs) {
    while (@(Get-Job -State Running).Count -gt 10) {
        Start-Sleep -Seconds 10
    }

    Start-Job { Start-Sleep -Seconds (Get-Random -Minimum 10 -Maximum 121)
}
    Get-Job -State Completed | Receive-Job | Export-Csv output.csv -Append
}

$jobs | Wait-Job | Receive-Job | Export-Csv output.csv -Append
```

The final line is required to wait for and then receive the jobs that were still running when the last job was started.

Reacting to events

Events in .NET occur when something of interest happens to an object. For instance, System.IO.FileSystemWatcher can be used to monitor a filesystem for changes; when something changes, an event will be raised.

Many different types of objects raise events when changes occur. Get-Member can be used to explore an instance of an object for Event members. For example, a Process object returned by the Get-Process command includes a number of events, shown as follows:

```
PS> Get-Process | Get-Member -MemberType Event


    TypeName: System.Diagnostics.Process

Name                    MemberType    Definition
----                    ----------    ----------
Disposed                Event         System.EventHandler
Disposed(System.Object, System.EventArgs)
ErrorDataReceived       Event
System.Diagnostics.DataReceivedEventHandler ErrorDataReceived(S...
Exited                  Event         System.EventHandler
Exited(System.Object, System.EventArgs)
OutputDataReceived      Event
System.Diagnostics.DataReceivedEventHandler OutputDataReceived(...
```

PowerShell can react to these events, executing code when an event occurs.

This section uses the events raised by `FileSystemWatcher` to demonstrate working with events. `FileSystemWatcher` is able to react to a number of different events, shown as follows:

```
PS> [System.IO.FileSystemWatcher]::new() | Get-Member -MemberType Event |
Select-Object Name

Name
----
Changed
Created
Deleted
Disposed
Error
Renamed
```

The `Changed` and `Created` events will be used in the following examples.

The Register-ObjectEvent and *-Event commands

`Register-ObjectEvent` is used to register interest in an event raised by a .NET object. The command creates a `PSEventSubscriber` object.

The `Register-ObjectEvent` command expects at least the name of the object that will be raising the event and the name of the event.

The following `FileSystemWatcher` instance watches the `C:\Data` folder. By default, the watcher will only watch for changes at that level, the `IncludeSubDirectories` property might be changed if this must change. Subscribers are created for the `Changed` and `Created` events in the following example:

```
$watcher = [System.IO.FileSystemWatcher]::new('C:\Data')
Register-ObjectEvent -InputObject $watcher -EventName Changed
Register-ObjectEvent -InputObject $watcher -EventName Created
```

If a file is created in the folder specified, an event will be raised. The `Get-Event` command can be used to view the event data:

```
PS> New-Item C:\Data\new.txt | Out-Null
PS> Get-Event

ComputerName      :
RunspaceId        : 46d2a562-2d07-4c58-9416-f82a3e9da5b8
EventIdentifier   : 3
Sender            : System.IO.FileSystemWatcher
```

```
SourceEventArgs  : System.IO.FileSystemEventArgs
SourceArgs       : {System.IO.FileSystemWatcher, new.txt}
SourceIdentifier : ff0784dc-1f0f-4214-b5e7-5d5516eaa13e
TimeGenerated    : 19/02/2019 17:29:53
MessageData      :
```

The `SourceEventArgs` property contains a `FileSystemEventArgs` object. This object includes the type of change, the path, and the filename.

The event remains until it is removed using `Remove-Event`. If another event is raised, it will be returned by `Get-Event` in addition to the existing event.

Depending on the operation performed, `FileSystemWatcher` may return more than one event. When using `Add-Content`, a single event will be raised as follows:

```
PS> Get-Event | Remove-Event
PS> Add-Content C:\Data\new.txt -Value value
PS> Get-Event | Select-Object -ExpandProperty SourceEventArgs

ChangeType   FullPath          Name
----------   --------          ----
   Changed   C:\Data\new.txt   new.txt
```

`Set-Content` is used when two events are raised. `Set-Content` makes two changes to the file, directly or indirectly. This will often be the case, depending on how an application interacts with the filesystem which is shown as follows:

```
PS> Get-Event | Remove-Event
PS> Set-Content C:\Data\new.txt -Value value
PS> Get-Event | Select-Object -ExpandProperty SourceEventArgs

ChangeType   FullPath          Name
----------   --------          ----
   Changed   C:\Data\new.txt   new.txt
   Changed   C:\Data\new.txt   new.txt
```

Whether an event will trigger once or twice depends on the type in use, the event raised, and the subsystem that caused the event to be raised in the first place.

If events are being handled in the foreground using `Get-Event`, `Wait-Event` might be used to wait until an event is raised.

Wait-Event does not return any output

`Wait-Event` stops as soon as an event is raised. `Wait-Event` does not return the event; any raised events must be retrieved using `Get-Event`.

The Get-EventSubscriber and Unregister-Event commands

The `Get-EventSubscriber` command may be used to view any existing event handlers created using `Register-ObjectEvent`. For example, `Get-EventSubscriber` will display the subscribers created for `FileSystemWatcher`:

```
PS> Get-EventSubscriber

SubscriptionId    : 4
SourceObject      : System.IO.FileSystemWatcher
EventName         : Changed
SourceIdentifier  : 6516aebc-d191-44b5-a38f-60314f606102
Action            :
HandlerDelegate   :
SupportEvent      : False
ForwardEvent      : False

SubscriptionId    : 5
SourceObject      : System.IO.FileSystemWatcher
EventName         : Created
SourceIdentifier  : ff0784dc-1f0f-4214-b5e7-5d5516eaa13e
Action            :
HandlerDelegate   :
SupportEvent      : False
ForwardEvent      : False
```

If the subscribers are no longer required, they can be removed using the `Unregister-Event` command. The following command removes all registered event subscribers:

```
Get-EventSubscriber | Unregister-Event
```

The Action, Event, EventArgs, and MessageData parameters

The `Action` parameter of `Register-ObjectEvent` allows a script block to be automatically triggered when an event is raised.

The script block can use a reserved variable, $event, which is equivalent to the output from Get-Event. In the following example, the event subscriber includes an action, which creates a log message. The log messages are written to file in a different folder; if they were written to the same folder, a loop would be created:

```
New-Item C:\Audit -ItemType Directory
$watcher = [System.IO.FileSystemWatcher]::new('C:\Data')
$params = @{
    InputObject = $watcher
    EventName   = 'Changed'
    Action      = {
        $event.SourceEventArgs | Export-Csv C:\Audit\DataActivity.log -
Append
    }
}
Register-ObjectEvent @params
```

If a file is created in the C:\Data folder, an event will be raised and an entry will be created in C:\Audit\DataActivity.log:

```
PS> Set-Content C:\Data\new.txt -Value new
PS> Import-Csv C:\Audit\DataActivity.log


ChangeType      FullPath            Name
----------      --------            ----
Changed         C:\Data\new.txt     new.txt
Changed         C:\Data\new.txt     new.txt
```

Additional information can be passed to the Action script block using the MessageData parameter. MessageData is an arbitrary object that contains user-defined information. Before continuing to the example, the event subscriber we just created should be removed. The log file is also deleted as the format of the file will be changed:

```
Get-EventSubscriber | Unregister-Event
Remove-Item C:\Audit\DataActivity.log
```

The following example adds a date stamp to the log entry, and a custom message which is supplied via MessageData. The values passed in using the MessageData parameter are made available as a MessageData property on the $event variable:

```
$watcher = [System.IO.FileSystemWatcher]::new('C:\Data')
$params = @{
    InputObject = $watcher
    EventName   = 'Changed'
    Action      = {
        $user = $event.MessageData |
            Where-Object { $event.SourceEventArgs.Name -match $_.Expression
```

```
    } |
                Select-Object -ExpandProperty User -First 1

            $event.SourceEventArgs |
                Select-Object @(
                    @{Name = 'Date'; Expression = { Get-Date -Format u }}
                    'ChangeType'
                    'FullPath'
                    @{Name = 'Responsible Person'; Expression = { $user }}
                ) |
                Export-Csv C:\Audit\DataActivity.log -Append
        }
        MessageData = @(
            [PSCustomObject]@{ Expression = '\.txt$'; User = 'Sarah' }
            [PSCustomObject]@{ Expression = '\.mdb';  User = 'Phil' }
        )
    }
    Register-ObjectEvent @params
```

Setting the content of a file in the `C:\Data` folder will trigger the event subscriber. An entry will be written to the log file using the entry from `MessageData`:

```
PS> Set-Content C:\Data\test.mdb 1
PS> Import-Csv C:\Audit\DataActivity.log

Date                    ChangeType      FullPath            Responsible
Person
----                    ----------      --------            -----------------
-
2019-02-19 18:30:04Z    Changed         C:\Data\test.mdb    Phil
```

The event subscribers should be removed if they are no longer required. Closing the PowerShell session will remove all event subscribers.

Using Runspaces and Runspace pools

Runspaces and Runspace pools are an efficient way of asynchronously executing PowerShell code. Runspaces are far more efficient than jobs as they execute in the same process. The main disadvantage is complexity: PowerShell does not include native commands to simplify working with these classes.

Fortunately, PowerShell is highly extensible. Two third-party modules have been created to work with Runspaces:

- PoshRSJob: https://www.powershellgallery.com/packages/PoshRSJob
- ThreadJob: https://www.powershellgallery.com/packages/ThreadJob

Both modules work with Windows PowerShell and PowerShell Core.

The PoshRSJob module is very mature and has a rich set of features. It is the most frequently recommended module, providing an alternative to the Start-Job command.

ThreadJob has promise; it interacts with the existing job commands, such as Get-Job, Wait-Job, and Receive-Job. However, the module is far less mature than PoshRSJob and does not include documentation.

When you need a bit more flexibility or efficiency, it's helpful to understand how PowerShell uses these component modules.

Creating a PowerShell instance

PowerShell instances are created using the Create static method of the System.Management.Automation.PowerShell type. A type accelerator exists for this type and the name can be shortened:

```
$psInstance = [PowerShell]::Create()
```

System.Management.Automation.PowerShell or PowerShell

The usage is slightly confusing as both the console host and the type used here are normally referred to as PowerShell.

References to instances of System.Management.Automation.PowerShell as PowerShell are highlighted in this section.

The object created by the Create method has a fluent interface. Methods can be chained one after another without assigning a value. The following example adds a single command and a parameter, and then runs the command:

```
[PowerShell]::Create().AddCommand('Get-Process').AddParameter('Name',
'powershell').Invoke()
```

A complex script can be built in this manner. If two commands are chained together, they are assumed to be part of the same statement, implementing a pipeline. The `AddStatement` method is used to start a new statement, ending the current command pipeline:

```
[PowerShell]::Create().AddCommand('Get-Process').AddParameter('Name',
'powershell').
                    AddStatement().
                    AddCommand('Get-Service').
                    AddCommand('Select-Object').AddParameter('First',
1).
                    Invoke()
```

The result of the preceding example is equivalent to the following script:

```
Get-Process -Name powershell
Get-Service | Select-Object -First 1
```

The `AddCommand`, `AddParameter`, and `AddStatement` methods demonstrated so far are particularly useful when assembling a script programmatically. If the script content is already known, the script can be added using the `AddScript` method:

```
$script = @'
    Get-Process -Name powershell
    Get-Service | Select-Object -First 1
'@
[PowerShell]::Create().AddScript($script).Invoke()
```

The script is added as a string, not as a script block. When creating the script, be mindful of variable interpolation. Interpolation is avoided in the following example by enclosing the script content in single quotes.

The `AddScript` method can be used in conjunction with any of the other methods used here to build a complex set of commands.

The Invoke and BeginInvoke methods

The `Invoke` method used with each of the following examples executes the code immediately and synchronously. The `BeginInvoke` method is used to execute asynchronously, that is, without waiting for the last operation to complete.

Both the `PowerShell` instance object and the `IASyncResult` returned by `BeginInvoke` must be captured. Assigning the values allows continued access to the instances and is required to retrieve output from the commands:

```
$psInstance = [PowerShell]::Create().AddCommand('Start-
Sleep').AddParameter('Seconds', 300)
$asyncResult = $psInstance.BeginInvoke()
```

While the job is running, the `InvocationStateInfo` property of the `PowerShell` object will show as `Running`:

```
PS> $psInstance.InvocationStateInfo

State       Reason
-----       ------
Running
```

This state is reflected on the `IASyncResult` object held in the `$asyncResult` variable:

```
PS> $asyncResult

CompletedSynchronously     IsCompleted     AsyncState     AsyncWaitHandle
----------------------     -----------     ----------     ---------------
                 False           False
System.Threading.ManualResetEvent
```

When the command completes, both objects will reflect that state:

```
PS> $psInstance.InvocationStateInfo.State
Completed

PS> $asyncResult.IsCompleted
True
```

Setting either (or both) of these variables to null does not stop the script executing in the `PowerShell` instance. Doing so only removes the variables assigned, making it impossible to interact with the Runspace:

```
$psInstance = [PowerShell]::Create().AddScript('
    1..60 | ForEach-Object {
        Add-Content -Path c:\temp\output.txt -Value $_
        Start-Sleep -Seconds 1
    }
')
$asyncResult = $psInstance.BeginInvoke()
$psInstance = $null
$asyncResult = $null
```

The script continues to execute, filling the output file. The following file may be using Get–Content:

```
Get-Content c:\temp\output.txt -Wait
```

If the work of the script is no longer required, the Stop method should be called instead of setting variables to null:

```
$psInstance = [PowerShell]::Create()
$psInstance.AddCommand('Start-Sleep').AddParameter('Seconds', 120)
$psInstance.Stop()
```

A terminating error is raised when the Stop method is called. If the output from the instance is retrieved using the EndInvoke method, a The pipeline has been stopped error message will be displayed.

The EndInvoke method and the PSDataCollection object

EndInvoke is one of two possible ways to get output from a PowerShell instance. The EndInvoke method may be called as follows:

```
$psInstance = [PowerShell]::Create()
$asyncResult = $psInstance.AddScript('1..10').BeginInvoke()
$psInstance.EndInvoke($asyncResult)
```

If the invocation has not finished, EndInvoke will block execution until it has completed.

The second possible method involves passing a PSDataCollection object to the BeginInvoke method:

```
$instanceInput =
[System.Management.Automation.PSDataCollection[PSObject]]::new()
$instanceOutput =
[System.Management.Automation.PSDataCollection[PSObject]]::new()

$psInstance = [PowerShell]::Create()
$asyncResult = $psInstance.AddScript('
    1..10 | ForEach-Object {
        Start-Sleep -Seconds 1
        $_
    }
').BeginInvoke(
    $instanceInput,
```

```
    $instanceOutput
)
```

The `$psInstance` and `$asyncResult` variables are still used to determine whether the script has completed. Results are available in `$instanceOutput` as they become available. Attempting to access `$instanceOutput` in the console will block execution until the script completes. New values added to the collection will be displayed as they are added.

The unused `$instanceInput` variable in the preceding example may be populated with values for an input pipeline if required, for example:

```
$instanceInput =
[System.Management.Automation.PSDataCollection[PSObject]](1..10)
$instanceOutput =
[System.Management.Automation.PSDataCollection[PSObject]]::new()

$psInstance = [PowerShell]::Create()
$asyncResult = $psInstance.AddCommand('ForEach-
Object').AddParameter('Process', { $_ }).BeginInvoke(
    $instanceInput,
    $instanceOutput
)
```

The `AddCommand` method was used in the preceding example as `ForEach-Object` will act on an input pipeline. A script can accept pipeline input within a process block; pipeline input is not implicitly passed to the commands within the script. The following example implements an input pipeline and uses the built-in `$_` variable to repeat the numbers from the input pipeline:

```
$instanceInput =
[System.Management.Automation.PSDataCollection[PSObject]](1..10)
$instanceOutput =
[System.Management.Automation.PSDataCollection[PSObject]]::new()

$asyncResult = $psInstance.AddScript('
    process {
        $_
    }
').BeginInvoke(
    $instanceInput,
    $instanceOutput
)
```

Each of the examples so far has concerned itself with running a single script or a set of commands.

Running multiple instances

As an individual instance is executing asynchronously with `BeginInvoke`, several may be started. In each case, both the `PowerShell` object and the `IASyncResult` object should be preserved:

```
$jobs = 1..5 | ForEach-Object {
    $instance = [PowerShell]::Create().AddScript('
        Start-Sleep -Seconds (Get-Random -Minimum 10 -Maximum 121)
    ')
    [PSCustomObject]@{
        Id          = $instance.InstanceId
        Instance    = $instance
        AsyncResult = $instance.BeginInvoke()
    } | Add-Member State -MemberType ScriptProperty -PassThru -Value {
        $this.Instance.InvocationStateInfo.State
    }
}
```

Each job will continue for a random number of seconds and then complete. As each job completes, the `State` property created by `Add-Member` will change to reflect that:

```
PS> $jobs | Select-Object Id, State

Id                                      State
--                                      -----
de79dcc3-8092-4592-a89e-271fc2b8b65e    Completed
85de5d4d-f754-461d-88da-ac5c7948c546    Running
eb8e0b84-2a47-4379-bd89-e7e523201033    Running
6357a4c3-b6d1-4a9f-8f88-ee3ac0891eb1    Running
3dc050fe-8ff9-4f93-afa9-86768bd3b407    Completed
```

The following snippet might be used to wait for all of the jobs to complete:

```
while ($jobs.State -eq 'Running') {
    Start-Sleep -Milliseconds 100
}
```

If the number of jobs is significantly larger, the system running the jobs might well become overwhelmed.

Using the RunspacePool object

RunspacePool can be used to overcome the problem of overwhelming a system. The pool can be configured with a minimum and maximum number of threads to execute at any point in time.

The RunspacePool object is created using the RunspaceFactory type, as follows:

```
[RunspaceFactory]::CreateRunspacePool(1, 5)
```

RunspacePool must be opened before it can be used. The same pool is set for each of the PowerShell instances that expects to use the pool:

```
$runspacePool = [RunspaceFactory]::CreateRunspacePool(1, 2)
$runspacePool.Open()
$jobs = 1..10 | ForEach-Object {
    $instance = [PowerShell]::Create().AddScript('Start-Sleep -Seconds 10')
    $instance.RunspacePool = $runspacePool
    [PSCustomObject]@{
        Id          = $instance.InstanceId
        Instance    = $instance
        AsyncResult = $instance.BeginInvoke()
    } | Add-Member State -MemberType ScriptProperty -PassThru -Value {
        $this.Instance.InvocationStateInfo.State
    }
}
```

Each of the jobs will show as running, but only two will complete at a time, based on the maximum set for the pool in the following example. After 10 seconds, the state of the jobs will be similar to the following:

```
PS> $jobs | Select-Object Id, State

Id                                      State
--                                      -----
63e2ab2d-613a-4c9c-8f21-d93c8a126008    Completed
781e4a08-04d6-4927-986a-e116fb16a852    Completed
1d80c45d-326b-423b-93d9-21703e747a93    Running
6840dfb1-f47d-4977-868f-697fcbb8af7e    Running
6f3aa668-f680-40b6-8a94-c9d04693b1ad    Running
868f324c-7ba5-4913-83a9-345d8f356aec    Running
318a44ec-b390-45a5-a2cc-0272c1e2ad20    Running
ced0f017-1a1c-42d0-9c53-9e09f9c8ace9    Running
9d003c91-6a2b-4d6f-820e-975fffeb57d8    Running
71818997-b55e-41d6-bdf2-e62426036863    Running
```

When all processing is finished, all objects should be explicitly disposed of to ensure they are closed down:

```
$jobs.Instance | ForEach-Object Dispose
$runspacePool.Dispose()
```

After `Dispose` has been run, the variables might be set to null. Objects that are no longer referenced will be removed by garbage collection. Garbage collection can be run immediately using the following command if a large amount of memory was committed when running the jobs:

```
[GC]::Collect()
```

Runspace pools are incredibly useful. To improve the utility of the pool, it can be seeded with modules, functions, and variables before the pool is opened.

About the InitialSessionState object

`InitialSessionState` is used by `Runspace` or `RunspacePool` to describe a starting point. The `InitialSessionState` object may have modules, functions, or variables added.

PowerShell provides several different options for creating `InitialSessionState`. This is achieved using a set of static methods. The most commonly used are `CreateDefault` and `CreateDefault2`. For example, `CreateDefault2` is used as follows:

```
$initialSessionState = [InitialSessionState]::CreateDefault2()
```

The difference between `CreateDefault` and `CreateDefault2` is that `CreateDefault` includes engine snap-ins, while `CreateDefault2` does not.

PowerShell Core does not use snap-ins

PowerShell Core does not include support for snap-ins. The difference between the two methods is therefore not apparent on PowerShell Core.

`CreateDefault2` is therefore slightly more lightweight and is more appropriate for more recent versions of PowerShell.

The difference may be shown by creating and comparing the list of snap-ins in each case:

```
PS>
[PowerShell]::Create([InitialSessionState]::CreateDefault()).AddCommand('Ge
t-PSSnapIn').Invoke().Name
```

```
Microsoft.PowerShell.Diagnostics
Microsoft.PowerShell.Host
Microsoft.PowerShell.Core
Microsoft.PowerShell.Utility
Microsoft.PowerShell.Management
Microsoft.PowerShell.Security
Microsoft.WSMan.Management
```

`CreateDefault2` only adds the `Microsoft.PowerShell.Core` snap-in, as follows:

```
PS>
[PowerShell]::Create([InitialSessionState]::CreateDefault2()).AddCommand('G
et-PSSnapIn').Invoke().Name

Microsoft.PowerShell.Core
```

Items can be added to `InitialSessionState` before `Runspace` (or `RunspacePool`) is opened.

Adding modules and snap-ins

Modules are added using the `ImportPSModule` method of `InitialSessionState`:

```
$initialSessionState = [InitialSessionState]::CreateDefault2()
$initialSessionState.ImportPSModule('Pester')
```

Several modules can be added with the same method. Modules can be specified by name, in which case the most recent will be used. A module may be specified using a hashtable that describes a name and version information:

```
$initialSessionState.ImportPSModule(@(
    'NetAdapter'
    @{ ModuleName = 'Pester'; ModuleVersion = '4.6.0' }
))
```

`MaximumVersion` and `RequiredVersion` may also be used with the hashtable.

A snap-in may be imported in Windows PowerShell using the `ImportPSSnapIn` method. The method requires the name of a single snap-in, and a reference to a variable to hold any warnings raised during import:

```
$warning =
[System.Management.Automation.Runspaces.PSSnapInException]::new()
$initialSessionState.ImportPSSnapIn('WDeploySnapin3.0', [Ref]$warning)
```

If multiple snap-ins are required, the `ImportPSSnapIn` method must be called once for each.

Adding variables

`InitialSessionState` objects created using `CreateDefault2` will include all of the built-in variables with default values. The value of these variables cannot be changed before the session is opened.

Additional variables can be added using the `Add` method of the `Variables` property. Variables are defined as a `SessionStateVariableEntry` object. An example of adding a variable is shown here:

```
$variableEntry =
[System.Management.Automation.Runspaces.SessionStateVariableEntry]::new(
    'Variable',
    'Value',
    'Optional description'
)

$initialSessionState = [InitialSessionState]::CreateDefault2()
$initialSessionState.Variables.Add($variableEntry)
```

Several overloads are available, each allowing the variable to be defined in greater detail. For example, a variable with the `Private` scope may be created:

```
$variableEntry =
[System.Management.Automation.Runspaces.SessionStateVariableEntry]::new(
    'PrivateVariable',
    'Value',
    'Optional description',
    [System.Management.Automation.ScopedItemOptions]::Private
)

$initialSessionState.Variables.Add($variableEntry)
```

Defining a fixed type for a variable is more difficult, the `ArgumentTypeConverterAttribute` needed to do this is private and difficult to create in PowerShell. To work around this problem, a variable might be created with the required attributes, then `SessionStateVariableEntry` can be created from the variable:

```
[ValidateSet('Value1', 'Value2')][String]$ComplexVariable = 'Value1'

$variable = Get-Variable ComplexVariable
$variableEntry =
```

```
[System.Management.Automation.Runspaces.SessionStateVariableEntry]::new(
    $variable.Name,
    $variable.Value,
    $variable.Description,
    $variable.Options,
    $variable.Attributes
)

$initialSessionState.Variables.Add($variableEntry)
```

Using this approach allows complex variables to be defined within the session.

Adding functions

Functions and other commands can be added to the InitialSessionState object in much the same way as variables. If a function is within a module, the module should be imported instead.

Functions, as SessionStateFunctionEntry objects, are added to the Commands property of the InitialSessionState object.

Simple functions can be added by defining the body of the function inline, as follows:

```
$functionEntry =
[System.Management.Automation.Runspaces.SessionStateFunctionEntry]::new(
    'Write-Greeting',
    'Write-Host "Hello world"'
)

$initialSessionState.Commands.Add($functionEntry)
```

Functions may be added with scope options in the same way as is done with variables. Scoping is rarely used with functions.

If the function already exists in the current session, the output of Get-Command might be used to fill the SessionStateFunctionEntry object:

```
function Write-Greeting {
    Write-Host 'Hello world'
}

$function = Get-Command Write-Greeting
$functionEntry =
[System.Management.Automation.Runspaces.SessionStateFunctionEntry]::new(
    $function.Name,
    $function.Definition
```

```
)

$initialSessionState.Commands.Add($functionEntry)
```

Once the `InitialSessionState` object is filled with the required objects, it may be used to create a `PowerShell` instance or a `RunspacePool`.

Using the InitialSessionState and RunspacePool objects

The `RunspacePool` object can be created using `RunspaceFactory`. `RunspacePool` can be created with either the minimum and maximum number of concurrent threads, or an `InitialSessionState` object. Creating the pool using an `InitialSessionState` object is shown here:

```
$initialSessionState = [InitialSessionState]::CreateDefault2()
$runspacePool = [RunspaceFactory]::CreateRunspacePool($initialSessionState)
```

Any extra entries required in the `InitialSessionState` must either be added using the `$intialSessionState` variable before `RunspacePool` is created, or extra entries must be added using `$runspacePool.InitialSessionState` after `RunspacePool` is created. Changes cannot be made after `RunspacePool` has been opened.

If `RunspacePool` is created with `InitialSessionState`, the `SetMinRunspaces` and `SetMaxRunspaces` methods can be used to adjust the minimum and maximum number of threads. The default value for both the minimum and maximum is 1. The following example changes the maximum:

```
$runspacePool.SetMaxRunspaces(5)
```

The `GetMinRunspaces` and `GetMaxRunspaces` methods may be used to retrieve the current values.

`RunspacePool` is then used as shown in the *Using the RunspacePool object* section.

Using Runspace-synchronized objects

A number of classes in .NET offer Runspace synchronization. This means that an instance of an object can be made accessible from Runspaces that share a common parent.

The most commonly used Runspace-synchronized object is a hashtable. The hashtable is created using the `Synchronized` static method of the `Hashtable` type:

```
$synchronizedHashtable = [Hashtable]::Synchronized(@{
    Key = 'Value'
})
```

The synchronized hashtable can be added to an `InitialSessionState` object and then used within a script or command that is running in a Runspace. The changes made to the hashtable within the runspace are visible outside:

```
$variableEntry =
[System.Management.Automation.Runspaces.SessionStateVariableEntry]::new(
    'synchronizedHashtable',
    $synchronizedHashtable,
    ''
)

$runspace =
[RunspaceFactory]::CreateRunspace([InitialSessionState]::CreateDefault2())
$runspace.InitialSessionState.Variables.Add($variableEntry)

$psInstance = [PowerShell]::Create()
$psInstance.Runspace = $runspace
$runspace.Open()

$psInstance.AddScript('$synchronizedHashtable.Add("NewKey",
"NewValue")').Invoke()
```

After the script has completed, the key added by the script will be visible in the parent Runspace, the current PowerShell session.

In addition to the Runspace-synchronized hashtable, an `ArrayList` might be created in a similar manner, as follows:

```
[System.Collections.ArrayList]::Synchronized([System.Collections.ArrayList]
::new())
```

.NET also offers classes in the `System.Collections.Concurrent` namespace, which offers similar cross-Runspace access: https://docs.microsoft.com/en-us/dotnet/api/system.collections.concurrent.

For example, `ConcurrentStack` might be used as follows:

```
$stack = [System.Collections.Concurrent.ConcurrentStack[PSObject]]::new()
$stack.Push('Value')

$variableEntry =
[System.Management.Automation.Runspaces.SessionStateVariableEntry]::new(
    'stack',
    $stack,
    ''
)

$runspace =
[RunspaceFactory]::CreateRunspace([InitialSessionState]::CreateDefault2())
$runspace.InitialSessionState.Variables.Add($variableEntry)

$psInstance = [PowerShell]::Create()
$psInstance.Runspace = $runspace
$runspace.Open()

$psInstance.AddScript('
    $value = 0
    if ($stack.TryPop([Ref]$value)) {
        $value
    }
').Invoke()
```

Each of the collection types in the `System.Collections.Concurrent` namespace offers similar `Try` methods to access elements.

Summary

In this chapter, we briefly explored the job commands built into PowerShell; since they are built in, they are a solid starting point for running asynchronous operations.

Event subscribers are used to reacting to events, or things of interest, that happen. The event commands are used to work with events on .NET objects.

Finally, we looked at how Runspaces and Runspace pools can be used in PowerShell as an efficient method of working asynchronously.

In the next chapter, we will explore the building blocks of larger scripts.

4
Section 4: Extending PowerShell

In this section, we will look at adding and implementing new functionality in PowerShell.

The following chapters are included in this section:

- Chapter 16, *Scripts, Functions, and Filters*
- Chapter 17, *Parameters, Validation, and Dynamic Parameters*
- Chapter 18, *Classes and Enumerations*
- Chapter 19, *Building Modules*
- Chapter 20, *Testing*
- Chapter 21, *Error Handling*

16
Scripts, Functions, and Filters

Functions can be described as building blocks in PowerShell. Functions are used to break up code into manageable sections. A function should strive to be good at one job. Functions are often used to build scripts; the script uses functions as a means of concisely describing the steps it is taking. Functions are often grouped together in modules. The functions within a module often share a common purpose or act on a single system. A filter is a specialized function, and are briefly explored in this chapter as they have been part of PowerShell since version 1.

This chapter explores the following topics:

- Introducing scripts, functions, and filters
- `Begin`, `Process`, and `End`
- Param, parameters, and `CmdletBinding`
- `ShouldProcess` and `ShouldContinue`

Introducing scripts, functions, and filters

Scripts, functions, and filters have equivalent functionality: all are considered to be commands. The most significant difference is how the command is stored and presented. A script is saved in a file with a `ps1` extension. Functions and filters can be created directly in the console, dot-sourced from a `ps1` file, or imported from a module.

The difference between a function and a filter is small and will be described when we explore `Begin`, `Process`, and `End` in this chapter. Filters are otherwise exactly like functions. Using filters is not recommended; they are extremely rare and may confuse others attempting to maintain a piece of code.

Scripts and Requires

The Requires statement is valid only in scripts and may be used to restrict a script from running if certain conditions are not met. For example, a script may require administrative rights, or certain modules.

The Requires statement must be the first line in the script; comments and other code may not appear before it.

An example of the Requires statement is shown here:

```
#Requires –RunAsAdministrator –Modules @{ ModuleName = 'TLS'; ModuleVersion = '2.0.0' }
```

Notice that there is no space between the comment character, #, and the Requires keyword.

PowerShell includes help for the Requires statement:

```
Get-Help about_Requires
```

In a script, the Requires statement may be used to declare a need for administrative rights, or certain modules.

Scripts and using statements

A function may benefit from using statements, provided they are declared in the parent scope. The parent scope includes code run on the console, a script that contains a function, or a module (psm1 file) that contains a function.

Using statements, introduced with PowerShell 5, appear throughout this book. An example of a using statement is shown here:

```
using assembly System.Xml.Linq
using namespace System.Xml.Linq
```

Nesting functions

In the same way that a script can contain functions, a function can contain other functions. This is shown in the following example:

```
function Outer {
    param (
        $Parameter1
    )

    function Inner1 {
    }
    function Inner2 {
    }

    Write-Host 'Hello world'
}
```

This technique can be used to isolate small repeated sections of code with a function.

Nested functions must appear before they are used, but otherwise can appear anywhere in the body of the function.

The disadvantage of nesting a function in this manner is that it becomes much harder to test as a unit of code. The function only exists in the context of its parent function; it cannot be called from the scope above that. This is an important consideration when developing a function as part of a module.

Comment-based help

Comment-based help was introduced with PowerShell 2 and allows the developer to provide content for Get-Help without needing to understand and work with the far more complex MAML help files.

About MAML

MAML stands for **Microsoft Assistance Markup Language** and is an XML format.

MAML must be used for binary modules (modules that contain commands compiled into a `dll`) that cannot support comment-based help.

The format offers greater control over help content, is used to deliver updateable help, and is the only way to support language localization. Further information on this topic can be found in Microsoft's module developer help content:

```
https://docs.microsoft.com/en-us/powershell/developer/module/
writing-help-for-windows-powershell-modules.
```

Tools such as the PlatyPS module (`https://github.com/PowerShell/platyPS`) can help. Help content can be written in markdown, which can be used to generate a MAML-based help file.

PowerShell includes help for authoring comment-based help:

```
Get-Help about_Comment_Based_Help
```

Comment-based help uses a series of keywords that match up to the different help sections. The most commonly used are listed here:

- `.SYNOPSIS`
- `.DESCRIPTION`
- `.PARAMETER <Name>`
- `.EXAMPLE`
- `.INPUTS`
- `.OUTPUTS`
- `.NOTES`
- `.LINK`

`.SYNOPSIS` and `.DESCRIPTION` are mandatory when writing help. Each of the other sections is optional.

`.PARAMETER`, followed by the name of a parameter, will be included once for each parameter.

`.EXAMPLE` may be used more than once, describing as many examples as desired.

The tag names are not case-sensitive; upper-case is shown here as it is one of the most widely adopted practices. Spelling mistakes in these section names may prevent help appearing altogether; it is important to be careful when writing comment-based help.

Comment-based help may be used with scripts, functions, and filters and is most often placed first in the body of a script. In a script, comment-based help is often written as follows:

```
<#
.SYNOPSIS
    Briefly describes the main action performed by script.ps1
.DESCRIPTION
    A detailed description of the activities of script.ps1.
#>
```

In a function, help is most commonly written as follows:

```
function Get-Something {
    <#
    .SYNOPSIS
        Briefly describes the main action performed by Get-Something
    .DESCRIPTION
        A detailed description of the activities of Get-Something.
    #>
}
```

Parameter help

Parameter help is most often written using the `.PARAMETER` tag, as shown in the following example:

```
function Get-Something {
    <#
    .SYNOPSIS
        Briefly describes the main action performed by Get-Something
    .DESCRIPTION
        A detailed description of the activities of Get-Something.
    .PARAMETER Parameter1
        Describes the purpose of Parameter1.
    .PARAMETER Parameter2
        Describes the purpose of Parameter2.
```

```
    #>

    param (
        $Parameter1,
        $Parameter2
    )
}
```

It is also possible to write the help for a parameter above the parameter itself:

```
function Get-Something {
    <#
    .SYNOPSIS
        Briefly describes the main action performed by Get-Something
    .DESCRIPTION
        A detailed description of the activities of Get-Something.
    #>

    param (
        # Describes the purpose of Parameter1.
        $Parameter1,

        # Describes the purpose of Parameter2.
        $Parameter2
    )
}
```

One possible advantage of this approach is that it is easy to see which parameters have help and which do not.

Regardless of where help is written for a parameter, Get-Help will read the value:

```
PS> Get-Help Get-Something -Parameter Parameter1

-Parameter1 <Object>
    Describes the purpose of Parameter1.

    Required? false
    Position? 1
    Default value
    Accept pipeline input? false
    Accept wildcard characters? false
```

Examples

`Get-Help` expects examples to start with one or more lines of code, followed by a description of the example, for example:

```
function Get-Something {
    <#
    .SYNOPSIS
        Briefly describes the main action performed by Get-Something
    .DESCRIPTION
        A detailed description of the activities of Get-Something.
    .EXAMPLE
        $something = Get-Something
        $something | Do-Something

        Gets something from somewhere.
    #>

    param (
        # Describes the purpose of Parameter1.
        $Parameter1,

        # Describes the purpose of Parameter2.
        $Parameter2
    )
}
```

The help parser is quite simple when it comes to comment-based help. Only the very first line of an example is considered to be code. This can be demonstrated by exploring the object returned by `Get-Help` based on the preceding example:

```
PS> (Get-Help Get-Something -Examples).examples[0].example.code
$something = Get-Something
```

The rest of the code is part of the remark. It is only possible to overcome this parsing problem by writing help in MAML.

Working with long lines

There are several techniques that can be used when writing scripts to avoid excessively long lines of code. The goal is to avoid needing to scroll to the right when reviewing code. A secondary goal is to avoid littering a script with the tick character, `` ` ``.

Adding extra line breaks is often a balancing act. Both too many and too few can make it harder to read a script.

Splatting was introduced in the first chapter of this book as a means of dealing with commands that require more than a couple of parameters. It remains an important technique for avoiding excessively long lines.

Line break after pipe

The most obvious technique is perhaps to add a line break after a pipe, for example:

```
Get-Process |
    Where-Object Name -match 'po?w(er)?sh(ell)?'
```

This is useful for long pipelines, but may be counterproductive for short pipelines. For example, the following short pipeline ends with `ForEach-Object`. The statement is not necessarily long enough to need extra line breaks:

```
Get-Service | Where-Object Status -eq Running | ForEach-Object {
    # Do work on the service
}
```

Line break after an operator

It is possible to add a line break after any of the operators. The most useful place for a line break is often after a logic operator is used to combine several comparisons, for example:

```
Get-Service | Where-Object {
    $_.Status -eq 'Running' -and
    $_.StartType -eq 'Manual'
}
```

One of the less obvious operators is the property dereference operator, . . A line break may be added after calling a method of accessing a property. This is shown in the following example:

```
{ A long string in a script block }.ToString().
                                    SubString(0, 15).
                                    Trim().
                                    Length
```

Using the array operator to break up lines

The array operator, @ (), can break up arrays that are used as arguments into operators, or values for parameters.

For example, the format operator, −f, may be used in place of sub-expressions or variable interpolation. @() may be used to define an array to hold the arguments for the operator. The following example shows two different ways of creating the same string:

```
$item = Get-Item C:\Windows\explorer.exe

# Sub-expressions and variable interpolation
"The file, $($item.Name), with path $item was last written on
$($item.LastWriteTime)"

# The format operator
'The file, {0}, with path {1} was last written on {2}' -f @(
    $item.Name
    $item
    $item.LastWriteTime
)
```

The same approach may be used for replace operations that use particularly long regular expressions. For example, this replace operation attempts to apply a standard format to a UK telephone number. The regular expression benefits from being on a new line:

```
$ukPhoneNumbers = '+442012345678', '0044(0)1234345678', '+44 (0) 20
81234567', '01234 456789'
$ukPhoneNumbers -replace @(
    '^(?:(?:\+|00)\d{2})?[ -]*(?:\(?0\)?[ -]*)?([138]\d{1,3}|20)[ -
]*(\d{3,4})[ -]*(\d{3,4})$'
    '+44 $1 $2 $3'
)
```

@() may also be used with arguments for commands, such as Select-Object:

```
Get-NetAdapter | Select-Object @(
    'Name'
    'Status'
    'MacAddress'
    LinkSpeed'
    @{ Name = 'IPAddress'; Expression = { ($_ | Get-NetIPAddress).IPAddress
}}
)
```

It is possible to add line breaks into the hashtable that describes the IPAddress property in the preceding example. Doing so may be beneficial if the Expression script grows to be complex.

Begin, process, and end

A script or function often begins with comment-based help, followed by a `param` block, and then one or more of the named blocks may be used.

In a script or function, if none of the blocks are declared, content is automatically placed in the `end` block.

In a filter, if none of the blocks are declared, content is automatically placed in the `process` block. This is the only difference between a function and a filter.

The named blocks refer to the processing of a pipeline and therefore make the most sense if the command is working on pipeline input.

This difference in default block is shown in the following pipeline example. The function must explicitly declare a `process` block to use the `$_` variable. The filter can leverage the default block:

```
PS> function first { process { $_ } }    # end block by default
PS> filter second { $_ }                 # process block by default
PS> 1..2 | first                         # Outputs the value of $_ from
explicit process
1
2
PS> 1..2 | second                        # Outputs the value of $_ from
implicit process
1
2
```

Misuse of begin, process, and end

It is not uncommon to see `begin`, `process`, and `end` blocks used as regions, grouping the code required to set up, run, and tear down a function or script.

Care must be taken if converting such a function to accept pipeline input. It is often the case that all of the content must be moved to the `process` block to make sense of a function in a pipeline.

It is wise to plan to support an input pipeline for a command. However, using named blocks is optional. If a command is not expected to work on a pipeline, the content can be left to fall into the default block.

Begin

The begin block runs before pipeline-processing starts. A pipeline that contains several commands will run each of the begin blocks for each command in turn first.

The following example shows a short function with a begin block:

```
function Show-Pipeline {
    begin {
        Write-Host 'Pipeline start'
    }
}
```

The content of the begin block runs before the pipeline starts, before any pipeline input is accepted.

If a parameter accepts pipeline input, that input is not available to the begin block.

Begin can be used to create things that are reused by the process block, in essence setting up the initial conditions for a loop.

Process

The content of the process block runs once for each value received from the pipeline. The built-in $_ variable may be used to access objects in the pipeline within the process block:

```
function Show-Pipeline {
    begin {
        $position = $myinvocation.PipelinePosition
        Write-Host "Pipeline position ${position}: Start"
    }

    process {
        Write-Host "Pipeline position ${position}: $_"
        $_
    }
}
```

When an object is passed to the pipeline, the start message will be shown before the numeric value:

```
PS> $result = 1..2 | Show-Pipeline
Pipeline position 1: Start
Pipeline position 1: 1
Pipeline position 1: 2
```

Adding Show-Pipeline to the end of the pipeline will show that begin executes twice before process runs:

```
PS> $result = 1..2 | Show-Pipeline | Show-Pipeline
Pipeline position 1: Start
Pipeline position 2: Start
Pipeline position 1: 1
Pipeline position 2: 1
Pipeline position 1: 2
Pipeline position 2: 2
```

The $result variable will contain the output of the last Show-Pipeline command.

End

The end block executes after process has acted on all objects in the input pipeline.

The end block cannot use the $_ automatic variable. Parameters that accept pipeline input will be filled with the last value from the process block:

```
function Show-Pipeline {
    begin {
        $position = $myinvocation.PipelinePosition
        Write-Host "Pipeline position ${position}: Start"
    }

    process {
        Write-Host "Pipeline position ${position}: $_"
        $_
    }

    end {
        Write-Host "Pipeline position ${position}: End"
    }
}
```

Running this command in a pipeline shows the end executing after all items in the input pipeline have been processed:

```
PS> $result = 1..2 | Show-Pipeline
Pipeline position 1: Start
Pipeline position 1: 1
Pipeline position 1: 2
Pipeline position 1: End
```

Commands that make extensive use of the `end` block include `Measure-Object`, `ConvertTo-Html`, and `ConvertTo-Json`. Such commands cannot return output until the end because the output is only valid when complete. The same is true of any other command that must gather input during a process, and output something on completion.

A simple command to count the number of elements in an input pipeline is shown here. The `process` block is unable to determine this; it must run again and again until the input pipeline is exhausted:

```
function Measure-Item {
    begin {
        $count = 0
    }

    process {
        $count++
    }

    end {
        $count
    }
}
```

Named blocks and return

The return keyword may be used to gracefully end the execution of a piece of code.

The return keyword is often confused with return in C#, where it explicitly returns a thing from a method. In PowerShell, return has a slightly different purpose.

When a named block is executing, the return keyword may be used to end the processing of a block early without stopping the rest of the pipeline.

For example, a return statement in the process block ends early in certain cases. The end block will continue to execute as normal:

```
function Invoke-Return {
    process {
        if ($_ -gt 2) {
            return
        }
        $_
    }

    end {
```

```
        'All done'
    }
}
```

When run, the process block will end early when the condition is met:

```
PS> 1..10 | Invoke-Return
1
2
All done
```

Leaky functions

PowerShell does not have a means of strictly enforcing the output from a script or function.

Any statement—composed of any number of commands, variables, properties, and method calls—may generate output. This output will be automatically sent to the output pipeline by PowerShell as it is generated. Unanticipated output can cause bugs in code.

The following function makes use of the `StringBuilder` type. Many of the methods on `StringBuilder` return the `StringBuilder` instance. This is shown here:

```
PS> using namespace System.Text
PS> $stringBuilder = [StringBuilder]::new()
PS> $stringBuilder.AppendLine('First')


Capacity MaxCapacity Length
-------- ----------- ------
      16  2147483647 7
```

This is useful in that it allows chaining to build up a more complex string in a single statement. The following function makes use of that chaining to build up a string:

```
using namespace System.Text

function Get-FirstService {
    $service = Get-Service | Select-Object -First 1
    $stringBuilder = [StringBuilder]::new()
    $stringBuilder.AppendFormat('Name: {0}', $service.Name).AppendLine().
                   AppendFormat('Status: {0}',
$service.Status).AppendLine().
                   AppendLine()
    $stringBuilder.ToString()
}
```

When the function is run, both the `StingBuilder` object and the assembled string will be written to the output pipeline:

```
PS> Get-FirstService

Capacity    MaxCapacity    Length
--------    -----------    ------
      64     2147483647        37
Name: aciseagent
Status: Running
```

This example is contrived and writing the function slightly differently would resolve the problem. However, this problem is not unique to the type used here.

When writing a function or script, it is important to be aware of the output of the statements used. If a statement generates output, and that output is not needed, it must be discarded. PowerShell will not automatically discard output from commands in functions and scripts.

There are a number of techniques available for dropping unwanted output.

The Out-Null command

The `Out-Null` command can be used at the end of a pipeline to discard the output from a statement.

The `Out-Null` command is relatively unpopular in Windows PowerShell as it is slow. In PowerShell Core, the speed issue is resolved, since `Out-Null` is one of the fastest—if not the fastest—of the available options.

Sticking with the `StringBuilder` example, the unwanted value might have dropped by appending `Out-Null`, as shown here:

```
using namespace System.Text

$stringBuilder = [StringBuilder]::new()
$stringBuilder.AppendFormat('Name: {0}', $service.Name).AppendLine().
              AppendFormat('Status: {0}', $service.Status).AppendLine().
              AppendLine() | Out-Null
$stringBuilder.ToString()
```

One criticism that might be leveled against `Out-Null` is that it appears at the end of the pipeline and is therefore more difficult to see.

Assigning to null

Assigning a statement to the null variable is a popular way of dropping unwanted output. It has the advantage of being obvious, in that it appears at the beginning of the statement. This method is fast in all versions of PowerShell:

```
using namespace System.Text

$stringBuilder = [StringBuilder]::new()
$null = $stringBuilder.AppendFormat('Name: {0}',
$service.Name).AppendLine().
                        AppendFormat('Status: {0}',
$service.Status).AppendLine().
                        AppendLine()
$stringBuilder.ToString()
```

Redirecting to null

Redirection to null, such as `Out-Null`, can be added at the end of a statement to discard output. This is shown here:

```
using namespace System.Text
$service = Get-Service | Select-Object -First 1
$stringBuilder = [StringBuilder]::new()
$stringBuilder.AppendFormat('Name: {0}', $service.Name).AppendLine().
                AppendFormat('Status: {0}', $service.Status).AppendLine().
                AppendLine() > $null
$stringBuilder.ToString()
```

Casting to Void

It is possible to cast to `System.Void` to discard output. When using the `StringBuilder` example, this is a clean approach:

```
using namespace System.Text

$stringBuilder = [StringBuilder]::new()
[Void]$stringBuilder.AppendFormat('Name: {0}', $service.Name).AppendLine().
                AppendFormat('Status: {0}',
$service.Status).AppendLine().
                AppendLine()
$stringBuilder.ToString()
```

However, when used with a command, it requires the use of extra parentheses, which can make it less appealing to use. This example uses `Void` to suppress the output from the `Get-Command` command:

```
[Void](Get-Command Get-Command)
```

Param, parameters, and CmdletBinding

The `param` block must appear before all other code with the exception of attributes. In a script, `using` statements, if present, must also be written before `param`.

The `param` block is used to define the parameters a Script or Function is willing to accept. The keyword is not case-sensitive, so the opening bracket may be placed immediately after (with no space), on the next line, or as shown in this simple example:

```
param (
    $Parameter1,
    $Parameter2
)
```

By default, parameters have the `System.Object` type. This means that you can pass just about anything into a parameter. It may be desirable to restrict values to those of a specific type.

Parameter types

The type assigned to a parameter is written before the parameter name.

For example, if the function expects a string, the parameter type might be set to `[String]`:

```
param (
    [String]$Parameter1
)
```

Any value passed to the parameter will be converted into a string. Within the function, it is therefore possible to know that the value is of that particular type.

When assigning a type to a parameter, it is important to remember that the type persists until a new type is assigned, or the variable is destroyed. Therefore, values assigned to the parameter within a function will be cast to a string.

Nullable types

In some rare cases, it may be desirable for a parameter to accept either null or a specific value type. For example, a parameter may need to accept either a date, or null.

A nullable type can be defined for the parameter:

```
function Test-Nullable {
    param (
        [Nullable[DateTime]]$Date
    )
}
```

The function can be called with a null value for Date:

```
Test-Nullable -Date $null
```

Without the nullable type, a type-conversion error message would be thrown.

> **Not everything is nullable**
>
> System.String is not a nullable type. The documentation for Nullable explains why:
>
>
>
> https://docs.microsoft.com/en-us/dotnet/api/system.nullable-1?
> view=netframework-4.7.2.
>
> In PowerShell, this is difficult to see. Assigning null to a variable with a String type will result in an empty string (not null). The result of the following statements is false:
>
> ```
> [String]$String = $null
> $null -eq $String
> ```

Default values

Parameters may be given default values by using assignment statements in the param block, such as the following, for example:

```
param (
    [String]$Parameter1 = 'DefaultValue'
)
```

If the assignment is the result of a command, the command must be placed in parentheses:

```
param (
    [String]$ProcessName = (Get-Process -Id $PID | Select-Object -
ExpandProperty Name)
)
```

Value types, such as `Boolean`, or `Int32` and other numeric types, are initialized with a default value for that type. For instance, a parameter of the `Boolean` type can never be null; it will default to false. Numeric values will default to `0`. Setting a default false value for a `Boolean` parameter is therefore unnecessary.

Assigning a default value was the basis for making parameters mandatory in PowerShell 1. The parameter would be assigned a `throw` statement by default, for example:

```
param (
    [String]$Parameter1 = (throw 'This parameter is mandatory')
)
```

This method of making parameters mandatory was replaced in PowerShell 2 by the `Mandatory` property of the `Parameter` attribute. The parameter attribute is explored in detail in the next chapter.

Cross-referencing parameters

When executing a param block, it is possible to cross-reference parameters. That is, the default value of a parameter can be based on the value of another parameter. This is shown here:

```
function Get-Substring {
    param (
        [String]$String,

        [Int]$Start,

        [Int]$Length = ($String.Length - $Start)
    )

    $String.Substring($Start, $Length)
}
```

The value of the `Length` parameter will use the default, derived from the first two parameters, unless the user of the function supplies their own value. The order of the parameters is important here: the `Start` parameter must be created before it can be used in the default value for `Length`.

The CmdletBinding attribute

The `CmdletBinding` attribute is used to turn a function into an advanced function. Advanced functions were introduced with PowerShell 2.

`CmdletBinding` may be used to do the following:

- Access common parameters, such as ErrorAction, Verbose, and Debug
- Gain access to the built-in `pscmdlet` variable
- Declare support for `WhatIf` and `Confirm` and define the impact level of the command

If a script or function has no parameters, and wishes to make use of the capabilities of `CmdletBinding`, an empty `param` block must be declared:

```
function Test-EmptyParam {
    [CmdletBinding()]
    param ( )
}
```

Common parameters

With `CmdletBinding` in place, a script or function may use common parameters. The common parameters are listed in PowerShell's help file:

```
Get-Help about_commonparameters
```

For example, the Verbose parameter is made available. Any verbose output written by the command will be displayed without the need to explicitly declare the Verbose parameter within the function:

```
function Show-Verbose {
    [CmdletBinding()]
    param ( )

    Write-Verbose 'Verbose message'
}
```

The verbose message will be displayed when the command is run with the -Verbose parameter.

In a similar way, parameters such as ErrorAction will effect Write-Error if it is used within the function.

CmdletBinding properties

The full set of possible values that may be assigned can be viewed by creating an instance of the CmdletBinding object:

```
PS> [CmdletBinding]::new()

PositionalBinding           : True
DefaultParameterSetName     :
SupportsShouldProcess       : False
SupportsPaging              : False
SupportsTransactions        : False
ConfirmImpact               : Medium
HelpUri                     :
RemotingCapability          : PowerShell
TypeId                      :
System.Management.Automation.CmdletBindingAttribute
```

For example, the output from the preceding command shows the existence of a PositionalBinding property. Setting this to false disables automatic position binding:

```
function Test-Binding {
    [CmdletBinding(PositionalBinding = $false)]
    param (
        $Parameter1
    )
}
```

When the preceding function is called, and a value for Parameter1 is given by position, an error will be thrown:

```
PS> Test-Binding 'value'
Test-Binding : A positional parameter cannot be found that accepts argument
'value'.
At line:1 char:1
+ test-binding 'value'
+ ~~~~~~~~~~~~~~~~~~~~~
  + CategoryInfo : InvalidArgument: (:) [Test-Binding],
ParameterBindingException
  + FullyQualifiedErrorId : PositionalParameterNotFound,Test-Binding
```

The most commonly used properties of CmdletBinding are SupportsShouldProcess and DefaultParameterSetName. DefaultParameterSetName will be explored in the next chapter.

ShouldProcess and ShouldContinue

ShouldProcess and ShouldContinue become available when a script or function has the CmdletBinding attribute, and the SupportsShouldProcess property is set.

Setting SupportsShouldProcess enables the ShouldProcess parameters, Confirm and WhatIf. These two parameters are used in conjunction with the ShouldProcess method that's exposed on the pscmdlet variable.

ShouldProcess

ShouldProcess is used to support WhatIf and is responsible for showing confirmation preferences based on the impact level of a command.

ShouldProcess is also used to prompt for confirmation when a command is performing a higher-risk action.

The following example will display a message instead of running the Write-Host statement when the WhatIf parameter is supplied:

```
function Test-ShouldProcess {
    [CmdletBinding(SupportsShouldProcess)]
    param ( )

    if ($pscmdlet.ShouldProcess('SomeObject')) {
        Write-Host 'Deleting SomeObject' -ForegroundColor Cyan
    }
}
```

When run using the WhatIf parameter, the command will show the following message:

```
PS> Test-ShouldProcess -WhatIf
What if: Performing the operation "Test-ShouldProcess" on target
"SomeObject".
```

The name of the operation, which defaults to the command name, can be changed using a second overload for ShouldProcess:

```
function Test-ShouldProcess {
    [CmdletBinding(SupportsShouldProcess)]
    param ( )

    if ($pscmdlet.ShouldProcess('SomeObject', 'delete')) {
        Write-Host 'Deleting SomeObject' -ForegroundColor Cyan
    }
}
```

This would change the message to the following:

```
PS> Test-ShouldProcess -WhatIf
What if: Performing the operation "delete" on target "SomeObject".
```

The next overload grants full control over the messages that display:

```
function Test-ShouldProcess {
    [CmdletBinding(SupportsShouldProcess)]
    param ( )

    if ($pscmdlet.ShouldProcess(
            'Message displayed using WhatIf',
            'Warning: Deleting SomeObject',
            'Question: Are you sure you want to do continue?')) {

        Write-Host 'Deleting SomeObject' -ForegroundColor Cyan
    }
}
```

Using the Confirm parameter instead of WhatIf forces the appearance of the second two messages and adds a prompt:

```
PS> Test-ShouldProcess -Confirm

Question: Are you sure you want to do continue?
Warning: Deleting SomeObject
[Y] Yes [A] Yes to All [N] No [L] No to All [S] Suspend [?] Help (default
is "Y"):
```

The different responses are automatically available without further code. If the request is within a loop, Yes to All may be used to bypass additional prompts. Replying Yes to All applies to all instances of ShouldProcess in the script or function:

```
function Test-ShouldProcess {
    [CmdletBinding(SupportsShouldProcess)]
    param ( )

    foreach ($value in 1..2) {
        if ($pscmdlet.ShouldProcess(
                "Would delete SomeObject $value",
                "Warning: Deleting SomeObject $value",
                'Question: Are you sure you want to do continue?')) {

            Write-Host "Deleting SomeObject $value" -ForegroundColor Cyan
        }
    }
}
```

Whether or not the confirmation prompt is displayed depends on the comparison between ConfirmImpact (medium by default), and the value in the $ConfirmPreference variable, which is High by default.

If the impact of the function is raised to High, the prompt will display by default instead of on demand. This is achieved by modifying the ConfirmImpact property of the CmdletBinding attribute:

```
function Test-ShouldProcess {
    [CmdletBinding(SupportsShouldProcess, ConfirmImpact = 'High')]
    param ( )

    if ($pscmdlet.ShouldProcess('SomeObject')) {
        Write-Host 'Deleting SomeObject' -ForegroundColor Cyan
    }
}
```

When the function is executed, the confirmation prompt will show unless the user either uses -Confirm:$false or sets $ConfirmPreference to None.

ShouldContinue

The ShouldContinue method is also made available when the SupportsShouldProcess property is set in CmdletBinding.

ShouldContinue differs from ShouldProcess in that it always prompts. This technique is used by commands such as Remove-Item to force a prompt when the Recurse parameter is not present and a directory name is passed.

ShouldContinue is rarely necessary, since ShouldProcess is the better option. It is available for the cases where a function must have a confirmation prompt that cannot be bypassed. Using ShouldContinue may make it impossible to run a function without user interaction unless also providing a means to bypass the prompt.

The use of ShouldContinue is similar to ShouldProcess. The most significant difference is that the Yes to All and No to All options are not automatically implemented:

```
function Test-ShouldContinue {
    [CmdletBinding(SupportsShouldProcess)]
    param ( )

    $yesToAll = $noToAll = $false
    if ($pscmdlet.ShouldContinue(
            "Warning: Deleting SomeObject $value",
            'Question: Are you sure you want to do continue?')) {

        Write-Host 'Deleting SomeObject' -ForegroundColor Cyan
    }
}
```

Running this function will show the confirmation prompt:

```
PS> Test-ShouldContinue

Question: Are you sure you want to do continue?
Warning: Deleting SomeObject
[Y] Yes [N] No [S] Suspend [?] Help (default is "Y"): y
```

Adding support for Yes to All and No to All means using three extra arguments. The first of these new arguments, hasSecurityImpact, affects whether the default option presented is Yes (when hasSecurityImpact is false) or No (when hasSecurityImpact is true):

```
function Test-ShouldContinue {
    [CmdletBinding(SupportsShouldProcess)]
    param ( )

    $yesToAll = $noToAll = $false
    if ($pscmdlet.ShouldContinue(
            "Warning: Deleting SomeObject $value",
            'Question: Are you sure you want to do continue?',
```

```
            $false,
            [Ref]$yesToAll,
            [Ref]$noToAll)) {

        Write-Host 'Deleting SomeObject' -ForegroundColor Cyan
    }
}
```

The confirmation prompt will now include the Yes to All and No to All options:

```
PS> Test-ShouldContinue

Question: Are you sure you want to do continue?
Warning: Deleting SomeObject
[Y] Yes [A] Yes to All [N] No [L] No to All [S] Suspend [?] Help (default
is "Y"):
```

If necessary, it is possible to provide a means of bypassing the prompt by implementing another switch parameter. For example, a Force parameter might be added:

```
function Test-ShouldContinue {
    [CmdletBinding(SupportsShouldProcess)]
    param (
        [Switch]$Force
    )

    $yesToAll = $noToAll = $false
    if ($Force -or $pscmdlet.ShouldContinue(
            "Warning: Deleting SomeObject $value",
            'Question: Are you sure you want to do continue?',
            $false,
            [Ref]$yesToAll,
            [Ref]$noToAll)) {

        Write-Host 'Deleting SomeObject' -ForegroundColor Cyan
    }
}
```

As the value of Force is evaluated before ShouldContinue, the ShouldContinue method will not run if the Force parameter is supplied.

Summary

In this chapter, we explored the basic differences between functions, filters, and scripts. We also looked at the structure of comment-based help, and a few strategies to use when working with long lines.

The use of `Begin`, `Process`, and `End` was explored as the starting point of developing a `pipeline-capable` function.

Parameters were briefly explored and a number of techniques for defining parameter values were introduced.

The `CmdletBinding` attribute was explored before we dived into the functionality of `SupportsShouldProcess`.

In the next chapter, we will explore parameters in detail, including pipeline binding, validation, and argument completers.

17
Parameters, Validation, and Dynamic Parameters

PowerShell has an extensive parameter handling and validation system that can be used in scripts and functions. The system allows a developer to make parameters mandatory; to define what, if any, positional binding is allowed; to fill parameters from the pipeline; to describe different parameter sets; and to validate the values passed to a parameter. The wealth of options available makes parameter handling a very involved subject.

This chapter explores the following topics:

- The `Parameter` attribute
- Validating input
- Pipeline input
- Defining parameter sets
- Argument-completers
- Dynamic parameters

The Parameter attribute

The `Parameter` attribute is an optional attribute that is used to define the behavior of a parameter within a script or function. Creating an instance of the `Parameter` object shows the different properties that might be set:

```
PS> [Parameter]::new()

Position                         : -2147483648
ParameterSetName                 : __AllParameterSets
Mandatory                        : False
ValueFromPipeline                : False
ValueFromPipelineByPropertyName : False
```

```
ValueFromRemainingArguments      : False
HelpMessage                      :
HelpMessageBaseName              :
HelpMessageResourceId            :
DontShow                         : False
TypeId                           :
System.Management.Automation.ParameterAttribute
```

A few of these properties should be ignored as they are not intended to be set directly, such as `HelpMessageBaseName`, `HelpMessageResourceId`, and `TypeId`.

A number of the more complex properties are explored in other sections in this chapter, such as `ParameterSetName`, `ValueFromPipeline`, and `ValueFromPipelineByPropertyName`.

The `Parameter` attribute is placed before the parameter itself. The following example shows the simplest use of the `Parameter` attribute:

```
[CmdletBinding()]
param (
    [Parameter()]
    $Paramter1
)
```

Using the `Parameter` attribute has the side-effect of turning a basic function into an advanced function, even when the `CmdletBinding` attribute itself is missing. `Get-Command` may be used to explore whether `CmdletBinding` is present:

```
PS> function Test-CmdletBinding {
>>      param (
>>          [Parameter()]
>>          $Parameter1
>>      )
>> }
PS> Get-Command Test-CmdletBinding | Select-Object CmdletBinding

CmdletBinding
-------------
        True
```

This means that the common parameters, including `Verbose` and `ErrorAction`, are available to any function that uses the `Parameter` attribute (for any parameter).

Starting with PowerShell 3, Boolean properties, such as `Mandatory` and `ValueFromPipeline`, may be written without providing an explicit argument. For example, `Parameter1` is made mandatory in the following code:

```
function Test-Mandatory {
    [CmdletBinding()]
    param (
        [Parameter(Mandatory)]
        $Parameter1
    )
}
```

Use of `Mandatory = $false`

The default value for `Mandatory` is `false`; setting an explicit value of a default provides no benefit and may be counterproductive.

`Mandatory` is significant and stands out, but the value assigned is less significant and, when reading rapidly, it might be assumed to be true simply because the property is present.

Position and positional binding

Position defaults to `-2147483648`, the smallest possible value for `Int32` (see `[Int32]::MinValue`). Unless an explicit permission is set, parameters may be bound in the order they are written in the parameter block. Setting the `PositionalBinding` property of `CmdletBinding` to false can be used to disable this behavior.

Automatic positional binding is shown in the following example:

```
function Test-Position {
    [CmdletBinding()]
    param (
        [Parameter()]
        $Parameter1,

        [Parameter()]
        $Parameter2
    )

    '{0}-{1}' -f $Parameter1, $Parameter2
}
```

When called, the command shows that `Parameter1` and `Parameter2` have been filled with the values supplied using position only:

```
PS> Test-Position 1 2
1-2
```

Automatic positional binding is available by default; the `Parameter` attribute is not required. An explicit definition of position allows greater control and effectively disables automatic positional binding:

```
function Test-Position {
    param (
        [Parameter(Position = 1)]
        $Parameter1,

        $Parameter2
    )
}
```

Exploring command metadata shows the positional binding is still enabled, but as this is an ordered operation, the default position no longer has meaning. The command metadata is shown as follows, showing that positional binding is still enabled:

```
PS> [System.Management.Automation.CommandMetadata](Get-Command Test-
Position)

Name                     : Test-Position
CommandType              :
DefaultParameterSetName  :
SupportsShouldProcess    : False
SupportsPaging           : False
PositionalBinding        : True
SupportsTransactions     : False
HelpUri                  :
RemotingCapability       : PowerShell
ConfirmImpact            : Medium
Parameters               : {[Parameter1,
System.Management.Automation.ParameterMetadata], [Parameter2,
System.Management.Automation.ParameterMetadata]}
```

Attempting to pass a value for `Parameter2` by position will raise an error:

```
PS> Test-Position 1 2
Test-Position : A positional parameter cannot be found that accepts
argument '2'.
 At line:1 char:1
 + test-position 1 2
 + ~~~~~~~~~~~~~~~~~
```

```
  + CategoryInfo : InvalidArgument: (:) [Test-Position],
ParameterBindingException
  + FullyQualifiedErrorId : PositionalParameterNotFound,Test-Position
```

PowerShell orders parameters based on the position value. The value must be greater than −2147483648. It is possible, but not advisable, to set Position to a negative value. The accepted practice has numbering starting at either 0 or 1.

The DontShow property

DontShow may be used to hide a parameter from tab completion and IntelliSense. This property is rarely used, but may be occasionally useful for short recursive functions. The following function recursively calls itself, comparing MaxDepth and CurrentDepth. The CurrentDepth parameter is owned by the function and a user is never expected to supply a value:

```
function Show-Property {
    [CmdletBinding()]
    param (
        # Show the properties of the specified object.
        [Parameter(Mandatory)]
        [PSObject]$InputObject,

        # The maximum depth when expanding properties of child objects.
        [Int32]$MaxDepth = 5,

        # Used to track the current depth during recursion.
        [Parameter(DontShow)]
        [Int32]$CurrentDepth = 0
    )

    $width = $InputObject.PSObject.Properties.Name |
        Sort-Object { $_.Length } -Descending |
        Select-Object -First 1 -ExpandProperty Length

    foreach ($property in $InputObject.PSObject.Properties) {
        '{0}{1}: {2}' -f
            (' ' * $CurrentDepth),
            $property.Name.PadRight($width, ' '),
            $property.TypeNameOfValue

        if ($CurrentDepth -lt $MaxDepth -and $property.Value -and
                -not $property.TypeNameOfValue.IsPrimitive) {

            Show-Property -InputObject $property.Value -CurrentDepth
```

```
($CurrentDepth + 1)
            }
        }
}
```

Marking a parameter as Dont Show hides the parameter to a degree, but it does nothing to prevent a user from providing a value for the parameter. In this preceding case, a better approach might be to move the body of the function into a nested function. Alternatively, if the function is part of a module, the recursive code might be moved to a function that is not exported from a module and exposed by a second, tidier, function.

The ValueFromRemainingArguments property

Setting the ValueFromRemainingArguments property allows a parameter to consume all of the other arguments supplied for a command. This can be used to make an advanced function act in a similar manner to a basic function.

For example, this basic function will fill the Parameter1 parameter with the first argument, and will ignore all others. The extra values are added to the $args automatic variable and are listed in the UnboundArguments property of the $MyInvocation automatic variable:

```
function Test-BasicBinding {
    param (
        $Parameter1
    )

    $MyInvocation.UnboundArguments
}
```

Calling the function with non-existent parameters will not raise an error. The additional values will be added to the UnboundArguments array (and the $args variable):

```
PS> Test-BasicBinding -Parameter1 value1 -Parameter2 value2
-Parameter2
Value2
```

Without a declared parameter in the param block, Parameter2 is just another value, it is not parsed as the name of a
parameter. The ValueFromRemainingArguments property can be used to make an advanced function behave in much the same way as the preceding basic function:

```
function Test-AdvancedBinding {
    [CmdletBinding()]
    param (
```

```
        $Parameter1,

        [Parameter(ValueFromRemainingArguments)]
        $OtherArguments
    )

    $OtherArguments
}
```

If the `$OtherArguments` parameter is not for the normal use of the function, the `DontShow` property might be added to make it less obvious and intrusive.

The HelpMessage property

`HelpMessage` is only applied to `Mandatory` parameters and is not particularly useful. If a parameter is mandatory and is not passed when a command is called, a prompt for the parameter value will appear. Typing `!?` in the prompt, instead of a value, will display the help message text:

```
PS> function Test-HelpMessage {
>>     param (
>>         [Parameter(Mandatory, HelpMessage = 'Help text for Parameter1')]
>>         $Parameter1
>>     )
>> }
PS> Test-HelpMessage

cmdlet Test-HelpMessage at command pipeline position 1
Supply values for the following parameters:
(Type !? for Help.)
Parameter1: !?
Help text for Parameter1
Parameter1:
```

Given that `HelpMessage` is only visible when explicitly requested in this manner, it is most often ignored entirely. It is better to spend time writing help content for a parameter than writing values for `HelpMessage`.

Validating input

PowerShell provides a variety of different ways to tightly define the content for a parameter. Assigning a .NET type to a parameter is the first of these. If a parameter is set as [String], it will only ever hold a value of that type. PowerShell will attempt to coerce any values passed to the parameter into that type.

The PSTypeName attribute

It is not uncommon in PowerShell to want to pass an object created in one command, as a PSObject (or PSCustomObject), to another. The PSTypeName attribute is able to test the type name assigned to a custom object. Type names are assigned by setting (or adding) a value to the hidden PSTypeName property. There are a number of ways to tag PSCustomObject with a type name. The simplest is to set a value for a PSTypeName property, shown as follows:

```
$object = [PSCustomObject]@{
    Property   = 'Value'
    PSTypeName = 'SomeTypeName'
}
```

The PSTypeName property remains hidden, but Get-Member will now show the new type name:

```
PS> $object | Get-Member

TypeName: SomeTypeName

Name          MemberType     Definition
----          ----------     ----------
Equals        Method         bool Equals(System.Object obj)
GetHashCode   Method         int GetHashCode()
GetType       Method         type GetType()
ToString      Method         string ToString()
Property      NoteProperty   string Property=Value
```

It is also possible to tweak the PSTypeNames array directory, shown as follows:

```
$object = [PSCustomObject]@{ Property = 'Value' }

# Add to the end of the existing list
$object.PSTypeNames.Add('SomeTypeName')
```

```
# Or add to the beginning of the list
$object.PSTypeNames.Insert(0, 'SomeTypeName')
```

Finally, Add-Member can add to PSTypeNames. If used, it adds the new type name at the top of the existing list:

```
$object = [PSCustomObject]@{ Property = 'Value' }
$object | Add-Member -TypeName 'SomeTypeName'
```

These tagged types may be tested using the PSTypeName attribute of a parameter, for example:

```
function Test-PSTypeName {
    [CmdletBinding()]
    param (
        [PSTypeName('SomeTypeName')]
        $InputObject
    )
}
```

This technique is used by many of the WMI-based commands implemented by Microsoft. For example, the Set-NetAdapter command uses a PSTypeName attribute for its InputObject parameter:

```
(Get-Command Set-NetAdapter).Parameters['InputObject'].Attributes |
    Where-Object  TypeId -eq ([PSTypeNameAttribute])
```

In the case of the WMI-based commands, this is used in addition to a .NET type name, an array of CimInstance. This type of parameter is similar to the following example:

```
function Test-PSTypeName {
    [CmdletBinding()]
    param (
        [Parameter(Mandatory, ValueFromPipeline, ParameterSetName =
'InputObject (cdxml)')]
[PSTypeName('Microsoft.Management.Infrastructure.CimInstance#MSFT_NetAdapte
r')]
        [CimInstance[]]$InputObject
    )
}
```

This technique is incredibly useful when the .NET object type is not sufficiently detailed to restrict input. This is true of `PSObject` input as much as the `CimInstance` array type used before.

Validation attributes

PowerShell offers a number of validation attributes to test the content of arguments passed to parameters. There are two general classes of validation attribute; the first validates the argument as a single object, which tests the value as a whole:

- `ValidateNotNull`
- `ValidateNotNullOrEmpty`
- `ValidateCount`
- `ValidateDrive`

The second validates enumerated arguments. These validation attributes can be applied to parameters that accept arrays. The validation step applies to each element in the array. The enumerated argument validation attributes are:

- `ValidateLength`
- `ValidatePattern`
- `ValidateRange`
- `ValidateScript`
- `ValidateSet`

The validation attributes are documented in `about_Functions_Advanced_Parameters` with the exception of the newer `ValidateDrive` attribute, which was introduced with PowerShell 5. The constructor for a validation attribute can be explored to determine the arguments it supports. This may be discovered using the `::new` static method in PowerShell 5 and newer, for example, `ValidateDrive`:

```
PS> [ValidateDrive]::new

OverloadDefinitions
-------------------
ValidateDrive new(Params string[] validRootDrives)
```

The ValidateNotNull attribute

ValidateNotNull may be used with parameters that are not flagged as mandatory. It is applicable where an object type is capable of accepting null input. Such types include object, CimInstance, and array types. The following is the simplest example of ValidateNotNull:

```
function Test-ValidateNotNull {
    [CmdletBinding()]
    param (
        [ValidateNotNull()]
        $Parameter1
    )
}
```

As Parameter1 is, by default, set to the Object type, it would ordinarily accept a null value. When applied to an array, it disallows null values but retains the ability to pass an empty array into a function, for example:

```
function Test-ValidateNotNull {
    [CmdletBinding()]
    param (
        [ValidateNotNull()]
        [String[]]$Parameter1
    )
}
```

If a null value is explicitly passed, an error will be raised:

```
PS> Test-ValidateNotNull -Parameter1 $null

Test-ValidateNotNull : Cannot validate argument on parameter 'Parameter1'.
The argument is null. Provide a valid value for the argument, and then try
running the command again.
 At line:1 char:34
 + Test-ValidateNotNull -Parameter1 $null
 +                                  ~~~~~
 + CategoryInfo : InvalidData: (:) [Test-ValidateNotNull],
ParameterBindingValidationException
 + FullyQualifiedErrorId : ParameterArgumentValidationError,Test-
ValidateNotNull
```

The ValidateNotNull attribute has no effect on String or numeric types (such as Byte, Int, or Int64).

The ValidateNotNullOrEmpty attribute

ValidateNotNullOrEmpty extends ValidateNotNull to disallow empty arrays and empty strings:

```
function Test-ValidateNotNullOrEmpty {
  [CmdletBinding()]
  param (
  [ValidateNotNullOrEmpty()]
  [String]$Parameter1,

  [ValidateNotNullOrEmpty()]
  [Object[]]$Parameter2
  )
}
```

An error will be thrown if either an empty string is supplied for Parameter1, or an empty array is supplied for Parameter2. Like ValidateNotNull, ValidateNotNullOrEmpty has no effect on numeric types.

The ValidateCount attribute

ValidateCount is used to test the size of an array supplied to a parameter. The attribute expects a minimum and maximum length for the array.

ValidateCount only has meaning when applied to an array-type parameter, for example:

```
function Test-ValidateCount {
    [CmdletBinding()]
    param (
        [ValidateCount(1, 1)]
        [String[]]$Parameter1
    )
}
```

ValidateCount may also be applied to parameters that accept more advanced array types, such as [System.Collections.ArrayList] or [System.Collections.Generic.List[String]].

The ValidateDrive attribute

ValidateDrive may be used to test the drive letter provided for a parameter that accepts a path. ValidateDrive handles both relative and absolute paths. A relative path is resolved to a full path before it is tested against the supplied drive letters. When using the ValidateDrive attribute, the parameter type must be String. The parameter cannot be omitted:

```
function Test-ValidateDrive {
    [CmdletBinding()]
    param (
        [ValidateDrive('C')]
        [String]$Parameter1
    )
}
```

ValidateDrive cannot act on an array of paths; if the parameter type is an array, an error will be thrown stating the path argument is invalid.

The ValidateLength attribute

ValidateLength can be applied to a String parameter or a parameter that contains an array of strings. Each string will be tested against the minimum and maximum length:

```
function Test-ValidateLength {
    [CmdletBinding()]
    param (
        [ValidateLength(2, 6)]
        [String[]]$Parameter1
    )
}
```

Any string with a length below the minimum, or above the maximum, will trigger an error.

The ValidatePattern attribute

ValidatePattern is used to test that a string, or the elements in an array of strings, matches the supplied pattern:

```
function Test-ValidatePattern {
    [CmdletBinding()]
    param (
        [ValidatePattern('^Hello')]
        [String]$Parameter1
```

```
        )
    }
```

In addition to the pattern argument, `ValidatePattern` accepts `RegexOptions` using the `Options` named parameter, for example:

```
function Test-ValidatePattern {
    [CmdletBinding()]
    param (
        [ValidatePattern('^Hello', Options = 'Multiline')]
        [String]$Parameter1
    )
}
```

The possible values for `Options` are described by the `System.Text.RegularExpressions.RegexOptions` enumeration, which is documented in the .NET reference (https://docs.microsoft.com/en-us/dotnet/api/system.text.regularexpressions.regexoptions?view=netframework-4.7.2).

Multiple options may be included as a comma-separated list, for example:

```
[ValidatePattern('^Hello', Options = 'IgnoreCase, Multiline')]
```

By default, the `IgnoreCase` option is set. If you want to make a pattern case-sensitive, the options can be set to `None`:

```
[ValidatePattern('^Hello', Options = 'None')]
```

A criticism that might be leveled against `ValidatePattern` is that there is no way to customize or define the error message in Windows PowerShell.

PowerShell Core adds an optional `ErrorMessage` parameter to tackle this problem. The default error message written by `ValidatePattern` is shown as follows:

```
PS> function Test-ValidatePattern {
>>      [CmdletBinding()]
>>      param (
>>          [ValidatePattern('^[A-Z]\S+ [A-Z]\S+\.', Options = 'None')]
>>          [String]$Greeting
>>      )
>> }
PS> Test-ValidatePattern -Greeting 'hello Jim.'

Test-ValidatePattern : Cannot validate argument on parameter 'Greeting'.
The argument "hello Jim." does not match the "^[A-Z]\S+ [A-Z]\S+\."
pattern. Supply an argument that matches "^[A-Z]\S+ [A-Z]\S+\." and try the
command again.
```

```
At line:1 char:34
+ Test-ValidatePattern -Greeting 'hello Jim.'
+                                  ~~~~~~~~~~~~~
    + CategoryInfo : InvalidData: (:) [Test-ValidatePattern],
ParameterBindingValidationException
    + FullyQualifiedErrorId : ParameterArgumentValidationError,Test-
ValidatePattern
```

In PowerShell Core, an alternative message may be supplied:

```
function Test-ValidatePattern {
    [CmdletBinding()]
    param (
        [ValidatePattern(
            '^[A-Z]\S+ [A-Z]\S+\.',
            Options     = 'None',
            ErrorMessage = 'The greeting and name must begin with a capital
letter.'
        )]
        [String]$Greeting
    )
}
```

The ValidateRange attribute

ValidateRange tests whether a value, or an array of values, fall within a specified range. ValidateRange is most commonly used to test numeric ranges. However, it is also able to test strings. For example, the z string can be said to be within the A to Z range. This approach is slightly harder to apply when testing strings as the Zz string is greater than Z. The following example uses ValidateRange to test an integer value:

```
function Test-ValidateRange {
    [CmdletBinding()]
    param (
        [ValidateRange(1, 20)]
        [Int]$Parameter1
    )
}
```

The ValidateScript attribute

ValidateScript executes an arbitrary block of code against each of the arguments for a parameter. If the argument is an array, each element is tested. One common use for ValidateScript is to test whether a path exists, for example:

```
function Test-ValidateScript {
    [CmdletBinding()]
    param (
        [ValidateScript( { Test-Path $_ -PathType Leaf } )]
        [String]$Path
    )
}
```

ValidateScript can contain just about anything a developer desires, although it is generally recommended to keep validation scripts short. In PowerShell Core, ValidateScript gains an optional ErrorMessage parameter that replaces the default message, which repeats the failed script to the end user:

```
function Test-ValidateScript {
    [CmdletBinding()]
    param (
        [ValidateScript(
            { Test-Path $_ -PathType Leaf },
            ErrorMessage = 'The path supplied must exist and must be a
file'
        )]
        [String]$Path
    )
}
```

In Windows PowerShell, throw may be used within the script to write a more friendly error message at the cost of a more complex script:

```
function Test-ValidateScript {
    [CmdletBinding()]
    param (
        [ValidateScript({
            if (Test-Path $_ -PathType Leaf) {
                $true
            } else {
                throw 'The path supplied must exist and must be a file'
            }
        })]
        [String]$Path
    )
}
```

The ValidateSet attribute

`ValidateSet` tests whether the specified argument, or each of an array of arguments, exists in a set of possible values:

```
function Test-ValidateSet {
    [CmdletBinding()]
    param (
        [ValidateSet('One', 'Two', 'Three')]
        [String]$Value
    )
}
```

The set of values must be hardcoded in the attribute, it cannot be derived from a variable or another command. By default, the set is not case-sensitive. If it is desirable, the set can be made case-sensitive by using the `IgnoreCase` named parameter:

```
function Test-ValidateSet {
    [CmdletBInding()]
    param (
        [ValidateSet('One', 'Two', 'Three', IgnoreCase = $false)]
        [String]$Value
    )
}
```

Like `ValidatePattern` and `ValidateSet`, `ValidateSet` gains an optional `ErrorMessage` parameter in PowerShell Core.

The Allow attributes

The `Allow` attributes are most commonly used when a parameter is mandatory. If a parameter is mandatory, PowerShell will automatically disallow assignment of empty values, that is, empty strings and empty arrays. The `Allow` attributes can be used to modify that behavior. The attributes make it possible to require a parameter, but still allow empty values.

The AllowNull attribute

`AllowNull` is used to permit explicit use of `$null` as a value for a `Mandatory` parameter:

```
function Test-AllowNull {
    [CmdletBinding()]
    param (
        [Parameter(Mandatory)]
```

```
        [AllowNull()]
        [Object]$Parameter1
    )
}
```

`AllowNull` is effective for array parameters, and for parameters that use `Object` as a type. `AllowNull` is not effective for string parameters as the null value is cast to an empty string, and an empty string is still not permitted.

The AllowEmptyString attribute

`AllowEmptyString` fills the gap, allowing both null and empty values to be supplied for a mandatory string parameter. In both cases, the resulting assignment will be an empty string. It is not possible to distinguish between a value passed as null and a value passed as an empty string:

```
function Test-AllowEmptyString {
    [CmdletBinding()]
    param (
        [Parameter(Mandatory)]
        [AllowEmptyString()]
        [String]$Parameter1
    )
}
```

The AllowEmptyCollection attribute

`AllowEmptyCollection`, as the name suggests, allows an empty array to be assigned to a mandatory parameter:

```
function Test-AllowEmptyCollection {
    [CmdletBinding()]
    param (
        [Parameter(Mandatory)]
        [AllowEmptyCollection()]
        [Object[]]$Parameter1
    )
}
```

This will allow the command to be called with an explicitly empty array:

```
Test-AllowEmptyCollection -Parameter1 @()
```

PSReference parameters

Many of the object types used in PowerShell are reference types. When an object is passed to a function, any changes made to that object will be visible outside the function, irrespective of the output generated by the command. For example, the following function accepts an object as input, then changes the value of a property on that object:

```
function Set-Value {
    [CmdletBinding()]
    param (
        [PSObject]$Object
    )

    $Object.Value = 2
}
```

When the function is passed an object, the change can be seen on any other variables that reference that object:

```
PS> $myObject = [PSCustomObject]@{ Value = 1 }
PS> Set-Value $myObject
PS> $myObject.Value
2
```

Strings, numeric values, and dates, on the other hand, are all examples of value types. Changes made to a value type inside a function will not be reflected in variables that reference that value elsewhere; a new value is created. Occasionally, it is desirable to make a function affect the content of a value type without either returning the value as output or changing the value of a property of an object. The PSReference type, [Ref], can be used to achieve this. The following function normally returns true or false depending on whether Get-Date successfully parsed the date string into a DateTime object:

```
function Test-Date {
    [CmdletBinding()]
    param (
        [String]$Date,

        [Ref]$DateTime
    )

    if ($value = Get-Date $Date -ErrorAction SilentlyContinue) {
        if ($DateTime) {
            $DateTime.Value = $value
        }
        $true
    } else {
```

```
            $false
        }
    }
```

When the function is run, a variable that holds an existing DateTime object might be passed as an optional reference. PowerShell can update the date via the reference, changing the value outside of the function:

```
PS> $dateTime = Get-Date
PS> Test-Date 01/01/2019 -DateTime ([Ref]$dateTime)
true
PS> $dateTime
01 January 2019 00:00:00
```

The same behavior can be seem with Boolean, string, and numeric types.

Pipeline input

Using the Parameter attribute to set either ValueFromPipeline or ValueFromPipelineByPropertyName sets a parameter up to fill from the input pipeline.

About ValueFromPipeline

ValueFromPipeline allows the entire object to be passed into a parameter from an input pipeline. The following function implements an InputObject parameter, which accepts pipeline input by using the ValueFromPipeline property of the Parameter attribute:

```
function Get-InputObject {
    [CmdletBinding()]
    param (
        [Parameter(Mandatory, ValueFromPipeline)]
        $InputObject
    )

    process {
        'Input object was of type {0}' -f $InputObject.GetType().FullName
    }
}
```

Remember that values read from an input pipeline are only available in the process block of a script or function. As the default type assigned to a parameter is Object, this will accept any kind of input that might be passed. This behaves in a similar manner to the InputObject parameter for Get-Member, for example.

Accepting null input

Commands such as `Where-Object` allow an explicit null value in the input pipeline. To allow null in an input pipeline, the `[AllowNull()]` attribute would be added to the `InputObject` parameter. There is a difference between supporting `$null | Get-InputObject` and implementing pipeline support originating from a command that returns nothing: `AllowNull` is only needed when an explicit null is in the input pipeline.

In the following example, the `Get-EmptyOutput` function has no body and will not return anything. This simulates a command that returns nothing because all of the output is filtered out. The `Get-InputObject` function can take part in a pipeline with `Get-EmptyOutput` without using `AllowNull`:

```
function Get-EmptyOutput { }
function Get-InputObject {
    [CmdletBinding()]
    param (
        [Parameter(Mandatory, ValueFromPipeline)]
        $InputObject
    )
}
# No output, no error
First | Second
```

If `Get-EmptyOutput` were to explicitly return null, which is not a good practice, `Get-InputObject` would raise a parameter binding error:

```
PS> function First { return $null }
PS> First | Second
Second : Cannot bind argument to parameter 'InputObject' because it is
null.
 At line:1 char:9
 + First | Second
 + ~~~~~~
 + CategoryInfo : InvalidData: (:) [Second],
ParameterBindingValidationException
 + FullyQualifiedErrorId :
ParameterArgumentValidationErrorNullNotAllowed,Second
```

Adding `AllowNull` would sidestep this error, but `Get-InputObject` would have to handle a null value internally:

```
function Get-EmptyOutput { return $null }
function Get-InputObject {
    [CmdletBinding()]
    param (
```

```
            [Parameter(Mandatory, ValueFromPipeline)]
            [AllowNull()]
            $InputObject
    )
    if ($InputObject) {
        # Do work
    }
}
# No output, no error
First | Second
```

If this were real output from a function, it may be better to consider the output from Get-EmptyOutput to be a bug and pass it through Where-Object to sanitize the input, which avoids the need to add AllowNull, for example:

```
Get-EmptyOutput | Where-Object { $_ } | Get-InputObject
```

Input object types

If a type is defined for the InputObject variable, the command will only work if the input pipeline contains that object type. An error will be thrown when a different object type is passed. The following example modifies the command to accept pipeline input from Get-Process; it expects objects of the System.Diagnostics.Process type only:

```
function Get-InputObject {
    [CmdletBinding()]
    param (
        [Parameter(Mandatory, ValueFromPipeline)]
        [System.Diagnostics.Process]$InputObject
    )

    process {
        'Process name {0}' -f $InputObject.Name
    }
}
```

Using ValueFromPipeline for multiple parameters

If more than one parameter uses `ValueFromPipeline`, PowerShell will attempt to provide values to each. The parameter binder can be said to be greedy in this respect. The following function can be used to show that both parameters are filled with the same value if the parameters accept the same type, or if the value can be coerced into that type:

```
function Test-ValueFromPipeline {
    [CmdletBinding()]
    param (
        [Parameter(ValueFromPipeline)]
        [Int]$Parameter1,

        [Parameter(ValueFromPipeline)]
        [Int]$Parameter2
    )

    process {
        'Parameter1: {0}:: Parameter2: {1}' -f $Parameter1, $Parameter2
    }
}
```

Providing an input pipeline for the command shows the values assigned to each parameter:

```
PS> 1..2 | Test-ValueFromPipeline
Parameter1: 1 :: Parameter2: 1
Parameter1: 2 :: Parameter2: 2
```

Filling variables is the job of the parameter binder in PowerShell. Using `Trace-Command` will show the parameter binder in action:

```
Trace-Command -Expression { 1 | Test-ValueFromPipeline } -PSHost -Name
ParameterBinding
```

The bind-pipeline section will display messages that show that the value was successfully bound to each parameter. If the two parameters expected different types, the parameter binding will attempt to coerce the value into the requested type. If that is not possible, it will give up on the attempt to fill the parameter. The next example declares two different parameters; both accept values from the pipeline and neither is mandatory:

```
function Get-InputObject {
    [CmdletBinding()]
    param (
        [Parameter(ValueFromPipeline)]
        [System.Diagnostics.Process]$ProcessObject,

        [Parameter(ValueFromPipeline)]
```

```
        [System.ServiceProcess.ServiceController]$ServiceObject
    )

    process {
        if ($ProcessObject) { 'Process: {0}' -f $ProcessObject.Name }
        if ($ServiceObject) { 'Service: {0}' -f $ServiceObject.Name }
    }
}
```

The command will, at this point, accept pipeline input from both Get-Process and Get-Service. Each command will fill the matching parameter, Get-Process fills ProcessObject, and Get-Service fills ServiceObject. This design is unusual and perhaps confusing; here, it is only demonstrated because it is possible. A parameter set can be used to make sense of the pattern, which we will explore in the *Defining parameter sets* section.

Using PSTypeName

The PSTypeName attribute may also be used to tightly define the objects acceptable for a parameter that uses ValueFromPipeline:

```
function Get-InputObject {
    [CmdletBinding()]
    param (
        [Parameter(ValueFromPipeline)]
        [PSTypeName('CustomTypeName')]
        $InputObject
    )

    process {
        $InputObject.Name
    }
}
```

This function would accept input from an object that declares the matching type name:

```
[PSCustomObject]@{
    Name      = 'Value'
    PSTypeName = 'CustomTypeName'
} | Get-InputObject
```

A .NET type may also be assigned to the InputObject parameter in addition to PSTypeName. However, in this case, the type would have to be either Object or PSObject. This is effectively pointless as absolutely any object type in PowerShell will satisfy either of those parameter types.

About ValueFromPipelineByPropertyName

ValueFromPipelineByPropertyName attempts to fill a parameter from the property of an object in the input pipeline. When filling a value by property name, the name and type of the property is important, but not the object that implements the property.

For example, a function might be created to accept a string value from a Name property:

```
function Get-Name {
    [CmdletBinding()]
    param (
        [Parameter(Mandatory, ValueFromPipelineByPropertyName)]
        [String]$Name
    )

    process {
        $Name
    }
}
```

Any command that returns an object which contains a Name property in a string is acceptable input for this function. Additional parameters might be defined, which would further restrict the input object type, assuming the new properties are mandatory:

```
function Get-Status {
    [CmdletBinding()]
    param (
        [Parameter(Mandatory, ValueFromPipelineByPropertyName)]
        [String]$Name,

        [Parameter(Mandatory, ValueFromPipelineByPropertyName)]
        [String]$Status
    )

    process {
        '{0}: {1}' -f $Name, $Status
    }
}
```

This new function would accept pipeline input from Get-Service, as the output from Get-Service has both Name and Status properties. Using Get-Member against Get-Service would show that the Status property is an enumeration value described by System.ServiceProcess.ServiceControllerStatus. This value is acceptable to the Get-Status function as it can be coerced into a string, which satisfies the Status parameter.

The previous function is not limited to a specific input object type. A PSCustomObject can be created with properties to satisfy the parameters for the Get-Status function:

```
[PSCustomObject]@{ Name = 'Name'; Status = 'Running' } | Get-Status
```

As with the ValueFromPipeline input, the parameter binder will attempt to fill as many of the parameters as possible from the input pipeline. Trace-Command, as used when exploring ValueFromPipeline, can be used to show the behavior of the parameter binder.

ValueFromPipelineByPropertyName and parameter aliases

We have not looked at parameter aliases yet. Any parameter may be given one or more aliases using the Alias attribute, as shown in the following example:

```
function Get-InputObject {
    [CmdletBinding()]
    param (
        [Parameter(ValueFromPipelineByPropertyName)]
        [Alias('First', 'Second', 'Third')]
        $InputObject
    )
}
```

The alias name is considered when determining whether a property on an input object is suitable to fill a parameter when filling a parameter by property name.

One of the more common uses of this is to provide support for a Path parameter via a pipeline from Get-Item or Get-ChildItem. For example, the following pattern might be used to expose a Path parameter. This is used in the short helper function that imports JSON content from a file:

```
function Import-Json {
    [CmdletBinding()]
    param (
        [Parameter(Mandatory, ValueFromPipelineByPropertyName)]
        [Alias('PSPath')]
        [String]$Path
    )

    process {
        Get-Content $Path | ConvertFrom-Json
    }
}
```

The PSPath property of the object returned by Get-Item or Get-ChildItem is used to fill the Path parameter from a pipeline. FullName is a possible alternative to PSPath, depending on how the path is to be used.

Converting relative paths to full paths

When using a path parameter, such as the one in the previous example, the following method on the PSCmdlet object can be used to ensure a path is fully qualified whether it exists or not:

```
$Path =
$PSCmdlet.GetUnresolvedProviderPathFromPSPath($Path)
```

This technique is useful if working with .NET types, which require a path as these are not able to resolve PowerShell paths (either relative or via a PS drive).

The New-TimeSpan command is an example of an existing command that uses the alias to fill a parameter from the pipeline. The Start parameter has an alias of LastWriteTime. When Get-Item is piped into New-TimeSpan, the time since the file or directory was last written will be returned as a TimeSpan via the aliased parameter.

Defining parameter sets

A parameter set in PowerShell groups different parameters together. In some cases, this is used to change the output of a command; in others, it provides a different way of supplying a piece of information. For example, the output from the Get-Process command changes if the Module parameter or, to a lesser extent, the IncludeUserName parameter are supplied. The Get-ChildItem command also has two parameter sets: one that accepts a Path with wildcard support, and another that accepts a LiteralPath that does not support wildcards. That is, it has two different ways of supplying essentially the same information. Parameter sets are declared using the ParameterSetName property of the Parameter attribute.

The following example has two parameter sets; each parameter set contains a single parameter:

```
function Get-InputObject {
    [CmdletBinding()]
    param (
        [Parameter(ParameterSetName = 'FirstSetName')]
        $Parameter1,
```

```
            [Parameter(ParameterSetName = 'SecondSetName')]
            $Parameter2
    )
}
```

As neither parameter set is the default, attempting to run the command using a positional parameter only will result in an error:

```
PS> Get-InputObject value
Get-InputObject : Parameter set cannot be resolved using the specified
named parameters.
At line:1 char:1
+ Get-InputObject value
+ ~~~~~~~~~~~~~~~~~~~~~
    + CategoryInfo : InvalidArgument: (:) [Get-InputObject],
ParameterBindingException
    + FullyQualifiedErrorId : AmbiguousParameterSet,Get-InputObject
```

This can be resolved by setting a value for the DefaultParameterSetName property in the CmdletBinding attribute:

```
[CmdletBinding(DefaultParameterSetName = 'FirstSetName')]
```

Alternatively, an explicit position might be defined for one of the parameters; the set will be selected on the basis of explicit position:

```
[Parameter(Position = 1, ParameterSetName = 'FirstSetName')]
$Parameter1
```

The name of the parameter set in use within a function is visible using the ParameterSetName property of the pscmdlet automatic variable, that is $pscmdlet.ParameterSetName. The value may be used to choose actions within the body of a function. The following example shows a possible implementation that tests the value of ParameterSetName. The function accepts the name of a service as a string, a service object from Get-Service, or a service returned from the Win32_Service class. The function finds the process associated with that service:

```
function Get-ServiceProcess {
    [CmdletBinding(DefaultParameterSetName = 'ByName')]
    param (
        [Parameter(Mandatory,  Position = 1, ParameterSetName = 'ByName')]
        [String]$Name,

        [Parameter(Mandatory, ValueFromPipeline, ParameterSetName =
'FromService')]
        [System.ServiceProcess.ServiceController]$Service,
```

```
        [Parameter(Mandatory, ValueFromPipeline, ParameterSetName =
'FromCimService')]
    [PSTypeName('Microsoft.Management.Infrastructure.CimInstance#root/cimv2/Win
32_Service')]
        [CimInstance]$CimService
    )

    process {
        if ($pscmdlet.ParameterSetName -eq 'FromService') {
            $Name = $Service.Name
        }
        if ($Name) {
            $params = @{
                ClassName = 'Win32_Service'
                Filter    = 'Name="{0}"' -f $Name
                Property  = 'Name', 'ProcessId', 'State'
            }
            $CimService = Get-CimInstance @params
        }
        if ($CimService.State -eq 'Running') {
            Get-Process -Id $CimService.ProcessId
        } else {
            Write-Error ('The service {0} is not running' -f
$CimService.Name)
        }
    }
}
```

The previous function accepts several different parameters. Each parameter is ultimately used to get to a value for the $CimService variable (or parameter), which has a ProcessID property associated with the service. Each of the examples so far has shown a parameter that is a member of a single, explicitly declared set. A parameter that does not describe a ParameterSetName is automatically part of every set.

In the following example, Parameter1 is part of every parameter set, Parameter2 is in a named set only:

```
function Test-ParameterSet {
    [CmdletBinding(DefaultParameterSetName = 'Default')]
    param (
        [Parameter(Mandatory, Position = 1)]
        $Parameter1,

        [Parameter(ParameterSetName = 'NamedSet')]
        $Parameter2
    )
}
```

Get-Command may be used to show the syntax for the command; this shows there are two different parameter sets, both of which require Parameter1:

```
PS> Get-Command Test-ParameterSet -Syntax

Test-ParameterSet [-Parameter1] <Object> [<CommonParameters>]

Test-ParameterSet [-Parameter1] <Object> [-Parameter2 <Object>]
[<CommonParameters>]
```

Parameters that do not use the Parameter attribute are also automatically part of all parameter sets. A parameter may also be added to more than one parameter set. This is achieved by using more than one Parameter attribute on a parameter:

```
function Test-ParameterSet {
    [CmdletBinding(DefaultParameterSetName = 'NamedSet1')]
    param (
        [Parameter(Mandatory)]
        $Parameter1,

        [Parameter(Mandatory, ParameterSetName = 'NamedSet2')]
        $Parameter2,

        [Parameter(Mandatory, ParameterSetName = 'NamedSet3')]
        $Parameter3,

        [Parameter(Mandatory, ParameterSetName = 'NamedSet2')]
        [Parameter(ParameterSetName = 'NamedSet3')]
        $Parameter4
    )
}
```

In the preceding example, Parameter1 is in all parameter sets. Parameter2 is in NamedSet2 only. Parameter3 is in NamedSet3 only. Parameter4 is mandatory in NamedSet2, and optional in NamedSet3.

This interplay of parameter sets is complex and difficult to describe without a complex command to use the parameters. Many existing commands use complex parameter sets and their parameter sets may be explored. For example, the parameter block for the Get-Process command may be shown by running the following command:

```
[System.Management.Automation.ProxyCommand]::GetParamBlock((Get-Command
Get-Process))
```

Argument-completers

Argument-completers have been around in a number of different forms since PowerShell 2. This section focuses on the implementation of argument-completers available in Windows PowerShell 5 and PowerShell Core.

An argument-completer is used by the tab completion system to provide a value for a parameter when *Tab* is pressed. For example, the Get-Module command cycles though module names when *Tab* is pressed after the command name. The argument-completer does not restrict the values that may be supplied; it is only used to offer values, to make the use of a command easier for an end user.

An argument-completer is a script block; the script block should accept the following parameters:

- commandName
- parameterName
- wordToComplete
- commandAst
- fakeBoundParameter

Any of these parameters may be used, but the most important and the most frequently used is wordToComplete.

The following example would suggest words from a fixed list:

```
param ( $commandName, $parameterName, $wordToComplete, $commandAst,
$fakeBoundParameter )

$possibleValues = 'Start', 'Stop', 'Create', 'Delete'
$possibleValues | Where-Object { $_ -like "$wordToComplete*" }
```

Notice that a wildcard, *, has been added on the end of wordToComplete. Arguably, ValidateSet might be a better option in this case as it also feeds tab completion. However, where ValidateSet enforces, ArgumentCompleter suggests. The argument-completer only suggests when the user is using tab to complete a parameter value so it cannot replace ValidateSet or any other parameter validation steps. Unlike ValidateSet, and perhaps more like ValidateScript, the list of possible values used in an argument-completer can be dynamic. That is, the list of possible values can be the result of running another command. PowerShell provides two different ways to assign an argument completer: the ArgumentCompleter attribute or the Register-ArgumentCompleter command.

The argument-completer attribute

The argument-completer attribute is used much like `ValidateScript`. The script block used previously is used as an argument for the attribute, shown as follows:

```
function Test-ArgumentCompleter {
    [CmdletBinding()]
    param (
        [Parameter(Mandatory)]
        [ArgumentCompleter( {
            param ( $commandName, $parameterName, $wordToComplete,
$commandAst, $fakeBoundParameter )

            $possibleValues = 'Start', 'Stop', 'Create', 'Delete'
            $possibleValues | Where-Object { $_ -like "$wordToComplete*" }
        } )]
        $Action
    )
}
```

When the user types `Test-ArgumentCompleter` and then presses *Tab*, the completer offers up each of the possible values with no filtering. If the user were to type `Test-ArgumentCompleters`, only start and stop would be offered when pressing *Tab*.

Using Register-ArgumentCompleter

The `Register-ArgumentCompleter` command has two advantages over the `ArgumentCompleter` attribute. First, it can be used to set an argument-completer for a number of parameters across a number of commands at once. And second, it can create argument-completers for native commands; for example, when used as an alternative to the `ArgumentCompleter` attribute, the command is used as follows:

```
function Test-ArgumentCompleter {
    [CmdletBinding()]
    param (
        [Parameter(Mandatory)]
        $Action
    )
}

$params = @{
    CommandName   = 'Test-ArgumentCompleter'
    ParameterName = 'Action'
    ScriptBlock   = {
        param ( $commandName, $parameterName, $wordToComplete, $commandAst,
```

```
$fakeBoundParameter )

        $possibleValues = 'Start', 'Stop', 'Create', 'Delete'
        $possibleValues | Where-Object { $_ -like "$wordToComplete*" }
    }
}
Register-ArgumentCompleter @params
```

The CommandName parameter used for Register-ArgumentCompleter accepts an array of command names. In one step, the completer can be added to several different commands that share a parameter. Register-ArgumentCompleter can also be used to add argument-completion to native commands. The following example offers a steadfast user of the wmic command automatic alias-completion:

```
Register-ArgumentCompleter -CommandName wmic -Native -ScriptBlock {
    param ( $wordToComplete, $commandAst, $cursorPosition )

    wmic /?:BRIEF |
        Where-Object { $_ -cmatch '^([A-Z]{2}\S+)+' } |
        ForEach-Object { $matches[1] } |
        Where-Object {
            $_ -notin 'CLASS', 'PATH', 'CONTEXT', 'QUIT/EXIT' -and
            $_ -like "$wordToComplete*"
        }
}
```

When using the -Native parameter, the arguments passed to the completer differ; the first argument becomes the word to complete.

Listing registered argument-completers

While it is possible to register argument-completers, PowerShell does not provide a way of listing them. This is somewhat frustrating as it makes exploration and finding examples more difficult.

The following script makes extensive use of reflection in .NET to explore classes that are not made publicly available, eventually getting to a property that holds the argument-completers:

```
$localPipeline =
[PowerShell].Assembly.GetType('System.Management.Automation.Runspaces.Local
Pipeline')
$getExecutionContextFromTLS = $localPipeline.GetMethod(
    'GetExecutionContextFromTLS',
    [System.Reflection.BindingFlags]'Static, NonPublic'
```

```
)
$internalExecutionContext = $getExecutionContextFromTLS.Invoke(
    $null,
    [System.Reflection.BindingFlags]'Static, NonPublic',
    $null,
    $null,
    $psculture
)
$customArgumentCompletersProperty =
$internalExecutionContext.GetType().GetProperty(
    'CustomArgumentCompleters',
    [System.Reflection.BindingFlags]'NonPublic, Instance'
)
$customArgumentCompletersProperty.GetGetMethod($true).Invoke(
    $internalExecutionContext,
    [System.Reflection.BindingFlags]'Instance, NonPublic, GetProperty',
    $null,
    @(),
    $psculture
)
```

Native argument-completers are held in a different property and will not be shown by the preceding snippet.

A more refined version of the previous snippet, which also supports the retrieval of native argument-completers, is available as a function at https://gist.github.com/indented-automation/26c637fb530c4b168e62c72582534f5b.

Dynamic parameters

Dynamic parameters allow a developer to define the behavior of parameters when a function is run, rather than hardcoding that behavior in advance in a `param` block. Dynamic parameters can be used to overcome some of the limitations inherent in a `param` block. For example, it is possible to change the parameters presented by a command based on the value of another parameter. It is also possible to dynamically write validation, such as dynamically assigning a value for the `ValidateSet` attribute.

Dynamic parameters remain unpopular in the PowerShell community. They are relatively complex; that is, they are hard to define, and difficult to troubleshoot as they tend to silently fail rather than raising an error. Dynamic parameters have a named block: `dynamicparam`. If `dynamicparam` is used, the default blocks for a script or function cannot be used; all code must be contained within explicitly declared named blocks. The `CmdletBinding` attribute must be explicitly declared when using `dynamicparam`, parameters will not be created without `CmdletBinding`, nor will an error message be shown to explain that.

The following example includes an empty `dynamicparam` block as well as an `end` block, which would have been implicit if `dynamicparam` were not present:

```
function Test-DynamicParam {
 [CmdletBinding()]
 param ( )

  dynamicparam { }
    end {
        Write-Host 'Function body'
    }
}
```

If the `end` block declaration is missing, a syntax error will be displayed. This is shown as follows, it does not state that the problem is the `dynamicparam` block, or because of a missing `named` block:

```
PS> function Test-DynamicParam {
>>      [CmdletBinding()]
>>      param ( )
>>      dynamicparam { }
>>      Write-Host 'Function body'
>> }
At line:1 char:28
+ function Test-DynamicParam {
+ ~
Missing closing '}' in statement block or type definition.
At line:4 char:1
+ }
+ ~
Unexpected token '}' in expression or statement.
 + CategoryInfo : ParserError: (:) [], ParentContainsErrorRecordException
 + FullyQualifiedErrorId : MissingEndCurlyBrace
```

The `dynamicparam` block must output a `RuntimeDefinedParameterDictionary` object. The dictionary should contain one or more `RuntimeDefinedParameter` objects.

Creating a RuntimeDefinedParameter object

A `RuntimeDefinedParameter` object describes a single parameter. The definition includes the name of the parameter, the parameter type, and any attributes that should be set for that parameter. PowerShell does not include type accelerators for creating `RuntimeDefinedParameter`; the full name, `System.Management.Automation.RuntimeDefinedParameter`, must be used. The constructor for `RuntimeDefinedParameter` expects three arguments: a string, which will be the parameter name, a .NET type for the parameter, and a collection or array of attributes that should be assigned. The attribute collection must contain at least one `Parameter` attribute.

The following example, which creates a parameter named `Action`, makes use of a `using namespace` statement to shorten the .NET type names:

```
using namespace System.Management.Automation
$parameter = [RuntimeDefinedParameter]::new('Action', [String],
[Attribute[]]@(
        [Parameter]@{ Mandatory = $true; Position = 1 }
        [ValidateSet]::new('Start', 'Stop', 'Create', 'Delete')
    )
)
```

The previous parameter is the equivalent of using the following in the `param` block:

```
param (
    [Parameter(Mandatory, Position = 1)]
    [ValidateSet('Start', 'Stop', 'Create', 'Delete')]
    [String]$Action
)
```

As the attributes are not being placed directly above a variable, each must be created as an independent object instance:

- The shorthand used for the `Parameter` attribute in the `param` block cannot be used; Boolean values must be written in full
- The `ValidateSet` attribute, and other validation attributes, must also be created as a new object rather than using the attribute syntax

The `Parameter` attribute declaration takes advantage of PowerShell's ability to assign property values to an object using a `hashtable`. This is feasible because a `Parameter` attribute can be created without supplying any arguments, that is, `[Parameter]::new()` can be used to create a `Parameter` attribute with default values. This technique cannot be used for the validation attributes, as each requires one or more arguments, therefore `::new` or `New-Object` must be used.

As with a normal parameter, `RuntimeDefinedParameter` can declare more than one parameter attribute. Each `Parameter` attribute is added to the attribute collection:

```
using namespace System.Management.Automation
$parameter = [RuntimeDefinedParameter]::new('Action', [String],
[Attribute[]]@(
        [Parameter]@{ Mandatory = $true; Position = 1; ParameterSetName =
'First' }
        [Parameter]@{ ParameterSetName = 'Second' }
    )
)
```

Any number of parameters might be created in this manner. Each parameter must have a unique name. Each parameter must be added to a `RuntimeDefinedParameterDictionary`.

Using the RuntimeDefinedParameterDictionary

`RuntimeDefinedParameterDictionary` is the expected output from the `dynamicparam` block. The dictionary must contain all of the dynamic parameters a function is expected to present.

The following example creates a dictionary and adds a single parameter:

```
using namespace System.Management.Automation

function Test-DynamicParam {
    [CmdletBinding()]
    param ( )

    dynamicparam {
        $paramDictionary = [RuntimeDefinedParameterDictionary]::new()

        $parameter = [RuntimeDefinedParameter]::new('Action', [String],
[Attribute[]]@(
                [Parameter]@{ Mandatory = $true; Position = 1 }
                [ValidateSet]::new('Start', 'Stop', 'Create', 'Delete')
```

```
            )
        )
        $paramDictionary.Add($parameter.Name, $parameter)

        $paramDictionary
    }
}
```

Using dynamic parameters

Dynamic parameters must be accessed using the PSBoundParameters variable within a function or script; dynamic parameters do not initialize variables of their own.

The value of the Action parameter used in the previous examples must be retrieved by using Action as a key, shown as follows:

```
using namespace System.Management.Automation

function Test-DynamicParam {
    [CmdletBinding()]
    param ( )

    dynamicparam {
        $paramDictionary = [RuntimeDefinedParameterDictionary]::new()

        $parameter = [RuntimeDefinedParameter]::new('Action', [String],
[Attribute[]]@(
                [Parameter]@{ Mandatory = $true; Position = 1 }
                [ValidateSet]::new('Start', 'Stop', 'Create', 'Delete')
            )
        )
        $paramDictionary.Add($parameter.Name, $parameter)

        $paramDictionary
    }

    end {
        Write-Host $psboundparameters['Action']
    }
}
```

As with parameters from the param block, the $psboundparameters.ContainsKey method may be used to find out whether a user has specified a value for the parameter. Dynamic parameters cannot have a default value; any default values must be created in begin, process, or end.

A dynamic parameter that accepts pipeline input, like a normal parameter that accepts pipeline input, will only have a value within the process and end blocks. The end block will only see the last value in the pipeline. The following example demonstrates this:

```
using namespace System.Management.Automation

function Test-DynamicParam {
    [CmdletBinding()]
    param ( )

    dynamicparam {
        $paramDictionary = [RuntimeDefinedParameterDictionary]::new()

        $parameter = [RuntimeDefinedParameter]::new('InputObject',
[String], [Attribute[]]@(
                    [Parameter]@{ Mandatory = $true; ValueFromPipeline = $true
}
              )
        )
        $paramDictionary.Add($parameter.Name, $parameter)

        $paramDictionary
    }

    begin {
        'BEGIN: Input object is present: {0}' -f @(
            $psboundparameters.ContainsKey('InputObject')
        )
    }

    process {
        'PROCESS: Input object is present: {0}; Value: {1}' -f @(
            $psboundparameters.ContainsKey('InputObject')
            $psboundparameters['InputObject']
        )
    }

    end {
        'END: Input object is present: {0}; Value: {1}' -f @(
            $psboundparameters.ContainsKey('InputObject')
            $psboundparameters['InputObject']
        )
    }
}
```

The function can be used with arbitrary input values, for example:

```
PS> 1..2 | Test-DynamicParam
```

```
BEGIN: Input object is present: False
PROCESS: Input object is present: True; Value: 1
PROCESS: Input object is present: True; Value: 2
END: Input object is present: True; Value: 2
```

The PSBoundParameters variable, and any other parameters, may be referenced inside the dynamicparam block.

Conditional parameters

One possible use of dynamic parameters is to change validation based on the value supplied for another parameter. Another use is to change which parameters are available, again based on the value of another parameter.

The following example changes validValues into ValidateSet depending on the value supplied for the Type parameter:

```
using namespace System.Management.Automation

function Test-DynamicParam {
    [CmdletBinding()]
    param (
        [Parameter(Mandatory, Position = 1)]
        [ValidateSet('Service', 'Process')]
        [String]$Type,

        [Parameter(Mandatory, Position = 3)]
        [String]$Name
    )

    dynamicparam {
        $paramDictionary = [RuntimeDefinedParameterDictionary]::new()

        [String[]]$validValues = switch ($Type) {
            'Service' { 'Get', 'Start', 'Stop', 'Restart' }
            'Process' { 'Get', 'Kill' }
        }
        $parameter = [RuntimeDefinedParameter]::new('Action', [String],
[Attribute[]]@(
                [Parameter]@{ Mandatory = $true; Position = 2 }
                [ValidateSet]::new($validValues)
            )
        )
        $paramDictionary.Add($parameter.Name, $parameter)

        $paramDictionary
```

```
        }
    }
```

Changing validation in this manner is entirely reliant on the user having typed a value for the `Type` parameter prior to attempting to use `Action`. Other comparisons can be made in dynamic parameter blocks, for example a parameter might only appear when a certain condition is met. `RuntimeDefinedParameterDictionary` is valid even if it is empty and no extra parameters need to be added.

Summary

In this chapter, we looked at working with parameters. We stared with an exploration of the `Parameter` attribute before moving on to validation techniques. We discussed `ValueFromPipeline` and `ValueFromPipelineByPropertyName` when working with pipeline parameters. We briefly looked at parameter sets before moving on to explore argument-completers. Finally, we explored the use of dynamic parameters.

In the next chapter, we will explore the classes and enumerations that were introduced in PowerShell 5.

18

Classes and Enumerations

PowerShell 5 introduced support for creating classes and enumerations within PowerShell directly. Prior to this, classes had to be imported from an assembly written in a language such as C#, or dynamically created using the dynamic module builders.

Classes and enumerations are undergoing a great deal of change in PowerShell Core. There are numerous enhancement issues open in the PowerShell project on GitHub that are slowly making their way into PowerShell Core. Examples include the addition of interfaces, support for using validation attributes on properties, and the ability to override getters and setters for properties.

This chapter will explore the following topics:

- Defining an enumeration
- Creating a class
- Argument transformation attribute classes
- Validation attribute classes
- Classes and DSC

Defining an enumeration

An enumeration is a set of named constants. The .NET framework is full of examples of enumerations. For example, the `System.Security.AccessControl.FileSystemRights` enumeration describes all of the numeric values that are used to define access rights for files or directories.

Enumerations are also used in PowerShell itself, for example, `System.Management.Automation.ActionPreference` contains the values for the preference variables, such as `ErrorActionPreference` and `DebugPreference`.

Enumerations are created using the enum keyword, and this is followed by a list of values:

```
enum MyEnum {
    First  = 1
    Second = 2
    Third  = 3
}
```

Each name must be unique within the enumeration, and must start with a letter or an underscore. The name may contain numbers after the first character. The name cannot be quoted and cannot contain the hyphen character.

The value does not have to be unique. One or more names in an enumeration can share a single value:

```
enum MyEnum {
    One    = 1
    First  = 1
    Two    = 2
    Second = 2
}
```

The style of the preceding enumeration is odd: it defines two sets of names in a single enumeration, which is not a good practice to adopt.

Enum and underlying types

In languages such as C#, enumerations can be given an underlying type, such as Byte or Int64. In PowerShell 5 and PowerShell Core 6.1 and older, the enumeration type is fixed to Int32. This type is shown using the following command:

```
PS> enum MyEnum {
>>     First = 1
>> }
PS> [MyEnum].GetEnumUnderlyingType()
```

IsPublic	IsSerial	Name	BaseType
True	True	Int32	System.ValueType

Any enumeration value may therefore be cast to its underlying type, or any numeric type capable of supporting the value:

```
[Int][MyEnum]::First
```

A new feature has been added to PowerShell Core that will grant you the ability to set the underlying type. This feature is likely to appear in PowerShell Core 6.2 but is not available in the preview versions at the time of writing. The notation that will be allowed is shown as follows:

```
enum MyEnum : UInt64 {
    First = 0
    Last  = 18446744073709551615
}
```

Automatic value assignment

An enumeration may be created without defining a value for a name. PowerShell will automatically allocate a sequence of values starting from 0. In the following example, the names Zero and One are automatically created with the values 0 and 1, respectively:

```
enum MyEnum {
    Zero
    One
}
```

If a value is assigned to a name, the sequence will continue from that point. The following example starts with the value 5; Six will automatically be given the value 6:

```
enum MyEnum {
    Five = 5
    Six
}
```

Automatic value assignment supports non-contiguous sets. The sequence may be restarted at any point, or values may be skipped. The following example demonstrates both restarting a sequence and skipping values in a sequence:

```
enum MyEnum {
    One    = 1
    Two
    Five   = 5
    Six
    First = 1
    Second
}
```

This example mixes two potentially different name sets in a single enumeration to demonstrate restarting the numeric sequence. This should be avoided outside of demonstrations as it makes the use of the enumeration ambiguous.

Enum or ValidateSet

In some cases, only the name of the value is important; enumerations are occasionally used in place of `ValidateSet`.

Class-based **Desired State Configuration (DSC)** resources provide one of the more obvious cases for this style. The `Ensure` parameter has two possible values: `Absent` and `Present`. `Ensure` can be expressed using an enumeration:

```
enum Ensure {
    Absent
    Present
}
```

`Absent` is placed first as this has the value of `0`, which might also be interpreted as false when casting to a `Boolean`:

```
[Boolean][Ensure]::Absent
```

The advantage of using an enumeration is that it can be shared across a script or module and would only need to be updated once in the event of a change.

The flags attribute

By default, an enumeration matches a single value. If the enumeration contains more than one name for a value, the first name will be chosen.

The flags attribute allows a value to describe more than one name. The flags attribute is placed before the `enum` keyword.

Typically, each value in the enumeration is given a value with a unique bit combination. This is shown in the following enumeration; the bit combination is shown in the comment after the value:

```
[Flags()]
enum MyEnum {
    First  = 1 # 001
    Second = 2 # 010
    Third  = 4 # 100
}
```

Automatic value assignment cannot be reasonably used to assign values for a flags enumeration at the time of writing.

When the flags attribute is present, PowerShell will cast a string that contains two or more names in a comma-separated list to the value that represents that combination:

```
[Int][MyEnum]'First,Second'
```

PowerShell will also cast a numeric value into a set of names. A value of 6 can be used to represent the Second and Third flags:

```
PS> [MyEnum] 6
Second, Third
```

Several enumerations that use the Flags attribute also provide named composite values. For example, the following enumeration contains a name that is used to represent the combination of the first and third flags:

```
[Flags()]
enum MyEnum {
    First        = 1 # 001
    Second       = 2 # 010
    Third        = 4 # 100
    FirstAndThird = 5 # 101
}
```

As FirstAndThird explicitly matches the value 5, any value the enumeration converts will use the FirstAndThird name instead of the individual values:

```
PS> [MyEnum] 7
Second, FirstAndThird

PS> [MyEnum] 'First, Second, Third'
Second, FirstAndThird
```

The System.Security.AccessControl.FileSystemRights enumeration makes use of this technique to summarise groups of rights. The Modify name can be represented as the 110000000110111111 binary string. The enumeration names that make up the value of Modify may be displayed by comparing individual bits in the value with other possible values of the enumeration. The following snippet isolates each bit in turn and attempts to convert that single bit into a FileSystemRight name:

```
$value = [Int64][System.Security.AccessControl.FileSystemRights]::Modify
$i = 0
do {
    if ($bit = $value -band 1 -shl $i++) {
        [System.Security.AccessControl.FileSystemRights]$bit
    }
} until (1 -shl $i -ge $value)
```

Using enumerations to convert values

Considering that enumerations are lists of names, each assigned a numeric value. A pair of enumerations to convert between two lists of names, linked only by a common value.

The following example defines two enumerations. The first is a list of values the end user will see, the second holds the internal name required by the code. This simulates, in part, the type of aliasing performed by the `wmic` command:

```
enum AliasName {
    OS
    Process
}

enum ClassName {
    Win32_OperatingSystem
    Win32_Process
}
```

A function might use the `AliasName` enumeration, as shown here:

```
function Get-CimAliasInstance {
    [CmdletBinding()]
    param (
        [Parameter(Mandatory, Position = 1)]
        [AliasName]$AliasName
    )

    Get-CimInstance -ClassName ([ClassName]$AliasName)
}
```

The command may now be used with the OS argument for the `AliasName` parameter. This will be converted to `Win32_OperatingSystem` by way of the enumeration. `Get-CimInstance` handles converting that value into a string.

A `hashtable` is a possible alternative way of providing the same lookup mechanism. Using an enumeration would potentially have an advantage if the enumerations used the `Flags` attribute, or if one of the enumerations was already present.

Creating a class

A class is used to describe an object. This may be any object, which means that a class in PowerShell might be used for any purpose you could dream up.

Classes in PowerShell are created using the `class` keyword. The following class contains a single property:

```
class MyClass {
    [String]$Property = 'Value'
}
```

The class may be created using either `new-object` or the `::new()` method:

```
PS> [MyClass]::new()

Property
--------
Value
```

This snippet creates an instance of the class using the default constructor, displaying the property that was defined for the class.

Properties

The properties defined in a class may define a .NET type and may have a default value if required. The following class has a single property with the String type:

```
class MyClass {
    [String]$Property = 'Value'
}
```

PowerShell automatically adds hidden get and set methods used to access the property, these cannot be overridden or changed at this time (within the class itself).

The get and set methods may be viewed using `Get-Member` with the `Force` parameter:

```
[MyClass]::new() | Get-Member get_*, set_* -Force

   TypeName: MyClass

Name         MemberType  Definition
----         ----------  ----------
get_Property Method      string get_Property()
set_Property Method      void set_Property(string )
```

The property itself may be accessed on an instance of the class:

```
$instance = [MyClass]::new()
$instance.Property
```

Constructors

A constructor is executed when either `New-Object` or `::new()` is used to create an instance of a class. If an explicit constructor is not declared, an implicit constructor is created for the class. The implicit or default constructor does not require arguments:

```
PS> [MyClass]::new

OverloadDefinitions
-------------------
MyClass new()
```

An explicit constructor may be created to handle more complex instantiation scenarios. The constructor must use the same name as the class. The following constructor makes use of the `$this` reserved variable to access other members of the class:

```
class MyClass {
    [String]$Property
    MyClass() {
        $this.Property = 'Hello world'
    }
}
```

Constructors may be overloaded, that is, more than one constructor might be declared. Each constructor must accept a unique set of arguments:

```
class MyClass {
    [String]$Property

    MyClass() {
        $this.Property = 'Hello world'
    }

    MyClass([String]$greeting) {
        $this.Property = $greeting
    }
}
```

When the first constructor is used, `Property` will be set to the default greeting. The second constructor allows the user to define a custom value for `Property`.

Methods

A method enacts a change to the object. This may be an internal change, such as opening a connection or stream, or it may take the object and change it into a different form as is the case with the ToString method.

The following class defines a simple ToString method that returns the value of the property:

```
class MyClass {
    [String]$Property

    MyClass() {
        $this.Property = 'Hello world'
    }

    [String] ToString() {
        return $this.Property
    }
}
```

When working with methods, and unlike functions in PowerShell, the return keyword is mandatory. Methods do not return output by default. An error will be raised if a method has an output type declared and it does not return output from each code path.

Methods can accept arguments in the same way as constructors. Methods can also be overloaded. For example, the ToString method might be overloaded, providing support for output formatting. An example of this is shown here:

```
class MyClass {
    [String]$Property = 'Hello world'

    [String] ToString() {
        return '{0} on {1}' -f  $this.Property, (Get-
Date).ToShortDateString()
    }
    [String] ToString($format) {
        return '{0} on {1}' -f $this.Property, (Get-Date).ToString($format)
    }
}
```

The arguments supplied will dictate which method implementation is used.

Inheritance

Classes in PowerShell can inherit from other classes (both classes in PowerShell and classes from the .NET Framework). The properties, constructors, and methods in a base class are available to an inheriting class.

The following example defines two classes – the second inherits from the first:

```
class MyBaseClass {
    [String]$BaseProperty = 'baseValue'
}
class MyClass : MyBaseClass {
    [String]$Property = 'Value'
}
```

The BaseProperty property is made available on instances of the child class:

```
PS> [MyClass]::new()

Property        BaseProperty
--------        ------------
Value           baseValue
```

Members may be overridden by re-declaring the member on the inheriting class. The ToString method implementation from the base class is overridden in the following example:

```
class MyBaseClass {
    [String] ToString() { return 'default' }
}
class MyClass : MyBaseClass {
    [String] ToString() { return 'new' }
}
```

Unlike C#, PowerShell does not require the use of an override modifier.

Constructor inheritance

Constructor inheritance allows a child class to tweak a constructor declared on a base class without re-implementing the constructor. The base keyword is used to reference the constructor on the inherited class. The constructor on the base class is executed before the constructor in the inheriting class:

```
class MyBaseClass {
    [String]$BaseProperty
```

```
    MyBaseClass() {
        Write-Host 'Executing base constructor'
        $this.BaseProperty = 'baseValue'
    }
}
class MyClass : MyBaseClass {
    [String]$Property

    MyClass() : base() {
        Write-Host 'Executing child constructor'
        $this.Property = 'value'
    }
}
```

It is possible to invoke a constructor in the base class with a different overload by passing arguments to the base keyword:

```
class MyBaseClass {
    [String]$BaseProperty
    MyBaseClass($value) {
        $this.BaseProperty = $value
    }
}
class MyClass : MyBaseClass {
    MyClass() : base('SomeValue') { }
}
```

The arguments passed to the base keyword may be either variable values, such as the parameters for the constructor on MyClass, fixed values, or expressions that invoke other functions and commands.

This form of inheritance only applies to constructors – the same technique cannot be used for methods.

Chaining constructors

Constructor chaining avoids the need to repeat the work a single constructor performs. Overloaded methods can be used to simulate constructor-chaining within a class.

In C#, constructor-chaining allows one constructor to call another using the this keyword. This would be similar to the use of the base keyword when invoking an inherited constructor. This form of chaining is not possible in PowerShell; a workaround is required.

Each constructor is given an associated method; the methods call each other depending on the arguments supplied:

```
class MyClass {
    [String]$FirstProperty
    [String]$SecondProperty

    MyClass()                                    { $this.Initialize() }
    MyClass([String]$First)                      { $this.Initialize($First) }
    MyClass([String]$First, [String]$Second) { $this.Initialize($First,
$Second) }

    [Void] Initialize()                { $this.Initialize('DefaultFirst',
'DefaultSecond') }
    [Void] Initialize([String]$First) { $this.Initialize($First,
'DefaultSecond') }

    [Void] Initialize([String]$First, [String]$Second) {
        $this.FirstProperty = $First
        $this.SecondProperty = $Second
    }
}
```

These methods can be invoked directly on an instance of a class. The `Initialize` methods are visible to the end user using `Get-Member` or to IntelliSense and tab completion which may not be desirable.

The Hidden modifier

The `Hidden` modifier may be used to hide a property or a method from casual discovery. Members marked as `Hidden` are still visible when using `Get-Member`, and may still be invoked. In many respects, this is similar to the `DontShow` property of the `Parameter` attribute: it hides the member from IntelliSense and tab completion, but does not prevent use.

In the following example, the `Initialize` method is hidden:

```
class MyClass {
    [String]$Property

    MyClass() { $this.Initialize() }

    Hidden [Void] Initialize() {
        $this.Property = 'defaultValue'
    }
}
```

By default, the `Initialize` method will be hidden from view. Using `Get-Member` with the `Force` parameter will show the method:

```
PS> [MyClass]::new() | Get-Member Initialize -Force

    TypeName: MyClass

Name          MemberType      Definition
----          ----------      ----------
Initialize    Method          void Initialize()
```

It is not possible to make members private in PowerShell at this time.

The Static modifier

All of the members demonstrated so far have required creation of an instance of a type using either `New-Object` or `::new()`.

Static members may be executed without creating an instance of a type (based on a class).

Classes may implement static properties and static methods using the `Static` modifier keyword:

```
class MyClass {
    static [String] $Property = 'Property value'
    static [String] Method() {
        return 'Method return'
    }
}
```

The static members are invoked as follows:

```
[MyClass]::Property
[MyClass]::Method()
```

The `Hidden` modifier may be used in conjunction with the `Static` modifier. The modifiers may be used in either order.

Argument-transformation attribute classes

Argument-transformation attributes may be added to parameters used in scripts and functions. An argument-transformation attribute is used to convert the value of an argument for a parameter. The transformation operation is carried out before PowerShell completes the assignment to the variable, side-stepping type mismatch errors.

A class must be created that inherits from `System.Management.Automation.ArgumentTransformationAttribute`. The class must implement a `Transform` method.

The `Transform` method must accept two arguments with the `System.Object` and `System.Management.Automation.EngineIntrinsics` types. The argument names are arbitrary, the names used in the following example follow the naming used in the .NET reference: `https://docs.microsoft.com/en-us/dotnet/api/system.management.automation.argumenttransformationattribute.transform?view=powershellsdk-1.1.0`.

Abstract methods must be implemented in inheriting classes. That the `Transform` method must be implemented in this class is indicated by the `abstract` modifier shown in the .NET documentation. The abstract modifier is discussed in the C# reference: `https://docs.microsoft.com/en-us/dotnet/csharp/language-reference/keywords/abstract`.

The following example implements an argument-transformation attribute that converts a date string in the `yyyyMMddHHmmss` format back to `DateTime` before the assignment to the parameter is completed:

```
using namespace System.Management.Automation

class DateTimeStringTransformationAttribute :
ArgumentTransformationAttribute {
    [Object] Transform(
        [EngineIntrinsics]$engineIntrinsics,
        [Object]$inputData
    ) {
```

```
        $date = Get-Date
        if ($InputData -is [String] -and
            [DateTime]::TryParseExact($inputData, 'yyyyMMddHHmmss', $null,
'None', [Ref]$date)) {

            return $date
        } elseif ($inputData -is [DateTime]) {
            return $inputData
        } else {
            throw 'Unexpected date format'
        }
    }
}
```

The class does not need to contain anything other than the `Transform` method implementation. If the transformation is more complex, it may implement other helper methods. The following example moves `DateTime.TryParseExact` into a new method:

```
using namespace System.Management.Automation

class DateTimeStringTransformationAttribute :
ArgumentTransformationAttribute {
    Hidden [DateTime] $date

    Hidden [Boolean] tryParseExact([String]$value) {
        $parsedDate = Get-Date
        $parseResult = [DateTime]::TryParseExact(
            $value,
            'yyyyMMddHHmmss',
            $null,
            'None',
            [Ref]$parsedDate
        )
        $this.date = $parsedDate

        return $parseResult
    }

    [Object] Transform(
        [EngineIntrinsics]$engineIntrinsics,
        [Object]$inputData
    ) {
        if ($inputData -is [String] -and $this.TryParseExact($inputData)) {
            return $this.date
        } elseif ($inputData -is [DateTime]) {
            return $inputData
        } else {
            throw 'Unexpected date format'
```

```
            }
        }
    }
```

The new class may be used with a parameter, as shown here. Note that the `Attribute` string at the end of the class name may be omitted when it is used:

```
function Test-Transform {
    param (
        [DateTimeStringTransformation()]
        [DateTime]$Date
    )

    Write-Host $Date
}
```

With this attribute in place, the function can be passed a date and time in a format that would not normally convert:

```
PS> Test-Transform -Date '20190210090000'
10/02/2019 09:00:00
```

As implementing a transformation attribute requires either restricting a command to PowerShell 5 or newer, or an implementation using C#, they rarely appear in code.

Validation attribute classes

PowerShell classes may be used to build custom validation attributes. This might act as an alternative to `ValidateScript` in some respects.

Validation attributes must inherit from either `ValidateArgumentsAttribute` or `ValidateEnumeratedArgumentsAttribute`.

Validators are most often used with parameters in scripts and functions, but they may be used with any variable.

ValidateArgumentsAttribute

Validators that inherit from `ValidateArgumentsAttribute` are somewhat difficult to define. The existing validators, such as `ValidateNotNullOrEmpty` and `ValidateCount`, catch most of the possible uses. Validation is more often interested in testing whether the value of parameter is an array.

Classes that inherit from `ValidateArgumentsAttribute` act on an argument as a single entity. If an argument is an array, the validation step applies to the array object rather than the individual elements of the array.

Classes that implement `ValidateArgumentsAttribute` must inherit from `System.Management.Automation.ValidateArgumentsAttribute`. The class must implement a `Validate` method that is marked as abstract in the `ValidateArgumentsAttribute` class.

The `Validate` method accepts two arguments with the `System.Object` and `System.Management.Automation.EngineIntrinsics` types. This is shown in the .NET reference: https://docs.microsoft.com/en-us/dotnet/api/system.management.automation.validateargumentsattribute.validate?view=powershellsdk-1.1.0.

The following example tests that the argument is not null or whitespace:

```
using namespace System.Management.Automation

class ValidateNotNullOrWhitespaceAttribute : ValidateArgumentsAttribute {
    [Void] Validate(
        [System.Object]$arguments,
        [EngineIntrinsics]$engineIntrinsics
    ) {
        if ([String]::IsNullOrWhitespace($arguments)) {
            throw 'The value cannot be null or white space'
        }
    }
}
```

The use of this validator is demonstrated in the following function:

```
function Test-Validate {
    [CmdletBinding()]
    param (
        [ValidateNotNullOrWhitespace()]
        [String]$Value
    )

    Write-Host $Value
}
```

This validator example will be more effective when defined as a validator that inherits from `ValidateEnumeratedArguments` and is implemented in the `ValidateElement` method.

ValidateEnumeratedArgumentsAttribute

Classes that inherit from `ValidateEnumeratedArgumentsAttribute` may be used to test each of the elements in an array (when associated with an array-based parameter), or a single item (when associated with a scalar parameter).

Classes that implement `ValidateEnumeratedArgumentsAttribute` must inherit from `System.Management.Automation.ValidateEnumeratedArgumentsAttribute`. The class must implement a `Validate` method that is marked as abstract in the `ValidateEnumeratedArgumentsAttribute` class.

The `ValidateElement` method accepts one argument with the `System.Object` type. This is shown in the .NET reference: `https://docs.microsoft.com/en-us/dotnet/api/system.management.automation.validateenumeratedargumentsattribute.validateelement?view=powershellsdk-1.1.0`.

The `ValidateElement` method does not return any output; it either runs successfully or throws an error. The error will be displayed to the end user.

The following validates that an IP address used as an argument falls in a private address range. If the address is not part of a private range, or not a valid IP address, the command will throw an error:

```
using namespace System.Management.Automation

class ValidatePrivateIPAddressAttribute :
ValidateEnumeratedArgumentsAttribute {
    Hidden $ipAddress = [IPAddress]::Empty

    Hidden [Boolean] IsValidIPAddress([String]$value) {
        return [IPAddress]::TryParse($value, [Ref]$this.ipAddress)
    }

    Hidden [Boolean] IsPrivateIPAddress([IPAddress]$address) {
        $bytes = $address.GetAddressBytes()
        $isPrivateIPAddress = switch ($null) {
            { $bytes[0] -eq 192 -and
              $bytes[1] -eq 168 } { $true; break }
            { $bytes[0] -eq 172 -and
              $bytes[1] -ge 16 -and
              $bytes[2] -le 31 } { $true; break }
            { $bytes[0] -eq 10 } { $true; break }
            default { $false }
        }
        return $isPrivateIPAddress
    }
```

```
    [Void] ValidateElement([Object]$element) {
        if (-not $element -is [IPAddress]) {
            if ($this.IsValidIPAddress($element)) {
                $element = $this.ipAddress
            } else {
                throw '{0} is an invalid IP address format' -f $element
            }
        }
        if (-not $this.IsPrivateIPAddress($element)) {
            throw '{0} is not a private IP address' -f $element
        }
    }
}
```

The attribute defined in the preceding code may be used with any parameter to validate IP addressing, as shown in the following short function:

```
function Test-Validate {
    [CmdletBinding()]
    param (
        [ValidatePrivateIPAddress()]
        [IPAddress]$IPAddress
    )

    Write-Host $IPAddress
}
```

Validation like this can be implemented with ValidateScript, which also inherits from ValidateEnumeratedArgumentsAttribute. ValidateScript can call functions, centralizing the validation code.

Classes and DSC

Classes in PowerShell exist because of **Desired State Configuration (DSC)**. DSC resources written as PowerShell classes are very succinct; they avoid the repetition inherent in script-based resources. Script-based resources must at least duplicate the param block. Class-based resources also avoid the need for a separately generated schema document and have a simpler module layout.

Class-based DSC resources in a module must be explicitly exported using the DscResourcesToExport key in a module manifest document.

The class must include a `DscResource` attribute. Each property a user is expected to set must have a `DscProperty` attribute. At least one property must be the `Key` property of the `DscProperty` attribute set. The class must implement the `Get`, `Set`, and `Test` methods.

Class-based resources may use inheritance to simplify an implementation as required; this is especially useful if a group of resources uses the same code to act out changes.

A basic DSC resource is defined as follows:

```
enum Ensure {
    Absent
    Present
}

[DscResource()]
class MyResource {
    [DscProperty(Key)]
    [Ensure]$Ensure

    [MyResource] Get() { return $this }

    [Void] Set() { }

    [Boolean] Test() { return $true }
}
```

This resource implements all of the required methods, but it performs no actions.

Like a good function, a good DSC resource should strive to be really good at one thing and one thing only. If a particular item has a variety of configuration options, it is often better to have a set of similar resources than a single resource that attempts to do it all.

The sections that follow will focus on the creation of a short resource that sets the computer description.

This resource will need to make a change to a single registry value. The computer description is set under the `HKLM:\SYSTEM\CurrentControlSet\Services\LanmanServer\Parameters` key using the `svrcomment` string value.

The starting point for the resource is shown here:

```
enum Ensure {
    Absent
    Present
}
```

```
[DscResource()]
class ComputerDescription {
    [DscProperty(Key)]
    [Ensure]$Ensure

    [DscProperty()]
    [String]$Description

    Hidden [String] $path =
'HKLM:\SYSTEM\CurrentControlSet\Services\LanmanServer\Parameters'
    Hidden [String] $valueName = 'svrcomment'

    [ComputerDescription] Get() { return $this }

    [Void] Set() { }

    [Boolean] Test() { return $true }
}
```

Each of the methods in the class must be implemented for the resource to function.

Implementing Get

The Get method should evaluate the current state of the resource. The registry key will exist, but the registry value may be incorrect, or may not exist.

The Get method will act as follows:

- If a the value is present, it will set the Ensure property to Present and update the value of the Description property.
- If the value is not present, it will set the Ensure property to Absent only.

The following snippet implements these actions:

```
[ComputerDescription] Get() {
    $key = Get-Item $this.Path
    if ($key.GetValueNames() -contains $this.valueName) {
        $this.Ensure = 'Present'
        $this.Description = $key.GetValue($this.valueName)
    } else {
        $this.Ensure = 'Absent'
    }
    return $this
}
```

The Get method must return an instance of the class. It can either return the existing instance, return $this, or generate a new instance, for instance by returning a hashtable:

```
[ComputerDescription] Get() {
    $computerDescription = @{}

    $key = Get-Item $this.Path
    if ($key.GetValueNames() -contains $this.valueName) {
        $computerDescription.Ensure = 'Present'
        $computerDescription.Description = $key.GetValue($this.valueName)
    } else {
        $computerDescription.Ensure = 'Absent'
    }
    return $computerDescription
}
```

The hashtable returned by the preceding function is automatically cast to the class, creating a new instance.

The Get method is only used when explicitly invoked. It is not used by either Set or Test.

Implementing Set

The Set method deals with making a change, if a change is required. Set can ordinarily assume that Test has been run, and therefore that a change is required.

As the resource allows a user to ensure a value is either present or absent, it must handle the creation and deletion of the value:

```
[Void] Set() {
    $params = @{
        Path = $this.path
        Name = $this.valueName
    }
    if ($this.Ensure -eq 'Present') {
        New-ItemProperty -Value $this.Description -Type String -Force
@params
    } else {
        $key = Get-Item $this.Path
        if ($key.GetValueNames() -contains $this.valueName) {
            Remove-ItemProperty @params
        }
    }
}
```

This version of `Set` uses the `Force` parameter of `New-ItemProperty` to overwrite any existing values of the same name. Using `Force` also handles cases where the value exists but the value type is incorrect.

Implementing Test

The `Test` method is used to determine whether `Set` should be run. DSC invokes `Test` before `Set`. The `Test` method returns a Boolean value.

The Test method must perform the following tests to ascertain the state of this configuration item:

- When `Ensure` is present, fail if the value does not exist.
- When `Ensure` is present, fail if the value exists, but the description does not match the requested value.
- When `Ensure` is absent, fail if the value name exists.
- Otherwise, pass.

The following snippet implements these tests:

```
[Boolean] Test() {
    $key = Get-Item $this.Path
    if ($this.Ensure -eq 'Present') {
        if ($key.GetValueNames() -notcontains $this.valueName) {
            return $false
        }
        return $key.GetValue($this.valueName) -eq $this.Description
    } else {
        return $key.GetValueNames() -notcontains $this.valueName
    }
    return $true
}
```

Each of these methods must be copied back into the resource class.

Using the resource

The complete class, ComputerDescription, incorporating each of the preceding methods, is shown here:

```
enum Ensure {
    Absent
    Present
}

[DscResource()]
class ComputerDescription {
    [DscProperty(Key)]
    [Ensure]$Ensure

    [DscProperty()]
    [String]$Description

    Hidden [String] $path =
'HKLM:\SYSTEM\CurrentControlSet\Services\LanmanServer\Parameters'
    Hidden [String] $valueName = 'svrcomment'

    [ComputerDescription] Get() {
        $key = Get-Item $this.Path
        if ($key.GetValueNames() -contains $this.valueName) {
            $this.Ensure = 'Present'
            $this.Description = $key.GetValue($this.valueName)
        } else {
            $this.Ensure = 'Absent'
        }
        return $this
    }

    [Void] Set() {
        $params = @{
            Path = $this.path
            Name = $this.valueName
        }
        if ($this.Ensure -eq 'Present') {
            New-ItemProperty -Value $this.Description -Type String -Force
@params
        } else {
            $key = Get-Item $this.Path
            if ($key.GetValueNames() -contains $this.valueName) {
                Remove-ItemProperty @params
            }
        }
    }
```

```
    [Boolean] Test() {
        $key = Get-Item $this.Path
        if ($this.Ensure -eq 'Present') {
            if ($key.GetValueNames() -notcontains $this.valueName) {
                return $false
            }
            return $key.GetValue($this.valueName) -eq $this.Description
        } else {
            return $key.GetValueNames() -notcontains $this.valueName
        }
        return $true
    }
}
```

DSC will only find the class using `Get-DscResource` if the following are true:

- The class is saved in a module.
- The module exports the DSC resource.
- The module is in one of the paths in `$env:PSMODULEPATH`.
- The module path is system-wide, accessible by the **Local Configuration Manager (LCM)**.

The following script creates the files and folders required to achieve under Program Files. The script will require administrative rights:

```
$modulePath = 'C:\Program Files\WindowsPowerShell\Modules'

$params = @{
    Path     = Join-Path $modulePath 'LocalMachine\1.0.0\LocalMachine.psm1'
    ItemType = 'File'
    Force    = $true
}
New-Item @params

$params = @{
    Path                 = Join-Path $modulePath
'LocalMachine\1.0.0\LocalMachine.psd1'
    RootModule           = 'LocalMachine.psm1'
    DscResourcesToExport = 'ComputerDescription'
}
New-ModuleManifest @params
```

The `LocalMachine.psm1` file should be edited, adding the `Ensure` enumeration and the `ComputerDescription` class.

Once the class is in a module, it can be used with the `using module` command:

```
using module LocalMachine

$class = [ComputerDescription]@{
    Ensure      = 'Present'
    Description = 'Computer description'
}
```

Individual methods may be invoked, for example, `Get` may be run:

```
PS> $class.Get()

Ensure     Description
------     -----------
Absent     Computer description
```

As the module is under a known module path, `Get-DscResource` should be able to find it immediately:

```
PS> Get-DscResource ComputerDescription

ImplementedAs      Name                    ModuleName       Version
Properties
-------------      ----                    ----------       -------    --------
--
PowerShell         ComputerDescription     LocalMachine     1.0        {Ensure,
DependsOn, Description,...
```

The `Invoke-DscResource` command may be used to run individual methods without creating a DSC configuration document:

```
$params = @{
    Name       = 'ComputerDescription'
    ModuleName = 'LocalMachine'
    Method     = 'Test'
    Property   = @{
        Ensure      = 'Present'
        Description = 'Some description'
    }
    Verbose    = $true
}
Invoke-DscResource @params
```

Running `Invoke-DscResource` will require administrative rights. `Invoke-DscResource` interacts with the LCM to execute the resource and will report back whether or not the configuration item is in the desired state.

Summary

In this chapter, we explored enumerations and classes in PowerShell. Classes were introduced with PowerShell 5.0 and continue to expand with PowerShell Core.

We covered how to create a class, including defining properties, constructors, and methods.

We looked at a few different uses of classes, starting with argument-transformation attributes and validation attributes, and finishing with class-based DSC resources.

In the next chapter, we will explore building modules, including how modules might be structured during development and assembled into a single file for use.

19
Building Modules

Modules were introduced with PowerShell 2. A module groups a set of commands together, most often around a common system, service, or purpose.

PowerShell uses several different types of module, such as manifest, binary, and script. A manifest module is typically made up of a set of nested modules. A binary module uses a compiled library (`.dll` file) to implement commands. This chapter focuses on script modules.

In this chapter we will cover the following topics:

- Module layout
- Multi-file module layout
- Module scope
- Module initialization and removal

Technical requirements

The final module content used in this chapter is available on GitHub at `https://github.com/indented-automation/LocalMachine`.

The content of the repository may be used to experiment with the different layouts explored in this chapter. The content may be used to ensure that any imported module content is functional.

Module layout

A module consists of a single file with a `psm1` extension, known as the root module, which contains all the functions of that module.

A module may include a manifest file with a `psd1` extension that contains extended information (metadata) about the module.

> The previous chapter ended with the creation of a DSC resource to set a description for a computer. This was made part of a `LocalMachine` module. The `LocalMachine` module will be rewritten in this chapter.
>
> If the `LocalMachine` module still exists under `C:\Program Files\WindowsPowerShell\Modules`, it can be deleted at this time.

Several modules exist to help with creating the initial layout of a module. The `Plaster` and `PSModuleDevelopment` modules are both reasonable examples:

- `Plaster`: https://github.com/PowerShell/Plaster
- `PSModuleDevelopment`: https://www.powershellgallery.com/packages/PSModuleDevelopment

The root module

The root module, a file with a `psm1` extension, is given the same name as the module itself and will be nested directly under a folder that bears the module name.

When a module is installed into one of the folders in `$env:PSModulePath`, it may have the following structure:

```
Modules
| -- LocalMachine
     | -- LocalMachine.psm1
```

The module can be imported immediately by passing the path to the `LocalMachine` folder to `Import-Module`. If the module content changes, the module should either be removed using `Remove-Module`, or the `Force` parameter should be used with `Import-Module`.

Adding temporary module paths

Environment variables modified using $env are not persistent; the change will disappear when PowerShell is closed. A temporary module path might be added to simplify testing while writing a module:

```
$env:PSMODULEPATH = 'C:\Workspace;{0}' -f
$env:PSMODULEPATH
```

Modules placed in C:\Workspace may be discovered using Get-Module and Get-Command.

The LocalMachine.psm1 file includes all of the functions that make up the module. The content of LocalMachine.psm1 is shown in the following example; the body of the functions has been omitted in this snippet:

```
function Get-ComputerDescription { }
function Set-ComputerDescription { }
```

All of the functions in a module are made available to a user by default. The names of the functions will be shown when Get-Module is run, shown as follows:

```
PS> Get-Module LocalMachine -ListAvailable

    Directory: C:\Workspace

ModuleType    Version    Name              PSEdition    ExportedCommands
----------    -------    ----              ---------    ----------------
Script        0.0        LocalMachine      Desk         {Get-
ComputerDescription, Set-ComputerDescription}
```

The example shows that both of the functions are exported. If either function is run, the module will be automatically imported.

The Export-ModuleMember command

All of the functions in a module are exported by default. The Export-ModuleMember command may be used to limit this to a named set of commands.

If the `Export-ModuleMember` command is used, certain functions can be hidden from view:

```
function Get-ComputerDescription { }
function Set-ComputerDescription { }
function GetRegistryValueInfo { }

Export-ModuleMember -Function Get-ComputerDescription, Set-
ComputerDescription
```

The result of this is a module that has a hidden, or private, `GetRegistryValueInfo` function.

Naming private functions

As private functions are not exported, they are not subject to the same discovery rules as exported commands.

My convention is to use verb-noun pairing with approved verbs, but to omit the hyphen.

Module information displayed using `Get-Module` is cached; if the module content does not display correctly, run `Get-Module LocalMachine -ListAvailable -Refresh` or restart the PowerShell session.

Wildcards may be used with `Export-ModuleMember`. Wildcards will affect the autoloader, and explicit names are preferred. For example:

```
Export-ModuleMember -Function *-ComputerDescription
```

`Export-ModuleMember` can be used to export functions, cmdlets, variables, and aliases. It cannot be used to export DSC resources, it cannot be used to version a module, and it cannot provide other information about the module. The module manifest greatly expands on the capabilities of `Export-ModuleMember`.

Module manifest

The module manifest is a PowerShell data file that contains metadata for the module. The manifest includes critical information, such as the version number, the files to import, and the commands, aliases, and classes that it contains. The manifest may include the software license and a project URL if they are applicable.

The use of a manifest is mandatory if a module will be published on the PowerShell Gallery or any other repository.

The `New-ModuleManifest` command may be used to create the manifest from scratch. The following example assumes the module is a `C:\workspace` path:

```
$params = @{
    Path               = 'C:\workspace\LocalMachine\LocalMachine.psd1'
    RootModule         = 'LocalMachine.psm1'
    ModuleVersion      = '1.0.0'
    FunctionsToExport = 'Get-ComputerDescription', 'Set-
ComputerDescription'
}
New-ModuleManifest @params
```

This manifest replaces much of the functionality of the `Export-ModuleMember` command. The manifest can be used to define functions to export; `Export-ModuleMember` is still required if variables are to be exported.

As with `Export-ModuleMember`, a wildcard pattern may be used for `FunctionsToExport`, however, this will make it impossible for the autoloader to do its job consistently.

The `New-ModuleManifest` command is complemented by `Test-ModuleManifest`. The `Test-ModuleManifest` command will import the data file and raise errors if problems are detected with the manifest. The `Import-PowerShellDataFile` command can also be used to import the content of the manifest.

In theory, in addition to creating a manifest for the first time, `New-ModuleManifest` can be used to update the content of an existing file. `Import-PowerShellDataFile` can be used to import the existing content and those values can be passed to `New-ModuleManifest`:

```
$path = 'C:\workspace\LocalMachine\LocalMachine.psd1'
$manifest = Import-PowerShellDataFile -Path
'C:\workspace\LocalMachine\LocalMachine.psd1'
$manifest.FunctionsToExport = '*'
New-ModuleManifest -Path 'C:\workspace\LocalMachine\LocalMachine-new.psd1'
@manifest
```

In practice, `New-ModuleManifest` will not correctly handle the nested `PrivateData` section. A similar problem applies to the `Update-ModuleManifest` command that comes with the `PowerShellGet` module.

The `Configuration` module on the PowerShell Gallery (`https://www.powershellgallery.com/packages/Configuration`) provides an alternative. Once installed, the command may be used to tweak content in an existing manifest, as follows:

```
Install-Module Configuration -Scope CurrentUser

$params = @{
    Path     = 'C:\workspace\LocalMachine\LocalMachine.psd1'
    Property = 'RootModule'
    Value    = 'LocalMachine.psm1'
}
Update-Metadata @params
```

The `Update-Metadata` command cannot write to commented keys in the manifest, and removing comment characters is beyond the scope of `Update-Metadata`.

Export-ModuleMember or FunctionsToExport

When using a manifest, the `Export-ModuleMember` command can be removed. Instead, the `FunctionsToExport` and the other export fields in manifest can be filled in.

It is possible to use wildcards in the `FunctionsToExport` field. However, this is a bad practice in production as it defeats the module's autoloader.

Side-by-side versioning

Multiple versions of the same module can exist on a system. As the version is only defined in the manifest, having a manifest is required to support side-by-side versioning.

When a versioned module is installed, a new folder is added to the hierarchy, as follows:

```
Modules
| -- LocalMachine
    | -- 1.0.0
        | -- LocalMachine.psd1
        | -- LocalMachine.psm1
```

Each new version of the module creates a new folder.

The preceding structure is used when a module is installed. The structure is not particularly useful when developing a module, especially if changes are being tracked using a source-control system. Every new release or update to the module would mean renaming the version folder, effectively changing everything.

Dependencies

A PowerShell module may have one or more dependencies. The dependencies should be included in the module manifest under the RequiredModules key.

Dependencies may be defined using a module name only, or alternatively as a module specification. For example:

```
RequiredModules = @(
    'Configuration'
    @{ ModuleName = 'Pester'; ModuleVersion = '4.6.0' }
)
```

The hashtable used in the preceding example may also use the MaximumVersion or RequiredVersion keys. If a module is loaded by name, the latest version will be used.

When publishing a module, the Publish-Module command will attempt to validate stated dependencies. The dependencies should be locally available or publishing may fail.

Multi-file module layout

PowerShell does not enforce a particular layout for a module in most cases, and there is a great deal of variety in the layout of modules on the internet.

An exception to this is script-based DSC resources. Script-based resources must be placed in a DscResources folder, and each resource is implemented as a separate module under that folder. For example:

```
LocalMachine
|  -- DscResources
|     |  -- LocalMachine
|           |  -- ComputerDescription.psd1 (Optional)
|           |  -- ComputerDescription.psm1
|           |  -- ComputerDescription.schema.mof
|  -- LocalMachine.psd1
|  -- LocalMachine.psm1
```

In some cases, a module will only have a root module file and perhaps a manifest. At the other extreme, a module may split every function in the module into a separate file. Other modules fall anywhere in between these two examples. There are advantages to using either of these approaches which:

- **A run-time consideration**: A module that has only a single root module file will import much more quickly than a module split into many files.
- **A development consideration**: It is easier to find content within a module that is split into many files. And it is easier to work on a multi-user project where content is broken down.

One of the most popular multi-file layouts is shown as follows:

```
LocalMachine (Project folder)
| -- LocalMachine (Module content folder)
    | -- classes
    |    | -- ComputerDescription.ps1
    | -- enum
    |    | -- Ensure.ps1
    | -- private
    |    | -- GetRegistryValueInfo.ps1
    | -- public
    |    | -- Get-ComputerDescription.ps1
    |    | -- Remove-ComputerDescription.ps1
    |    | -- Set-ComputerDescription.ps1
    | -- LocalMachine.psd1
    | -- LocalMachine.psm1
```

The project folder is most often named after the module. It exists to host content that is not part of the published module, such as source-control specific files (such as `.gitignore`), readme files, or scripts used to build and test the module.

A popular variation in the preceding structure names the module content folder `Source`, or `Src`, instead of using the name of the module. Complex modules will often add sub-folders to each of those used in the preceding example to group common elements together.

Dot-sourcing module content

When a module is divided in this manner, the root module must contain everything required to load the module content. This is most often achieved by dot-sourcing each of the files in the sub-folders adjacent to the root module. One possible way to do this is to use `Get-ChildItem` to find all of the `ps1` files beneath a certain point and dot-source those.

The following snippet uses this approach:

```
Get-ChildItem (Join-Path $psscriptroot 'private') {
    . $_.FullName
}
$functionsToExport = Get-ChildItem (Join-Path $psscriptroot 'public') {
    . $_.FullName
    $_.BaseName
}
Export-ModuleMember -Function $functionsToExport
```

The snippet assumes Export-ModuleMember is to be used, and that the manifest has FunctionsToExport set to *. As the files are named after the functions, the BaseName property of each item is used to build an array of functions to pass to Export-ModuleMember.

The disadvantage of this approach is that it loads all ps1 files without further consideration. Any additional files dropped into the module will load as well. While a module is undergoing development, this behavior may be desirable, but it represents a small risk for anyone installing the module.

An alternative, but higher-maintenance, approach, is to name the files to import instead of allowing any file at all to load. For example:

```
$private = 'GetRegistryValueInfo'
$public = @(
    'Get-ComputerDescription'
    'Remove-ComputerDescription'
    'Set-ComputerDescription'
)

foreach ($item in $private) {
    . '{0}\private\{1}.ps1' -f $psscriptroot, $item
}
foreach ($item in $public) {
    . '{0}\public\{1}.ps1' -f $psscriptroot, $item
}
Export-ModuleMember -Function $public
```

With this version, module content is loaded with an explicit name. Additional files that are erroneously placed in the module folder will not be processed.

Merging module content

Dot-sourcing module content is useful when a module is being developed, it allows a developer to realize the benefits of having module content split into separate files. It is possible to leave the module as it is, it can be published; many popular modules are. To realize the benefit of a single root module file, the content might be merged. This operation can be performed when testing a module, or when preparing a module for release.

There are a number of modules available that can be used to perform this step. For example, the `ModuleBuilder` module is capable of merging module content. The `ModuleBuilder` module requires a `build.psd1` file in the root of the module (adjacent to `LocalMachine.psd1`). The `build.psd1` file does not need to contain more than an empty `hashtable`; it can be used to customize the merge process.

With the file present, the following command may be used to merge the module content:

```
Install-Module ModuleBuilder -Scope CurrentUser

Build-Module -SourcePath
C:\Workspace\LocalMachine\LocalMachine\LocalMachine.psd1
```

If the command is run from the same directory as `build.psd1`, the `SourcePath` argument can be omitted. For example:

```
Set-Location C:\Workspace\LocalMachine\LocalMachine
Build-Module
```

The resulting module file is placed in the output folder under the project folder. The output path is configurable. The merge process itself is not very complicated. The following script can be used to achieve a similar result when running from the project root folder (`C:\Workspace\LocalMachine`):

```
$configuration = @{
    ModuleName      = Split-Path $psscriptroot -Leaf
    FoldersToMerge = @(
        'enum*'
        'class*'
        'private*'
        'public*'
    )
    FilesToCopy     = '*.ps1xml', '*.psd1'
    FilesToExclude = 'build.psd1'
}

try {
    $ErrorActionPreference = 'SilentlyContinue'
```

```
    if (Test-Path 'output') {
        Remove-Item 'output' -Recurse -Force
    }
    $outputPath = New-Item 'output' -ItemType Directory

    Push-Location (Join-Path $psscriptroot $configuration.ModuleName) -
StackName build

    Get-ChildItem $configuration.FilesToCopy -Exclude
$configuration.FilesToExclude |
        Copy-Item -Destination $outputPath -Verbose

    Get-ChildItem $configuration.FoldersToMerge -Directory |
        Get-ChildItem -Filter *.ps1 -File -Recurse |
        Get-Content -Raw |
        ForEach-Object {
            $_.Trim()
            ''
        } |
        Add-Content ('{0}\{1}.psm1' -f $outputPath,
$configuration.ModuleName)
} finally {
    Pop-Location -StackName build
}
```

As a module grows in complexity, it may be desirable to perform additional tasks during the build step. For example, tests might be run, help files might be regenerated, the module might be published. A more extensive build script might perform these actions.

Module scope

The content of the root module file executes when a module is imported. Functions are imported into the module scope and exported into global scope if they are included in the list of functions to export.

Variables may be created in the module scope, functions within the module may consume those variables. Such variables might be created in the root module, or they may be created when a command is run.

The $Script: scope prefix may be used to explicitly access the scope and it clearly identifies such variables where they are used. Helper functions might be created to provide obvious access to the variable content.

This approach is illustrated in the following example. This pattern is common for modules that interact with services that require an authentication token, such as a REST web service:

```
function Connect-Service {
    [CmdletBinding()]
    param (
        [Parameter(Mandatory)]
        [String]$Server
    )

    $Script:connection = [PSCustomObject]@{
        Server = $Server
        PSTypeName = 'ServiceConnectionInfo'
    }
}

function Get-ServiceConnection {
    [CmdletBinding()]
    param ( )

    if ($Script:connection) {
        $Script:connection
    } else {
        throw [InvalidOperationException]::new('Not connected to the
service')
    }
}

function Get-ServiceObject {
    [CmdletBinding()]
    param (
        [PSTypeName('ServiceConnectionInfo')]
        $Connection = (Get-ServiceConnection)
    )
}
```

Considering the preceding snippet:

- `Connect-Service` stores the connection object in the module scope.
- `Get-ServiceConnection` retrieves that cached connection or throws an error if the connection does not exist.
- The `Get-ServiceObject` and any other function use that cached value as the default value for a `Connection` parameter. The end user may override that value by providing their own service connection.

Module-scoped variables can also be created by creating a variable in the root module file.

Accessing module scope

It is possible to access module scope from the global scope by passing a module information object to the call operator.

The following snippet is used to demonstrate accessing module scope. The module consists of one public function, one private function, and a module-scoped variable:

```
function GetModuleServiceConnection {
    [CmdletBinding()]
    param ( )

    $Script:connection
}

function Connect-ModuleService {
    [CmdletBinding()]
    param (
        [String]$Name
    )

    $Script:connection = $Name
}

$Script:connection = 'DefaultConnection'

Export-ModuleMember -Function Connect-ModuleService
```

The following snippet should be saved to a file named ModuleService.psm1, then the module should be imported using Import-Module .\ModuleService.psm1.

By default, only the Connect-ModuleService function is available. The value of the script/module-scoped connection variable may be retrieved as follows:

```
PS> & (Get-Module ModuleService) { $connection }
DefaultConnection
```

If the Connect-ModuleService command is used, the value returned by the preceding command will change. The same approach may be used to interact with functions that are not normally exported by the module. For example, the GetModuleServiceConnection function can be called:

```
& (Get-Module ModuleService) { GetModuleServiceConnection }
```

Finally, as the command is executing in the scope of the module, this technique may be applied to list the commands within the module, as follows:

```
& (Get-Module ModuleService) { Get-Command -Module ModuleService }
```

This technique is useful when debugging modules that heavily utilize module scope.

Initializing and removing modules

The content of the root module executes every time a module is imported. A root module file may be used to perform initialization steps, perhaps filling cache files, importing static data, or setting a default configuration. These steps are extra code that must be added to the root module, perhaps at the beginning or end of the file.

If a module is being built, and the root module is automatically generated, the additional content would need to be drawn in by the merge script. The `ModuleBuilder` module, introduced when exploring merging content in this chapter, achieves this by using the `Prefix` and `Suffix` parameters. Values for this parameter may be supplied when running `Build-Module` or added to the `build.psd1` file. These parameters allow the developer to inject the content of a named script at the beginning (prefix), or end (suffix), of the root module file.

The ScriptsToProcess key

The `RequiredAssemblies` and `RequiredModules` keys of the module manifest both execute before the root module is imported, accounting for normal prerequisites.

In rare cases, it is desirable to run commands in the users scope before importing the module. The `ScriptsToProcess` key in the module manifest is present for this purpose. Scripts placed here are executed in the users scope and cannot access commands and variables internal to the module.

The OnRemove event

The `ModuleInfo` object provides access to an `OnRemove` event handler. This event is triggered if the module is removed from the user's session using the `Remove-Module` command. The event is not triggered if the session is closed. This event handler may be used to trigger a cleanup of the artifacts created by the module, if any are required.

The following module creates a global variable in the user's scope. Exporting the variable from the module using `VariablesToExport` and `Export-ModuleMember` may have been a better approach, the variable would have been automatically removed. An `OnRemove` handler is added to the module to forcefully remove the global variable with the module and the handler is created in the root module file:

```
$Global:VariableName = 'Value'
$executionContext.SessionState.Module.OnRemove = {
 if (Test-Path variable:VariableName) {
 Remove-Variable VariableName -Scope Global
 }
}
```

If the preceding module content is placed in `TestOnRemove.psm1`, and the module file is imported, the `VariableName` variable will be present:

```
PS> Get-Variable VariableName

Name            Value
----            -----
VariableName    Value
```

When the module is removed, using `Remove-Module`, the variable is removed as well:

```
PS> Remove-Module TestOnRemove
PS> Test-Path variable:VariableName
False
```

`Remove-Module` and the `OnRemove` event handler cannot overcome limitations such as the inability to unload assemblies. If the module contains an assembly, `.dll` file, and that is loaded by the module; the assembly will remain loaded until the PowerShell session is closed.

Summary

This chapter explored the creation of modules, starting with a basic module that contained only a root module, extending upward into modules that contained a number of functions. We explored using modules with many files while developing as well as merging a module for publication. Finally, working inside module scope, we looked at initialization and removal.

In the next chapter, we will explore static analysis and unit testing with `Pester` to validate and verify the behavior of a module before it is publicly released.

20
Testing

The goal of testing in PowerShell is to ensure that the code works as intended. Automatic testing ensures that this continues to be the case as code is changed over time.

Testing often begins before code is ready to execute. `PSScriptAnalyzer` can look at code and provide advice on best practices. This is known as static analysis.

Unit tests pick up when the code is ready to execute. Tests may exist before the code when you are following practices such as **Test-Driven Development (TDD)**. A unit test focuses on the smallest parts of a script, function, module, or class. A unit test strives to validate the inner workings of a unit of code, ensuring that conditions evaluate correctly, that it terminates or returns where it should, and so on.

Testing might extend into systems and acceptance testing, although this often requires a test environment to act against. Acceptance testing may include black-box testing, used to verify that a command accepts known parameters and generates an expected set of results. Black-box testing, as the name suggests, does not concern itself with understanding how a block of code arrives at a result.

The following topics will be covered in this chapter:

- Static analysis
- Testing with Pester

Technical requirement

Pester version 4.6.0 is required by this chapter.

Static analysis

Static analysis is the process of evaluating code without executing it. In PowerShell, static analysis makes use of an **Abstract Syntax Tree (AST)**: a tree-like representation of a block of code. AST was introduced with PowerShell 3.

AST

The AST in PowerShell is available for any script block; an example is as follows:

```
{ Write-Host 'content' }.Ast
```

The script block that defines a function can be retrieved via Get-Command:

```
function Write-Content { Write-Host 'content' }
(Get-Command Write-Content).ScriptBlock
```

Or, the script block defining a function can be retrieved using Get-Item:

```
function Write-Content { Write-Host 'content' }
(Get-Item function:\Write-Content).ScriptBlock
```

It is possible to work down through the content of the script block using AST. For example, the first argument for the Write-Host command might be accessed, as follows:

```
{ Write-Host 'content' }.Ast.
                        Endblock.
                        Statements.
                        PipelineElements.
                        CommandElements[1]
```

The preceding approach is rough, and simply extracts the second command element from the first statement in the end block.

A visual approach

The ShowPSAst module, available in the PowerShell Gallery, may be used to visualize the AST tree. Install the module with: Install-Module ShowPSAst -Scope CurrentUser.

It can be run against a function, a module, a script block, and so on: Show-Ast { Write-Host 'content' }.

Rather than following the tree so literally, it is possible to execute searches against the tree. For example, the `Write-Host` command is not necessarily a sensible inclusion; a search for occurrences of the command can be constructed as follows:

```
{ Write-Host 'content' }.Ast.FindAll(
    {
        param ( $ast )

        $ast -is [Management.Automation.Language.CommandAst] -and
        $ast.GetCommandName() -eq 'Write-Host'
    },
    $true
)
```

In the preceding example, the `FindAll` method expects two arguments.

The first argument is a script block; a predicate. The predicate accepts a single argument: a node from the tree. A parameter may be declared to give the argument a name; alternatively, the node can be referenced using `$args[0]`. The argument is tested by a comparison that will return `true` or `false`.

The second argument is used to decide whether the search should extend to include nested script blocks.

Tokenizer

In addition to the AST, PowerShell can also convert a script into a series of `tokens`, each representing an element of a script.

In PowerShell 2, the `Tokenize` static method of `System.Management.Automation.PSParser` may be used; an example is as follows:

```
$script = @'
# A short script
if ($true) {
 Write-Host 'Hello world'
}
'@
$errors = @()
$tokens = [System.Management.Automation.PSParser]::Tokenize($script,
[Ref]$errors)
```

The `tokens` array contains objects describing each part of the script. The first of these is shown as follows; it describes the comment at the start of the script:

```
Content     : # A short script
Type        : Comment
Start       : 0
Length      : 16
StartLine   : 1
StartColumn : 1
EndLine     : 1
EndColumn   : 17
```

With PowerShell 3, two static methods on the `System.Management.Automation.Language.Parser` Parser type may be used: `ParseInput` and `ParseFile`. The two methods return an AST; `tokens` are returned via a reference to an array. An example is as follows:

```
$script = @'
# A short script
if ($true) {
    Write-Host 'Hello world'
}
'@
$tokens = $errors = @()
$ast = [System.Management.Automation.Language.Parser]::ParseInput(
    $script,
    [Ref]$tokens,
    [Ref]$errors
)
```

The token that's returned is structured differently from the token returned by the `Tokenize` method in PowerShell 2. The comment token is shown as follows:

```
Text       : # A short script
TokenFlags : ParseModeInvariant
Kind       : Comment
HasError   : False
Extent     : # A short script
```

Both AST nodes and the PowerShell 3 token objects are used by `PSScriptAnalyzer`.

PSScriptAnalyzer

The evaluation of elements in the AST is the method used by the PSScriptAnalyzer tool. The tool can be installed using the following code:

```
Install-Module PSScriptAnalyzer -Scope CurrentUser
```

PSScriptAnalyzer can be used to inspect a script with the Invoke-ScriptAnalzyer command. For example, the tool will flag warnings and errors about use of the Password parameter and variable, as it is not considered to be a good practice:

```
[CmdletBinding()]
param (
    [Parameter(Mandatory)]
    [String]$Password
)

$credential = [PSCredential]::new(
    '.\user',
    ($Password | ConvertTo-SecureString -AsPlainText -Force)
)
$credential.GetNetworkCredential().Password
```

The script is saved to a file named Show-Password.ps1, and the analyzer is run against the file , as shown here:

```
PS> Invoke-ScriptAnalyzer .\Show-Password.ps1 | Format-List

RuleName : PSAvoidUsingConvertToSecureStringWithPlainText
Severity : Error
Line     : 9
Column   : 18
Message  : File 'Show-Password.ps1' uses ConvertTo-SecureString with
plaintext. This will expose
           secure information. Encrypted standard strings should be used
instead.

RuleName : PSAvoidUsingPlainTextForPassword
Severity : Warning
Line     : 3
Column   : 5
Message  : Parameter '$Password' should use SecureString, otherwise this
will expose
           sensitive information. See ConvertTo-SecureString for more
information.
```

The script analyzer raises one error and one warning. The error notes that `ConvertTo-SecureString` is used, exposing information that is supposed to be secure.

The warning suggests that password parameters should accept `SecureString` values rather than a plain text string.

Suppressing rules

It is rarely realistic to expect any significant piece of code to pass all of the tests that `PSScriptAnalyzer` will throw at it.

Individual tests can be suppressed at the function, script, or class level. The following demonstrative function creates a `PSCustomObject`:

```
function New-Message {
    [CmdletBinding()]
    param (
        $Message
    )

    [PSCustomObject]@{
        Name  = 1
        Value = $Message
    }
}
```

Running `PSScriptAnalyzer` against a file containing the function will show the following warning:

```
PS> Invoke-ScriptAnalyzer -Path .\New-Message.ps1 | Format-List

RuleName  : PSUseShouldProcessForStateChangingFunctions
Severity  : Warning
Line      : 1
Column    : 10
Message   : Function 'New-Message' has verb that could change system state.
Therefore, the function
            has to support 'ShouldProcess'.
```

Given that this function creates a new object in the memory, and does not change the system state, the message might be suppressed. This is achieved by adding a `SuppressMessage` attribute before a `param` block:

```
function New-Message {
    [Diagnostics.CodeAnalysis.SuppressMessage(
```

```
        'PSUseShouldProcessForStateChangingFunctions',
        ''
    )]
    [CmdletBinding()]
    param (
        $Message
    )

    [PSCustomObject]@{
        Name  = 1
        Value = $Message
    }
}
```

VS Code snippets

VS Code will offer to automatically complete the suppress message attribute when starting to type the word suppress.

Rules are often suppressed as it becomes evident one will be triggered. The list of rules may be viewed using the `Get-ScriptAnalyzerRule` command.

Custom script analyzer rules

The script analyzer utility allows custom rules to be defined and used. Custom rules might be used to test for personal or organization-specific conventions when striving for a consistent style; such conventions may not necessarily be widely adopted best practices.

Script analyzer rules must be defined in a module `psm1` file. The path to the module file may be passed in by using the `CustomRulePath` parameter, or may be defined in a script analyzer configuration file.

Creating a custom rule

A script analyzer rule is a function within a module. A script analyzer allows rules to be written to evaluate AST nodes or tokens.

The name of the function is arbitrary. The community examples use the verb *measure*; however, use of this verb is not mandatory and does not affect discovery. The script analyzer engine examines each function in the custom rule module, looking for parameters following a particular style. If the such a parameter is found, the function is deemed to be a rule.

If a rule is expected to act based on an AST node, the first parameter name must end with `ast`. The parameter must use an AST type, such as `System.Management.Automation.Language.ScriptBlockAst`.

If a rule is expected to act based on a token, the first parameter name must end with token and must accept an array of tokens.

AST-based rules

Script analyzer rules are often very simple; it is not always necessary for a rule to perform complex AST searches.

The following example evaluates the named blocks `dynamicparam`, `begin`, `process`, and `end`. If such a block is declared in a function, script, or script block, and it is empty, the rule will respond. The rule only accepts `NamedBlockAst` nodes; the script analyzer only passes matching nodes to the rule, and therefore, the rule itself does not have to worry about handling other node types:

```
using namespace Microsoft.Windows.PowerShell.ScriptAnalyzer.Generic
using namespace System.Management.Automation.Language

function PSAvoidEmptyNamedBlocks {
    [CmdletBinding()]
[OutputType([Microsoft.Windows.PowerShell.ScriptAnalyzer.Generic.Diagnostic
Record])]
    param (
        [NamedBlockAst]$ast
    )

    if ($ast.Statements.Count -eq 0) {
        [DiagnosticRecord]@{
            Message  = 'Empty {0} block.' -f $ast.BlockKind
            Extent   = $ast.Extent
            RuleName = $myinvocation.MyCommand.Name
            Severity = 'Warning'
        }
    }
}
```

The rule returns `DiagnosticRecord` when it is triggered. The record is returned by the script analyzer as long as the rule is not suppressed.

Token-based rules

Rules based on tokens evaluate an array of tokens to make a decision. The following example looks for empty single-line comments in a block of code. Comments are not a part of the syntax tree, so using `tokens` is the only option:

```
using namespace Microsoft.Windows.PowerShell.ScriptAnalyzer.Generic
using namespace System.Management.Automation.Language

function PSAvoidEmptyComments {
    [CmdletBinding()]
[OutputType([Microsoft.Windows.PowerShell.ScriptAnalyzer.Generic.Diagnostic
Record])]
    param (
        [Token[]]$token
    )

    $ruleName = $myinvocation.MyCommand.Name
    $token.Where{ $_.Kind -eq 'Comment' -and $_.Text.Trim() -eq '#'
}.ForEach{
        [DiagnosticRecord]@{
            Message  = 'Empty comment.'
            Extent   = $_.Extent
            RuleName = $ruleName
            Severity = 'Information'
        }
    }
}
```

As the name suggests, the rule will trigger when it encounters an empty comment.

Using custom rules

Custom rules may be used with the `CustomRulePath` parameter. If the two rules were saved in a `Rules.psm1` file, they can be used as follows:

```
$script = @'
function Get-CurrentProcess {
    [CmdletBinding()]
    param ( )

    begin { }
    process { }
    end {
        #
        # Get the current process
```

```
        #
        Get-Process -Id $PID
    }
}
'@

Invoke-ScriptAnalyzer -ScriptDefinition $script -CustomRulePath
.\Rules.psm1
```

The script analyzer will show each triggered rule, as follows:

RuleName	Severity	ScriptName	Line	Message
PSAvoidEmptyComments	Information		9	Empty comment.
PSAvoidEmptyComments	Information		11	Empty comment.
PSAvoidEmptyNamedBlocks block.	Warning		5	Empty Begin
PSAvoidEmptyNamedBlocks block.	Warning		6	Empty Process

The script analyzer also allows custom rules to be defined by using a configuration file. The configuration file may be either explicitly or implicitly referenced, as described in the script analyzer's documentation (https://github.com/PowerShell/PSScriptAnalyzer).

VS Code allows a settings path to be globally defined (across any PowerShell project) by defining a value for powershell.scriptAnalysis.settingsPath.

Testing with Pester

The PowerShell Pester module can be used to build unit tests for scripts and functions. Unit tests target the smallest possible unit of code, which, in PowerShell, is likely to be a function or a method in a PowerShell class.

Pester tests are saved in a file name ending with .tests.ps1 and executed using the Invoke-Pester command. Invoke-Pester finds files named *.tests.ps1 under a given path and executes all of the tests in each.

Describe and Should statements may also be entered in the console when exploring syntax, but this is not the normal method of defining and running tests.

While Pester is included with Windows 10, it is not the latest version. The latest version may be installed from `PSGallery`, as follows:

```
Install-Module Pester -Force
```

Why write tests?

A set of tests can prevent a bug making it out of the development environment, whether as the result of a change, or as a part of a new feature. This is especially important if several people are working on the same project.

Refactoring, or restructuring, existing code has a high chance of introducing bugs. If a script or function already has tests, the risk is reduced. Tests that verify the overall functionality (not necessarily unit tests) should continue to pass after refactoring.

To a degree, tests may also show how a piece of code is expected to work to someone reviewing or looking to contribute to the code.

What to test

How extensive tests should be is debatable. Striving for 100% code coverage does not necessarily mean that a block of code has been effectively tested.

Consider testing the following:

- Parameters
- Any complex conditions
- Acceptance of different input or expected values, including complex parameter validation
- Exit conditions (especially raised errors or exceptions)

When writing a unit test, resist the temptation to test other functions or commands. A unit test is not responsible for making sure that every command that it calls works. That comes later.

Describe and It

Groups of tests are written within a Describe block. The Describe block must be given a name. A Describe block is often named after the subject of the tests.

Tests are declared using It, followed by a description. The It statement contains assertions that are declared using Should.

Pester 4

Pester 3 expected assertion keywords (Be, BeLike, and so on) to be written as a bare word; for example: $value | Should -Be 0.

Pester 4 supports the syntax used by Pester 3 as legacy syntax. The assertion names are now also presented as dynamic parameters; for example: $value | Should -Be 0.

This allows tools such as ISE and Visual Studio Code to provide auto completion when Should is typed. The tests that are used as examples in this section use the syntax native to Pester 4.

The following function calculates the square root of a value. This particular function does not draw in information, except from the single parameter; testing is limited to validating output:

```
function Get-SquareRoot {
    param (
        [Decimal]$Value
    )

    if ($Value -lt 0) { throw 'Invalid value' }

    $result = $Value
    $previous = 0
    while ([Math]::Abs($result - $previous) -gt 1e-300) {
        $previous = $result
        $result = ($result + $Value / $previous) / 2
    }
    $result
}
```

Tests may be written to verify that the function does what it is expected to do, as follows:

```
Describe Get-SquareRoot {
    It 'Returns a square root of 0 for a value of 0' {
```

```
        Get-SquareRoot 0 | Should -Be 0
    }

    It 'Returns simple square root values' {
        Get-Squareroot 1 | Should -Be 1
        Get-SquareRoot 4 | Should -Be 2
        Get-SquareRoot 9 | Should -Be 3
        Get-SquareRoot 16 | Should -Be 4
    }
}
```

Pester displays the output showing the state of each of the tests:

```
Describing Get-SquareRoot
  [+] Returns a square root of 0 for a value of 0 43ms
  [+] Returns simple square root values 12ms
```

Each test, defined using It, returns a single line expressing the result of the test. A test may fail for two reasons, as follows:

- The subject of the test has an error.
- The test has an error.

For example, if an error is injected into the first test, the result will change, showing what about the test failed:

```
PS> Describe Get-SquareRoot {
>>      It 'When the value is 9, returns 3' {
>>          Get-SquareRoot 9 | Should -Be 1
>>      }
>> }

Describing Get-SquareRoot
  [-] Returns a square root of 0 for a value of 0 42ms
  Expected 1, but got 3.0000000000000000000000000000.
  3: Get-SquareRoot 9 | Should -Be 1
```

If a single test contains multiple Should assertions, the conditions are evaluated in order until the first fails, or all of them pass.

For example, if two errors are injected into the last test, Pester is expected to indicate the test fails when it reaches the assertion that the square root of 9 is 33:

```
Describe Get-SquareRoot {
    It 'Returns simple square root values' {
        Get-Squareroot 1 | Should -Be 1
        Get-SquareRoot 4 | Should -Be 2
```

```
            Get-SquareRoot 9 | Should -Be 33
            Get-SquareRoot 16 | Should -Be 44
    }
}
```

Executing the tests shows an error once `Pester` reaches the third assertion, that the square root of 9 should be 33:

```
Describing Get-SquareRoot
  [-] Returns simple square root values 30ms
    Expected 33, but got 3.000000000000000000000000000.
    5:            Get-SquareRoot 9 | Should -Be 33
```

In this context, `Pester` will never execute the last assertion; the test has already failed.

Test cases

When the input and output of a function are being repetitively tested, the `TestCases` parameter of `It` can be used. Test cases are defined in a hashtable, which is splatted into `It` as a set of parameters.

The four test cases used in the preceding example might be rewritten as follows:

```
Describe Get-SquareRoot {
    It 'When the value is <Value>, the square root is <ExpectedResult>' -
TestCases @(
        @{ Value = 1;  ExpectedResult = 1 }
        @{ Value = 4;  ExpectedResult = 2 }
        @{ Value = 9;  ExpectedResult = 33 }
        @{ Value = 16; ExpectedResult = 44 }
    ) {
        param (
            $Value,
            $ExpectedResult
        )

        Get-SquareRoot $Value | Should -Be $ExpectedResult
    }
}
```

The preceding tests still contain errors; the advantage of this approach is that `Pester` will report a success or failure for each of the test cases individually:

```
Describing Get-SquareRoot
  [+] Calculates the square root of 1 to be 1 52ms
  [+] Calculates the square root of 4 to be 2 7ms
```

```
[-] Calculates the square root of 9 to be 33 10ms
    Expected 33, but got 3.0000000000000000000000000000.
    10: Get-SquareRoot $Value | Should -Be $ExpectedResult
[-] Calculates the square root of 16 to be 44 13ms
    Expected 44, but got 4.0000000000000000000000000000.
    10: Get-SquareRoot $Value | Should -Be $ExpectedResult
```

Pester automatically replaces values enclosed in angular braces (< and >) with names from the hashtable describing each test case.

Using test cases can save time spent debugging code and tests, as fewer runs are needed to highlight problems.

Independent verification

It is common to find that there is more than one way to achieve a result in PowerShell. In the case of the Get-SquareRoot function, .NET has a Math.Sqrt static method that can be used to produce a similar result.

The availability of an alternative approach (which is known to work) allows a result to be dynamically validated, either in place of, or in addition to, statically defined values.

The set of test cases might be adjusted to use Math.Sqrt to verify that the function is working as intended:

```
Describe Get-SquareRoot {
    It 'When the value is <Value>, the square root is <ExpectedResult>' -
TestCases @(
            @{ Value = 81;              ExpectedResult = [Math]::Sqrt(81) }
            @{ Value = 9801;            ExpectedResult = [Math]::Sqrt(9801) }
            @{ Value = 3686400;         ExpectedResult = [Math]::Sqrt(3686400)
}
            @{ Value = 212255761;       ExpectedResult =
[Math]::Sqrt(212255761) }
            @{ Value = 475316482624; ExpectedResult =
[Math]::Sqrt(475316482624) }
    ) {
        param (
            $Value,
            $ExpectedResult
        )

        Get-SquareRoot $Value | Should -Be $ExpectedResult
    }
}
```

Independent verification has limitations if two approaches return different data types. For example, the following assertion will fail, despite using the same input values:

```
PS> Get-SquareRoot 200 | Should -Be ([Math]::Sqrt(200))
Expected 14.142135623731, but got 14.1421356237309504880168887242.
At ...
```

It may be possible to overcome the limitation of the verification by converting both to the same data type. Whether this action is appropriate depends on the nature of, and reason for, the test.

Assertions

Pester comes with support for a variety of assertion types. These assertion types are exposed as parameters for Should. Several of these assertion types grant access to additional parameters. These assertions are, for the most part, similar to PowerShell's comparison operators.

 Details of the available assertions are available on the Pester wiki, under the description for Should, at https://github.com/pester/Pester/wiki/Should.

Assertions are most frequently used to test the actions and output of the subject of a test. The simplest of these, -Be, was used in the examples for Get-SquareRoot. The -Be assertion is the equivalent of the -eq comparison operator, with one difference: -Be can compare arrays for equality.

Testing for the errors raised by a command is one of the more advanced testing cases.

Testing for errors

The -Throw assertion is used to test whether a block of code throws a terminating error. Throw has a number of different usage scenarios. The simplest is detecting whether a terminating error (of any kind) is thrown at all:

```
function Invoke-Something {
    throw
}

Describe Invoke-Something {
    It 'Throws a terminating error' {
        { Invoke-Something } | Should Throw
```

```
    }
}
```

When testing for terminating errors, the subject of the test is placed in a script block (curly braces).

The next step might be to get `Pester` to test the error message, to ensure that the right error is thrown:

```
function Invoke-Something {
    throw 'an error'
}

Describe Invoke-Something {
    It 'Throws a terminating error' {
        { Invoke-Something } | Should Throw 'an error'
    }
}
```

If a module is written with localization in mind, the error message might not be particularly reliable. A trivial change to the message, such as a punctuation change, may break the test. Two alternative approaches are available: testing the exception type and testing the error ID.

Testing the exception type may be useful if the command raises different exception types for each operation. For example, this command raises one of two different exceptions, depending on the value of a parameter:

```
function Invoke-Something {
    param (
        $value
    )

    if ($value -isnot [Int32]) {
        throw [ArgumentException]::new('The value must be an integer')
    }
    if ($value -ge 100) {
        throw [ArgumentOutOfRangeException]::new('The value must be less
than 100')
    }
}

Describe Invoke-Something {
    It 'When the value is not an integer, throws an ArgumentException' {
        { Invoke-Something -Value none } | Should -Throw -ExceptionType
ArgumentException
    }
```

```
    It 'When the value is greater or equal to 100, throws an
ArgumentOutOfRange exception' {
        { Invoke-Something -Value 100 } | Should -Throw -ExceptionType
ArgumentOutOfRangeException
    }
}
```

This is bad parameter validation

The preceding example is contrived. It demonstrates testing errors raised by a common in Pester. This example should not be considered a reasonable way to constrain and validate a parameter value.

Pester also allows for the testing of the fully qualified error ID. For this approach to be beneficial, the subject of the test must define a reasonable set of fully qualified error IDs:

```
function Invoke-Something {
    $errorRecord = [System.Management.Automation.ErrorRecord]::new(
        [InvalidOperationException]::new('an error'),
        'AUniqueErrorID',
        'OperationStopped',
        $null
    )
    throw $errorRecord
}
Describe Invoke-Something {
    It 'Throws a terminating error' {
        { Invoke-Something } | Should -Throw -ErrorId 'AUniqueErrorId'
    }
}
```

If a function is written such that it writes a non-terminating error (using Write-Error), and the generation of that error must be tested, two possible approaches are available.

The ErrorVariable parameter might be used to capture, and then test, as follows:

```
function Invoke-Something {
    [CmdletBinding()]
    param ( )
    Write-Error 'Error' -ErrorId 'NonTerminating'
}

Describe Invoke-Something {
    It 'Throws a non-terminating error' {
        Invoke-Something -ErrorAction SilentlyContinue -ErrorVariable
testError
        $testError.Count | Should -Be 1
```

```
        $testError.FullyQualifiedErrorId | Should -Match 'NonTerminating'
    }
}
```

Or, `ErrorAction` may be used, influencing whether the error is raised:

```
function Invoke-Something {
    [CmdletBinding()]
    param ( )
    Write-Error 'Error' -ErrorId 'NonTerminating'
}
Describe Invoke-Something {
    It 'Throws a non-terminating error' {
        { Invoke-Something -ErrorAction SilentlyContinue } | Should -Not -
Throw -ErrorId 'NonTerminating'
        { Invoke-Something -ErrorAction Stop } | Should -Throw -ErrorId
'NonTerminating'
    }
}
```

Context

`Context` blocks are nested under `Describe`. `Context` blocks allowing tests to be grouped together.

`Context` blocks are useful when there is a fundamental difference in how groups of tests should be handled; for example, where the setup method for each test is more extensive than the parent `Describe` block.

Before and after

Pester includes keywords that hold code that will execute before or after either each test or all of the tests. The following keywords are available:

- `BeforeAll`: Executed once, before all other content
- `AfterAll`: Executed once, after all other content
- `BeforeEach`: Executed immediately, before each individual test
- `AfterEach`: Executed immediately, after each individual test

Each of the keywords should be followed by a script block.

When using `Before` or `After`, it is important to be aware of the order in which a section is executed. In the following list, `Loose code` refers to anything that is not part of a `Before`, `After`, or `It`:

- `Describe\BeforeAll`
- `Describe\Loose code`
- `Context\BeforeAll`
- `Context\Loose code`
- `Describe\BeforeEach`
- `Context\BeforeEach`
- `Context\Loose code`
- `It`

- `Context\AfterEach`
- `Describe\AfterEach`
- `Context\AfterAll`
- `Describe\AfterAll`

It is important to note that if `Mocks` are created under a `Describe` block, they are categorized as `Loose code` in the context of this list. A command called in `Describe\BeforeAll` will not have access to mocks that are only created further down the list.

Loose code

When using `Before` or `After`, consider enclosing `Mocks` in `BeforeAll` or `It` (if `Mocks` are specific to a single test), to ensure that `Mocks` are always available where they might be used.

The following function is used to demonstrate how `Before` and `After` might be used. The function deletes files in a specified path where the last access time was defined at least a certain number of days ago:

```
function Remove-StaleFile {
    param (
        [Parameter(Mandatory = $true)]
        [String]$Path,
        [String]$Filter = '*.*',
        [Int32]$MaximumAge = 90
    )

    Get-ChildItem $Path -Filter $Filter |
```

```
        Where-Object LastWriteTime -lt (Get-Date).AddDays(-$MaximumAge) |
        Remove-Item
}
```

To test the function, a number of test cases might be constructed. `BeforeAll`, `BeforeEach`, and `AfterAll` might be used to ensure that everything is ready for an individual test. Each of the following elements is contained within a single `Describe` block.

`BeforeAll` is used to create a temporary working path:

```
BeforeAll {
    $extensions = '.txt', '.log', '.doc'
    $Path = 'C:\Temp\StaleFiles'
    $null = New-Item $Path -ItemType Directory
    Push-Location $Path
}
```

`AfterAll` is used to clean up:

```
AfterAll {
    Pop-Location
    Remove-Item C:\Temp\StaleFiles -Recurse -Force
}
```

`BeforeEach` is used to create a known set of files before each test executes:

```
BeforeEach {
    foreach ($extension in $extensions) {
        $item = New-Item "stale$extension" -ItemType File -Force
        $item.LastWriteTime = (Get-Date).AddDays(-92)
    }
    foreach ($extension in $extensions) {
        $item = New-Item "new$extension" -ItemType File -Force
        $item.LastWriteTime = (Get-Date).AddDays(-88)
    }
}
```

The tests themselves only contain the code required to execute and test the impact of the function:

```
It 'Removes all files older than 90 days' {
    Remove-StaleFile $Path
    "stale.*" | Should -Not -Exist
    "new.*" | Should -Exist
}

It 'Removes all <Extension> files older than 90 days' -TestCases (
    $extensions | ForEach-Object { @{ Extension = $_ } }
```

```
) {
    param ( $Extension )

    Remove-StaleFile $Path -Filter "*$Extension"
    "stale$Extension" | Should -Not -Exist
    "stale.*" | Should -Exist
    "new.*" | Should -Exist
}
```

All of these sections are combined to produce a set of tests describing the behavior of Remove-StaleFile:

```
Describe Remove-StaleFile {
    BeforeAll {
        $extensions = '.txt', '.log', '.doc'
        $Path = 'C:\Temp\StaleFiles'
        $null = New-Item $Path -ItemType Directory
        Push-Location $Path
    }

    AfterAll {
        Pop-Location
        Remove-Item C:\Temp\StaleFiles -Recurse -Force
    }

    BeforeEach {
        foreach ($extension in $extensions) {
            $item = New-Item "stale$extension" -ItemType File -Force
            $item.LastWriteTime = (Get-Date).AddDays(-92)
        }
        foreach ($extension in $extensions) {
            $item = New-Item "new$extension" -ItemType File -Force
            $item.LastWriteTime = (Get-Date).AddDays(-88)
        }
    }

    It 'Removes all files older than 90 days' {
        Remove-StaleFile $Path

        "stale.*" | Should -Not -Exist
        "new.*" | Should -Exist
    }

    It 'Removes all <Extension> files older than 90 days' -TestCases (
        $extensions | ForEach-Object { @{ Extension = $_ } }
    ) {
        param ( $Extension )
```

```
Remove-StaleFile $Path -Filter "*$Extension"

"stale$Extension" | Should -Not -Exist
"stale.*" | Should -Exist
"new.*" | Should -Exist
        }
    }
```

Pester will run four tests against the `Remove-StaleFile` function; each should pass.

TestDrive

When testing commands that work with the filesystem, Pester provides `TestDrive`. `TestDrive` is a temporary folder created in the current user's temporary directory.

The folder is created when `Describe` runs, and is destroyed afterwards.

Using `TestDrive` simplifies the setup process for the `Remove-StaleFile` function; for example, `BeforeAll` might become the following:

```
BeforeAll {
    $extensions = '.txt', '.log', '.doc'
    Push-Location 'TestDrive:\'
}
```

`AfterAll` becomes the following:

```
AfterAll {
    Pop-Location
}
```

In the event that a command cannot work with the `TestDrive` label, as is the case with .NET types and methods, as well as non-PowerShell commands, the full path can be discovered by using `Get-Item`. This can be executed anywhere inside of a `Describe` block:

```
(Get-Item 'TestDrive:\').FullName
```

Mock

The ability to mock commands is a prominent feature of Pester. Mocking is used to reduce the scope of a set of tests.

Creating a Mock overrides a command by taking a partial copy. The copy includes the param and dynamicparam blocks, but excludes any command implementations.

Mocks can be created under the Describe or Context keywords.

Commands are mocked by using the Mock keyword:

```
Describe Subject {
    Mock Get-Date
}
```

If a command returns a value, a body can be defined for the Mock to simulate the normal operation of the command. In the following example, the string 01/01/2017 is returned in place of a normal response from Get-Date:

```
Describe Subject {
    Mock Get-Date {
        [DateTime]::new(2017, 1, 1)
    }
}
```

In the preceding example, the script block is a positional argument for the MockWith parameter. The mock might also be written as follows:

```
Describe Subject {
    Mock Get-Date -MockWith {
        [DateTime]::new(2017, 1, 1)
    }
}
```

Assert-MockCalled

Pester tracks calls made to mocked commands. The number of times a Mock has been called by a command can be tested by using the Assert-MockCalled command. The following function makes a single call to Get-CimInstance:

```
function Get-OperatingSystemName {
    (Get-CimInstance Win32_OperatingSystem).Caption
}
```

If a Mock of Get-CimInstance is created, the number of times that the command is called can be tested. In this example, the test asserts that Get-CimInstance is called at least once:

```
Describe Get-OperatingSystemName {
    BeforeAll {
```

```
        Mock Get-CimInstance {
            [PSCustomObject]@{
                Caption = 'OSName'
            }
        }
    }

    It 'Gets the name of the operating system' {
        Get-OperatingSystemName | Should -Be 'OSName'
        Assert-MockCalled Get-CimInstance
    }
}
```

If a test is to verify that a mocked command is never called, the `Times` parameter of `Assert-MockCalled` can be set to `0`:

```
Assert-MockCalled Get-CimInstance -Times 0
```

If a command is used in several different ways, it might be important to ensure that the command is called a specific number of times. In this instance, the `Exactly` parameter can be added to ensure that the `Mock` is called that number of times only:

```
Assert-MockCalled Get-CimInstance -Times 1 -Exactly
```

Parameter filtering

Parameter filters can be applied to mocks to limit the scope of the `Mock`.

A parameter filter is a script block that tests the parameters passed when the `Mock` is called. For example, a mock for `Test-Path` might only apply to a specific path:

```
Mock Test-Path { $true } -ParameterFilter { $Path -eq 'C:\Somewhere' }
```

If Pester cannot find a `Mock` with a matching parameter filter, it will default to a mock without a parameter filter. If there are no mocks available, the real command will be called.

In the following example, when the value of the `Path` parameter is `C:\`, the value will be returned from the `Mock`. Otherwise, the value returned by the `real` command will be used:

```
Describe TestPathMocking {
    BeforeAll {
        Mock Test-Path { $false } -ParameterFilter { $Path -eq 'C:\' }
    }

    It 'Uses the mock' {
        Test-Path 'C:\' | Should -Be $false
```

```
    }

    It 'Uses the real command' {
        Test-Path 'C:\Windows' | Should -Be $true
    }
}
```

Mocking non-local commands

In some cases, it is desirable to mock commands that are not available on the test system. One possible approach in these circumstances is to create a function that reflects the command first, then mock the function.

For example, consider a function that creates and configures a DNS zone with a predefined set of parameter values:

```
function New-DnsZone {
    [CmdletBinding()]
    param (
        [Parameter(Mandatory)]
        [String]$Name
    )

    $params = @{
        Name              = $Name
        DynamicUpdate     = 'Secure'
        ReplicationScope  = 'Domain'
    }
    if (-not (Get-DnsServerZone $Name -ErrorAction SilentlyContinue)) {
        Add-DnsServerPrimaryZone @params
    }
}
```

It may not be desirable to install the DNS module on a development system when testing the script. To mock and verify that `Add-DnsServerPrimaryZone` is called, a function must be created first:

```
Describe CreateDnsZone {
    BeforeAll {
        function Get-DnsServerZone { }
        function Add-DnsServerPrimaryZone { }

        Mock Get-DnsServerZone
        Mock Add-DnsServerPrimaryZone
    }
```

```
It 'When the zone does not exist, calls Add-DnsServerPrimaryZone' {
    New-DnsZone -Name name

    Assert-MockCalled Add-DnsServerPrimaryZone
}
}
```

Creating the function first is enough to satisfy the tests, but the approach is basic. The test will not fail if the parameter names that are used are incorrect.

A more advanced function to mock may be created by visiting a system with the command installed and retrieving the following param block:

```
$command = Get-Command Add-DnsServerPrimaryZone
[System.Management.Automation.ProxyCommand]::GetParamBlock($command)
```

The first of the parameters from the block is shown as follows:

```
[Parameter(ParameterSetName='ADForwardLookupZone',
ValueFromPipelineByPropertyName=$true)]
[Parameter(ParameterSetName='ADReverseLookupZone',
ValueFromPipelineByPropertyName=$true)]
[Parameter(ParameterSetName='FileForwardLookupZone',
ValueFromPipelineByPropertyName=$true)]
[Parameter(ParameterSetName='FileReverseLookupZone',
ValueFromPipelineByPropertyName=$true)]
[ValidateNotNull()]
[ValidateNotNullOrEmpty()]
[string]
${ResponsiblePerson},
```

Adding a reasonable parameter block will improve the overall quality of the tests. The tests will fail if a non-existent parameter is used, or if an invalid parameter combination is used.

Stub commands

I refer to the functions used like this as stub commands, and have written a module that will interrogate other modules and generate a psm1 file, which can be imported by a stub module. This approach is based on, but is more detailed than, the method described previously.

The module is available in the PowerShell Gallery and can be installed as follows: Install-Module Indented.StubCommand -Scope CurrentUser.

Mocking objects

It is not uncommon for a function to expect to work with the properties and methods of another object returned by a command. Mocked commands must often return rich objects, simulating the value that would normally be returned.

Fabricating objects

Objects with specific properties can be simulated by creating a PS custom object (or PSObject):

```
[PSCustomObject]@{
    Property = "Value"
}
```

Methods can be added to an object using Add-Member:

```
[PSCustomObject]@{} | Add-Member MethodName -MemberType ScriptMethod -Value
{ }
```

This approach can be extended to include objects instantiated by New-Object. The following function creates and uses instances of two different .NET types:

```
function Write-File {
    $fileStream = New-Object System.IO.FileStream(
        "C:\Temp\test.txt",
        'OpenOrCreate'
    )
    $streamWriter = New-Object System.IO.StreamWriter($fileStream)
    $streamWriter.WriteLine("Hello world")
    $streamWriter.Close()
}
```

The following mocks replace the first call made to New-Object in the preceding script with null. The second call is replaced with an object that supports the methods used by the script:

```
Mock New-Object -ParameterFilter { $TypeName -eq 'System.IO.FileStream' }
Mock New-Object -ParameterFilter { $TypeName -eq 'System.IO.StreamWriter' }
-MockWith {
    [PSCustomObject]@{} |
        Add-Member WriteLine -MemberType ScriptMethod -Value { } -PassThru
    |
        Add-Member Close -MemberType ScriptMethod -Value { } -PassThru
}
```

At this point, it is possible to assert that the function creates each of the objects, but the test is blind to how the methods are used. If it is not desirable to let the methods act on a real object, it may be worth considering what could be done inside of a method implementation to signal activity to Pester. The following example changes the methods to make a change to a script-scoped variable. The variable can be accessed within the other tests. The content of the script-scoped variables is cleared before each test:

```
Describe Write-File {
    BeforeAll {
        Mock New-Object -ParameterFilter { $TypeName -eq
'System.IO.FileStream' }
        Mock New-Object -ParameterFilter { $TypeName -eq
'System.IO.StreamWriter' } -MockWith {
            [PSCustomObject]@{} |
                Add-Member WriteLine -MemberType ScriptMethod -PassThru -
Value {
                    $Script:WriteLine = $args[0]
                } |
                Add-Member Close -MemberType ScriptMethod -PassThru -Value
{
                    $Script:Close = $true
                }
        }
    }

    BeforeEach {
        $Script:WriteLine = ''
        $Script:Close = $false
    }

    It 'Creates a file stream' {
        Write-File

        Assert-MockCalled New-Object -ParameterFilter { $TypeName -eq
'System.IO.FileStream' }
        Assert-MockCalled New-Object -ParameterFilter { $TypeName -eq
'System.IO.StreamWriter' }
    }

    It 'Writes a line and closes the file stream' {
        Write-File

        $Script:WriteLine | Should -Be 'Hello world'
        $Script:Close | Should -Be $true
    }
}
```

Mocking existing members

If an object is completely replaced with a made-up PSCustomObject, the object type is lost; this is important when another command requires an object of a specific type as input. Attempting to override properties and methods on a real instance of the object may be used to work around this problem.

The following snippet creates an instance of an SQL connection object, then overrides the Open method and State properties:

```
$sqlConnection = [System.Data.SqlClient.SqlConnection]::new()
$sqlConnection | Add-Member State -MemberType NoteProperty -Force -Value
'Closed'
$sqlConnection | Add-Member Open -MemberType ScriptMethod -Force -Value {
    $this.State = 'Open'
}
```

The State property cannot be set by default, so overriding both is required to simulate use. The normal methods may be seen by looking beneath the PowerShell object; an example is as follows:

```
PS> $sqlConnection = [System.Data.SqlClient.SqlConnection]::new()
PS> $sqlConnection | Add-Member State -MemberType NoteProperty -Force -
Value 'Open'
PS> $sqlConnection.State
Open

PS> $sqlConnection.PSBase.State
Closed
```

This technique can be used to create a disarmed object of the correct type.

The following function expects an SQL connection object as input:

```
function Invoke-SqlQuery {
    [CmdletBinding()]
    param (
        [Parameter(Mandatory)]
        [String]$Query,

        [Parameter(Mandatory)]
        [System.Data.SqlClient.SqlConnection]$Connection
    )
    try {
        $Connection.Open()

        $sqlCommand = $Connection.CreateCommand()
```

```
    $sqlCommand.CommandText = $Query

    $dataTable = New-Object System.Data.DataTable
    $sqlDataAdapter = New-Object
System.Data.SqlClient.SqlDataAdapter($sqlCommand)
    $sqlDataAdapter.Fill($dataTable) | Write-Verbose

    $dataTable
} catch {
    $pscmdlet.ThrowTerminatingError($_)
} finally {
    if ($Connection.State -eq 'Open') {
        $Connection.Close()
    }
}
}
```

To create unit tests for the Invoke-SqlQuery function, an SQL connection object must be created and supplied. In addition, SqlDataAdapter must be mocked.

The tests shown as follows provide a modified SQL connection object, and a version of the data adapter with the Fill method replaced:

```
Describe Invoke-SqlQuery {
    BeforeAll {
        Mock New-Object -ParameterFilter { $TypeName -like
'*SqlDataAdapter' } -MockWith {
            [System.Data.SqlClient.SqlDataAdapter]::new() |
                Add-Member Fill -MemberType ScriptMethod -Force -PassThru -
Value {
                    $null = $args[0].Columns.Add('ColumnName')
                    $row = $args[0].NewRow()
                    $row.ColumnName = 'value'
                    $args[0].Rows.Add($row)

                    $args[0].Rows.Count
                }
        }

        $defaultParams = @{
            Query = 'SELECT * FROM Table1'
            Connection = [System.Data.SqlClient.SqlConnection]::new() |
                Add-Member State -MemberType NoteProperty -Force -PassThru
-Value { 'Closed' } |
                Add-Member Open -MemberType ScriptMethod -Force -PassThru
-Value {
                    $this.State = 'Open'
                } |
```

```
                         Add-Member Close -MemberType ScriptMethod -Force -PassThru
    -Value {
                             $this.State = 'Closed'
                     }
            }
    }

    It 'Executes a query and returns the results' {
        $output = Invoke-SqlQUery @defaultParams

        $output.Rows.Count | Should -Be 1
        $output[0].ColumnName | Should -Be 'value'
    }

    Context 'Error handling' {
        BeforeAll {
            $contextParams = $defaultParams.Clone()
            $contextParams.Connection = $contextParams.Connection |
                Add-Member Open -MemberType ScriptMethod -Force -PassThru -
    Value {
                    throw 'Connection failed'
                }
        }

        It 'When the connection fails, throws an error' {
            { Invoke-SqlQUery @contextParams } | Should -Throw 'Connection
    failed'
        }
    }
}
```

Using New-MockObject

The New-MockObject command provides a way to create an uninitialized version of a type. An instance of an uninitialized type has all of the properties and methods of the initialized instance, but without any of the code behind and potentially without some default values.

It is possible to use New-MockObject to generate an instance of the sqlConnection object used in the previous example. As the object is uninitialized, errors are likely when attempting to use the methods that the type provides:

```
PS> $sqlConnection = New-MockObject System.Data.SqlClient.SqlConnection
PS> $sqlConnection.Open()
Exception calling "Open" with "0" argument(s): "Object reference not set to
an instance of an object."
```

```
At line:1 char:1
+ $sqlConnection.Open()
+ ~~~~~~~~~~~~~~~~~~~~~
  + CategoryInfo : NotSpecified: (:) [], MethodInvocationException
  + FullyQualifiedErrorId : NullReferenceException
```

In this case, the `Open` and `Close` methods, and the `State` property, must still be overridden by using `Add-Member` before the object can be used. `New-MockObject` comes into its own when working with objects that you cannot easily create: objects that either have no constructor at all, or are very complex to create otherwise.

For example, the following function expects a `CimSession` object. `New-MockObject` provides a convenient way to create a `CimSession` to satisfy the parameter during testing:

```
function Get-CurrentUser {
    [CmdletBinding(DefaultParameterSetName = 'UsingComputerName')]
    param (
        [Parameter(ParameterSetName = 'UsingComputerName')]
        [String]$ComputerName,

        [Parameter(Mandatory, ParameterSetName = 'UsingCimSession')]
        [CimSession]$CimSession
    )

    (Get-CimInstance Win32_ComputerSystem -Property UserName
@psboundparameters).UserName
}
```

A test may be created that ensures that a `CimSession` provided to the function is passed on to `Get-CimInstance`:

```
Describe Get-CurrentUser {
    Context 'Using a CIM session' {
        BeforeAll {
            Mock Get-CimInstance -ParameterFilter { $CimSession } -MockWith
{
                [PSCustomObject]@{ UserName = 'UserFromCimSession' }
            }
        }

        It 'When a CimSession is supplied, passes the CimSession to Get-
CimInstance' {
            Get-CurrentUser -CimSession (New-MockObject CimSession) |
                Should -Be 'UserFromCimSession'
        }
    }
}
```

Mocking CIM objects

CIM-based commands that accept pipeline input, such as Set-NetAdapter, require a CIM instance with a specific PSTypeName. The PSTypeName is a string property normally hidden from Get-Member.

Exploring the InputObject parameter of Set-NetAdapter shows that it accepts a CIM instance type. Expanding the PSTypeName attribute shows that it also requires an object that includes the type
name Microsoft.Management.Infrastructure.CimInstance#MSFT_NetAdapter:

```
PS> (Get-Command Set-
NetAdapter).Parameters['InputObject'].ParameterType.Name
CimInstance[]

PS> (Get-Command Set-NetAdapter).Parameters['InputObject'].Attributes.
>>     Where{ $_.TypeId -match 'PSType' }.PSTypeName
Microsoft.Management.Infrastructure.CimInstance#MSFT_NetAdapter
```

There are two ways to create an object that will satisfy the InputObject parameter of Set-NetAdapter.

The first is to create a ClientOnly instance of the type. This requires the namespace of the class; the namespace is exposed as a property of the object returned by Get-NetAdapter:

```
PS> Get-NetAdapter | Select-Object CimClass -First 1

CimClass
--------
ROOT/StandardCimv2:MSFT_NetAdapter
```

The namespace may be used to create the client-only instance with all the properties of a normal net adapter object:

```
New-CimInstance MSFT_NetAdapter -Namespace ROOT/StandardCimv2 -ClientOnly
```

The second method omits the namespace. If the namespace is omitted, an object that is visually the same is created:

```
New-CimInstance MSFT_NetAdapter -ClientOnly
```

The output of the command is described by a format applied because of the type name. The created object lacks most of the members. Passing the output from each command to Get-Member will show the difference.

If the members are not important, or the real CIM class is not available where the tests are executing, the version without a namespace may be used. The properties needed to satisfy testing may be added by using Add-Member.

Pester in practice

The following function sets a computer description by modifying values in the registry:

```
function Set-ComputerDescription {
    [CmdletBinding()]
    param (
        [Parameter(Mandatory = $true)]
        [AllowEmptyString()]
        [String]$Description
    )

    $erroractionpreference = 'Stop'

    try {
        $path =
'HKLM:\System\CurrentControlSet\Services\LanmanServer\Parameters'

        if ((Get-Item $path).GetValue('srvcomment') -ne $Description) {
            if ($Description) {
                Set-ItemProperty $path -Name 'srvcomment' -Value
$Description
            } else {
                Remove-ItemProperty $path -Name 'srvcomment'
            }
        }
    } catch {
        throw
    }
}
```

When the function interacts with the registry, it does so using the following commands:

- `Get-Item`
- `Set-ItemProperty`
- `Remove-ItemProperty`

Testing the actions undertaken by each of the previous commands is not the responsibility of a unit test for `Set-ComputerDescription`. Unit tests are limited to ensuring that each of the commands has the right parameters, and at the right time. Each of the commands used by the function will be mocked.

The function reacts to a combination of the value of the `Description` parameter and the current state of the value.

A set of context blocks is appropriate for this division of the test. The difference between the blocks is the response from `Get-Item`, and is therefore the implementation of the `Mock`:

```
Describe Set-ComputerDescription {
    BeforeAll {
        Mock Set-ItemProperty
        Mock Clear-ItemProperty
        Mock Remove-ItemProperty
    }
}
```

The first context is used to describe what happens when the current description is blank. A `Mock` for `Get-Item` is created, which returns a blank result. Tests are added, describing the behavior of the command:

```
Describe Set-ComputerDescription {
    BeforeAll {
        Mock Set-ItemProperty
        Mock Clear-ItemProperty
        Mock Remove-ItemProperty
    }

    Context 'Description is not set' {
        BeforeAll {
            Mock Get-Item {
                [PSCustomObject]@{} | Add-Member GetValue -MemberType
ScriptMethod -Value { '' }
            }
        }

        It 'When the description differs, sets a new value' {
            Set-ComputerDescription -Description 'New description'
```

```
            Assert-MockCalled Set-ItemProperty -Scope It
        }

    It 'When the description matches, does nothing' {
            Set-ComputerDescription -Description ''

            Assert-MockCalled Set-ItemProperty -Times 0 -Scope It
            Assert-MockCalled Remove-ItemProperty -Times 0 -Scope It
        }
    }
}
```

The previous tests may be enhanced to ensure that Remove-ItemProperty is not called when updating with a new value. Given that the code paths are mutually exclusive, it should not be possible to call both. Extending the test ensures that future logic changes do not inadvertently trigger both commands.

The following context tests the actions that should be taken if a description is set. The Mock for Get-Item is replaced with one that returns a value:

```
Describe Set-ComputerDescription {
    BeforeAll {
        Mock Set-ItemProperty
        Mock Clear-ItemProperty
        Mock Remove-ItemProperty
    }

    Context 'Description is set' {
        BeforeAll {
            Mock Get-Item {
                [PSCustomObject]@{} | Add-Member GetValue -MemberType
ScriptMethod -Value {
                    return 'Current description'
                }
            }
        }

    It 'When the description differs, sets a new value' {
            Set-ComputerDescription -Description 'New description'

            Assert-MockCalled Set-ItemProperty -Scope It
        }

    It 'When the description matches, does nothing' {
            Set-ComputerDescription -Description 'Current description'

            Assert-MockCalled Set-ItemProperty -Times 0 -Scope It
```

```
                    Assert-MockCalled Remove-ItemProperty -Times 0 -Scope It
        }

    It 'When the description is empty, removes the value' {
    Set-ComputerDescription -Description ''

    Assert-MockCalled Remove-ItemProperty -Times 1 -Scope It
    }
    }
}
```

The preceding tests might be enhanced to verify that an error will trigger the catch statement. For example, if Set-ItemProperty were to throw a non-terminating error with ErrorActionPreference set to Stop, a non-terminating error would be raised as a terminating error. The terminating error can be tested, as follows:

```
Describe Set-ComputerDescription {
    BeforeAll {
        Mock Set-ItemProperty
        Mock Clear-ItemProperty
        Mock Remove-ItemProperty
    }

    Context 'Error handling' {
        BeforeAll {
            Mock Set-ItemProperty {
                Write-Error -Message 'Non-terminating error'
            }
        }

        It 'When Set-ItemProperty throws, raises a terminating error' {
            { Set-ComputerDescription -Description 'New description' } |
    Should Throw
        }
    }
}
```

The following snippet combines each of the sections described previously:

```
Describe Set-ComputerDescription {
    BeforeAll {
        Mock Set-ItemProperty
        Mock Clear-ItemProperty
        Mock Remove-ItemProperty
    }

    Context 'Description is not set' {
        BeforeAll {
```

```
            Mock Get-Item {
                [PSCustomObject]@{} | Add-Member GetValue -MemberType
ScriptMethod -Value { '' }
            }
        }

        It 'When the description differs, sets a new value' {
            Set-ComputerDescription -Description 'New description'
            Assert-MockCalled Set-ItemProperty -Scope It
            Assert-MockCalled Remove-ItemProperty -Times 0 -Scope It
        }

        It 'When the description matches, does nothing' {
            Set-ComputerDescription -Description ''
            Assert-MockCalled Set-ItemProperty -Times 0 -Scope It
            Assert-MockCalled Remove-ItemProperty -Times 0 -Scope It
        }
    }

    Context 'Description is set' {
        BeforeAll {
            Mock Get-Item {
                [PSCustomObject]@{} | Add-Member GetValue -MemberType
ScriptMethod -Value {
                    return 'Current description'
                }
            }
        }

        It 'When the description differs, sets a new value' {
            Set-ComputerDescription -Description 'New description'
            Assert-MockCalled Set-ItemProperty -Scope It
        }

        It 'When the description matches, does nothing' {
            Set-ComputerDescription -Description 'Current description'
            Assert-MockCalled Set-ItemProperty -Times 0 -Scope It
            Assert-MockCalled Remove-ItemProperty -Times 0 -Scope It
        }

        It 'When the description is empty, removes the value' {
            Set-ComputerDescription -Description ''
            Assert-MockCalled Remove-ItemProperty -Times 1 -Scope It
        }
    }

    Context 'Error handling' {
        BeforeAll {
```

```
            Mock Set-ItemProperty { Write-Error -Message 'Non-terminating
error' }
        }

        It 'When Set-ItemProperty throws, raises a terminating error' {
            { Set-ComputerDescription -Description 'New description' } |
Should Throw
        }
    }
}
```

Summary

This chapter explored static analysis with PSScriptAnalyzer. PSScriptAnalyzer makes use of the AST to examine a script or function. The creation of custom rules for the script analyzer was briefly demonstrated.

Testing with Pester was explored in detail, including the use of the different named blocks. This included a demonstration of building tests for a function.

The next chapter will explore error handling in PowerShell, including terminating and non-terminating errors and the use of try, catch, and finally, the trap statement.

21
Error Handling

Errors are used to communicate unexpected conditions or exceptional circumstances. Errors often contain useful information that can be used to diagnose a condition.

PowerShell has two different types of errors, terminating and non-terminating, and several different ways to raise and handle them.

During the course of this chapter, self-contained blocks of code are described as scripts. The terms function, `ScriptBlock`, and script can be considered interchangeable in the context of error handling.

The following topics are covered in this chapter:

- Error types
- Error actions
- Raising errors
- Catching errors

Error types

PowerShell defines two different types of errors: terminating and non-terminating errors.

Each command in PowerShell may choose to raise either of these, depending on the operation.

Terminating errors

A terminating error stops a pipeline processing; once an error is thrown, everything stops. A terminating error might appear as the result of using throw. In the following function, the second Write-Host statement will never execute:

```
PS> function ThrowError {
>>      Write-Host 'First'
>>      throw 'Error'
>>      Write-Host 'Second'
>> }
PS> ThrowError
First
Error
At line:3 char:5
+ throw 'Error'
+ ~~~~~~~~~~~~~
+ CategoryInfo : OperationStopped: (Error:String) [], RuntimeException
+ FullyQualifiedErrorId : Error
```

Terminating errors are typically used to convey that something unexpected and terminal has occurred, such as a catastrophic failure that prevents a script continuing.

Non-terminating errors

A non-terminating error, a type of informational output, is written without stopping a script. Non-terminating errors are often the result of using the Write-Error command. The following function shows that processing continues after the error:

```
PS> function WriteError {
>>      Write-Host 'First'
>>      Write-Error 'Error'
>>      Write-Host 'Second'
>> }
PS> WriteError
First
WriteError : Error
At line:1 char:1
+ WriteError
+ ~~~~~~~~~~
+ CategoryInfo : NotSpecified: (:) [Write-Error], WriteErrorException
+ FullyQualifiedErrorId :
Microsoft.PowerShell.Commands.WriteErrorException,WriteError
Second
```

Non-terminating errors are used to notify the user that something went wrong, but that it didn't necessarily warrant shutting down a script. A user may choose to stop processing when a non-terminating error is raised.

Error actions

The `ErrorAction` parameter and the `ErrorActionPreference` variable are used to control what happens when a non-terminating error is written.

`ErrorAction` **parameter requires** `CmdletBinding`.

The `ErrorAction` parameter is only available if a function declares the `CmdletBinding` attribute. `CmdletBinding` automatically added is if the `Parameter` attribute is used.

By default, `ErrorAction` is set to continue. Any non-terminating errors will be displayed, but a script or function will continue to run.

If `ErrorAction` is set to `SilentlyContinue`, errors will be added to the `$error` automatic variable, but the error won't be displayed.

The following function writes a non-terminating error using `Write-Error`:

```
function SilentError {
    [CmdletBinding()]
    param ( )

    Write-Error 'Something went wrong'
}
 SilentError -ErrorAction SilentlyContinue
```

The error is written, but hidden from view. The error may be viewed as the latest entry in the `$error` variable:

```
PS> $Error[0]
SilentError : Something went wrong
At line:1 char:1
+ SilentError -ErrorAction SilentlyContinue
+ ~~~~~~~~~~~~~~~~~~~~~~~~~~~~~~~~~~~~~~~~~~~
+ CategoryInfo : NotSpecified: (:) [Write-Error], WriteErrorException
+ FullyQualifiedErrorId :
Microsoft.PowerShell.Commands.WriteErrorException,SilentError
```

If the error action is set to `Stop`, a non-terminating error becomes a terminating error, as in the following example:

```
PS> function StopError {
>>      [CmdletBinding()]
>>      param ( )
>>
>>      Write-Error 'Something went wrong'
>> }
PS> StopError -ErrorAction Stop
StopError : Something went wrong
At line:1 char:1
+ StopError -ErrorAction Stop
+ ~~~~~~~~~~~~~~~~~~~~~~~~~~~~
+ CategoryInfo : NotSpecified: (:) [Write-Error], WriteErrorException
+ FullyQualifiedErrorId :
Microsoft.PowerShell.Commands.WriteErrorException,StopError
```

Raising errors

When writing a script, it may be desirable to use errors to notify the person running the script of a problem. The severity of the problem will dictate whether an error is non-terminating or terminating.

If a script makes a single change to a large number of diverse, unrelated objects, a terminating error might be frustrating for anyone using the script.

On the other hand, if a script fails to read a critical configuration file, a terminating error is likely the right choice.

Error records

When an error is raised in PowerShell, an `ErrorRecord` object is created (explicitly or implicitly).

An `ErrorRecord` object contains a number of fields that are useful for diagnosing an error. `ErrorRecord` can be explored using `Get-Member`. For example, an `ErrorRecord` will be generated when attempting to divide by `0`:

```
100 / 0
$record = $Error[0]
```

The `ErrorRecord` object that was generated includes `ScriptStackTrace`.
`ScriptTrackTrace` is extremely useful when debugging problems in larger scripts:

```
PS> $record.ScriptStackTrace
at <ScriptBlock>, <No file>: line 1
```

The `Exception` in the error record also includes a .NET stack trace:

```
PS> $record.Exception.StackTrace
at System.Management.Automation.IntOps.Divide(Int32 lhs, Int32 rhs)
at System.Dynamic.UpdateDelegates.UpdateAndExecute2[T0,T1,TRet](CallSite
site, T0 arg0, T1 arg1)
at
System.Management.Automation.Interpreter.DynamicInstruction`3.Run(Interpret
edFrame frame)
at
System.Management.Automation.Interpreter.EnterTryCatchFinallyInstruction.Ru
n(InterpretedFrame frame)
```

In some cases, the `TargetObject` property of `ErrorRecord` might contain the object being
worked on.

For example, if the values for a division operation were dynamically set, `ErrorRecord`
might be created to return those values to assist with debugging:

```
$numerator = 10
$denominator = 0
try {
    $numerator / $denominator
} catch {
    $errorRecord = [System.Management.Automation.ErrorRecord]::new(
        [Exception]::new($_.Exception.Message),
        'InvalidDivision',    # ErrorId
        'InvalidOperation',   # ErrorCategory
        [PSCustomObject]@{  # TargetObject
            Numerator   = $numerator
            Denominator = $denominator
        }
    )
    Write-Error -ErrorRecord $errorRecord
}
```

The values pushed into `ErrorRecord` may be viewed by exploring the `TargetObject` property:

```
PS> $Error[0].TargetObject

Numerator       Denominator
---------       -----------
       10                 0
```

The `try-catch` statement used previously is covered in detail while exploring `try`, `catch`, and `finally` later in this chapter.

Write-Error

The `Write-Error` command can be used to write non-terminating error messages.

The `Write-Error` command can be used with nothing more than a message:

```
Write-Error 'Message'
```

Or it might include additional information, such as a category and error ID to aid diagnosis by the person using the script:

```
Write-Error -Message 'Message' -Category 'InvalidOperation' -ErrorId
'UniqueID'
```

The following example shows a non-terminating error that was raised while running a loop:

```
function Test-Error {
    for ($i = 0; $i -lt 5; $i++) {
        Write-Error -Message "Iteration: $i"
    }
}
Test-Error
```

The error will be displayed five times without stopping execution.

Setting the value of `ErrorAction` to `Stop` will cause `Write-Error` to throw a terminating error, ending the function within the first iteration of the loop:

```
PS> function Test-Error {
>>      [CmdletBinding()]
>>      param ( )
>>
>>      for ($i = 0; $i -lt 5; $i++) {
```

```
>>           Write-Error -Message "Iteration: $i"
>>    }
>> }
>>
PS> Test-Error -ErrorAction Stop
Test-Error : Iteration: 0
At line:1 char:1
+ Test-Error -ErrorAction Stop
+ ~~~~~~~~~~~~~~~~~~~~~~~~~~~~~
+ CategoryInfo : NotSpecified: (:) [Write-Error], WriteErrorException
+ FullyQualifiedErrorId :
Microsoft.PowerShell.Commands.WriteErrorException,Test-Error
```

Alternatively, the error might be silent (`SilentlyContinue`) or ignored (`Ignore`), depending on the context in which the error appears.

Setting the `ErrorActionPreference` variable (either globally or within the function scope) will have the same effect on the `Write-Error` command.

throw and ThrowTerminatingError

The `throw` keyword raises a terminating error, as in the following example:

```
throw 'Error message'
```

Existing exception types are documented in the .NET framework; each is ultimately derived from the `System.Exception` type found in the .NET reference:

```
https://docs.microsoft.com/en-us/dotnet/api/system.exception?view=netframework-
4.7.2
```

`throw` may be used with a string or a message, as shown previously. `throw` may also be used with an exception object:

```
throw [ArgumentException]::new('Unsupported value')
```

Or it may be used with `ErrorRecord`:

```
throw [System.Management.Automation.ErrorRecord]::new(
    [InvalidOperationException]::new('Invalid operation'),
    'AnErrorID',
    [System.Management.Automation.ErrorCategory]::InvalidOperation,
    $null
)
```

Commands in binary modules (cmdlets) cannot use `throw`; it has a different meaning in the languages that might be used to author a cmdlet. Cmdlets use the `PSCmdlet.ThrowTerminatingError` .NET method.

The `ThrowTerminatingError` method can be used in PowerShell in conjunction with an `ErrorRecord` object, provided the `CmdletBinding` attribute is declared, as in the example:

```
function Invoke-Something {
    [CmdletBinding()]
    param ( )

    $errorRecord = [System.Management.Automation.ErrorRecord]::new(
        [InvalidOperationException]::new('Failed'),
        'AnErrorID',
        [System.Management.Automation.ErrorCategory]::OperationStopped,
        $null
    )
    $pscmdlet.ThrowTerminatingError($errorRecord)
}
```

Error and ErrorVariable

The `Error` variable is a collection (`ArrayList`) of handled and unhandled errors raised in the PowerShell session.

Testing the content of error variables

Testing the content of an error variable is not a robust way to test for error conditions.
As the variable fills with both handled and unhandled errors, it's indeterminate at best. `Error` variables continue to have value when debugging less obvious problems with code.

The error collection can be cleared using the `Clear` method:

```
$Error.Clear()
```

The most recent error is first in the list:

```
$Error[0]
```

Errors will be added to the collection except when `ErrorAction` is set to `Ignore`.

The `ErrorVariable` parameter can be used to name a variable that should be used, as well as `Error` for a specific command. The `Error` variable, the value in the variable name, is an `ArrayList`.

The following function writes an `Error` variable. When `ErrorVariable` is used, the errors are added to the named variable:

```
function Invoke-Something {
    [CmdletBinding()]
    param ( )

    Write-Error 'Failed'
}
Invoke-Something -ErrorVariable InvokeError -ErrorAction SilentlyContinue
```

The errors stored in the variable can be inspected:

```
PS> $InvokeError
Invoke-Something : Failed
At line:1 char:1
+ Invoke-Something -ErrorVariable InvokeError -ErrorAction SilentlyCont ...
+ ~~~~~~~~~~~~~~~~~~~~~~~~~~~~~~~~~~~~~~~~~~~~~~~~~~~~~~~~~~~~~~~~~~~~~~~
+ CategoryInfo : NotSpecified: (:) [Write-Error], WriteErrorException
+ FullyQualifiedErrorId :
Microsoft.PowerShell.Commands.WriteErrorException,Invoke-Something
```

ErrorVariable is never null

If no errors occur, the variable will still be created as an `ArrayList`, but the list will contain no elements. That the list exists means using the variable as an implicit Boolean is flawed, that is, the `$null -eq` `$InvokeError` statement will return `false`.
The `Count` property might be inspected instead, using `$InvokeError.Count -eq 0`.

Error messages written to an `ErrorVariable` are duplicated in `Error`:

```
PS> $error[0]
Invoke-Something : Failed
At line:1 char:1
+ Invoke-Something -ErrorVariable InvokeError -ErrorAction SilentlyCont ...
+ ~~~~~~~~~~~~~~~~~~~~~~~~~~~~~~~~~~~~~~~~~~~~~~~~~~~~~~~~~~~~~~~~~~~~~~~
+ CategoryInfo : NotSpecified: (:) [Write-Error], WriteErrorException
+ FullyQualifiedErrorId :
Microsoft.PowerShell.Commands.WriteErrorException,Invoke-Something
```

Catching errors

PowerShell provides two different ways to handle terminating errors: using `try-catch-finally`, or using `trap`.

try, catch, and finally

PowerShell 2.0 introduced `try-catch-finally` as a means of handling terminating errors.

try

A `try` block must be followed by either one or more `catch` blocks, a `finally` block, or both. Each of the following patterns is valid:

```
try { <script> } catch { <script> }
try { <script> } finally { <script> }
try { <script> } catch { <script> } finally { <script }
```

An error occurring within `try` will trigger the execution of `catch`.

catch

`catch` is used to respond to terminating errors raised within `try`. `catch` can be used to respond to any exception, or a specific set of exception types. Each of the following is valid, if incomplete:

```
try { } catch { 'Catches any exception' }
try { } catch [ExceptionType] { 'Catch an exception type' }
try { } catch [ExceptionType1], [ExceptionType2] {
    'Catch exception type 1 and 2'
}
```

In the following example, calling the `ToString` method on the `null` variable will throw an exception that triggers `catch`:

```
try {
    $null.ToString()
} catch {
    Write-Host 'This exception has been handled'
}
```

When working with `catch`, the error record that was thrown is made available by using either the `$_` variable or `$PSItem`:

```
try {
    $null.ToString()
} catch {
    Write-Host $_.Exception.Message        # This is the same as...
    Write-Host $PSItem.Exception.Message # ... this.
}
```

`ForEach-Object` and `catch`

If `ForEach-Object` is used, the current object in the pipeline is stored in the `$_` variable. For the object from the input pipeline to be available inside `catch`, it must be assigned to another variable first.

`catch` statements can be limited to handle specific exception types:

```
$ErrorActionPreference = 'Stop'
try {
    # If the file does not exist, this will raise an exception of type
ItemNotFoundException
    $content = Get-Content C:\doesnotexist.txt
} catch [System.Management.Automation.ItemNotFoundException] {
    Write-Host 'The item was not found'
}
```

If more than one type of error might be thrown by a block of code, multiple `catch` statements are supported. In the following example, an unauthorized access exception is thrown in response to an attempt to read a directory like a file:

```
$ErrorActionPreference = 'Stop' try { Get-ChildItem
C:\Windows\System32\Configuration -Filter *.mof | ForEach-Object { $content
= $_ | Get-Content } } catch [System.IO.FileNotFoundException] { Write-Host
'The item was not found' } catch
[System.Management.Automation.ItemNotFoundException] { Write-Host 'Access
denied' }
```

In a similar manner, `catch` statements can be layered, starting with the most specific error type, working down to a broader condition. The first matching `catch` block will be used:

```
using namespace System.Management.Automation

try {
    throw [ItemNotFoundException]::new('Item not found')
} catch [ItemNotFoundException] {
    Write-Host 'Item not found exception thrown'
```

```
} catch {
    Write-Host 'Error thrown'
}
```

finally

The `finally` block will invoke whether an error is thrown or not. This makes it ideal for handling situations where things must always be cleanly closed down.

The following function ignores errors, but will always close down an open SQL connection, whether the `ExecuteReader` method succeeds or not:

```
using namespace System.Data.SqlClient

$connectionString = 'Data Source=dbServer;Initial Catalog=dbName'
try {
    $sqlConnection = [SqlConnection]::new($connectionString)
    $sqlConnection.Open()
    $sqlCommand = $sqlConnection.CreateCommand()
    $sqlCommand.CommandText = 'SELECT * FROM Employee'
    $reader = $sqlCommand.ExecuteReader()
} finally {
    if ($sqlConnection.State -eq 'Open') {
        $sqlConnection.Close()
    }
}
```

When `catch` is used with `finally`, the content of `finally` is executed before errors are returned, but after the body of `catch` has executed. This is demonstrated by the following example:

```
try {
    Write-Host "Try"
    throw 'Error'
} catch {
    Write-Host "Catch, after Try"
    throw
} finally {
    Write-Host "Finally, after Catch, before the exception"
}
```

Re-throwing errors

An error might be re-thrown within a `catch` block. This technique can be useful if a `try` block performs a number of dependent steps in a sequence where one or more might fail.

Re-throwing an error raised by a script can be as simple as using `throw` in a `catch` block:

```
try {
    'Statement1'
    throw 'Statement2'
    'Statement3'
} catch {
    throw
}
```

`ThrowTerminatingError` might be used instead, depending on the desired behavior:

```
function Invoke-Something {
    [CmdletBinding()]
    param ( )
    try {
        'Statement1'
        throw 'Statement2'
        'Statement3'
    } catch {
        $pscmdlet.ThrowTerminatingError($_)
    }
}
```

When an error is re-thrown in this manner, the second instance of the error (within the `catch` block) is not written to either `Error` or an error variable. In cases where the error is re-thrown without modification, this doesn't present a problem.

If the re-thrown error attempts to add information, such as an error ID, the modified error record won't be available to error variables, as in the example:

```
try {
    throw 'Error'
} catch {
    Write-Error -Exception $_.Exception -ErrorId 'GeneratedErrorId' -
Category 'InvalidOperation'
}
```

The error raised in the `try` block is added to the error variables but isn't displayed in a console (since it's been handled). The second error is displayed on the console but isn't added to error variables.

To resolve this problem, the new error record may return the original exception as an inner exception:

```
try {
    throw 'Error'
} catch {
    $exception = [InvalidOperationException]::new(
        $_.Exception.Message,
        $_.Exception
    )
    Write-Error -Exception $exception -ErrorId 'GeneratedErrorId' -Category
'InvalidOperation'
}
```

In the case of exception and most, if not all, exception types, the first argument of the constructor is a message, and the second (optional) argument is an inner exception.

Using an inner exception has a number of advantages:

- try-catch statements that test the outcome of the preceding snippet will trigger based on either the exception type or inner exception type
- The other properties of the exception remain available (via the inner exception), such as the stack trace

When using an inner exception, it's important to note that PowerShell can't catch based on the inner exception type in most cases. The following example has three nested exceptions. PowerShell can't react to either the inner or intermediate exceptions:

```
try {
    throw [InvalidOperationException]::new(
        'OuterException',
        [ArgumentException]::new(
            'IntermediateException',
            [UnauthorizedAccessException]::new('InnerException')
        )
    )
} catch [UnauthorizedAccessException] {
    'Inner'
} catch [ArgumentException] {
    'Intermediate'
} catch [InvalidOperationException] {
    'Outer'
}
```

An exception to this rule is `MethodInvocationException`. PowerShell raises `MethodInvocationException` when a method call fails. For example, the `DaysInMonth` method of the `DateTime` type will fail if the month number isn't between 1 and 12. The exception raised by PowerShell is `MethodInvocationException`:

```
PS> [DateTime]::DaysInMonth(2019, 13)
Exception calling "DaysInMonth" with "2" argument(s): "Month must be
between one and twelve.
Parameter name: month"
At line:1 char:2
+ [DateTime]::DaysInMonth(2019, 13)
+ ~~~~~~~~~~~~~~~~~~~~~~~~~~~~~~~~~
    + CategoryInfo : NotSpecified: (:) [], MethodInvocationException
    + FullyQualifiedErrorId : ArgumentOutOfRangeException
```

However, it's possible to catch the inner exception, `ArgumentOutOfRangeException`, in this and similar cases:

```
try {
    [DateTime]::DaysInMonth(2019, 13)
} catch [ArgumentOutOfRangeException] {
    Write-Host 'Out of range'
}
```

When a command raises an error, and only the inner most exception is interesting, the `InnerException` property becomes useful. It allows access to each inner exception in turn. In the following example, the property is used to access the intermediate exception:

```
try {
  throw [InvalidOperationException]::new(
  'OuterException',
  [ArgumentException]::new(
  'IntermediateException',
  [UnauthorizedAccessException]::new('InnerException')
  )
  )
} catch {
  Write-Host $_.Exception.InnerException.Message
}
```

The `Exception` class (and all derived classes) include a `GetBaseException` method. This method provides simple access to the innermost exception and is useful when the number of nested exceptions is unknown or variable:

```
try {
    throw [InvalidOperationException]::new(
        'OuterException',
```

```
        [ArgumentException]::new(
            'IntermediateException',
            [UnauthorizedAccessException]::new('InnerException')
        )
    )
} catch {
    Write-Host $_.Exception.GetBaseException().Message
}
```

If and Switch statements may be used inside the catch block to further refine the handling of a specific error.

Inconsistent error behavior

The different methods PowerShell exposes to terminate a script aren't entirely consistent and may lead to confused behavior.

When throw is used to raise a terminating error, it'll stop the current script and anything that called it. In the following example, child2 will never execute:

```
$ErrorActionPreference = 'Continue'
function caller {
    child1
    child2
}
function child1 {
    throw 'Failed'
    'child1'
}
function child2 {
    'child2'
}
caller
```

When the ThrowTerminatingError method is used, processing within child1 stops, but the caller function continues. This is demonstrated as follows:

```
function caller {
    child1
    child2
}
function child1 {
    [CmdletBinding()]
    param ( )

    $errorRecord = [System.Management.Automation.ErrorRecord]::new(
```

```
        [Exception]::new('Failed'),
        'ID',
        'OperationStopped',
        $null
    )
    $pscmdlet.ThrowTerminatingError($errorRecord)
    'child1'
}
function child2 {
    'child2'
}
```

Executing the `caller` function shows that `child2` is executed:

```
child1 : Failed
At line:2 char:5
+ child1
+ ~~~~~~
+ CategoryInfo : OperationStopped: (:) [child1], Exception
+ FullyQualifiedErrorId : ID,child1
child2
```

The behavior of the preceding example is equivalent to the behavior seen when calling cmdlets. For example, the `ConvertFrom-Json` command raises a terminating error when the content it's asked to convert is invalid.

When a cmdlet throws a terminating error within another function, the caller script continues to execute unless `ErrorAction` is set to `Stop`. In the following example, `ConvertFrom-Json` will raise a terminating error, but won't stop the `caller` function:

```
function caller {
    ConvertFrom-Json -InputObject '{{'
    child1
}
function child1 {
    'Called'
}
caller
```

The same behavior is seen when calling .NET methods, shown as follows. The `static` method, `IPAddress.Parse`, will raise an exception because the use of the method isn't valid. The function continues on from this error and calls `child1`:

```
function caller {
    [IPAddress]::Parse('this is not an IP')
    child1
}
```

```
function child1 {
    'Called'
}
caller
```

The interaction between `Throw` and `ErrorAction` is explored in greater detail in the following section, which describes patterns for raising and handling errors.

throw and ErrorAction

The `throw` keyword raises a terminating error; terminating errors aren't supposed to be affected by `ErrorAction` or `ErrorActionPreference`.

Unfortunately, errors raised by `throw` are affected by `ErrorAction` when `ErrorAction` is set to `SilentlyContinue`. This behavior is an important consideration when designing commands for others to use.

The following function throws an error first; the second command should never run:

```
function Invoke-Something {
    [CmdletBinding()]
    param ( )

    throw 'Error'
    Write-Host 'No error'
}
```

Running the function normally shows that the error is thrown, and the second command doesn't execute:

```
PS> Invoke-Something
Error
At line:5 char:5
+ throw 'Error'
+ ~~~~~~~~~~~~~
+ CategoryInfo : OperationStopped: (Error:String) [], RuntimeException
+ FullyQualifiedErrorId : Error
```

If `ErrorAction` is set to `SilentlyContinue`, `throw` will be ignored:

```
PS> Invoke-Something -ErrorAction SilentlyContinue
No error
```

Enclosing `throw` in a `try-catch` block will trigger `catch`, ending the script as it should regardless of the `ErrorAction` setting:

```
PS> function Invoke-Something {
>>      [CmdletBinding()]
>>      param ( )
>>
>>      try {
>           throw 'Error'
>>          Write-Host 'No error'
>>      } catch {
>>          Write-Host 'An error occurred'
>>      }
>> }
PS> Invoke-Something -ErrorAction SilentlyContinue
An error occurred
```

The problem described here also applies when `throw` is used within the `catch` block, although, in this case, the script is still terminated. The script below should result in an error being displayed as the error is terminating, however no error is displayed. The error raised in try does still prevent the script for progressing to the `Write-Host` command:

```
PS> function Invoke-Something {
>>      [CmdletBinding()]
>>      param ( )
>>
>>      try {
>>          throw 'Error'
>>          Write-Host 'No error'
>>      } catch {
>>          throw 'An error occurred'
>>      }
>> }
PS> Invoke-Something -ErrorAction SilentlyContinue
```

For scripts that declare the `CmdletBinding` attribute, `ThrowTerminatingError` can be used. The `ThrowTerminatingError` method doesn't suffer from the same problem; it isn't affected by `ErrorAction`:

```
PS> function Invoke-Something {
>>      [CmdletBinding()]
>>      param ( )
>>
>>      try {
>>          throw 'Error'
>>          Write-Host 'No error'
>>      } catch {
```

```
>>            $pscmdlet.ThrowTerminatingError($_)
>>      }
>> }
PS> Invoke-Something -ErrorAction SilentlyContinue
Invoke-Something : Error
At line:12 char:1
+ Invoke-Something -ErrorAction SilentlyContinue
+ ~~~~~~~~~~~~~~~~~~~~~~~~~~~~~~~~~~~~~~~~~~~~~~~~
+ CategoryInfo : OperationStopped: (Error:String) [Invoke-Something],
RuntimeException
+ FullyQualifiedErrorId : Error,Invoke-Something
```

In the preceding example, throw is used to raise the original error condition (which will create an error record). ThrowTerminatingError is used to re-throw the terminating error correctly.

If a function doesn't use the CmdletBinding attribute, care should be taken when writing error handling. For example, the following function cannot use ThrowTerminatingError or the ErrorAction parameter, but it's still subject to ErrorActionPreference:

```
PS> function Invoke-Something {
>>      throw 'Error'
>>      Write-Host 'No error'
>> }
PS> $ErrorActionPreference = 'SilentlyContinue'
PS> Invoke-Something
No error
```

Workarounds for this problem for standard functions include using Write-Error with ErrorAction set to Stop, however it's often best to simply add the CmdletBinding attribute and make the function advanced.

The following statements encompass a possible best practice:

- When using throw, ensure throw is within a try block
- Use PSCmdlet.ThrowTerminatingError to raise a terminating error from a script
- Use advanced functions to get most predictable behavior from ErrorAction

Nesting try-catch-finally

One try-catch-finally statement can be nested beneath another. This is most appropriate when a different approach is required by a smaller section of code.

A script which performs setup actions, then works on a number of objects in a loop, is a good example a script that might benefit from more than one `try-catch` statement. The script should terminate cleanly if something goes wrong during setup, but it might only notify you if an error occurs within the loop.

The following functions can be used as a working example of such a script. The setup actions might include connecting to a management server of some kind:

```
function Connect-Server {}
```

Once the connection is established, a set of objects might be retrieved:

```
function Get-ManagementObject {
    1..10 | ForEach-Object {
        [PSCustomObject]@{
            Name     = $_
            Property = "Value$_"
        }
    }
}
```

The `Set` filter accepts an input pipeline and changes a value on the object:

```
function Set-ManagementObject {
    [CmdletBinding()]
    param (
        [Parameter(Mandatory, ValueFromPipeline)]
        $InputObject,

        $Property
    )

    process {
        $InputObject.Property = $Property
    }
}
```

The following script uses the preceding functions. If a terminating error is raised during either the `Connect` or `Get` commands, the script will stop. If a terminating error is raised during `Set`, the script writes about the error and moves onto the next object:

```
try {
    Connect-Server
        Get-ManagementObject | ForEach-Object {
        try {
            $_ | Set-ManagementObject -Property 'NewValue'
        } catch {
```

```
            Write-Error -ErrorRecord $_
        } finally {
            $_
        }
    }
} catch {
    throw
}
```

Changing individual functions to throw errors will show how each block triggers.

Terminating or non-terminating

One of the challenges of writing error handling is determining whether the error is terminating or non-terminating.

A possible solution is to force all errors to be terminating by setting ErrorActionPreference to Stop.

Setting ErrorActionPreference to Stop is equivalent to adding -ErrorAction Stop to every command that supports it.

When exploring nesting try-catch-finally, the following example was used:

```
try {
    Connect-Server
    Get-ManagementObject | ForEach-Object {
        try {
            $_ | Set-ManagementObject -Property 'NewValue'
        } catch {
            Write-Error -ErrorRecord $_
        } finally {
            $_
        }
    }
} catch {
    throw
}
```

Setting ErrorActionPreference to Stop would remove the need to set an ErrorAction parameter on each of the commands (if those commands wrote non-terminating errors). However, doing so would also cause any informational errors written by Write-Error to completely stop the script.

For a script that implements a process, where the error handling can be strictly defined, the following workaround might be used. ErrorAction for Write-Error is forcefully set to Continue, overriding the value held in the preference variable:

```
$ErrorActionPreference = 'Stop'
try {
    Connect-Server
    Get-ManagementObject | ForEach-Object {
        try {
            $_ | Set-ManagementObject -Property 'NewValue'
        } catch {
            Write-Error -ErrorRecord $_ -ErrorAction Continue
        } finally {
            $_
        }
    }
} catch {
    throw
}
```

Setting ErrorActionPreference to Stop is harder to apply when writing tools, such as when writing the commands used by this script; doing so would remove the choice from the end user.

A need for complex error handling is often a sign that a script should be broken down into smaller units.

trap

PowerShell 1.0 came with trap. trap is used to catch errors raised anywhere within the scope of the trap declaration. that is, the current scope and any child scopes.

trap is a useful tool for capturing errors that aren't accounted for by try-catch blocks. Much of its use has been superseded by try-catch-finally.

Using trap

trap is declared in a similar manner to the catch block:

```
trap { <script> }
trap [ExceptionType] { <script> }
trap [ExceptionType1], [ExceptionType2] { <script> }
```

A script may contain more than one `trap` statement, for example:

```
trap [InvalidOperationException] {
    Write-Host 'An invalid operation'
}
trap {
    Write-Host 'Catch all other exceptions'
}
```

The ordering of the preceding `trap` statements doesn't matter; the statement with the most specific error type is used to handle a given error.

PowerShell, as a script-based language normally executes statements in the order written. However, when using a script, function, or script block, the `trap` statement can appear anywhere; `trap` doesn't have to appear before the code it acts against. For example, the `trap` implemented at the bottom of the script block will used when the preceding code raises an error:

```
& {
    Write-Host 'Statement1'
    throw 'Statement2'
    Write-Host 'Statement3'

    trap { Write-Host 'An error occurred' }
}
```

The error raised by `throw` causes the `trap` statement to execute, and then execution stops; `Statement3` is never written.

trap, scope, and continue

By default, if an error is handled by `trap`, script execution stops. The `continue` keyword can be used to resume a script at the next statement.

The following example handles the error raised by `throw` and continues onto the next statement:

```
& {
    Write-Host 'Statement1'
    throw 'Statement2'
    Write-Host 'Statement3'

    trap {
        Write-Host 'An error occurred'
        continue
```

```
        }
    }
```

The behavior of continue is dependent on the scope the trap statement is written in. In the preceding example, continue moves onto writing Statement3 as the trap statement, and the statements being executed are in the same scope.

The following script declares a function that throws an error. trap is declared in the parent scope of the function:

```
& {
    function Invoke-Something {
        Write-Host 'Statement1'
        throw 'Statement2'
        Write-Host 'Statement3'
    }

    Invoke-Something
    Write-Host 'Done'

    trap {
        Write-Host 'An error occurred'
        continue
    }
}
```

The continue keyword is used, but Statement3 isn't displayed. Execution can only continue in the same scope as the trap statement.

Summary

This chapter explored the different ways to raise and handle errors in PowerShell. Then, we looked at the difference between terminating and non-terminating errors.

We discussed using try-catch-finally, introduced with PowerShell 2, as the preferred means of handling terminating errors.

Then we demonstrated the use of trap, the type of error handling available with PowerShell 1, which we can add to our error-handling toolset.

Other Books You May Enjoy

If you enjoyed this book, you may be interested in these other books by Packt:

Learn PowerShell Core 6.0
David das Neves, Jan-Hendrik Peters

ISBN: 978-1-78883-898-6

- Get to grips with Powershell Core 6.0
- Explore basic and advanced PowerShell scripting techniques
- Get to grips with Windows PowerShell Security
- Work with centralization and DevOps with PowerShell
- Implement PowerShell in your organization through real-life examples
- Learn to create GUIs and use DSC in production

PowerShell Core for Linux Administrators Cookbook
Prashanth Jayaram, Ram Iyer

ISBN: 978-1-78913-723-1

- Leverage the object model of the shell, which is based on .NET Core
- Administer computers locally as well as remotely using PowerShell over OpenSSH
- Get to grips with advanced concepts of PowerShell functions
- Use PowerShell for administration on the cloud
- Know the best practices pertaining to PowerShell scripts and functions
- Exploit the cross-platform capabilities of PowerShell to manage scheduled jobs, Docker containers and SQL Databases

Leave a review - let other readers know what you think

Please share your thoughts on this book with others by leaving a review on the site that you bought it from. If you purchased the book from Amazon, please leave us an honest review on this book's Amazon page. This is vital so that other potential readers can see and use your unbiased opinion to make purchasing decisions, we can understand what our customers think about our products, and our authors can see your feedback on the title that they have worked with Packt to create. It will only take a few minutes of your time, but is valuable to other potential customers, our authors, and Packt. Thank you!

Index

Printed in Great Britain
by Amazon